GUIDE TO
PREHISTORIC SCOTLAND

GUIDE TO
PREHISTORIC
SCOTLAND

RICHARD FEACHEM

B. T. BATSFORD LTD

LONDON

First published 1963
Second edition 1977
Reprinted 1983, 1988, 1992

ISBN: 0-7134-3264-0

PRINTED IN GREAT BRITAIN BY
BUTLER & TANNER LTD, FROME, SOMERSET
FOR THE PUBLISHERS
B. T. BATSFORD LTD
4 FITZHARDINGE STREET, LONDON, W1H 0AH

TO
RICHARD CHARLES ALEXANDER

PREFACE

The structural remains which constitute the visible record of the human occupation of Scotland in prehistoric times are spread in profusion throughout the mainland and the islands. A great many of them, and of the relics of bone, stone, pottery and metal which were used, and in many cases made, by their builders, are well known both locally and over a wider field. In some parts of the country, however, little or no systematic recording or investigation of the virtually unlimited store of prehistoric material which these structures and relics represent has been undertaken, so that considerable areas are still archaeologically unexplored, and our knowledge of the distribution and nature of even some of the major classes of monuments is little more than rudimentary.

Comprehensive modern accounts of Scotland's prehistory began with Gordon Childe's work in the twenties and thirties of this century. Later researches by the same scholar and by his successor at Edinburgh, Stuart Piggott, provide sources from which the enquiring reader can obtain a sound and complete picture of the place of prehistoric Scotland in the European scene, and an appreciation of the manner in which the nature of the land and its resources affected early settlement. There are also available, or becoming available, both general and specific studies of various monuments and relics, published by Government departments and Universities, and in the proceedings and transactions of national and local archaeological societies.

Sources such as these have been drawn upon in the formation of this Guide. It has of course been necessary to limit the number of examples of most types of monument described and listed, but the aim has been to provide for the first time a broad picture of the best preserved and most significant of those which have survived. After an introductory chapter, the main body of the work is arranged as far as possible in chronological order, the system adopted being based on the classification of monuments under ten headings. Five of these cover the period from the earliest times down to the middle of the 1st millennium B.C.—the era of the primary exploration and exploitation of the land and its resources—and the other five cover the remaining half millennium which saw the construction of many of the dwellings and enclosures of which the often magnificent ruins still survive, and ended with the arrival of the Romans in certain parts of Scotland during the 1st century A.D.

Each of the sections comprises first, a general account of the monuments contained in it, and then descriptions of as many individual examples as space allows. The introductory chapter is thus restricted to a short summary of the local course of prehistory. Although the main narrative ends at the beginning of the Christian era, a short section on early mediaeval Pictish Symbol Stones has been appended.

At the time of writing a great many questions about the content and chronology of the prehistory of Scotland remain unsettled. It is not the purpose of a work of this kind to enter the field of controversy or to attempt to elaborate conclusions already established or to explore new ground. The aim is rather to provide a general account of the principal types of actual structural remains of prehistoric date that can be seen by the resident or visiting traveller in Scotland, and to offer a concise description of the monuments themselves and a hint of the place they occupy in the lengthening story of the human occupation of the country.

PREFACE TO SECOND EDITION

Since this *Guide* was first published important additions have been made to our knowledge of certain categories of the prehistoric antiquities of Scotland, most notably as a result of the major work on chambered tombs by Miss Audrey Henshall, on vitrified forts and brochs by Dr Euan MacKie and on the hitherto unsuspected but widespread remains of prehistoric agricultural communities by the Archaeology Division of the Ordnance Survey which has extended throughout Scotland as well as over the highland areas of England and Wales. In addition to these advances, various excavations of antiquities of all periods have enhanced general knowledge and revealed many interesting peculiarities in particular examples. References to a selection of these have been added to the Bibliography and introduced into the Gazetteer.

Although the counties of Scotland have now been grouped into Regions the old names survive within these and are therefore retained throughout the *Guide*.

CONTENTS

ACKNOWLEDGMENT

The Author and Publishers wish to thank the following for permission to reproduce the illustrations appearing in this book:

Figs. 9–17, 19–24, 31, 36–41 and 47–50 and the illustration on the dust jacket are Crown Copyright, and are reproduced by permission of the Controller of Her Majesty's Stationery Office, and the Department of the Environment.

Figs. 29, 30 and 32–5 are Crown Copyright, and are reproduced by permission of Dr J. K. S. St Joseph and the Cambridge University Collection.

Fig. 28 is Crown Copyright, and is reproduced by the Royal Commission on the Ancient and Historical Monuments of Scotland.

THE ILLUSTRATIONS

0   50
MILES

0   80
KILOMETRES

SHETLAND

☐ FAIR ISLE

ORKNEY

•STROMA

CAITHNESS

SUTHERLAND

LEWIS

HARRIS

BERNERAY H.

NORTH
UIST

BENBECULA

SOUTH
UIST

SKYE   RAASAY

ROSS & CROMARTY   MORAY   BANFF

NAIRN

ABERDEEN

CANNA

BARRA

SANDRAY

PABBAY

BERNERAY

EIGG

MUCK

I N V E R N E S S

KINCARDINE

COLL

TIREE

NORTH
ARGYLL

ANGUS

MULL

L O R N

PERTH

IONA

COLONSAY

MID-ARGYLL

CLACKMANNAN   F I F E

KINROSS

COWAL   DUNBARTON

STIRLING

ISLAY   KNAPDALE

RENFREW

W.
LOTHIAN

MIDLOTHIAN

EAST
LOTHIAN

BERWICK

ARRAN

LANARK   PEEBLES

KINTYRE

AYR

SELKIRK

ROXBURGH

DUMFRIES

WIGTOWN   KIRKCUDBRIGHT

RWF

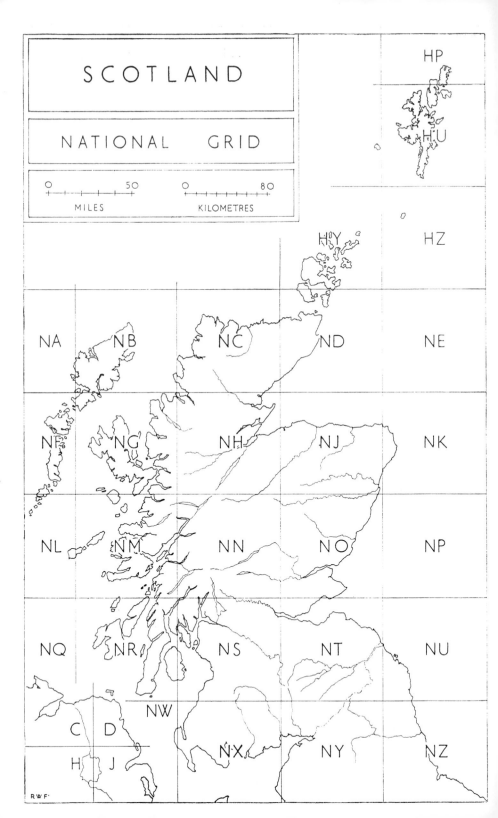

INTRODUCTION

"These Castles ruines when we did consider,
We saw that wasting time makes all things wither"
Henry Adamson, *The Muses Threnodie, or Mirthfull
Mournings on the death of Master Gall.* Edinburgh, 1638.

A certain number of structural and material relics has survived in Scotland by random chance, to bear witness to the more solid and enduring incidentals of those countless human lives which are not otherwise recorded. It is these monuments which form the staple of this Guide. The ruins of houses, settlements, strongholds, places of forgotten ceremonial, tombs and graves—and the relics found in them—can be translated into history by inference and comparison, and only thus can any contact at all be made with the nameless generations who opened up the land. A widespread fame attaches to some of the structural remains which are listed below; but that of a majority is local, or even absent.

Relics of the earliest settlers in Scotland are few and insubstantial. Some of the nomadic squatters, gathering their food entirely from natural sources, lived in coastal caves and on beaches where their presence has been recognised by the discovery of tools and implements of stone and bone. Others, traced only by mislaid or discarded fragments, sheltered in simple refuges among brushwood and forest trees. The remains of untold meals of fish, birds and small animals, secured with arrows or spears or harpoons, and of shell-fish dredged from the teeming sea-bed, are represented in their middens, some of which have been estimated to contain several million shells. There is evidence too that when whales were stranded in the broad, shallow estuaries of the Forth and Tay their carcases were stripped of blubber by avid strokes of mattocks made for the purpose, their monstrous frames left on the muddy foreshore to be picked clean by scouring brutes and birds.

Much of the travelling undertaken by these people was by water, and the dug-out vessel, and perhaps the skin-covered framework of the coracle type, must have been familiar sights in the virgin rivers and short sea passages of the 5th millennium B.C.

While study of the lives of these wanderers is a rewarding and select branch of archaeological research, the nature of the remains of this period is such that nothing further need be said in this context. During

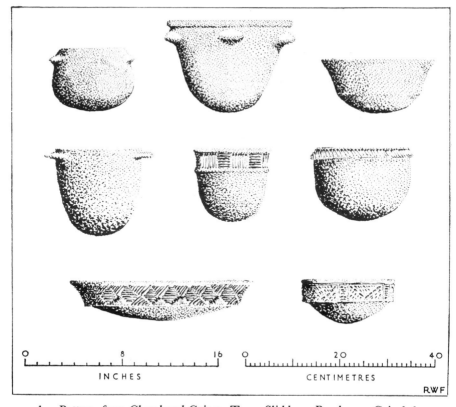

1 *Pottery from Chambered Cairns.* Top, *Sliddery, Beacharra, Cairnholy.*
Centre, *Clettraval, Clettraval, Rudh' an Dunain.*
Bottom, *Onstan* (*Unstan*), *Taversoe Tuack*

the ensuing period, however, a different kind of settler arrived; and before long some of the most impressive and enduring monuments which survive today had been erected throughout the country. The peasant farmers who now began to come in from time to time over a considerable period, both over land and by water, may not at first have effected much of a change even in the vicinity of their settlements. But as they made their grip on the country secure, their social organisation developed and the habit of building elaborate and costly tombs was indulged. The flesh of this mode of living has withered like that of its predecessors; the woven cloth, the articles of hide and wood and basketry, the ripe grain and the savoury stew and the warmth of the fires have gone with the echoes of practical and philosophical talk and the colour and motion both of everyday life and of special routines. The pattern of cultivation is largely lost, and most of the houses, built of timber, are no longer recognisable. In some districts, however, where timber was less plentiful than stone, houses have survived, as described below, while their plenishing—pots, stone implements, objects of bone and other relics—is in the museums.

Tombs of several varieties have, however, survived in those parts of the country in which communities were established during the 4th and 3rd millennia B.C. These include representatives of varieties of the two widespread basic types; the Gallery-Grave, a virtually rectangular chamber covered by a long cairn of stones, and the Passage-Grave, a virtually round chamber entered by way of a passage and placed within a round cairn. Numerous different modifications were evolved, while there were also in use such practices as burial in holes in the ground and in timber tombs under earthen mounds. Evidence of both inhumation and cremation has been found among the various burials of the period, together with such an eccentricity as the burial of animals alongside humans and the regular ritual of depositing vessels and ornaments with the dead. It is usually found that the entrances of the tombs

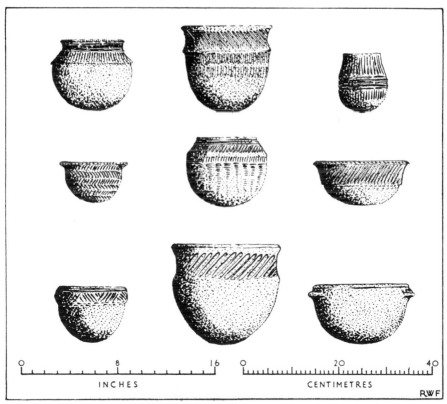

2   *Pottery from North Uist.* Top 2 rows, *Uneval Chambered Cairn.*
Bottom, *Eilean An Tighe Pottery Workshop*

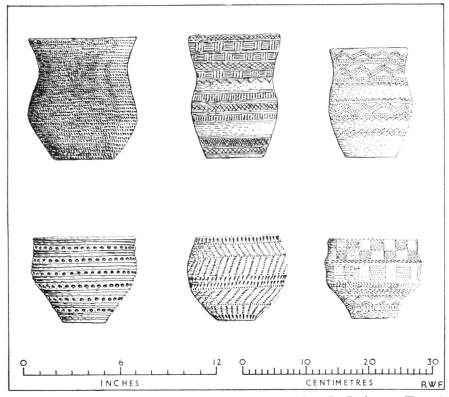

3   *Beaker and Food Vessel Pottery.* Top, *Beakers—Type B, Bathgate; Type A (Ca), Dairsie; Type C (Cb), Cairnpapple.* Bottom, *Food Vessels—Type B, Duncra; Type A, Duncra; Type C, Larkhall*

remained open, or were periodically reopened, for successive burials over a great number of years.

Fresh incursions of peoples still largely of the former habit, but distinguishable by their use of different kinds of pottery and by the new settings the requirement for which presumably arose from their practising different rites, have been traced by structural remains and by relics. Late in the 3rd and in the 2nd millennium B.C. the accumulation of clearances must have produced considerable areas of pasture land associated with arable. With the changes which now took place new monuments again appeared. The large open-air places of ceremonial known as henges were constructed at various populous centres, with their high banks and internal ditches and often with a central feature in stone and possibly in wood. Circles and alignments of tall stones were erected, securely enough to have survived in dumb, outmoded magnificence until today. Paired or single monoliths were raised to mark sanctified spots. And many of

18

these, and of natural rock-faces and boulders, were carved with symbols which are known, after the designs which occur most frequently, as cup-and-ring markings. Collective burial finally gave place to individual inhumation, and the re-used chambered tomb was succeeded by the large cist.

Copper and bronze gradually came into limited use, and both imported and locally made implements and ornaments of these and of gold began to accumulate. By the middle of the 2nd millennium B.C. a far-reaching trade in these and other objects and in raw metal had developed, which played a significant part in opening up the country. At about this time, too, cremation cemeteries were inaugurated, in which the burnt bones were deposited in cinerary urns. As the 2nd millennium drew towards its close, the population of parts at least of Scotland must have been considerable, but at present not much is known about where the people lived before they were settled into their urns. In certain fringe

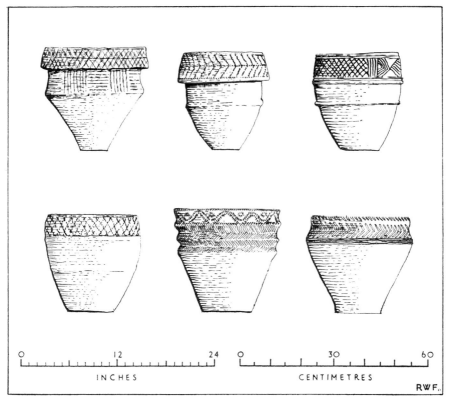

4   *Cinerary Urn Pottery.* Top, *Childe's Types II, III, IV.*
Bottom, *V, Encrusted Urn, enlarged Food Vessel*

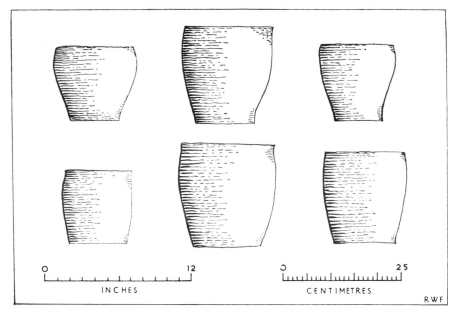

5 *"Flat-rimmed" Pottery*. Top, *Old Keig, Loanhead of Daviot, Loanhead of Daviot*. Bottom, *Covesea, Green Knowe, Forvie*

areas the remains of small stone houses not dissimilar to some of those of earlier periods have been recognised, but over most of the country hardly any work has been done towards discovering the settlements.

Whatever the homes of the people were like, their continuing absence from modern records suggests that they were insubstantial, and that a modified continuation of a largely nomadic life may be indicated. By this time, however, various specialists such as smiths must have had a permanent place throughout society, while a thin but inferentially resilient thread of trade must have formed a network of communication. For even in this place so far distant from the ebullience of the Mediterranean, enough vainglorious and costly relics have survived to reveal the superior, barbaric character of some at least among an otherwise rather undemanding population. These, and the occasional appearance of a working horse, would seem to have provided what occasional relief there might have been over a period of several otherwise quiet centuries.

The question of the arrival of the Celtic languages to Britain and Ireland is still very much a matter of debate. But if we regard a Celt as a non-mediterranean European we can surmise, if no more, that the Celtic languages arrived in Britain, and so in Scotland, at least with the Beaker peoples if not with the Neolithic. The introduction in the first millennium B.C. of various new classes of monuments such as hill-forts and enclosed settlements and, very possibly, the great acreages of open agricultural settlements, and of imported technical and material items including the use of iron—all these denote the reflection in this geographically remote region of what was going on in Continental Europe. Stock rearing probably continued to predominate over the production of crops, but the new social order and material culture led to increase in population and in prosperity. And though iron may long have been scarce among them, it was with this that they hewed their way into the alders in the valley floors in search of timbers for the new houses and settlements, and drew at will upon the unlimited supplies of fuel awaiting them in the turbaries.

The ruins of their works form the largest group of monuments, and contain the mightiest structures, of any period before the introduction of lime mortar in the Middle Ages. The sequence in which the various categories of these structures developed, and subsequently fell into disuse, is by no means clear in every part of the country. In the Southern Uplands there exist the remains of hundreds of buildings of this period,

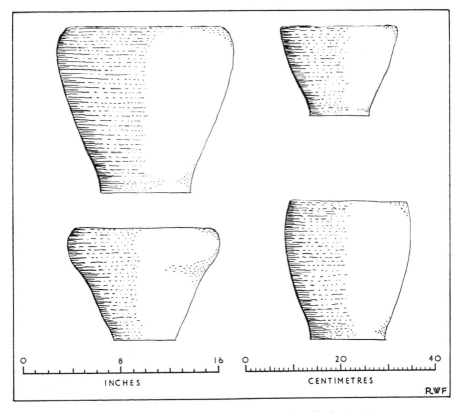

6 *Pottery of late Prehistoric Forms from S. Scotland*

the laborious recording and study of which has at last led to a considerable degree of enlightenment about the order in which they were
developed and the social conditions they reflect. They start with unassuming timber structures and continue through a floruit of walled
settlements—many of them very large—to reach a climax, and a
dénouement, with the arrival in the vicinity of the Roman armies in
Lowland Scotland towards the end of the 1st century A.D.

In the far north, in Shetland, a sequence of comparable structures of
quite different designs has been worked out, broadly covering the same
period but extending a little later into proto-historical times. It may be
generally true to say that the pattern of development during the second
half of the 1st millennium A.D. in the eastern part of the country corres-
ponded with that in the south, while the way of life in the west had more
affinity with the north.

The flowering of architectural and engineering skill, combined with a
degree of logistical and political sophistication to which all these hundreds of ruins bear witness is remarkable. They provide the background
against which social advancement accelerated during a period of less
than half a millennium by the end of which so-called tribal organisations
had been developed which were to form the basis of the ever fewer and
larger "kingdoms" which were themselves ultimately to merge, in
historical times, into mediaeval Scotland.

By the end of the 1st millennium B.C., mainland Scotland had been
divided in some unspecified way among two supra-tribal groups—the
Picts, north of the Forth-Clyde isthmus, the Britains south of it. These
people may have been considerably less well off materially than their
continental relatives, though presumably generally similar in speech,
customs and beliefs, embodying their own version of chiefs and Druids,
the moustachioed, trousered cattleman riding about inspecting herds,
buying and selling from a variety of traders, or feasting beside the open
fire in his large circular house. A large group were free men of mixed
stock, many of whose dwellings are now known, who practised the arts
of living such as farming, carpentry and metal-working. The number of
tribal groupings on record in Scotland at the turn of the eras is large
when considered against the background of the available inhabitable
land. Many must surely have been numerically small, with rulers little
raised above the men of the next lower state; but some must have been
both numerous and politically well knit, under men of substance and
of effective power.

It was into the territories of some of these definable groups that the
Roman armies marched in the year A.D. 79 and continued to manoeuvre
for several years thereafter. The effect of these military units was limited

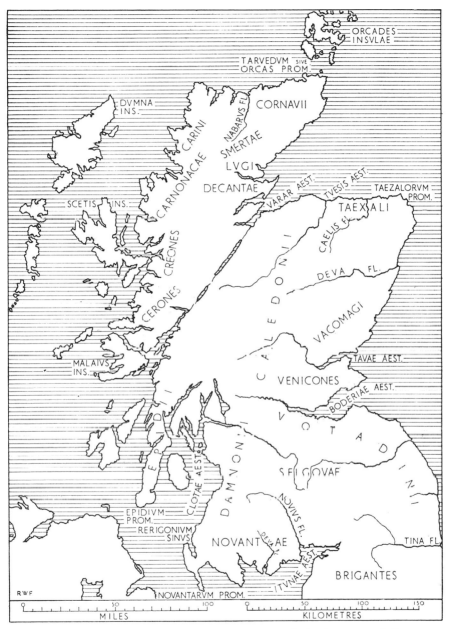

ORCADES
INSVLAE

TARVEDVM SIVE
ORCAS PROM.

DVMNA
INS.

CORNAVII

NABARVS FL.

CARINI

SMERTAE

CARNONACAE

LVGI

DECANTAE

VARAR AEST.

TVESIS AEST.

TAEZALORVM
PROM.

SCETIS INS.

TAEXALI

CAELIS FL.

CRECNES

DEVA FL.

CERONES

VACOMAGI

MALAIVS
INS.

TAVAE AEST.

AEST.

VENICONES

BODERIAE AEST.

CALEDONII

V O T A D I N I

EPIDII

SELGOVAE

CLOTAE AEST.

DAMNONII

NOVIVS FL.

EPIDIVM
PROM.

RERIGONIVM
SINVS

NOVANTAE

DEVAE

TINA FL.

ITVNAE AEST.

BRIGANTES

RWF

NOVANTARVM PROM.

MILES

KILOMETRES

7   *The Tribes and Natural Features of North Britain, 1st century A.D.,
by Claudius Ptolemaus.* After Richmond

23

at the most to the southern shore of the Moray Firth, and it would have been possible at that time to have lived in Kintyre or in Caithness, and neither to have seen or heard more of the Romans than the occasional glimpse of the sail of a military ship or the story of a raid, embellished by the proud evidence of a piece of terra sigillata or an enamelled fibula. It is not the purpose of this Guide, however, to enter into Roman times. It will suffice to emphasise that, outside the areas of established Roman penetration, a provincial version of a local Celtic way of life must have proceeded along its uneven way until the new invasions brought Scots, Saxons and Christianity.

It has nevertheless been considered appropriate to include a section dealing with some of the Pictish Symbol Stones, which are of early mediaeval, and not of prehistoric, date.

THE GAZETTEER

The monuments listed in each of the ten sections of the Gazetteer are arranged in alphabetical order by counties, with the exception of those which are situated on islands off the west coast. In the latter cases it is more convenient to know upon which island a monument is located rather than the county in which the island is incorporated. Accordingly, the names of the following 23 islands are used where appropriate, with no county name: Arran, Barra, Benbecula, Berneray, Berneray (Harris), Canna, Coll, Colonsay, Eigg, Harris, Iona, Islay, Lewis, Muck, Mull, North Uist, Pabbay, Raasay, Sandray, Skye, South Uist, Stroma and Tiree. Further, any confusion which might arise from the existence of such great numbers of islands in both the Orkney and the Shetland groups, together with the fact that the principal island in each group is called Mainland, has been avoided by including in the title of every monument in those groups the group name, the name of the island upon which the monument is situated, and the word "island". Thus— "Orkney, Mainland island": "Shetland, Yell island". It is of course understood that the word "island" is rarely if ever actually used in this way.

Every individual monument can be located by National Grid Reference on a specified sheet of the 50 000 Ordnance Survey map, and the position of each is further indicated by the inclusion of the Ministry of Transport road number (where applicable) and, in most cases, by a description of the nature of the final approach. Permission to have access to any monument other than those under guardianship by the Department of the Environment or the National Trust should be sought from the landowner or tenant upon whose ground the monument stands, and in the case of a monument situated far out on open moorland, it is advisable to enquire about the presence and disposition of any cattle which may be at large in the vicinity.

The great majority of the relics found in monuments and by chance discovery are housed in the National Museum of Antiquities of Scotland, Edinburgh. Other museums are located in Aberdeen, Campbel-

25

town, Dumfries, Dundee, Elgin, Falkirk, Fort William, Glasgow (Kelvingrove and Hunterian), Hawick, Inverness, Paisley, Peterhead, Perth and Stirling, and in a few other centres.

A reference to every monument is included in the bibliography, which is arranged territorially, while the monuments are listed in alphabetical order in the index.

EARLY SETTLEMENTS

Two groups of dwellings in Orkney, broadly contemporary with certain chambered tombs and henge monuments, have been preserved to a remarkable degree. Houses of this and of the ensuing period were almost universally of timber construction, and the few such so far discovered in Britain have been represented merely by the remains of floors and by post-holes. No complete plan of such a house has yet been recorded in Scotland: At the two places in Orkney, however, and at others more recently discovered, the dwellings were built almost entirely of stone. The settlements at Skara Brae, on the Mainland island, and at Rinyo, on Rousay, would no doubt have been despoiled for their stones after they had fallen into decline, had they not been overwhelmed by drifting sand, scree and washed soil, and so lost to view for centuries. It is possible that the existing dwellings, described below, were preceded by others, even including some of wood.

The settlements were occupied over a considerable period by pastoralists who raised sheep and cattle, and eked out their diet with hunting and fishing. The equipment found in the settlements embraces a great range of different kinds of objects of stone, bone, antler, whale-bone, cetacean ivory and pottery. Relationships are apparent between certain of these and others of contemporary cultures, particularly the Clacton element in the Secondary Neolithic Rinyo-Clacton culture.

In addition to these Orkney communities, numerous detached houses, together with a few examples of small amalgamated groupings, have been recognised in Shetland. The small finds recovered from them indicate that some were probably built before the use of metal was introduced locally, while others were occupied and probably built at various times thereafter throughout the rest of the 2nd and even the earlier part of the 1st millennium B.C. Houses of this class, of which well over 50 have been recorded already, have been systematically explored only since 1949, but the work achieved during the ensuing decades both at Jarlshof and over the rest of Shetland has provided solid foundations for future research.

One of the first of the detached Shetland houses to have been examined was the structure known as the Temple at Stanydale, in west Shetland. The details in which this differs from palpable houses are many, the most striking being the concave line, reminiscent of a

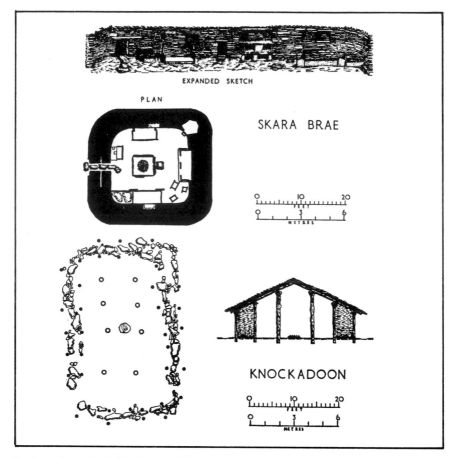

EXPANDED SKETCH

PLAN

SKARA BRAE

KNOCKADOON

8 *Skara Brae Early Settlement: House 1, simplified plan and reconstruction to roof level*

sepulchral monument, followed by the outer face of the wall on either side of the entrance.

Unexcavated houses of this type appear on the surface as mounds of stones, oval in shape and slightly hollowed. In many cases the stone banks or the terraces defining field systems can be seen on the moorland in the vicinity of the houses, together with clearance cairns. This pattern of tillage is at present the most widely known and best documented in the prehistoric north of Britain.

Skara Brae, Settlement (HY 230187), 6½ miles N. of Stromness, Sheet 6 (A.967, B.9056). *Orkney, Mainland island.*
This neolithic settlement of houses built largely if not entirely of stone was buried under a mixture of midden material and blown sand, and so mercifully lost to view until recently. It consists of several houses set close together, so that when viewed on plan they appear to have been squeezed and kneaded into a mass through which a random intes-

9 *Skara Brae Early Settlement; House 1, showing Hearth, Box Bed, Dresser, Tanks, Quernstones*

tinal passage threads its way. The individual house is inclined to the subrectangular in shape, with approximately equal axes and very rounded corners. It measures about 15 ft. in both width and length, more or less, and the thick drystone wall of varying width is faced on both sides. Entrance is gained through a low and narrow hole once fitted with a door, as jambs, sill and bar-holes attest. The roof is corbelled at the corners, and must have been spanned by a frame of some such article as whale ribs, and then covered with skins or thatch.

Various articles of built-in furniture have survived, among them a seat beside a central hearth, pairs of box beds, dressers with two shelves and wall-cupboards. All these are made entirely of planks of the fine-grained flagstone which is exposed over much of the island, as are the luted tanks let into the floor to hold live fish and crustaceans.

The settlement does not all date from one period of construction, and there were gaps of uncertain length between at least three principal phases of occupation. The sequence of finds, however, shows no recognisable change in the direction of the economy based on stock-raising and fishing. Great quantities of relics have been found both during excavations and casually. Some are to be seen at the settlement, which is under the charge of a Department of the Environment guide, but most are in the national collection.

Rinyo, Settlement (HY 440321), 3 miles N. by E. of Brinyan Pier, Sheet 6 (B.9065, B.9064 and by-road).

Orkney, Rousay island.

This settlement, partially excavated in 1938, was found to be of a very similar type to that at Skara Brae. The results of the trial excavation provided useful information and promised more, but since the parts uncovered were filled in to await a better opportunity, no further work has been done. The cultural tradition displayed by the relics is strictly parallel to that of Skara Brae. These consist of numerous potsherds, including some of beaker ware; flint implements to the number of 250, including a polished knife; stone axes and balls, a mortar, what was described as a paint pot, and so-called pot-lids. No evidence of agriculture was adduced, even though the occupants were evidently sedentary. Some of the pottery added confirmation to what Childe called Piggott's very acute recognition in 1936 of the connection between pottery from Orkney settlements and the East Anglian Grooved Ware.

Jarlshof, Early Settlements, Broch, etc. (HU 397096), ¼ mile S. of Sumburgh airport, Sheet 4.

Shetland, Mainland island.

The remarkable sequence of occupations at Jarlshof starts with houses of Skara Brae type probably dating from the early or middle part of the 2nd millennium B.C., and continues with houses occupied in the Late Bronze Age but closely similar in plan to some of the houses in the four main Shetland groups, such as Stanydale. Next came people with a very early Iron Age culture,

building circular houses divided radially and sometimes appointed with little souterrains. After an interval of unknown length, there followed the builders of the broch, with its walled garth. This was succeeded by a whole series of other structures, beginning with an aisled round-house and a wheel-house.

This display of so many monuments of so many different periods provides a splendid opportunity of seeing examples of all before setting out to visit other individuals or groups. As at Mousa and Clickhimin, the Official Guide is a most valuable necessity for a visitor to or a student of Jarlshof.

Stanydale, "Temple" (HU 285503), 1½ miles ESE. of Bridge of Walls, Sheet 3 (A.971 and by-road).

Shetland, Mainland island.

This monument has been called a temple reasonably enough, because its remains combine characteristics of both domestic and sepulchral buildings without conforming very closely with recognisable works of either of those types. It

10   *Jarlshof Early Settlement; Houses attributed to the First Part of the 1st Millennium* B.C.

is a handsome and pleasing structure, consisting of a wall averaging 12 ft. in thickness built of large undressed blocks, which encloses an oval area measuring about 40 ft. in length by about 20 ft. in width. The regularity of the outline of the outside of this is broken by a concave front 30 ft. long which was constructed in place of the regular curve which would have made the SW. end symmetrical with the opposite one. The entrance into the interior opens from the centre of this façade. It leads into the plain SW. part of the chamber which contrasts with the NE. part, the wall of which is diversified by six beautifully built shallow recesses. The only other major internal features are two post sockets for 10-in. timbers, placed in the floor of the chamber at points on its longer axis.

It is a matter of some interest that the fragments of wood found in these post sockets were of spruce, a tree which was not introduced into Scotland until A.D. 1548. The nearest sources are said to have been Scandinavia—which would indicate deliberate importation—and lands on the other side of the Atlantic—which would imply that the wood had come to Shetland as driftwood. If, as seemed more probable to the excavator, the amount of wood required was such that the builders are most unlikely to have relied on driftwood supplies, and therefore must have brought the wood with them, then another most interesting question arises. If spruce must have come from Scandinavia, did expeditions deliberately set out from Shetland, knowing this, to collect it? It is, of course, the same distance from Shetland to the western islands and coasts of Norway as it is to Aberdeen, and there is no reason why such journeys over the North Sea should not have been commonplace. Even today, though now nominally a part of Scotland, Shetland maintains warm affinities to the east.

The small finds from the "temple" include fragments of several huge pottery vessels which were considered to belong in a period very late in the Neolithic, and fragments of a beaker virtually contemporary with this. Several objects of stone were recorded, including an adze-shaped pendant of pumice-stone (a common drift-article on the beaches of Shetland and Orkney) which has been compared to one found in the chambered tomb at Uneval, in North Uist, for which a distribution based on the Central Mediterranean was postulated. In addition, several articles reflecting occupation or at least prolonged visitation of the monument at later dates were found.

It cannot be denied that the designation "temple" is used with a certain amount of reserve, as the quotes imply. The monument is clearly not a house like all the other houses of comparable period and situation, nor of course is it a heel-shaped chambered cairn. It is only reasonable to conclude that its size, excellence of build, lack of early occupation material and details of design all add up to an exceptional, probably public rather than private building, possibly devoted to practices of a formal nature which are most likely to have been associated with religious ritual. Beyond this it is impossible to go, except in so far as the so-called temples in Malta provide the closest known parallels. The rarity of dwellings and other buildings of this period is such that it will always be difficult to find any considerable number of settlements of a comparable nature to those in Shetland. But future work might well establish that such a public building regularly formed part of a settlement, or a group of settlements, of this kind and at this period. At the present, questions arise on all sides, the two most ready are, how extensive was the "parish" served by Stanydale, and do the other groups of houses already known in Shetland have temples too?

Quite apart from the interesting possibilities raised by the existence of this structure, it is of great importance as it stands, together with the neighbouring houses and the field-systems preserved around it.

Stanydale, House (HU 288503), 1¾ miles ESE. of Bridge of Walls, Sheet 3 (A.971 and by-road).

Shetland, Mainland island.

The "temple" of Stanydale stands among the ruins of five houses presumably contemporary with it, and not far from four more. This example stands half-way between the "temple" and the bridge which carries the by-road from the A.971 road over the Burn of Scutta Voe, just below the Loch of Gruting. The

11 *Stanydale "Temple" after excavation. The Cubicles can be distinguished against the Inner Face of the Wall*

house is oval on plan, measuring internally 30 ft. by 15 ft. within a wall up to 9 ft. thick standing to an average height of 2 ft. 6 in. The interior is reached by an entrance the outer end of which is covered by a protrusion from the house wall forming a porch or baffle against the wind and rain. This feature is not found on all the houses of this type. Inside, the house is divided into a large room with two small recesses in the E. wall, a bench along the W. wall and a hearth not far from the middle; and a small inner room, almost circular on plan. A sub-rectangular enclosure, a modification to the original plan which may not be contemporary with the primary occupation of the house, adheres to the outside of the porch wall.

A second house among those of this group, situated 100 yds. NE. of Gruting School, was also excavated, but found to be in a much more ruinous condition than the one here described. Although very similar in size and shape to the latter, it did not have a porch. **Ness of Gruting,** House (HU 280483), 2¼ miles SE. of Bridge of Walls, Sheet 3

(A.971 and by-road).

Shetland, Mainland island.

This house is one of a group of five which lie on the Ness of Gruting among widely spread clearance cairns and traces of field boundaries. It was excavated early in the 1950s, when it was found to be oval in shape, containing a room with an apsidal appendage at the end opposite the entrance—a slight variant on the almost completely circular inner rooms recorded at other houses. The chamber measured about 30 ft. in length by about 20 ft. in breadth, the apse about 5 ft. measured down the long axis of the house and 10 ft. across this. The wall was about 9 ft. thick, the entrance at the SE. being covered by a porch.

A secondary occupation of the house saw the reduction of the size of the main room to a length of 20 ft. and a width of 15 ft., and the construction of a new apse measuring 7 ft. 6 in. by 6 ft. 9 in. The reduced house re-used the SE. part of the old one, including the entrance, though only with the reassurance of a very substantial buttress. At some stage in its career the space between the faces of the wall of the original house was filled with peat ash over much of its length and for a considerable depth. It was suggested that this would be as good a material as any for the purpose of insulation, the result aimed at in the filling of a dry-stone house wall.

The finds recorded from this house included the particularly interesting one of 28 lb. of carbonised barley; a lot of stone articles, both rude and otherwise, among them models of battle-axes copying in miniature artefacts of that significant type which belong to early post-neolithic times; and great quantities of domestic pottery, the unusual amount of which may be due to the house having been used by a potter apparently with a higher rate of production than one household could require. The commonest sherds, decorated with diamonds, chevrons and herring-bone patterns, reflect a ceramic tradition of the builders of the Hebridean chambered tombs, while the appearance of lugs is consistent with western neolithic origins.

Mavis Grind, Houses (HU 3368), 20 miles NNW. of Lerwick, Sheet 2 (A.970).
Shetland, Mainland island.

Very nearly all the 57 early houses known in Shetland at the time of compilation of the distribution map in 1956 occur in four groupings on Mainland and another on Whalsay. The northernmost grouping lies immediately N. and S. of Mavis Grind, the narrow isthmus which connects the greater part of Mainland with Northmaven at the point where these are nearly separated by Sullom Voe and the waters of St Magnus Bay.

Eight houses have been recorded in this area, four each to N. and S. of the Grind. One among the former is situated ¼ mile SSW. of Islesburgh, close to the shore near the Minn (HU 334685). A feature of Shetland life which is still in use, though not so widely as heretofore, is the minute stone-walled enclosure built as a wind-break and a defence against animals for the rearing of a rather limited variety of young vegetables. This is called a plantie-crub, and such an object is by no means infrequently found on or close to the ruin of a house or cairn from the dead body of which material has been so easily derived for the new structure. Such a plantie-crub stands within the ruin of this house, which is nevertheless quite substantial, measuring about 52 ft. by 42 ft. over the bank of debris. The house stands within a U-shaped enclosure formed by a stone wall 5 ft. in thickness and, in places, as much in height. The S. extremities of the wall rest on the shore. Such an enclosure, which in this case measures about 200 ft. along either axis, is not found elsewhere in such a context, and may not belong together with the house.

Another ruin in this northern group is situated on the Ness of Islesburgh, 60 yds. from the W. shore of Mangaster Voe (HU 333698). It consists of an oval bank measuring axially from crest to crest 50 ft. by 35 ft. Outlines of the partition between the main and inner rooms and of a recess in the NE. arc of the inner face of the wall can be distinguished on the surface.

South of the Grind the four houses on the land of Culsetter include one hollowed out of the steep slope about 200 yds. NE. of the loch called Bays Water (HU 332677). This appears as a spread stony bank which encloses an area about 45 ft. in length and 25 ft. in width, larger than most houses but not far from the Stanydale "temple" in its superficial proportions. A secondary structure overlies the middle of the house.

Clumlie, House (HU 397185), 15 miles S. of Lerwick, Sheet 4 (A.968).
Shetland, Mainland island.

The nine early houses recorded in the S. part of Shetland include one situated only 45 yds. E. of the main road, about 500 yds. S. of the junction of the by-road to Clumlie. This consists of a grass-covered bank enclosing a hollow and measuring 45 ft. in length by 36 ft. in width over all. The bank, which stands to as much as 18 in. in height, is studded with protruding stones, and the entrance gap is clearly distinguishable in the SSE.

Isbister, House (HU 584646), 3 miles NE. of Symbister, Sheet 3 (by-road and moorland). *Shetland, Whalsay island.*

The few early houses on Whalsay include the ruin NE. of Isbister which is locally known as "The Gairdie". It consists of the ruin of a house with three apses at the far end of the main room; the latter measures 23 ft. in either direction, excluding the apses. The central apsidal recess, the largest, measures 10 ft. both in width and depth and contains what looks like the base of a dresser made of stone slabs of the kind which is found at Skara Brae. The other two recesses are only 6 ft. wide and 4 ft. deep.

Scord of Brouster, Houses and Fields (HU 256516), 1¼ miles WNW. of Bridge of Walls, Sheet 3 (A.971).

Shetland, Mainland island.

Another of the four principal groupings of houses lies in the W. part of Mainland, 12 houses lying E. of Gruting Voe and one, with possibly at least two more, to the W. The later lies among field boundaries and clearance cairns on the flanks of the Scord of Brouster a short distance N. of the A.971 road about 300 yds. WSW. of Brouster. The ruin of the certain house consists of a heavy grass-covered, stony bank which encloses an oval area measuring 24 ft. by 18 ft., at the NW. end of which, opposite the entrance, four deep recesses can be distinguished. There is a superficial suggestion of the Stanydale "temple" in the shallowness of the recesses and the flattened SE. end of the ruin.

The field systems in which the house stands comprise five or six enclosures covering altogether an area of about 2¾ acres. Two oval banks which lie among them may represent ruined houses, while a subrectangular stony mound might be a cairn or a building.

CHAMBERED TOMBS

Knowledge of the earliest peasant farmers who lived in Scotland in the 4th millennium B.C. and into the ensuing period depends at present almost entirely upon information derived from their tombs, as so little has yet been established about the dwellings of the living. And while this must of necessity mean that the picture is incomplete, the structures themselves hold much that is of interest. The tombs themselves were usually built of large blocks of stone, where these were plentiful, or of walling made up of smaller slabs when the material locally available so dictated. They were collective in character, and in general they seem to have remained in use, as occasion demanded, throughout a considerable number of years. All the chambered tombs in Scotland are described, with plans, in Miss Audrey Henshall's two magnificent volumes, their characteristics and structural history being discussed in the second. One of the most interesting conclusions demonstrated here is that in many cases tombs originally built on a comparatively modest scale were later made grand and imposing by the addition of enormous tonnages of stones in the form of tails and horns.

It has been mentioned above that such tombs have been classified in two main categories—passage-graves and gallery-graves. The principal groups of chambered tombs in Scotland are the Clyde–Carlingford gallery-graves and the Hebridean, the Orkney Cromarty, the Shetland and the Clava groups, all of which are passage-graves, even though gallery-grave influences occur in some of them. The Clyde–Carlingford group is recognised to have been among the earliest, pottery with Windmill Hill affinities being found in several examples. Links have been observed in certain structural details among tombs of the Clyde–Carlingford group and the Hebridean tombs, and between the latter and the Orkney–Cromarty class. The passage-graves of Clava, like those of Shetland, reveal no distinct connection with any of the others.

The *Clyde–Carlingford* group of tombs is disposed, as its name suggests, on either side of the North Channel between south-western Scotland and Ulster. The majority of the principal Scottish examples occur in Galloway, Arran, Bute and the southern part of the large but spidery county of Argyll, while a subsidiary group occurs in Central Scotland. It has been suggested that the people who brought in what is called the Clyde–Carlingford culture came from Western Europe by sea, and probably settled first round the Clyde estuary, later expanding to Ireland.

Although these tombs vary very greatly on plan, the typical character-istic feature by which their identity can be established is a rectangular burial-chamber roofed with large slabs or with a corbelled vault. The chamber, divided internally into separate compartments by low slab walls, is usually set near one end of a long cairn, its entrance opening into the middle of a façade. In most cases this is concave, its horns running out some way towards embracing a forecourt.

Individual tombs vary in shape, size, details of the structure of the chamber, the entrance and the façade, in orientation and in every other conceivable way, while the burial ritual carried on inside them varied both from one place to another and between one period and another. Some of the Clyde–Carlingford tombs were used right on into the times when beaker and food-vessel pottery were in use.

The *Hebridean* tombs mostly lie in Skye and the Outer Hebrides, although several passage-graves belonging with the others have been recognised on the western coasts of the mainland. Some among this group are long, but the majority incline towards a circular plan. The chambers tend to be oval or polygonal, and the passages connecting them with the entrances are more often than not short. Hybrids between true passage-graves and the Clyde–Carlingford gallery-graves occur among members of the group. Very little work has been done among tombs of the Hebridean group, but what information there is points to the familiar succession of burials, most of them by inhumation, accompanied by pottery vessels and by stone objects.

The *Orkney–Cromarty* tombs comprise a broad and varied class occur-ring in Orkney, Caithness, Sutherland and the Cromarty district which embraces north-eastern Invernesshire and the eastern part of Ross and Cromarty. From among them all three principal varieties have been extracted: the long cairns, taking their name from the *Yarrows* cairn, in Caithness; the round *Camster* cairns, named from another Caithness monument, and their elongated derivatives the Stalled Cairns of Orkney; and the *Maes Howe* group.

The Yarrows cairns show affinities with Clyde–Carlingford gallery-graves of the type which have curved or horned façades, but the lofty corbelled and stalled chambers are of passage-grave type. Some of the Yarrows cairns which have horns at either end are long, others so short that on plan the forecourt is indistinguishable from the other end or the sides.

The round Camster cairns may represent the primary immigrant movement into the NE. region, very probably up the Great Glen. The Camster cairn itself, with its tholos tomb with an antechamber, reflects examples in Spain.

Camster chambers, modified by elongation, appear in long or oval cairns with, in some cases, the passage entering them in a long side instead of an end. In the true Stalled Cairns this lengthening became exaggerated until as many as 24 stalls (12 compartments) were constructed in one chamber. Such a process naturally led to a change in the outline of the cairn, and the development of an oblong structure with rounded corners.

The Maes Howe tomb itself is a passage-grave with a rectangular corbelled chamber with three side-chambers. The other members of the group show variations on this theme, some of them seeming to show evidence of a desire to extend the useful life of the cairn by multiplying the internal accommodation, in a manner already described in connection with the Camster Stalled Cairn derivatives. Copying, if not indeed independently originating, this modification, the designers of this group increased the number of lateral cells until an oblong external form was achieved. It has been suggested that the people to whom Maes Howe tombs belonged came to western Orkney direct from the west coast of Scotland rather than up the Great Glen or from further south still.

Burials in tombs of the Orkney–Cromarty group seem to have been both by inhumation and by cremation; grave goods and accompanying material include pottery vessels, animal bones and a great variety of objects of stone.

The distinctive character of the *Shetland* group is the heel-shaped plan, seen in small oval cairns with curved façades. Some of these contain a cruciform or trefoil chamber, reached by a passage leading in from the centre of the façade, and are therefore true chambered cairns of the passage-grave category. A variety of the heel-shaped cairn is the circular or oval structure with an external facing of well-laid blocks which rises vertically from a heel-shaped platform, as exemplified at Vementry. Others, however, contain no passage, but enclose a chamber or cist with no formal entrance. For convenience, these as well as those known to have a passage are included in this section.

Tombs of the compact *Clava* group are clustered round the lower reaches of the rivers Spey, Nairn, Ness, Enrick and Beauly. Two sub-groups have been distinguished among the 50 or so structures which make up the group, one a corbelled passage-grave in a round cairn, the other an annular cairn enclosing an apparently unroofed area into which there is no formal means of access from the outside. Tombs of both these sub-groups are set within a ring of free-standing stones.

In addition to the several types of true chambered tombs described above, this section includes a few less distinctive long cairns which have been recorded in central eastern Scotland and the Lowlands, a distribution which is complementary to that of the chambered tombs. Some of these may be related to certain generally similar monuments farther south; but so little work has been done on them that no generalisations about their characteristics or affinities can be elaborated very far.

Certain funerary monuments seem to stand between chambered tombs and simple burials under round cairns of one kind or another. These include the so-called ring cairns, such as the well-known group in Kincardineshire, the members of which, though very small, stand in rings of upright stones in the Clava manner. Likewise, the recumbent-stone circles have been considered as parallel phenomena to, if not indeed derivatives from, the Clava cairns. More than 100 of these, at best, impressive monuments are crowded into Aberdeenshire and the borders of adjacent counties, and representative examples are included here.

Cloghill, Long Cairn (NJ 851071), 5 miles W. of Aberdeen, Sheet 38 (A.944 and by-road). *Aberdeenshire.*
The remains of this unchambered long cairn are very dilapidated, the scatter of stones stretching over a distance of 170 ft., with a general width of 38 ft. It has been damaged both by the robbery of stones and by the addition to it of small stones cleared from fields, as it was described in the 1790s as being only 108 ft. long but of the same width.

Balnagowan, Long Cairn (NJ 500000), 2 miles WNW. of Aboyne, Sheet 37 (A.93, farm road and footpath). *Aberdeenshire.*

This long cairn in Balnagowan Wood now consists of a series of piles of stones which stretch altogether over a distance of 230 ft., and include among them at least one earthfast quadrangular boulder. The shape is such as to have inspired its original recorder to observe that "the plan shows a general resemblance to the outlines of the Milky Way at the section occupied by the constellations of Cassiopeia and Cygnus".

Knapperty Hill, Long Cairn (NJ 945504), 2¼ miles NE. of Maud, Sheet 30 (B.9106, farm road and pasture land). *Aberdeenshire.*
The remains of this long cairn are not

12   *Loanhead of Daviot Recumbent-stone Circle*

now very impressive in themselves, but are of interest in that some neolithic pottery was found in them. This was lodged in the Arbuthnot Museum at Peterhead.

Loanhead of Daviot, Recumbent-stone Circle (NJ 747288), 4 miles W. by N. of Old Meldrum, Sheet 38 (B.9000 and by-road). *Aberdeenshire.*

The recumbent-stone circle consists basically of a ring cairn surrounded by a circle of standing stones among which one huge boulder is placed in a horizontal position. In some cases the standing stones are set in a bank, but this may not be an original feature; in others a narrow ring replaces the true broad ring of a ring cairn. More than 60 such monuments have been superficially examined in some detail out of a known total of more than 100, and two were excavated in the 1930s.

One of these, at Daviot, occupies a broad shelf near the summit of a gentle hill which is nevertheless conspicuous from a fair distance round about. The excavation showed that this cairn, like the similar monument at Old Keig, had been lived in by people using pottery attributable to the end of the first half of the 1st millennium B.C., but that its primary use, for burial, dated from at least 1000 years before that.

The central area of the cairn was found to measure about 12 ft. in diameter, the ring about 20 ft. in thickness, and the outer ring of 10 upright stones and the recumbent monster stood 5 ft. outside this. Beaker sherds were found at various places both in the central area and round the periphery of the cairn, the wide dispersal being due in part at least to the fact that the cairn had been used as a quarry.

Tomnaverie, Recumbent-stone Circle (NJ 478034), ¼ mile SE. of Tarland, Sheet 37 (B.9094). *Aberdeenshire.*

This recumbent-stone circle stands on the brink of a now disused quarry on the opposite side of the road to Mill of Wester Coull, and is under guardianship. The outer ring in which the recumbent stone is placed measures 56 ft. in diameter, and the remains of the inner ring 28 ft.

Ardmarnock, Chambered Cairn (NR 915726), 4 miles S. by W. of Kilfinnan, Sheet 62 (A.886 and farm road).
Argyll, Cowal.

The ruins of this Clyde-Carlingford tomb stand on a ridge a short distance E. of Ardmarnock farmhouse. The principal feature is a cist 4 ft. 9 in. long, up to 3 ft. 3 in. wide and 5 ft. 6 in. deep formed by side slabs respectively 5 ft. 7 in. and 6 ft. 4 in. in length, an end slab and a septal stone. The line of the top of the last named dips 3 in. in the middle, possibly as a result of hammering, and the broad faces are each marked by a single cup the axes of which match. Outside this slab are two further earthfast slabs which may have served as portal stones or may represent a ruined second chamber.

Beacharra, Chambered Cairn (NR 692434), 16 miles NNW. of Campbeltown, Sheet 62 (A.83). *Argyll, Kintyre.*

This cairn was opened in 1892, when the famous pottery, now in Campbeltown Museum, was recovered. The ruin of the cairn was examined afresh in 1959. The chamber was found to be over 20 ft. in length and up to 5 ft. in width, and the E. portal stone and a sill stone remained *in situ*. The E. part of the façade was found to be perfectly straight, in the form of a dry-stone wall standing in places over 2 ft. in height. At the far end a right-angled corner merged the façade with the long side of the cairn. It is virtually certain that the W. part of the façade was constructed in the same manner.

Brackley, Chambered Cairn (NR 794418), 4 miles NW. of Carradale, Sheet 62 (B.842). *Argyll, Kintyre.*

This comparatively well preserved Clyde-Carlingford chambered cairn stands in spectacular ruin near the farmhouse, in Carradale Glen, where its low elevation in relation to the public road renders it visible from a considerable distance. It had long been known as a large and presumably important structure when, in 1952, it was chosen for excavation partly because of its situation in what was described as "the heartland of the Clyde-Carlingford culture in Scotland", and partly because it could be expected to provide evidence of the relationship between the Clyde-Carlingford tombs of Arran and those of Kintyre. It was found to contain a megalithic chamber (with two sets of portal stones), in which inhumed burials had been made, probably accompanied by

39

Beacharra pottery. At a later period, well into the 2nd millennium B.C., the floor of the chamber had been paved and a cremated burial deposited on it, accompanied by food vessel pottery and beads from at least two "jet necklaces".

Ardnacross, Chambered Cairn (NR 768261), 5 miles NE. of Campbeltown, Sheet 68 (B.842).   *Argyll, Kintyre.*

The remains of this Clyde-Carlingford chambered cairn sprawl on the brink of the descent to the sea-shore at the far side of a small field bordering the road. The mass of stones, the shape of which has probably been altered by robbing, now measures about 60 ft. in diameter. Several large upright boulders and a slab protruding through the turf just outside the spread of stones to the NE. probably represent the remains of a megalithic cist.

Crarae, Chambered Cairn (NR 987974), 3 miles SW. of Furnace, Sheet 55 (A.83).   *Argyll, Mid.*

The Clyde-Carlingford chambered cairn, situated in the grounds of Crarae Lodge, one of Scotland's famous gardens, was excavated in 1955, 1956 and 1957, when it was found to measure at least 115 ft. in length and 60 ft. in greatest width. Part of the forecourt area had been paved, and the dry-stone walling of the façade, originally 35 ft. in length, was revealed standing in parts to a height of 3 ft. The chamber, built of massive slabs, measures 16 ft. in length and up to 4 ft. in width. Although much mutilated, the cairn was described by the excavators as being comparable to some of the larger Clyde-Carlingford cairns in Arran.

Dunan Beag, Chambered Cairn (NS 027330), 2 miles SSE. of Brodick, Sheet 69 (A.841 and moorland).   *Arran.*

This cairn, lying a little below Dunan Mor, is somewhat rectangular in outline, measuring about 120 ft. in length by 65 ft. in width. It is abnormal in that it contains a chamber at either end and has no façade or other feature at the entrances. Beaker sherds and the triangular terminal of a crescentic jet necklace were found in the S. chamber.

Dunan Mor, Chambered Cairn (NS 028322), 2 miles SSE. of Brodick, Sheet 69 (A.841 and moorland).   *Arran.*

This Clyde-Carlingford cairn, situated close to its neighbour Dunan Beag on the Clauchland Hills N. of Lamlash, contains the remains of three chambers placed radially, apparently without special entrances. A plano-convex flint knife representing an earlier use of the tomb and beaker sherds representing a later have been recovered from it.

Giants Graves, Chambered Cairn (NS 043246), 7 miles S. by E. of Brodick, Sheet 69 (A.841 and moorland).   *Arran.*

This Clyde-Carlingford chambered cairn overlooking Whiting Bay from the S. is a denuded structure the chamber of which is divided into four compartments with overlapping wall-slabs and fitted with a septal slab immediately inside the portal stones. Leaf-shaped arrowheads and plano-convex flint knives were found in it, together with some beaker sherds indicating a continuing series of burials.

Cairn Ban, Chambered Cairn (NR 991262), 6½ miles SSW. of Brodick, Sheet 69 (A.841, by-road, footpath and moorland).   *Arran.*

This Clyde-Carlingford chambered cairn, situated 900 ft. above sea level in the heart of the hill forming the S. part of the Isle of Arran, is naturally enough well preserved. It consists of a mound of stones 100 ft. long and 60 ft. wide with the deep bay of the forecourt and crescentic façade forming the E. end. The chamber, divided into three compartments and measuring 15 ft. in length, retains its original roofing—a slab set on corbelling at a height of 8 ft. above the floor. It has been suggested that originally there was a completely circular setting of stones at the E. end of the cairn, half represented by the stones of the façade and half by a free-standing arc.

Tormore, Chambered Cairn (NR 903310), 7¼ miles SW. of Brodick, Sheet 69 (B.880, by-road, A.841 and peat track).   *Arran.*

When the tripartite chamber of this Clyde-Carlingford cairn was searched 60 years ago, relics recovered included a sherd of Rinyo I ware, a plano-convex flint knife, a flint knife with a polished edge and a small perforated stone macehead with a straight cylindrical perforation—an assemblage which has led to the suggestion that the tomb indicates settlement from the Orkney-Cromarty region.

Sliddery, Chambered Cairn (NR 943238), 9 miles SSW. of Brodick, Sheet 69 (A.841, by-road and moorland).

Arran.

The remains of this cairn reveal a tripartite chamber the portal of which has been removed. An unornamented Beacharra A vessel, a leaf-shaped arrowhead and a plano-convex flint knife were recovered from it.

East Bennan, Chambered Cairn (NR 994207), 9½ miles S. by W. of Brodick, Sheet 69 (A.841 and farm land). *Arran.*

This Clyde-Carlingford cairn situated near the S. shore of the island is notable for the large flat slabs forming the five-compartment gallery 20 ft. long and sections of the façade. The portals are backed by a septal slab.

Clachaig, Chambered Cairn (NR 950214), 10 miles SSW. of Brodick, Sheet 69 (A.841, by-road, A.841 and farm land). *Arran.*

This Clyde-Carlingford chambered cairn, less than 1 mile W. of another at Torlin, is oval on plan, measuring axially about 60 ft. by 50 ft. It contains a simple bipartite segmented chamber the septal slab of which rises, as is common to such tombs, to only about one-third of the height of the chamber. It is recorded that the remains of 12 adults and two children were found in the tomb, together with unornamented Beacharra A pottery and a cord-ornamented C bowl, a stone axe over 8 in. long and a plano-convex flint knife. A secondary short cist also found in the cairn produced a food vessel and a scraper.

Torlin, Chambered Cairn (NR 955211), 10 miles SSW. of Brodick, Sheet 69 (A.841, by-road, A.841 and farm land). *Arran.*

This chambered cairn, in which the remains of six adults and a child together with those of otter, birds and fish were identified, produced also Beacharra A pottery and a plano-convex flint knife. The cairn originally took the shape of a short oval mound enclosing a chamber of four compartments without a façade.

Balmalloch, Chambered Cairn (NX 264845), 9¼ miles SE. of Girvan, Sheet 76 (A.714, farm road and moorland). *Ayrshire.*

Parts of two megalithic cists or chambers arranged radially protrude from the ruin of the circular cairn. That to the S.

appears to be a cist 6 ft. 6 in. long by 2 ft. 6 in. wide, the walls formed by a combination of slabs and dry-stone masonry leading up through corbelling to a slab roof. The other, in the E., is represented by a capstone 6 ft. long and wide below which parts of the wall of the cist can be descried.

Longman Hill, Long Cairn (NJ 738620), 3½ miles ESE. of Banff, Sheet 29 (A.98 and farm road). *Banff.*

This cairn appears to be made of earth. It measures a little over 200 ft. in length, and in profile gives the impression of a round cairn, 65 ft. in diameter and 11 ft. high, joined on the SW. by a narrow neck to a long mound standing about 7 ft. high and tapering from 36 ft. to 28 ft. in width.

Dun Bharpa, Chambered Cairn (NF 672018), 2¼ miles N. of Castlebay, Sheet 31 (A.888, by-road and footpath). *Barra.*

This circular chambered cairn measuring about 85 ft. in diameter is encircled by the remains of an intermittent peristalith of upright slabs standing individually to as much as 7 ft. in height. The top cover-slab of the chamber, nearly 10 ft. long, 5 ft. 8 in. wide and 1 ft. thick, is exposed near the crest of the cairn at a height of 17 ft. above ground level. The passage is in the E.

Airidh na h'aon Oidhche, Chambered Cairn (NF 816525), 2¾ miles NNE. of Creagorry, Sheet 22 (A.865 and moorland). *Benbecula.*

This chambered cairn stands near the summit of a small hill, 550 yds. ESE. of another on Stiaraval. It is circular, a little over 50 ft. in diameter and 11 ft. high, and the ruin of the central chamber can be seen in the top. The passage is in the ESE.

Stiaraval, Chambered Cairn (NF 812526), 2¾ miles N. by E. of Creagorry, Sheet 22 (A.865 and moorland). *Benbecula.*

This robbed chambered cairn measures about 60 ft. in diameter within the scanty remains of a peristalith of earth-fast slabs. The ruin of the chamber can be seen in the centre and that of the passage in the SSE. The chamber is nearly circular, measuring about 12 ft. in diameter.

Cladh Maolrithe, Chambered Cairn (NF 912805), 1 mile SW. of Berneray

Post Office, Sheet 18 (by-road and moorland). *Berneray, Harris.*

The remains of the chamber of this cairn, the rest of which has been robbed, consist of two upright slabs—4 ft. 6 in. long by 2 ft. 2 in. high and 5 ft. long by 3 ft. 9 in. high respectively—and two prostrate slabs one 5 ft. 7 in. and the other 7 ft. 4 in. long.

The Mutiny Stones, Long Cairn (NT 623590), 4½ miles WNW. of Longformacus, Sheet 74 (farm road and walk). *Berwickshire.*

This long cairn, aligned E. and W., lies on Byrecleugh Ridge at a height of 1250 ft. O.D., 250 ft. above the old Byrecleugh shooting lodge. It measures 280 ft. in length, 25 ft. in width at the W. end and 75 ft. at the E. It attains a height of 12 ft. near the E. extremity. The cairn has been damaged by the construction of a sheep fold out of its material and by other robbing and by illicit excavations, and has actually been cut through at a point 100 ft. from the W. end. It was excavated most recently in 1924, when the only discovery reported was a stretch of internal walling of uncertain purpose.

This cairn, like others in Dumfriesshire, Roxburghshire and eastern Scotland, can be numbered among the long cairns which seem to belong to no group of chambered tombs, and whose distribution is indeed complementary to the latter. It has been suggested that they may possibly be the counterparts of unchambered long barrows further south.

The name of this cairn has varied from "The Mittenfull of Stones" in 1794 by way of "The Meeting Stones" to the present version.

Bicker's Houses, Chambered Cairn (NS 060604), 3¼ miles SW. of Rothesay, Sheet 63 (B.878, A.844, farm road and hill). *Bute.*

The chamber of this Clyde-Carlingford chambered cairn constitutes the principal feature of the robbed remains. It measures 15 ft. by 3 ft. 4 in., and is divided into two compartments by two septal slabs. The large portal stones stand 2 ft. 6 in. apart, and the opening between them is diminished by a septal slab immediately within them.

Glecknabae, Chambered Cairn (NS 007683), 5½ miles WNW. of Rothesay, Sheet 63 (A.844 and farm road). *Bute.*

This Clyde-Carlingford chambered cairn lies on a mesolithic midden which had already been covered with turf before the cairn was built. Two chambers set radially occur in the remaining part of the cairn, while a third probably originally existed in the robbed part. The chambers both have openings diminished by a slab inside the portal stones. Pottery of the Beacharra A group in the form of bowls with flattened rims has been recovered from this cairn, while beaker-like sherds attest the continuing sequence of burials.

Carn Ban, Chambered Cairn (NS 005693), 6 miles NW. of Rothesay, Sheet 63 (A.844, farm road and hill). *Bute.*

The remains of this cairn lie mostly in the SE. limit of South Wood of Lenihuline. They appear as a much pillaged pile of stones about 180 ft. long and 30 ft. wide. This cairn displays the abnormality of having a chamber at each end but no façade or other feature. A side chamber can be distinguished near the E. end.

Michael's Grave, Chambered Cairn (NR 994704), 7 miles NW. of Rothesay, Sheet 63 (A.844 and farm road). *Bute.*

The chamber is virtually all that remains of this Clyde-Carlingford chambered cairn situated 1 mile NW. of Carn Ban. It is bipartite, each compartment measuring 5 ft. in length. The portal stones stand as little as 1 ft. apart to form a symbolic aperture, and this is not fitted with a septal slab.

Earl's Cairn, Chambered Cairn (ND 263697), 2¼ miles SW. of Mey, Sheet 12 (by-roads). *Caithness.*

This round cairn with a Camster chamber was excavated many years ago. It measures about 40 ft. in diameter and 6 ft. in length, and the base has been kerbed with boulders. The passage, in the ESE., is 15 ft. 6 in. long; it gives access to a first compartment measuring 2 ft. by 5 ft., a second measuring 6 ft. by 7 ft., and a third 3 ft. by 3 ft.

Ham, Chambered Cairn (ND 235738), 3¼ miles W. by N. of Mey, Sheet 12 (A.836 and by-road). *Caithness.*

This round chambered cairn with a Camster-type chamber was mistaken for a souterrain just over 200 years ago by Bishop Pococke, but the plan and description published in 1911 reveal the true identity of the monument while perpetuating the episcopal error in the title. The grass-grown mound, 60 ft. in diameter, and 8 ft. high, stands near the cliffs a quarter of a mile NW. of Ham. It has been cut about over the last two centuries, and the passage, now 13 ft. long but somewhat truncated, can barely be perceived to enter the chamber which is 15 ft. long and up to 6 ft. wide, with a corbelled roof closed with flags at a height of 6 ft. 6 in. above the floor. This is the most northerly chambered cairn recorded on the mainland of Britain.

Shebster, Chambered Cairn (ND 013646), 3 miles E. of Reay, Sheet 11 (by-road and pasture land). *Caithness.*

This round cairn, occupying the summit of Shebster Hill, measures over 80 ft. in diameter. It is entered by a passage in the ESE. leading to a chamber which, judging from the slabs protruding from the body of the cairn, is about 20 ft. long and divided into three compartments, in the Camster style.

Shebster, Chambered Cairns (ND 013653, 014654), 3 miles E. of Reay, Sheet 11 (By-roads and pasture land). *Caithness.*

Two long horned cairns lie 100 yds apart on the N. summit of Shebster Hill which is called the Ward Hill or Cnoc Freiceadan. The more southerly of the two, aligned WNW. and ESE., has an extreme length of 255 ft. over the horns. The body of the cairn measures on average 40 ft. in width and stands to a height of 5 ft. It expands towards the ESE. to a width of 60 ft. and a height of 10 ft., and towards the WNW. to 56 ft. and 7 ft. respectively.

The other cairn, aligned NNE. and SSW., measures over all 240 ft. and attains a maximum height of 8 ft. and width of 53 ft., towards the SSW. end.

Shurrery, Chambered Cairn (ND 048587), 6½ miles SE. of Reay, Sheet 11 (by-roads). *Caithness.*

The remains of the chamber of a cairn stand in the rear of the house called Monadh nan Carn at Shurrery. The original shape of the cairn is not easy to determine, the spread of stones being suitable for either a round or a short horned original. Several of the wall slabs of a long chamber survive *in situ*, some standing to a height of 5 ft.

Dorrery, Chambered Cairn (ND 075554), 9 miles SE. of Reay, Sheet 11 (A.836 and by-road). *Caithness.*

The remains of this chambered cairn, situated ¼ mile N. by E. of Dorrery Lodge, consist of a turf-covered stony mound about 42 ft. in diameter and 5 ft. high. The start of the entrance passage is marked by two upright slabs in the W. quadrant, and 16 ft. in from this another such slab marks the beginning of the first compartment of a Camster tripartite chamber. Other slabs reveal the outlines of the rest of the chamber.

Camster, Chambered Cairn (ND 260442), 6¼ miles S. of Watten, Sheet 11 (by-road to Lybster). *Caithness.*

This long horned cairn, and its large round neighbour 200 yds. to the SSE., are known as the Grey Cairns of Camster. A third cairn, 140 yds. WSW. of the round Grey cairn, measures 27 ft. in diameter and 2 ft. in height, and is not included in the sonorous appellation. The long cairn, with its four horns, fits into a space measuring 200 ft. by 65 ft., and is thus one of the largest cairns in the country. The main chamber, reached by a passage leading in from the long E. side, is a tripartite Camster type chamber. The cairn also has a minor chamber, a small cell about 5 ft. in diameter with a corbelled roof 6 ft. from the floor, reached by a narrow passage 20 ft. long which leads in from a point 30 ft. SW. of the tip of the E. horn.

Camster, Chambered Cairn (ND 260440), 6¼ miles S. of Watten, Sheet 11 (by-road to Lybster). *Caithness.*

This round cairn forms, with its long neighbour, the Grey Cairns of Camster. It is the prototype and eponym of the Camster cairns, a round structure of loose stones measuring about 55 ft. in diameter and 12 ft. in height. The passage, 20 ft. long, leads in from the SE. Its side walls are interrupted by four opposed pairs of slabs which project after the manner of door-jambs. The chamber is in three parts on plan, though the first to be reached at the end of the passage is roofed with flat slabs, while the remaining two both lie together beneath one corbelled roof through a modern hole in the top of which the interior of the chamber can be conned today. The excavators found the remains of cremations, of Western Neolithic pottery and of several artefacts including a polished knife.

Ormiegill, Chambered Cairn, (ND 332429), 5 miles SSW. of Wick, Sheet 12 (A.9 and footpath). *Caithness.*

The short horned cairn on the Hill of Ulbster has been famous since Joseph Anderson described it 100 years ago. It now appears as a dilapidated pile of stones among which slabs forming parts of the tripartite Camster chamber can be distinguished. It was found to measure 75 ft. by 70 ft. between the tips of the four horns. The façade out of which the passage opens is in the S. It is a little larger than that formed between the two horns at the N. end of the cairn. In this as in other such monuments the outline of the cairn was originally secured by duplicating the wall faces, while an innermost face held the stones packed round the slabs forming the chamber and the passage. The excavators found charred bones, western neolithic pottery, objects of flint and a mace-head comparable to one from Taversoe Tuack cairn, on Rousay, Orkney.

Yarrows, Chambered Cairn (ND 304432), 5½ miles SSW. of Wick, Sheet 12 (A.9, farm road and moorland). *Caithness.*

Two long horned chambered cairns originally stood about 300 yds. apart on a ridge ½ mile SSW. of the Loch of Yarrows, but after excavations 100 years ago one was demolished beyond recognition by stone-robbers. The other remains impressive only by the enduring evidence it provides of great size. It measures 240 ft. in length, 92 ft. between the tips of the horns at the E., and 53 ft. at the W. end. It was 12 ft. high at the E., 5 ft. at the W. Access to the Camster tripartite chamber was gained by a short passage set in the focus of the E. façade. The E. horns of the cairn were found to be defined by double lines of kerb-boulders, the rest of the cairn by a single line.

Garrywhin, Chambered Cairn (ND 313411), 7 miles SSW. of Wick, Sheet 12 (A.9, by-road and moorland). *Caithness.*

This short horned cairn is situated within ¼ mile to the W. of Ulbster station on the disused track of the old Wick and Lybster Light Railway Company. It is ruinous, but a certain amount of the structure of the cairn and of the chamber can be distinguished among the debris.

The chamber, reached by a passage from the façade in the S. (which is only slightly larger than that in the N.), is in two parts, an outer small one and an inner larger and almost circular compartment. The latter feature contrasts with the normal tripartite Camster chamber as found at Ormiegill. Evidence of cremations as well as of unburnt skeletons came from this cairn, together with western neolithic pottery.

Windy Edge, Long Cairn (NY 429839), 4 miles E. of Longholm, Sheet 79 (unclassified road and moorland). *Dumfriesshire.*

This long cairn standing on the watershed between the Liddel and Tarras Waters is reached with the least difficulty from the unfenced road running from the A.7 just N. of Langholm over the hills to join the B.6357 at Newcastleton. It is much mutilated by the construction of a large fold and several small refuges, but the general form of a huge pile of stones stretching for over 200 ft. in length testifies to the original shape, and a cist can be discerned in the W. end.

Stidriggs, Long Cairn (NY 041987), 3¼ miles SW. of Beattock, Sheet 78 (A.701, by-road and footpath). *Dumfriesshire.*

This long cairn stands on the N. toe of Broadshaw Rig on the moors which are now desolate but which were probably more widely used in the 2nd and perhaps the 3rd millennium B.C., as patches of clearance cairns and burial cairns in the vicinity testify. It measures a little less than 100 ft. in length, 30 ft. in width near the N. end and 60 ft. near the S. where it attains an elevation of 6 ft.

Clonfeckle, Long Cairn (NX 958867), 1½ miles NE. of Dalswinton, Sheet 78 (by-road and moorland). *Dumfriesshire.*

This member of the non-chambered long cairns lies in the SE. extremity of Dalswinton Common, 270 yds. W. of the Duncow Burn. It measures 110 ft. in length by a greatest width of as much as 84 ft. Many of the boulders forming the peristalith are visible.

Capenoch, Long Cairn (NX 838926), 1½ miles SSW. of Penpont, Sheet 78 (farm land and moorland). *Dumfriesshire.*

This long cairn is situated 3¼ miles N. by W. of its companion at Fleuchlarg. It measures 120 ft. in length by 31 ft. in width near the NE. end and 57 ft. near the S., and now attains a height of no more than 11 ft.

Fleuchlarg, Long Cairn (NX 854874), 2 miles NNW. of Dunscore, Sheet 78 (B.729 and farm land). *Dumfriesshire.*

The rather scanty remains of this, one of the westernmost of the not strictly chambered long cairns, lie in a field 200 yds. W. by S. of Fleuchlarg farmhouse. It measures 140 ft. in length from N. to S., 30 ft. in width near the N. end and 80 ft. near the S., where it stands to a height of 12 ft.

Walton, Chambered Cairn (NS 363782) 1¼ miles NE. of Cardross, Sheet 63 (A.814 and by-road). *Dunbartonshire.*

This ruinous Clyde-Carlingford chambered cairn, standing on a hillside overlooking the estuary of the River Clyde from the N., was examined in 1954. Most of the material of the cairn had been robbed for building purposes, but two portal stones and two side slabs survive to indicate the former presence of a chamber about 15 ft. long. Some 50 quartz pebbles, thought to have been a ritual deposit, were discovered in the ruined chamber, together with part of a polished axe.

Corrimony, Chambered Cairn (NH 381304), 8 miles W. of Drumnadrochit, Sheet 26 (A.831). *Inverness-shire.*

This passage grave of the Clava group, situated at the head of Glen Urquhart beside the River Enrick, was excavated in 1952. It is roughly circular, with a diameter of about 60 ft., and stands nearly 8 ft. in greatest height. The base is kerbed, and the interior structures comprise a passage, 23 ft. in length, and a circular chamber 12 ft. in diameter. The latter shows the remains of a corbelled roof which might originally have attained an internal height of 8 ft., beneath a massif capstone upon which cup-markings are carved. A free-standing circle of 11 stones surrounds the cairn at a distance of some 12 ft. Cleared of filling, the chamber floor was found to be of sand, with a central area paved with flat slabs intermingled with charcoal. On raising these, signs of a crouched inhumation burial were revealed in the sand below, representing the last interment in the useful life of the tomb.

Balnuaran of Clava, Ring Cairn (NH 756443), 10½ miles SW. of Nairn, Sheet 27 (B.9091, B.851 and by-road).
Inverness-shire.

This member of the Ring Cairn subgroup of the Clava cairns actually stands between the two passage graves of the other sub-group from which the whole series derive their name. It appears as a slightly oval, thick ring of stones and rubble, bounded by a kerb outside and a set of upright slabs inside and measuring 16 ft. to 22 ft. in thickness. The central space is almost circular—21 ft. by 18 ft.—and the external axial measurements are 70 ft. and 64 ft. This substantial ring lies within nine standing stones set on the circumference of a circle about 100 ft. in diameter. The stones vary tremendously in appearance, from as little as 1 ft. in height, for example, to as much as 7 ft. 6 in. Three of them—on the E., SSE. and W. are connected to the outer kerb of the circle by paths of small stones about 7 ft. wide, but this has not been recorded elsewhere among cairns of this class.

Culdoich, Ring Cairn (NH 752438), 11 miles SW. of Nairn, Sheet 27 (B.9091, B.851 and by-road). *Inverness-shire.*

This Ring Cairn, belonging to the sub-group of the Clava cairns, measures 57 ft. in diameter within its boulder kerb and contains a central hollow about 22 ft. in diameter. Only one stone of the circle which originally surrounded the cairn survives, a slab 12 ft. high situated 25 ft. SW. of the kerb and so indicating an original diameter of about 100 ft. for the circle.

Excavation of the central hollow showed that the slabs surrounding this rose to a height of 5 ft. above the original ground level and that they contained within them a deposit of stones and earth up to 3 ft. in depth. At the centre of the latter, on the old ground surface, a patch about 7 ft. in diameter was found to be heavily impregnated with charcoal and cremated human bones.

Cragabus, Chambered Cairn (NR 329451), 2 miles W. of Port Ellen, Sheet 60 (by-road through the Oa). *Islay.*

This cairn lies among crofts, the material for the walls of which was partly derived from it, so that little remains but the slabs of the tripartite chamber and one isolated stone 9 ft. high, distant 9 ft. 6 in. to the NE. The single remaining internal septal slab rises as high as do those of the walls of the chamber, indicating that the latter may originally have been carried up in the form of corbelled dry-stone walling to the level of the capstones.

Raedykes, Ring Cairns (NO 833906), 4 miles NW. of Stonehaven, Sheet 38 (A.957 and by-road).   *Kincardineshire.*

At present, no information is available about the number and distribution of the little ring cairns of which four examples have been noted in Kincardineshire in the moorland E. of the Mounth. These are situated ¼ mile NW. of West Raedykes, on the opposite side from the well-known curiously shaped Roman temporary camp of that name. The north-westernmost cairn consists of a ring 12 ft. thick with an internal diameter of 8 ft. and an external one of 32 ft. Several slabs and pillars of the inner and outer kerbs are still *in situ.* Three earthfast and two loose standing stones still survive from a complete ring which surrounded the cairn at a distance of 7 ft. 6 in., adding considerably to the Clava-like impression which these monuments give. The next cairn to the S., distant 50 yds. from the first, also has a central hollow 8 ft. in diameter, but the ring is only 7 ft. thick. No stones of any external circle which may ever have existed are apparent. The third cairn, 10 yds. to the E., repeats the internal diameter of 8 ft., but the ring is 10 ft. thick. The fourth cairn, 25 yds. to the SE., measures 9 ft. internally, its ring 12 ft. in thickness, and the slabs and stones defining it are still comparatively plentiful. As many as eight earthfast and several loose standing stones belonging to the external circle remain, at a distance of 12 ft. from the cairn.

Gourdon, Long Cairn (NO 818707), 1½ miles SSW. of Inverbervie, Sheet 45 (A.92 and farm land).   *Kincardineshire.*

This member of the eastern group of long cairns which cannot be classified as chambered cairns proper measures 155 ft. in length, 25 ft. in width at the S. end and 40 ft. at the N., and attains a general height of 9 ft.

Boreland, Chambered Cairn (NX 405690), 1½ miles N. of Minnigaff, Sheet 77 (by-road and footpath).
Stewartry of Kirkcudbright.

This Clyde-Carlingford chambered cairn with a terminal chamber is in good condition, standing to a height of 6 ft. and measuring 70 ft. in length by a maximum of 40 ft. near the SE. where four stones of the crescentic forecourt survive. The peristalith is also marked by more than a dozen boulders, but there are no visible signs of the passage or chamber.

Dranandow, Chambered Cairn (NX 408714), 3 miles N. of Minnigaff, Sheet 77 (by-road and footpath).
Stewartry of Kirkcudbright.

This Clyde-Carlingford chambered cairn belongs to the class which has lateral as well as axial chambers. It measures 95 ft. on the long axis, aligned from E. to W., and up to 60 ft. transversely. The axial chamber lies centrally near the E. end, and the four lateral chambers are regularly disposed in square formation W. of this. The peristalith is of small boulders.

Cairn Avel, Long Cairn (NX 559925), ½ mile S. of Carsphairn, Sheet 77 (farm road and footpath).
Stewartry of Kirkcudbright.

This cairn has lost some 50 ft. of its W. end, and now measures only a little over 50 ft. in length by a maximum of 65 ft. near the E. end, where it stands to a height of 10 ft. While no upright stones or slabs are exposed in the remaining part of the cairn, its general appearance is similar to that of the unchambered long cairns which are distributed farther to the E. and N.

White Cairn, Bargrennan, Chambered Cairn (NX 353784), 9 miles NNW. of Newton Stuart, Sheet 77 (A.714).
Stewartry of Kirkcudbright.

This small, ruinous passage grave, situated within ½ mile E. of another cairn of unknown type but called by the same name, was excavated in 1949. It is circular, about 45 ft. in diameter, and stands nearly 5 ft. in height near the centre. The megalithic chamber and the passage form a single, undifferentiated unit, near the entrance to which a fire-pit had been used, and bones and a flint tool burned. Though the chamber and the passage had been robbed and gutted, the excavators were able to reach an undisturbed area of paving in the passage, where they found cremated bones and sherds of a neolithic type of pottery. They suggested that a link might have existed between the builders of the cairn and

13 *Cairnholy I Clyde–Carlingford Chambered Cairn during Excavation. The Chamber is in the foreground, the Façade and Forecourt beyond*

people of the Ronaldsway culture of the Isle of Man.

Cairnderry, Chambered Cairn (NX 315799), 11 miles NW. of Newton Stewart, Sheet 77 (A.714).
Stewartry of Kirkcudbright.

This chambered cairn, situated close to the N. side of the road, is the only representative in Galloway of a more or less circular type of Clyde-Carlingford cairn, with three chambers set radially within the body of the cairn, to show affinity with others in Bute and Arran. It measures about 92 ft. from N. to S. by about 81 ft. transversely, and a few boulders of the peristalith are still preserved in the SW. Several slabs forming the chambers are visible *in situ*, particularly those of the S. chamber.

Newton, Chambered Cairn (NX 550526), 3¾ miles SW. of Gatehouse of Fleet, Sheet 83 (A.75).
Stewartry of Kirkcudbright.

Four elegant monoliths in a field ½ mile SW. of Newton represent all that is left of the chamber of what was probably a Clyde-Carlingford cairn. Traces of slab walling connect the bases of the pillars to define an area 7 ft. long by 3 ft. wide. The highest stone reaches 5 ft. 4 in., the next 4 ft. 11 in.; the other two, which are tilted, are of comparable size.

Cairnholy I and II, Chambered Cairns (NX 517538), 4 miles SE. of Creetown, Sheet 83 (A.75). *Stewartry of Kirkcudbright*

These Clyde-Carlingford chambered cairns, which are situated 150 yds. apart on a hillside overlooking the E. shore of Wigtown Bay, were excavated in 1949.

The southern cairn, Cairnholy I, is a conspicuous monument measuring axially about 170 ft. by 50 ft., with a monumental crescentic façade and a ruined chamber. The forecourt blocking was found to cover hearths, a stone-hole and western neolithic sherds. The chamber is bipartite; the outer section contained a fragment of a jadeite ceremonial axe, probably attributable to the earliest burials, together with sherds of western neolithic pottery and a leaf-shaped arrowhead. Late grave-goods comprised Peterborough and Beaker sherds and a plano-convex flint knife. The rear compartment, though robbed, contained a secondary cist, with food vessel sherds and a cup-and-ring carved stone.

The northern cairn, Cairnholy II, is a less spectacular structure, measuring axially about 70 ft. by 40 ft., with a bipartite chamber exposed, opening between portal stones. The rear compartment had been robbed, and the outer disturbed, but a leaf-shaped arrowhead and a flint knife of Arran type came from the filling, together with secondary sherds of beaker pottery.

Coll, Chambered Cairn (NB 450382), 3½ miles NE. of Stornoway, Sheet 8 (A.857, B.895 and moorland).   *Lewis.*

The remains of this cairn lie on the moor 1 mile SW. of Coll farmhouse. The cairn measures 50 ft. in diameter and 4 ft. in height, and the remains of a cur-

circumference of a circle 70 ft. in diameter, and an internal setting representing the chamber. The latter comprises four large slabs and a fallen capstone. Two other earthfast slabs 12 ft. SE. of these may represent part of the passage.

Gress, Chambered Cairn (NB 472438), 7½ miles NNE. of Stornoway, Sheet 8 (A.857, B.895 and footpath).   *Lewis.*

14   *Callanish: the Chambered Cairn lies immediately beyond the Great Central Pillar Stone*

vilinear chamber about 6 ft. in diameter are visible in the E. quadrant. Two large lintels lie upon it.

Garrabost, Chambered Cairn (NB 523330), 6 miles E. of Stornoway, Sheet 8 (A.866 and moorland).   *Lewis.*

This cairn, robbed of most of its material, now appears as a setting of seven kerb stones lying roughly on the

This cairn stands on a site which may have been levelled, at a point about 2 miles NW. of Gress Lodge. It consists of a mass of stones measuring 92 ft. by 77 ft. along the axes and standing to a height of 10 ft. The remains of a kerb of earthfast boulders still survive round the SW. margin. while several large slabs situated in the SE. quadrant probably represent parts of the passage and chamber.

Steinacleit, Chambered Cairn (NB 396540), 13 miles N. by W. of Stornoway, Sheet 8 (A.857 and track). *Lewis.*

The remains of this tomb consist of a peristalith of 10 upright slabs on the circumference of a circle 50 ft. in diameter enclosing much-robbed cairn material through which three earthfast slabs comprising part of the chamber protrude. The cairn stands in an oval enclosure 270 ft. long by 180 ft. wide formed by closely set earthfast boulders.

Callanish, Chambered Cairn and Standing Stones (NB 213330), 13 miles W. of Stornoway, Sheet 8 (A.858 and by-road). *Lewis.*

The setting of tall thin megaliths at Callanish constitutes the most spectacular part of a remarkable composite monument. The focus is a pillar 15 ft. 7 in. high, 5 ft. wide and 1 ft. thick which stands near the centre of a circle 37 ft. in diameter delineated by 13 slabs placed with their broad faces on the line of the perimeter and standing to a mean height of 10 ft. A double avenue 27 ft. wide runs N. from this for a distance of 270 ft. This may originally have contained 20 monoliths on either side, but only 10 have survived on the W. side and nine on the E. A single row of five monoliths runs S. from a point outside the S. arc of the circle on the line of the W. side of the double avenue, the last member lying at a distance of 90 ft. from the circle. A single stone 12 ft. E. of the innermost of this line may be the only remnant of a parallel row. Short lines of monoliths radiate to E. and W. of the circle, each comprising four stones; the W. line ends 40 ft. from the circle, that to the E., 50 ft.

The roofless remains of the chambered cairn lie between the central pillar and the monoliths forming the E. arc of the circle in a manner which strongly suggests that the two were designed to go together, even if one preceded the other. The design of the chamber has been said to suggest comparison with Camster type chambers. A second and so-called cairn, however, presents a far less satisfactory appearance. It is a very low mound measuring 18 ft. by 14 ft. which is situated immediately NE. of the chambered cairn. Its nature has not been

ascertained; but at least one of the slabs forming the circle is planted in it.

Breasclete, Chambered Cairn (NB 211355), 13¼ miles W. by N. of Stornoway, in Breasclete township, Sheet 8 (A.858). *Lewis.*

The remains of the chamber of this cairn, crowning a low hill W. of Breasclete, consist of four contiguous upright slabs forming an arc about 8 ft. long facing the NE. Most of the rest of the cairn has been removed.

Port Donain, Chambered Cairn (NM 738292), 5 miles SSE. of Craignure, Sheet 49 (B.8035 and by-road). *Mull.*

This cairn, probably a Clyde-Carlingford tomb but situated in territory bordering on that of the Hebridean group, stands close to the sea-shore at Port Donain, near the E. extremity of Mull. It measures about 100 ft. in length and 50 ft. in greatest width, and stands to a height of 5 ft. Portal stones flanking a gap in the middle of the façade at the E. end of the cairn form the opening to a chamber about 14 ft. long. Other chambers or cists, possibly secondary, may exist in the W. part of the cairn.

Barpa nam Feannag, Chambered Cairn (NF 856721), 4¼ miles NW. of Lochmaddy, Sheet 18 (A.865 and moorland). *North Uist.*

This cairn appears as a mound of stones measuring 165 ft. from WNW. to ESE. and 46 ft. in breadth near the latter end where it stands to a height of 8 ft. A flat slab measuring at least 6 ft. by 3 ft. appears near the centre of the ESE. end, and a slab on end protrudes some distance W. of this.

Barpa Langass, Chambered Cairn (NF 837656), 5¼ miles WSW. of Lochmaddy, Sheet 18 (A.867). *North Uist.*

This is one of the better preserved chambered cairns on North Uist. It is a circular pile of stones measuring about 80 ft. in diameter and standing to a height of 14 ft., with the remains of a peristalith of small flat slabs. The passage, in the E. quadrant, leads into a polygonal chamber in a good state of repair. This measures a little over 9 ft. from E. to W. by 6 ft. from N. to S., and up to 7 ft. in height. The walls consist of five large slabs, the spaces between and around them being filled with dry-stone walling. The roof is formed by two large lintels, a third covering the gap between them. Pottery, a barbed arrow-head, a scraper and a pierced talc disc recovered from the chamber are in the national collection.

Craonaval, Chambered Cairn (NF 842625), 6 miles SW. of Lochmaddy, Sheet 22 (A.867, B.894 and moorland). *North Uist.*

This much pillaged chambered cairn is almost circular in shape, measuring about 55 ft. in diameter. Remains of passage and chamber can be seen in the form of earthfast slabs standing out above the scanty debris in the E. quadrant.

Uneval, Chambered Cairn (NF 800669), 7 miles W. by S. of Lochmaddy, Sheet 18 (A.867, A.865 and moorland). *North Uist.*

The remains of this chambered tomb, excavated in 1935 and 1939, consist of a polygonal chamber and short passage and several earthfast slabs of the façade and peristalith. A considerable amount of neolithic pottery of several kinds was obtained from the chamber, in addition to beaker.

A two-compartment dwelling of the Early Iron Age subsequently built in the NE. corner of the cairn was considered to incorporate a corn-drying room.

Clettraval, Chambered Cairn and Dun (NF 749714), 10¼ miles W. by N. of Lochmaddy, Sheet 18 (A.867, A.865 and moorland). *North Uist.*

This Hebridean chambered cairn with marked Clyde-Carlingford connections, was excavated in 1934. It was then established that a circular dun measuring 26 ft. in internal diameter within a wall 7 ft. thick had been built of and over the W. end of the cairn, which was in this manner almost entirely destroyed. After the dun had fallen into decay, "some secondary occupation of the broch period" was recorded by the excavator among the dun's ruins.

The cairn had originally been wedge-shaped on plan, measuring about 90 ft. in greatest width, at the E. end, by at least an estimated 150 ft. in length. The façade was found to be rectilinear, or straight, and to bend back on either side of the middle at a little more, or less, than a right-angle to the axis of the entrance to the chamber. The chamber is in five sections, the innermost being larger than the others and so suggesting

a passage-grave influence. The sections are formed by septal slabs which stand to heights above the floor varying between 1 ft. 6 in. and 2 ft. 6 in. The floor is of natural rock (gneiss). The roof has all been taken away, but its original position may be estimated by the fact that the orthostatic wall of the innermost chamber is 7 ft. high, and that of the outermost chamber 4 ft. 6 in. The cairn was bordered on ground level by an elaborate, beautifully built peristalith. Considerable quantities of pottery of both neolithic and beaker periods was recovered.

Maes Howe, Chambered Cairn (HY 317127), 4½ miles NE. of Stromness, Sheet 6 (A.965). *Orkney, Mainland island.*

This chambered tomb, representing a standard of design and workmanship which is not otherwise known to have been reached in neolithic Britain—or indeed in any place N. and W. of the Mediterranean—has suffered from a certain amount of damage during its 35 or more centuries of life, but by far the greater part of it is still in good condition.

The outward appearance of the monument is a domical mound 24 ft. high and 115 ft. in diameter, standing on a level space varying in width from 40 ft. to 70 ft. This is in turn surrounded by a shallow ditch from less than 25 ft. to 60 ft. wide. A low mound which borders the outer lip of the ditch is of recent construction, although it is possible that quite by chance it replaced an original wall, slabs thought to belong to which have been dug out of the ditch. The ditch itself is about 3 ft. to 4 ft. deep, flat bottomed and cut down through clay and stones to a surface of bed-rock.

The surface of the space between the inner lip of the ditch and the outer margin or base of the cairn was levelled artificially before the cairn was built.

The cairn may originally have been bounded by a bank of sods from which a wooden fence may have risen. The main body of the cairn consists of a very obdurate mixture of clay and stones. Internal walls or stretches of masonry are incorporated into the mass; their function may have been both to add rigidity during the process of building up the cairn and to ensure stability after the material was all in place. The chamber at the centre of the cairn is contained under the mass of cairn material, in a strong skin comprising tiers of walling based on a plinth and rising in a series of narrow steps. In the E. part of the cairn this casing wall has been found by excavation to be standing to a height of 14 ft.

The entrance to the interior of the chamber is on the SW. side of the mound. It opens into a passage 36 ft. long, checked after 6 ft. 6 in. for a door at a point where the passage is 4 ft. 6 in. high and 3 ft. wide. The door-slab rests in a recess in the wall a short distance inside the door. In the vicinity of the door, the walls of the passage are built of ordinary coursed masonry, but thereafter each wall and the roof are formed by a slab of stone averaging 18 ft. 6 in. in length, 4 ft. 4 in. in width and 7 in. thick. There is then a slight contraction, formed by portal stones, before the chamber proper is reached. This is 15 ft. square. The four walls rise vertically for 4 ft. 6 in. and then begin to converge in overlapping courses.

It is in this corbelling that the technical ability of the builders is revealed at its most attractive. The natural angle of splitting of the stone has allowed them to lay the successive members of the roofing in such a way that the resulting surface is as smooth as if each stone had been most accurately dressed. A pillar in each corner of the chamber helps to keep the roof in place. The original structure survives to a height of 12 ft. 6 in. The top 5 ft. of the vaulting must have been extremely stable, but latter-day vandals managed to tear it off when they attempted to rob the cairn in 1861, and it has been replaced by a concrete dome. The structural details of the chamber bear long and careful examination.

The wall opposite the entrance and the side walls each have a rectangular recess leading off them into the body of the cairn; the openings into these are raised nearly 3 ft. above the floor of the chamber. A massive block of stone lies on the floor outside each of them, in witness

15   *Maes Howe Chambered Cairn. The passage from the Interior, illustrating the use of beams of sedimentary rock*

of the violation of the burials and grave-goods which must once have lain in the recesses.

Apart from the wanton damage of 1861, however, the tomb had several times been entered on earlier occasions, although without receiving any damage to its structure. No less than 24 runic inscriptions carved on various stones in the chamber testify to the former presence of Norse and other piratical bands. One of these, usually supposed to have been that led by Rognvald and Eindrid the Younger, which wintered in Orkney in 1150-1, must have represented the first people to have entered the tomb since the last obsequious priest backed out and sealed up the door getting on for 3000 years earlier. For they recorded that they had looted the tomb of a great treasure which can only have been composed of gold articles of Mediterranean and more local origin. Later comers may have picked up trifles left by the earlier arrivals, and eventually the last scraps were removed and the tomb allowed to remain quiet until the unwelcome feet of Farrer and his band arrived to add destruction to robbery.

Besides inscriptions, the earlier marauders left certain other engravings—a serpent knot, an animal which is usually called a walrus but is more likely to be a seal, and a splendid beast known as the lion and assigned to a date early in the 12th century A.D.

Onstan, Chambered Cairn (HY 282117), 2 miles NE. of Stromness, Sheet 6 (A.965). *Orkney, Mainland island.*

The alteration in the name of this place may appear unnecessary and is undoubtedly very inconvenient, as the so-called UNSTAN pottery—named at the time of excavations in 1884—occupies an important place in the neolithic series. By 1934 the name had become Onston on the maps, and today it is Onstan.

The cairn is an almost circular stalled cairn, a Camster derivative, the lengthening of the chamber just affecting the regularity of the outline of the exterior. The chamber, measuring 20 ft. in length by 6 ft. in width, is divided into five compartments or 10 cells, into one cf which the passage opens and out cf another of which a little cell is entered. The cairn itself consists of an innermost

cylinder of stones which contains the chamber, its outer face well laid and vertical; and two contiguous outer skins which encase this.

Ring of Bookan, Chambered Cairn (HY 285147), 3¼ miles NNE. of Stromness, Sheet 6 (A.965, B.9055).
Orkney, Mainland island.

The cairn called the Ring of Bookan has been virtually obliterated, but there is reason to believe that it was of the Maes Howe type. Nevertheless the monument is of considerable interest by reason of the presence of the broad, shallow ditch which surrounds the central plateau. The latter measures 146 ft. by 124 ft. along the axes; the ditch is 44 ft. wide and 6 ft. deep. While the central area, and presumably therefore the cairn which once stood upon it, are smaller than those at Maes Howe, the ditch is of precisely the same proportions. Such ditches betoken a relationship, even if of an attenuated nature, with henges and with disc barrows and other, distant, cultures.

Via, Chambered Cairn (HY 259160), 4¼ miles N. of Stromness, Sheet 6 (A.967). *Orkney, Mainland island.*

This is an example of the principal stones of the chamber of a chambered cairn having been denuded of all cairn material—comparatively uncommon in this part of the country but well known as dolmen or cromlech elsewhere. The displaced coverstone still rests partly on two earthfast stones of the wall of the chamber, while five other such stones which have been displaced lie about in the immediate vicinity.

Head of Work, Chambered Cairn (HY 483138), 3 miles NE. of Kirkwall, Sheet 6 (by-road, farm road).
Orkney, Mainland island.

This long horned cairn of the Yarrows type, horned at either end, measures 160 ft. by 80 ft. over all extremities, the actual body being 105 ft. long and at the most 45 ft. wide. It appears as a grass-grown mound; evidence of slight and informal excavation rests in an exploratory depression near the E. end in which slabs belonging to what is probably a secondary cist are exposed. It is hardly likely that a primary chamber would appear so high above ground level.

Wideford Hill, Chambered Cairn (HY 409121), 3 miles E. by N. of Kirkwall,

Sheet 6 (A.965). *Orkney, Mainland island.*

This chambered cairn of the Maes Howe type contains a main chamber with a cell opening from each wall, except the W. long side into which the passage opens. The structural entity comprising the chambers and passage is encased within a cylindrical mass of laid stones, the carefully made outer face of which rises vertically as far as it still exists—a maximum height of 5 ft. 6 in. above the floor of the passage. This mass is in turn enveloped by two concentric and contiguous vertical-faced annular walls, each about 4 ft. thick. When new, the lower part of the exterior of the cairn would have appeared like a stone drum 45 ft. in diameter, but there is no knowing how far the vertical sides were carried up or how the top of the monument was finished off.

The passage is 17 ft. 6 in. in length. The main chamber measures 10 ft. 4 in. in length by 4 ft. 6 in. in width at floor level. Its walls converge gradually as they rise, until the gap is reduced to 6 ft. 9 in. by 1 ft. 9 in., and could have been covered with no more than three stone slabs, at a height of 8 ft. 3 in. above the floor.

Cuween, Chambered Cairn (HY 364127), ¼ mile S. of Finstown, Sheet 6 (farm road). *Orkney, Mainland island.*

This chambered cairn of the Maes Howe sub-group has been broken into more than once, but has now been repaired and is under guardianship. The cairn measures 55 ft. in diameter and stands to a height of 8 ft. 6 in. A passage with a total length of 18 ft. and measuring 2 ft. 8 in. in height and 2 ft. 4 in. in width, leads in from the SE. to the oblong main chamber. This is about 10 ft. long and 5 ft. wide, and the replacement roof, situated a little lower than the original, is 7 ft. 6 in. above the floor. Four cells, one with a subsidiary cell, open off the main chamber.

Taversoe Tuack, Chambered Cairn (HY 426276), ¾ mile W. of Brinyan pier, Sheet 6 (B.9064). *Orkney, Rousay island.*

This, the only two-decked chambered cairn known apart from Huntersquoy, on Eday, is a Camster cairn in which the entrance passage reaches a long side of the chamber, rather than an end. Its small size places it early in the secession series.

The cairn measures 30 ft. in diameter and is apparently all of one build rather than constructed in skins. The lower chamber, reached by a passage 19 ft. long, is 12 ft. 3 in. long, 5 ft. wide and 5 ft. 3 in. high, and includes four cells. It contained several skeletons, pieces of six Unstan (Onstan) bowls and a perforated mace-head of secondary neolithic type. The upper chamber, the floor of which is formed by the roofing slabs of the lower, is reached by a passage 11 ft. long. The chamber consists of two compartments, one 9 ft. 4 in. by 6 ft. 6 in. and the other 4 ft. 3 in. by 3 ft. 8 in. A recess in the wall carries on the line of the passage for 4 ft. 7 in. Cremated bone and some Onstan sherds were found in cists situated in the main chamber.

A curious feature of this monument is a drain which continues the line of the entrance passage of the lower chamber outwards for a further 18 ft. 9 in., to end near a small rock-cut chamber, oval on plan and measuring 5 ft. by 3 ft. 10 in. axially and 2 ft. 10 in. in height. Two complete Onstan bowls and fragments of a third were found in it.

Blackhammer, Chambered Cairn (HY 414276), 1¼ miles W. of Brinyan pier, Sheet 6 (B.9064). *Orkney, Rousay island.*

A neighbour to the little Yarso stalled cairn, Blackhammer is of interest because the passage leads in to a long side of the chamber instead of an end. The chamber, measuring 42 ft. 6 in. in length and about 6 ft. in width, is divided by six pairs of opposing septal slabs into seven compartments or 14 stalls, into one of which the short passage emerges from the S. The chamber is encased in a stone skin about 7 ft. thick, and this in turn is protected by another of comparable weight. The roof has been removed along with the upper part of the cairn.

Knowe of Yarso, Chambered Cairn (HY 404281), 2 miles W. of Brinyan, Sheet 6 (B.9064 and footpath).
Orkney, Rousay island.

This stalled cairn with four compartments, excavated in 1934 and now under guardianship, measures 50 ft. in length by 25 ft. in width. It contained the bones of 20 adults and one adolescent as well as those of 30 individual red-deer, some sheep and a dog. Relics included fragments of food-vessel and beaker pottery, four arrowheads and more than 60 other

16   *Mid Howe Stalled Chambered Cairn, now preserved beneath a protective covering*

flint implements, and five bone tools, all now in the national collection.

Knowe of Lairo, Chambered Cairn (HY 400277), 2½ miles W. of Brinyan pier, Sheet 6 (B.9064).

Orkney, Rousay island.

The presence of this long four-horned cairn of the Yarrows type on the island of Rousay, among all the stalled and other chambered cairns, emphasises the fact that some among several classes of monuments which are now recognised as having been broadly contemporary, must nevertheless have been erected at quite different times and under very different circumstances from others.

Although it has been mutilated, this cairn still appears as a long mound, higher at the ESE. end, measuring about 180 ft. in length and up to 72 ft. in width. It is 16 ft. high at the highest—above the chamber. The entrance passage, 18 ft. long, leads into the tripartite chamber which is about 17 ft. long, 8 ft. wide and as much as 13 ft. 8 in. high. The chamber has been altered by the insertion of later structures, but the original work can easily be distinguished.

Mid Howe, Chambered Cairn (HY 371306), 4½ miles WNW. of Brinyan pier, Sheet 6 (B.9064 and by-road).

Orkney, Rousay island.

This is the largest stalled cairn. It measures 106 ft. 9 in. in length by 42 ft.

6 in. in width and contains an inner dry-stone structure encasing the chamber, and an outer skin faced with coursed slabs set on a slant. The chamber measures 76 ft. in length and 7 ft. in width, and is divided into 12 compartments each of two opposing cells, 24 cells in all. The 12 cells along the E. range are fitted with slab platforms on which bones representing a total of 25 skeletons were found. The pottery is of the Unstan type.

Sandyhill Smithy, Chambered Cairn (HY 561327), 2 miles NNW. of Bay of Backaland pier, Sheet 6 (B.9063).

Orkney, Eday island.

This monument was excavated in 1937, when it was found to be a small stalled Camster cairn measuring 26 ft. 6 in. in average external diameter. The method of building such a structure, by first casing the chamber and then casing the casing, was brought out during the excavation. The passage, in the SE., is 7 ft. long. It leads into the rectangular chamber which measures 11 ft. 6 in. in length and from 5 ft. 3 in. to 6 ft. 6 in. in width. It is divided into three parts, the two innermost of which at least are provided with slab shelves 1 ft. above the floor.

The roof and many of the uprights supporting it have been destroyed for a very long time, but scraps of neolithic pottery were found among the debris on the floor.

Huntersquoy, Chambered Cairn (HY 562377), 4¾ miles N. by W. of Bay of Backaland pier, Sheet 5 (B.9063 and by-road). *Orkney, Eday island.*

This cairn, a storeyed stalled cairn comparable so far as is known only to the Taversoe Tuack cairn, is situated ¼ mile SW. of Carrick House. It is now marked chiefly by the stumps of the remains of the upper chamber. When excavated in 1937 it was found that the almost circular cairn, measuring about 35 ft. in diameter, contained a lower chamber, reached by a passage from the E., immediately above which was an upper chamber entered from the W. The upper chamber, measuring axially 11 ft. 6 in. by 6 ft. 6 in., contained six stalls, three on either side of the central space. The entrance passage, 10 ft. long, leads into the W. end of the chamber.

The roof of the upper chamber has gone, but its floor is formed by a layer of clay 10 in. thick placed upon the lintels forming the roof of the lower chamber. This is aligned N. and S., its passage entering the middle of the E. side. The chamber, the floor of which is solid rock, measures 12 ft. 10 in. in length, 8 ft. 4 in. in width and 7 ft. in height. The ends of the chamber are each divided off by a pair of opposed slabs which may be said to form either a pair of recesses or two pairs of stalls. In either case a simple stall is formed opposite the entrance. Subsidiary compartments and aumbries are built beneath the roof; one of them above the innermost lintel of the passage, one at the upper rear part of the central stall and one in the same place in the S. stall, and a double one in the N. stall.

Neolithic pottery and other small finds were recovered from this monument.

Vinquoy Hill, Chambered Cairn (HY 560382), 5 miles N. by W. of Bay of Backaland pier, Sheet 5 (B.9063 and by-road). *Orkney, Eday island.*

This chambered cairn of the Maes Howe type now appears only as an irregular stony mound overgrown with heather and with only occasional traces of building. The chamber has survived, except for the inevitable hole smashed through the apex of the corbelled roof to show that Farrer was here.

The tomb is built of sandstone, which here overlies the flagstone exposed elsewhere. The entrance passage is 13 ft. in length at the least and 2 ft. in width, while its height is at the most 2 ft. 6 in. It leads in to the chamber from the S. The latter is polygonal, measuring axially 8 ft. by 6 ft. and rising to a height of 9 ft. It has four cells, two each on the E. and W. All the entrances to the cells are on floor level, and the cells average 5 ft. 6 in. in height.

Calf of Eday, Chambered Cairn (HY 579387), 200 yds. from the W. shore of Calf of Eday, Sheet 5. *Orkney, Calf of Eday island.*

After removing the debris of a thick but secondary stone wall from the mound, excavators in 1936 went on to recover the original shape of the mound and the remarkable contents thereof. The first thing that strikes the eye on the finished plan is that the cairn not only contained a stalled chamber but overlay a small house of the type now, but not then, widely known in Shetland. This latter structure, however, measures only 10 ft. in length internally by 6 ft. 9 in. in width, and is subdivided into two unequal parts. It contained peaty soil blackened by fire and a few thin, undecorated sherds. Its long axis runs W. by N. and E. by S. The entrance was found to have been blocked with stones. Whether this little structure had been a house or a tomb, or both, it had evidently been robbed by the time the site came to be disused, because its walls were stripped of their facers.

There was now built a stalled chamber, entered from the E. end by a passage 11 ft. long. Three pairs of subdivisions form four compartments or eight stalls within the chamber, which measures 23 ft. in length by a maximum of 7 ft. in width. This structure has a wall about 4 ft. thick, one corner of which overlies and has obliterated one belonging to the little house-like structure.

The stalled chamber and the other structure were then encased in one oblong mass of stone, aligned on the longer axis of the stalled chamber. The casing measures 66 ft. by 27 ft., the faces of the sides and ends all being slightly convex. It seems inescapable that the casing and the stalled chamber represent one phase of construction and the little oval building an earlier, independent, one which was not, however, to be completely destroyed when the cairn casing was assembled and erected.

Other monuments on the Calf of Eday include what appear to be the remains of a house of Skara Brae type, and two souterrains.

Holm of Papa, Papa Westray, Chambered Cairn (HY 509518), W. coast of the Holm of Papa, Sheet 5.

Orkney, Holm of Papa island.

This cairn, now covered with a concrete roof through manholes in which the persistent visitor can gain access to the interior, is the end-product of the Maes Howe derivatives along the line characterised by a side-entrance to the chamber. The original outer appearance of the cairn is uncertain, but it was described as an oblong with rounded corners measuring 104 ft. in length by 41 ft. in breadth. The chamber is 67 ft. long and 5 ft. wide. It is subdivided by two cross-walls which are open at ground level to admit passage between the compartments thus formed, but solid above. The central compartment is 45 ft. long, the W. compartment 12 ft. and the E., 7 ft. Mural cells open off the compartments, entered from ground level. The two end compartments have three each, the central compartment four single and two double.

Several designs are engraved or carved upon the stonework of the chamber, including circular depressions and zig-zags, and two rectilinear devices which have even been interpreted as *eta* and *theta*.

It is interesting to note that a small stalled cairn with the passage leading into the end of the chamber is found on the same small island.

Quoyness, Chambered Cairn (HY 676378), 2 miles SSW. of Roadside, Sheet 5 (B.9069 and links).

Orkney, Sanday island.

This chambered cairn of the Maes Howe group, standing on the E. side of Els Ness, was excavated by Childe in 1951 and 1952. The roughly rectangular chamber measures 13 ft. 6 in. in length, 6 ft. 6 in. in width and 13 ft. in height, with an entrance passage 12 ft. long. It has six cells in the walls. It is encased in an ovoid cairn, supported by two retaining walls, the whole being covered with cairn material supported by a third wall standing on a raised platform. The original entrance to the chamber must have been blocked by the cairn material. Sherds of neolithic pottery found on the floor show affinity with Rinyo and Skara Brae settlements. A slate disc discovered in the chamber is comparable to finds in western Scotland, Wales, Spain and Portugal, thus supporting the belief that ritual traditions embodied in such tombs reached Britain by way of Atlantic seaways.

Isbister, Chambered Cairn (ND 469844), 7 miles S. of St Margaret's Hope, Sheet 7 (A.961, B.9041).

Orkney, South Ronaldsay island.

The remains of this chambered cairn of the Camster subdivision of the Orkney–Cromarty group, standing near the E. cliffs of South Ronaldsay 450 yds. ESE. of Isbister farmhouse, were partly opened in 1958. In view of the discoveries then made, officers of the Ministry of Works were despatched to the site to record what was visible and close the wounds. The cairn appears as a turf-covered mound about 135 ft. long by 50 ft. wide, and stands to a greatest height of 10 ft. It contains a stalled chamber of unknown extent, the three proximal segments of which had been uncovered. The rear wall of the ultimate one consists of a single slab, the side-walls of horizontally coursed dry masonry. A few bones were found in this part of the chamber. Pottery fragments, a cylindrical bone bead, three pairs of skulls and a great many other bones came from the second compartment; leg bones were found in the passage of a side chamber leading off the main chamber, and 10 skulls and numerous other bones lay in the side chamber itself, together with a deposit containing three axes, a mace-head, a knife and a V-bored button. Other holes in the body of the cairn revealed walling. The human remains are described as the most complete and best preserved yet found in a neolithic context in Scotland.

The Dwarfie Stane, Rock-cut Tomb (HY 243005), 1½ miles S. of Bay of Quoys, Sheet 7 (B.9049 and by-road).

Orkney, Hoy island.

The Dwarfie Stane is a block of sandstone which rests on a steep hillside a quarter of a mile S. of the road between Quoys and Rackwick. It measures 28 ft. in length and half as much in width, and is about 8 ft. or more deep. A passage and two cells have been cut in it, or hollowed out of it. The passage is 7 ft. 6 in. long, 2 ft. 4 in. high and 2 ft. 10 in. wide. It is flanked on either side by a cell about 5 ft. wide, 3 ft. deep and 2 ft. 6 in. high. A square block of stone lying just outside the entrance and measuring 5 ft. 1 in. by 2 ft. 8 in. by 2 ft. 1 in. was originally used to stop the entrance.

In the British Isles, the only structure possibly comparable to the Dwarfie Stane is the rock-cut St Kevin's Bed at Glendalough, 25 miles S. of Dublin; but the technique of cutting a tomb out of solid rock rather than erecting it above ground level is paralleled on a rather grander scale in the lower floors of the two-storeyed stalled cairns on Eday and Rousay, as well at at places in France, Iberia and the Mediterranean among which affiliations must be sought.

Clach na Tiompan, Chambered Cairn (NN 830330), 7 miles SW. of Amulree, Sheet 52 (A.822 and private road).
Perthshire.

The substantial remains of this example of the central-Scotland version of the Clyde-Carlingford chambered cairn were excavated in 1954. The cairn measures nearly 200 ft. in length, the E. end being the larger. A segmented chamber with two septal slabs and a portal is situated 35 ft. from the E. end; a second chamber, also with two septal slabs, was found 20 ft. farther W.; and a

third chamber 40 ft. E. of the W. end. A fourth chamber, destroyed in comparatively recent times, once existed between the second and third chambers. The first chamber consisted of an inner compartment the floor of which was slightly lower than those of the two outer compartments. The façade at the mouth of the chamber appeared at first sight to have formed part of the exterior of the cairn, but the excavators decided that the weight of the cairn material was such that this could not have been the case, and that it must have been concealed.

Kindrochat, Chambered Cairn (NN 723230), 3 miles W. of Comrie, Sheet 52 (A.85 and farm road).
Perthshire.

This cairn is a member of the Central Scotland group of modified Clyde-Carlingford chambered cairns, one of the four which occur in the middle part of Strathearn. The others are Rottenreoch, Clathick and Cultoquhey. It stands just S. of the disused railway track, 300 yds. S. of the farmhouse, on the flood-plain of the River Earn, appearing as a straggling mass of stones and boulders among which various internal features can still be readily distinguished. It was excavated by Childe in 1929 and 1930, when it was found to be made of large waterworn boulders and to measure 135 ft. by a greatest width of 36 ft. within a kerb embedded in virgin soil. Laid out with the long axis E. and W., it contained

17   *The Dwarfie Stane Rock-cut Chamber. The entrance with the displaced Blocking Stone*

three cists, one opening into the central sector of the E. end, one at about the middle and one between this and the W. end. The latter two were built parallel to the short axis, at a right angle to the E. cist. The central cist, the best preserved, was easily recognisable as a segmented cist. It contained a leaf-shaped arrow-head.

Rottenreoch, Chambered Cairn (NN 843206), 2 miles SW. of Crieff, Sheet 52 (A.822, by-road and farm road).
Perthshire.

This chambered cairn with Clyde-Carlingford affinities measures about 190 ft. in length, 37 ft. in width near the SW. end and 43 ft. near the NE. Slabs protruding through the turf near the latter indicate an axial chamber, while others near the far end may represent another.

Edderton, Chambered Cairn (NH 684858), 1¾ miles NW. of Edderton, Sheet 21 (A.9 and farm roads).
Ross & Cromarty.

This chambered cairn, measuring some 50 ft. in diameter, contains traces of a chamber oriented E. and W. comprising both upright stones and slabs and dry-stone walling. Another such cairn, more denuded, stands 100 yds. to the SE.

Ardvanie, Chambered Cairn (NH 681874), 2¼ miles NW. of Edderton, Sheet 21 (A.9). *Ross & Cromarty.*

This denuded passage grave, about 70 ft. in diameter, is situated between the road and the railway. It contains the remains of a polygonal chamber 11 ft. long and 6 ft. wide, the entrance being in the E.

Kilcoy, Carn Glas (Kilcoy I) Chambered Cairn (NH 578522), 4 miles NE. of Beauly, Sheet 26 (B.9162).
Ross & Cromarty.

This chambered cairn of the Camster group has been very much reduced by the removal of stone for building during the last century. It measured some 70 ft. in diameter, and when excavated in 1955 was found to have contained a bipartite chamber. Relics comprised secondary neolithic and beaker pottery, a leaf-shaped arrow-head and a barbed arrow-head; this would seem to imply two successive burials or periods of burial, the interval between them being indeterminate.

Long Knowe, Long Cairn (NY 527862), 3 miles W. of Newcastleton, Sheet 79 (B.6357, then forest tracks).
Roxburghshire.

This long cairn is one of the somewhat enigmatic structures which lie E. of the territories of the Clyde-Carlingford chambered cairns, and are probably not related to these or any other chambered cairns. The Long Knowe cairn is hard to find, as it lies in a small clearing in a comparatively young forest, but the remains justify the visit. It now appears as a pile of stones, shaped like an elongated pear and measuring 175 ft. in length by up to 45 ft. in width. Various slabs which protrude from the tumbled mass represent the remains of cists and vestigial burial chambers. The cairn may not have been very extensively robbed of stone, but it was burgled in the 19th century, with unrecorded results.

Seli Voe, Chambered Cairn (HU 297485), 2½ miles SE. of Bridge of Walls, Sheet 3 (farm road).
Shetland, Mainland island.

Although considerably robbed of material, this cairn retains enough earth-fast slabs to reveal the heel-shaped plan and the central chamber, or cist. The façade, the SW. end of which rests on a natural rock, measures 24 ft. in length. The chamber or cist, represented by six embedded slabs, measures 9 ft. by 5 ft.

Hill of Dale, Chambered Cairn (HU 409699), 4 miles N. of Voe, Sheet 3 (A.968). *Shetland, Mainland island.*

This cairn stands on the saddle of the Hill of Dale overlooking Dales Voe from the W. It is a heel-shaped cairn of which the large stones flanking the concave façade are preserved, together with much of the outline of the rest of the cairn. The façade measures 23 ft. 6 in. and is broken by no visible entrance to a passage. It is possible that here, as in some other examples, the cairn contained a cist rather than a full-scale chamber.

Punds Water, Chambered Cairn (HU 325713), 7 miles NW. of Voe, Sheet 3 (A.970 and moorland).
Shetland, Mainland island.

This heel-shaped cairn is one of the largest and the best preserved of its class. It is built of white quartzite boulders. The façade is over 50 ft. long, the converse axis 32 ft. A trefoil chamber, now roofless, occupies the centre of the cairn, being entered by a passage 12 ft. long opening out in the middle of the façade. The cairn is heel-shaped, but the two corners at either end of the façade are pinched out in a manner recalling the horns of such cairns as the Yarrows group.

March Cairn, Chambered Cairn (HU 223789), 4 miles WNW. of Hillswick, Sheet 3 (A.970, B.9078).

Shetland, Mainland island.

The possibility that some heel-shaped cairns would verge, on plan, towards a squarer outline than is common to most heels is of course admissible, and it is realised in the March Cairn, and in a few other known examples. This cairn measures 33 ft. 6 in. along the façade and 34 ft. 6 in. over the transverse axis. The façade runs on a somewhat sinuous line between the two corner stones, but the sides and the rear are straight, and the curves joining them very small and tight. The March Cairn has been excavated, and a report on the results will appear in the Proceedings of the Society of Antiquaries of Scotland.

Ronas Hill, Chambered Cairn (HU 305835), 5 miles NNE. of Hillswick, Sheet 3 (A.970 and moorland).

Shetland, Mainland island.

This cairn is superbly situated close to the pinkish summit of Ronas Hill, the highest peak in all Shetland (1486 ft. O.D.). It originally measured about 45 ft. in extent either way, but is now (even here!) somewhat mutilated, although the debris stands to a height of 10 ft. The chamber consists of a single compartment 5 ft. 6 in. wide, 3 ft. deep and 4 ft. high, entered by a short passage which opens into one of the long sides.

Vementry, Chambered Cairn (HU 294610), 7 miles WSW. of Voe, Sheet 3 (boat). *Shetland, Vementry island.*

This magnificent heel-shaped cairn is so constructed that the chamber is encased in a circular—possibly originally domical—stone-faced stone mass rising from a heel-shaped platform with which it is of one build. The heel-shaped base measures 37 ft. across the façade by 33 ft. along the transverse axis. The façade is faced with large slabs set on end, and is unbroken by any gap.

The chamber structure is set back 2 ft. from the rounded end of the heel-shaped base, continuing its circular form accord-

ing to a diameter of 26 ft. It is entered by a passage 12 ft. long, and the chamber is a typical trefoil shape, built of large stones and measuring 10 ft. 6 in. by 9 ft. at the most.

Setter, Chambered Cairn (HU 173603), ½ mile SW. of Gardie pier, Sheet 3 (pasture land). *Shetland, Papa Stour island.*

This cairn is now a grass-grown mound 80 ft. in length by 50 ft. in width, standing to a maximum height of 3 ft. 6 in. The size singles it out from the majority in Shetland, and the presence of two rows of slabs 9 ft. apart running for a distance of 46 ft. along the long axis suggests that it may be a stalled cairn, a type of which all the other examples are in Orkney.

Muckle Heog, Chambered Cairn (HP 631108), 1¼ miles NE. of Baltasound, Sheet 1 (A.968 and moorland).

Shetland, Unst island.

The Muckle Heog, a hill which stands between Balta Sound and Harold's Wick, has the remains of four cairns upon it. The one on the summit is a ruinous cairn the debris of which covers an area about 60 ft. in diameter, and little can be deduced from its remains beyond the probability that it was a cairn of a Shetland type. The cairn which is situated a little to the W., however, at the foot of the steep face of an outcrop of serpentine, is readily identifiable as a heel-shaped cairn. Many of the outer stones have been robbed from it to build a now ruinous field boundary which crosses its N. extremity from E. to W., but the arc of set stones defining the façade can be traced over its full 41 ft. 6 in., between the large upright terminal stones. The cairn must originally have measured about 35 ft. along the axis transverse to the façade. No surface traces of the chamber can be seen, but two either primary or secondary cists are exposed among the debris of the body of the cairn.

Vatten, Chambered Cairn (NG 298440), 3½ miles SE. of Dunvegan, Sheet 23 (A.863). *Skye.*

Several cairns survive W. of the head of Loch Caroy, among them this circular one which measures 90 ft. in diameter and 20 ft. in height. Part of a peristalith of blocks set edge to edge survives in the E. While no indications of a passage or a chamber appear on the surface of the mound, it is reasonably certain that this is a chambered cairn of the Hebridean class.

Ullinish Lodge, Chambered Cairn (NG 323378), 2 miles W. by S. of Bracadale, Sheet 23 (by-road). *Skye.*

The remains of this cairn, 200 yds. NNW. of Ullinish Lodge, consist of a denuded circle of boulders about 76 ft. in diameter near the centre of which are eight slabs representing the walls of the sub-oval chamber, 17 ft. long by 9 ft. wide.

Rudh' an Dunain, Chambered Cairn (NG 393164), 3¼ miles SSW. of Glenbrittle House, Sheet 32 (footpath). *Skye.*

This cairn measures 65 ft. in diameter and stands to a height of 11 ft. Access to a bipartite antechamber and a polygonal chamber is gained from a crescentic forecourt in the E., all these features being in a good state. Fragments of Windmill Hill pottery were recovered from the floor, in addition to a beaker representing later use of the tomb.

Carn Liath, Chambered Cairn (NG 420514), 6 miles NW. of Portree, Sheet 23 (A.850). *Skye.*

This cairn, close to the right bank of the lowest reach of the River Haultin, measures about 80 ft. in diameter and 18 ft. in height. No trace of the passage or chamber is visible, but a secondary cist lies in the NE. quadrant.

Loch a Barp, Chambered Cairn (NF 777215), 1¾ miles NW. of Lochboisdale, Sheet 31 (A.865 and moorland). *South Uist.*

This circular chambered cairn has had its passage and part of the S. quadrant pillaged for stones, but the rest can be recognised as having measured about 86 ft. in diameter, and still attains a height of 19 ft. The remains of a slab peristalith also survive. The chamber is oval, measuring at least 12 ft. along the major axis. Displaced lintel stones up to 9 ft. long lie among the ruins, and other blocks and slabs are scattered on the S. part of the cairn.

Reineval, Chambered Cairn (NF 755260), 5 miles NW. of Lochboisdale, Sheet 22 (A.865 and moorland track). *South Uist.*

This almost circular chambered cairn measures about 75 ft. in diameter and stands to a height of 12 ft. It has had a peristalith of pillar stones as much as 7 ft. in height and as little as 3 ft. A cover stone of the chamber is exposed in the E. quadrant, and traces of the passage can be followed to the E. of it.

Stockie Muir, Chambered Cairn (NS 479812), 6 miles NW. of Milngavie, Sheet 64 (A.809 and walk 2 miles). *Stirlingshire.*

The remains of this cairn appear as a long spread-out mound of stones on almost level ground, and are conspicuous from a considerable distance. The cairn may originally have measured about 60 ft. in length on the longer axis, nearly due E. and W., by about 30 ft. at the greatest width, but the outline is now lost beneath the tumble. Two large earthfast boulders protrude from the debris near the E. end, and the remains of a chamber about 13 ft. long by about 3 ft. wide can be distinguished a few feet W. of them. One lintel stone remains *in situ,* others have fallen into the chamber. Three depressions occur in the rest of the body of the cairn, but their nature has not been ascertained. The cairn is one of the Central Scotland group of Clyde-Carlingford cairns.

Stroma, Chambered Cairn (ND 353791), 1¾ miles N. of Uppertown pier, Sheet 7 (boat and farm road). *Stroma island.*

This round cairn measures about 50 ft. in diameter and stands to a height of 5 ft. It has been broken open to expose the remains of what may be a tripartite chamber of the Camster type.

Achu, Chambered Cairn (NH 671910), ¾ mile N. by W. of Spinningdale, Sheet 21 (by-road and moorland). *Sutherland.*

This cairn was excavated in 1910, when it was found to be a short horned cairn measuring about 50 ft. over all, in either direction. The passage to the chamber leads in from the ESE. façade for a distance of 12 ft. The chamber, which is polygonal, measures 8 ft. 9 in. in length by 7 ft. in width, the bases of the walls being formed of seven large slabs the interspaces of which are filled with dry-stone walling. Above the level of these slabs the walls are corbelled in, the roof of the chamber having been closed with flat slabs at a height of 8 ft. above the floor.

Another similar cairn lies ½ mile to the W. at Kyleoag.

Killin, Chambered Cairn (NC 857077), 4 miles NW. of Brora, Sheet 17 (by-road). *Sutherland.*

This chambered cairn lies in a wood 30 yds. E. of the road up the E. side of Loch Bora, at a point ½ mile N. of Killin. It is a stony mound measuring about 50 ft. in diameter, containing a tripartite Camster-type chamber, entered from the W. Most of the passage, about 20 ft. long, has suffered mutilation, but several details of the chamber are preserved. The first compartment, measuring about 7 ft. in width by 5 ft. in length, is built of dry-stone masonry. It is separated from the second by a pair of large partition stones set vertically and 2 ft. apart. The second compartment too is built of laid stones, and the portals leading to the innermost can be distinguished at its E. end. The last compartment, however, is choked.

Torboll, Chambered Cairn (NH 740995), 5¼ miles W. of Golspie, Sheet 21 (A.9 and moorland). *Sutherland.*

This is one of the many ruined monuments known as Carn Liath. It stands on a hill ¾ mile NW. of Torboll, among clearance cairns and some so-called hut-circles on the nose of the ridge dividing Strathcarnaig and Strathfleet. It is a circular stony mound 60 ft. in diameter, with a chamber and passage which have at some time been cleared of debris. The passage, 14 ft. 6 in. in length, runs in from the SE. to the bipartite chamber. The outer compartment is rectangular, measuring almost 4 ft. 6 in. square, the inner polygonal, 6 ft. 2 in. by 5 ft. 4 in. The walls are composed of slabs with dry-stone interfilling.

Kinbrace, Chambered Cairn (NC 875283), 2¼ miles SSE. of Kinbrace, Sheet 17 (A.897). *Sutherland.*

Numerous chambered cairns, both long and round, have been recorded in the section of the Strath of Kildonan immediately S. of Kinbrace. This one, on an elevated angle between the Kinbrace Burn and the River Helmsdale, has a tripartite chamber reached by a passage 25 ft. long from the E. The outer compartment measures 3 ft. by 5 ft., defined at the ends by upright slabs and walled with drystone masonry. The next compartment is polygonal on plan, measuring 6 ft. 6 in. by 7 ft. 9 in. The innermost measures 3 ft. by 5 ft. This

and the outermost are very low, their slab roofs placed only 2 ft. from the floor, but the central compartment has had a corbelled roof which did not begin until above a height of 3 ft. from the floor.

The cairn appears as a mass of tumbled boulders, and it is difficult to decide whether it was originally round or whether it was a short horned cairn.

Achany, Chambered Cairn (NC 571018), 4 miles N. of Invershin, Sheet 16 (A.837, B.864). *Sutherland.*

This cairn, situated beside the road on the right bank of the Grudie Burn, has been robbed of material, but the chamber is fully exposed. The cairn has been about 60 ft. in diameter, and the entrance has been in the NE., the position being marked by a section of a kerb and an inner arc of boulders. The chamber is rectangular, over 12 ft. long and 6 ft. wide, divided into two roughly equal parts. This is an unusual structure which does not seem to conform closely to any recognised category.

Skelpick, Chambered Cairn (NC 723566), 3 miles S. by E. of Bettyhill, Sheet 10 (A.836 and by-road). *Sutherland.*

This long horned cairn lies near the right bank of the Skelpick Burn with its long axis N. and S. It measures about 200 ft. in length, and the passage, about 15 ft. long, enters from the façade between the N. horns. The outermost compartment of the chamber is 6 ft. 6 in. long, 4 ft. wide and 4 ft. 3 in. high. It opens into the middle compartment through a portal surmounted by a lintel 10 ft. long. This compartment measures 10 ft. by 8 ft. and is separated from the innermost compartment by another portal surmounted by a lintel of similar proportions to the other. The innermost compartment measures 12 ft. by 10 ft. axially, and is polygonal. It is formed by six huge slabs with dry-stone walling in the interspaces.

Skail, Chambered Cairn (NC 711465), 9 miles S. of Bettyhill, Sheet 10 (A.836, B.871). *Sutherland.*

This round cairn lies between the road and the river at Skail. It has been robbed after being ravished by a shooting tenant, but it is still possible to discern an original diameter of about 65 ft. and a polygonal chamber with its axis NE. and

SW. Several slabs show the outline of the various compartments of the chamber.

Altnacealgach, Chambered Cairn (NC 262112), 6¼ miles S. of Inchnadamph, Sheet 15 (A.837). *Sutherland.*

Several chambered cairns in various states of ruin occur in the significant area where the route leading from the NE. coastal area up Strathoykel meets the Inchnadamph-Ullapool section of the route leading from N. to S. up the W. coastal strip. One of these, situated 100 yds. NE. of and 100 ft. above the Strathoykel road as this skirts the NE. shore of Loch Borralan, is a stony mound 45 ft. in diameter and 6 ft. 6 in. high with a polygonal chamber 10 ft. long and 6 ft. wide. This feature, which occupies a position a little off the centre, is constructed of six large slabs, the interspaces of which are filled with dry-stone walling. It is aligned from WNW. to ESE., the blocked entrance facing the latter quarter. A recess in the NNW. corner measuring 4 ft. 6 in. by 2 ft. 6 in. is roofed by overlapping slabs.

Cnoc an Daimh, Chambered Cairn (NC 165428), 1¼ miles SSE. of Scourie, Sheet 9 (A.894). *Sutherland.*

This round cairn, some 40 ft. in diameter, lies on a rocky knoll 100 yds. E. of the road. It appears as a stony mound from which several slabs and boulders protrude to indicate the existence of a polygonal chamber.

Badnabay, Chambered Cairn (NC 219467), 4 miles ENE. of Scourie, Sheet 9 (A.894). *Sutherland.*

The remains of this cairn, originally about 40 ft. in diameter, stand close to the N. side of the road just before this reaches sea level at Traigh Bad na Baighe, 1 mile W. of Laxford Bridge. The cairn material has been taken away, leaving only the embedded stones of the chamber standing in the short pasture-grass. The entrance measures 13 ft. in length, the polygonal inner compartment 10 ft. by 9 ft. The slabs outlining these structures stand to as much as 3 ft. 8 in. in height and form a most impressive monument.

Cairnscarrow, Chambered Cairn (NX 136650), 2¼ miles W. of New Luce, Sheet 82 (moorland). *Wigtownshire.*

This monument consists of a megalithic burial chamber which may have formed part of a Clyde-Carlingford cairn, but which may be nothing more than a particularly massive cist of a later date.

Mid Gleniron, Chambered Cairns (NX 187610), 2¼ miles N. by W. of Glenluce, Sheet 82 (by-road and farm road). *Wigtownshire.*

The better preserved of these two Clyde-Carlingford chambered cairns with terminal chambers and crescentic forecourt settings measures 108 ft. in length by 27 ft. in width near the S. and 36 ft. near the N. Excavations between 1963 and 1966 revealed that an original Early Neolithic chambered cairn, and another probably of the same period, constructed close to it, were eventually joined to form a long cairn with a facade at the N. and with an additional chamber in the middle. Nine cremations in cinerary urns were later inserted in the cairn. The cairn was bisected by a later track.

The other chambered cairn has been more severely pillaged. The excavations showed that this too was of multiple construction, the original round cairn being enlarged to a subrectangular shape with a facade on the S.

Caves of Kilhern, Chambered Cairn (NX 198644), 4 miles N. of Glenluce, Sheet 82 (by-road and hill track). *Wigtownshire.*

The remains of this broad Clyde-Carlingford chambered cairn lie beyond the head of the Cruise Burn on open moorland. The body of the cairn measures about 100 ft. from ENE. to WSW., 60 ft. in width near the former end and 30 ft. near the latter. The principal axial chamber, near the ESE. end, is well preserved, standing out from the robbed cairn material and still capped by its cover. Two lateral chambers lie behind this and another, aligned on the axis, farther towards the WSW. end of the cairn.

High Gillespie, Chambered Cairn (NX 255525), 4¼ miles SE. of Glenluce, Sheet 82 (A.747 and farm road). *Wigtownshire.*

This ruinous Clyde-Carlingford chambered cairn, marked as a graveyard on the old edition of the O.S. 6-in. map, lies 100 yds. W. of the right bank of the Gillespie Burn at a point less than one mile from the main road. Like the examples at Dranandow and the Caves of Kilhern, it has lateral chambers, in this case numbering as many as seven, together with the remains of an axial chamber near the broad E. end. The cairn now measures about 75 ft. in width near the E. end and 115 ft. in length. The cairn material has been severely robbed, so that the remains of the chambers appear virtually uncovered.

HENGE MONUMENTS

The name henge applies to a class of monument which, as was recently pointed out, was only first established as forming a recognisable group some 40 years ago, even though the most famous henge of all carries the distinction of having excited written comment 800 years earlier. It is a commonplace that only at Stonehenge itself is there any existing evidence of the presence of the horizontal lintel stones, the "hanging" stones, which gave rise to the name. Among the other 70 or so henge monuments there are examples in which free-standing stones still remain, but none which show signs of having supported lintels.

The classic henge monument comprises a circular ditch with an external bank, the level interior being reached by either one or two entrances consisting of a gap or gaps in the bank and a causeway or causeways in the ditch. Several very small structures conform to this principle, while at the other end of the scale there are three which are very much larger than the rest. If the very small and the very large examples are excluded, the remainder fall into two groups defined by the measurement of diameter. The lower group includes measurements between 110 ft. and 385 ft., and the upper group those between 465 ft. and 600 ft. Henge monuments have been classified by number of entrances into Class I henges with a single entrance and Class II henges with two opposed entrances. It has been observed that all the Class I henges occur in the group with the lower measurements of diameter.

In Scotland, three henge monuments of Class I have been recorded, each with a diameter of about 300 ft. In addition, three of the very small and possibly atypical type have been noted. The Class II monuments, however, are much more widely spread, nine examples being known between Orkney and Dumfriesshire. Others are suspected, although at the present time their identity has not been proved; while still more may well have been entirely obliterated by the plough.

Broomend of Crichie, Henge and Pictish Symbol Stone (NJ 779196), 1 mile S. of Inverurie, Sheet 38 (A.96).
Aberdeenshire.
This Class II henge is situated on the S. outskirts of Port Elphinstone on level ground between the main road and the Great North of Scotland Railway, at a point distant ¼ mile from the present position of the right bank of the River Don. Measuring 110 ft. in diameter, it approximates very closely to the Muir of Ord and Ballymeanoch henges. The interior contains three standing stones. Two, near the inner lip of the ditch, belong to a circular setting contemporary

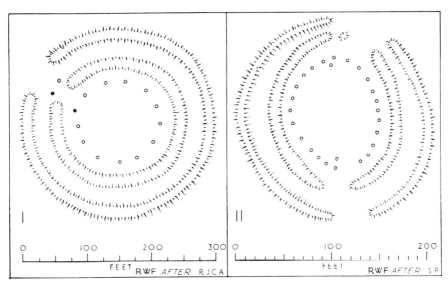

18 *Plans of typical Henges of Classes I and II*

with the henge, but the third was erected near the centre in modern times when it was removed from a bank 50 yds. to the NE. which was being used for ballast for the railway. Several standing stones existed in the neighbourhood of the henge, and it is only likely that this one was originally one of them which was re-used in Early Christian times. It bears very well preserved examples of the so-called elephant symbol and the crescent and V rod symbol.

Two double crouched beaker burials were found in two cists a few hundred yards S. of the henge in 1866, one of them including a now famous horn spoon.

Ballymeanoch, Henge (NR 833963), 5¼ miles N. by W. of Lochgilphead, Sheet 55 (A.816).   *Argyll, Mid.*

This monument, little more than 100 yds. SW. of the Ballymeanoch Standing Stones, consists of a low cairn 70 ft. in diameter surrounded by the ditch and bank of a henge probably of Class II. Two cists were found in the cairn, the smaller containing parts of a beaker, the larger robbed.

Overhowden, Henge (NT 487524), 4 miles NW. of Lauder, Sheet 66 (A.68, by-road and farm road).   *Berwickshire.*

This Class I henge is almost ploughed out, but the swelling of the bank is spread over more than 20 ft. even though it rises only to 1 ft. in height. The ditch is entirely filled and levelled. The entrance gap, in the NW., is recognisable as an interruption more than 30 ft. in width. The henge was proved by excavation in 1950, when it was found to measure 320 ft. across the crest of the bank, and to have a ditch 12 ft. wide and 4 ft. deep.

Numerous flint implements have been and still are found on the fields in the vicinity of the henge, especially round a low knoll 170 yds. away to the NW.

Balfarg, Henge (NO 281032), 1¼ miles NW. of Markinch, Sheet 59 (A.911, A.92).   *Fife.*

All that remains of this Class I henge on the surface are two upright standing stones and a faint swelling in the ground. The stone to the NW. stands to a height of 6 ft. 6 in. and the other to 5 ft. 3 in. The existence of the henge connected with them was discovered from an air photograph and confirmed by probing and surveying the site. The henge was found to have measured nearly 300 ft. from side to side over the crest of the bank. The NW. stone is one of a pair set in the entrance gap, and the other a survivor of a ring of stones set 20 ft. within and concentric to the inner lip of the ditch.

65

Normangill, Henge (NS 972221), 1½ miles NE. of Crawford, Sheet 72 (by-road).   *Lanarkshire.*

This Class II henge has recently been cut across by the remodelled road leading from Crawford to the Camps Reservoir. The N. and S. arcs, which include the entrances, can nevertheless still be seen, albeit in a somewhat eroded condition.

Ring of Brodgar, Henge (HY 294134), 4 miles NE. of Stromness, Sheet 6 (A.965, B.9055).   *Orkney, Mainland island.*

This large Class II henge is magnificently placed on a low neck of land between the Lochs of Harray and Stenness, and is remarkably well preserved. The ring of upright slabs still has 27 out of the original 60, and they stand to an average height of 7 ft. between limits of 15 ft. and 9 in. This ring is placed about 10 ft. from the inner lip of the ditch, the slabs being erected so that their longer axes are parallel with this. The ditch is 30 ft. wide and 6 ft. deep, and encloses an area 370 ft. in diameter. It is broken by causeways in the NW. and SE., the one 10 ft. and the other 12 ft. in width. No trace remains of the external bank which by definition forms part of a henge —an oddity as remarkable as the reverse positions of the ditch and bank at Stonehenge itself.

One stone has a runic inscription incised upon it.

Stenness, Henge (HY 306125), 4 miles ENE. of Stromness, Sheet 6 (A.965, B.9055).   *Orkney, Mainland island.*

The remains of the earthwork of this henge are now so slight that excavation would be necessary to determine whether or not it belongs to Class I or Class II. One entrance certainly occurs in the NW., but there is doubt about another in the SE., even though this is the usually accepted form. The henge measures about 200 ft. in diameter from crest to crest of the bank.

Today, however, the henge is rightly noted more particularly for the four stones just within the central space defined by the inner lip of the ditch. They survive from an original circular setting 104 ft. in diameter which possibly contained 13 stones. Three of the survivors rise to heights of 17 ft., 15 ft. 6 in. and 15 ft. above ground level respectively, and the other is broken off short. They are all taken from local beds of flagstone, and so measure no more than 1 ft. in thickness.

What has been described as a modern and wholly fanciful addition to the monument takes the form of an egregious stone bench which mars the validity of this otherwise sincere ruin.

Muir of Ord, Henge (NH 527497), ¼ mile S. by W. of Muir of Ord, Sheet 26 (A.9 and on golf course).

Ross & Cromarty.

This structure is the third Class II henge of this particular size to have been recorded in Scotland, the other two being at Crichie and at Ballymeanoch. The mean measurement of the extreme diameters taken from crest to crest of the bank gives a figure between 110 ft. and 115 ft. The monument has been used as a green on the Muir of Ord golf course.

19   *Ring of Brodgar Henge. The fourth stone from the left stands to a height of 15 ft. and measures 9½ in. in thickness*

and a short stretch of the NW. arc of the ditch has been filled to allow easy access and egress. The wasting of the bank may also be due in some measure to the exigencies of the game, but the general state of preservation is moderate. The interior measures about 85 ft. by about 65 ft. and the two segments of the ditch measure about 18 ft. in width and 4 ft. in depth. The axis of the henge lies a little S. of E. and N. of W.

originally fully annular or whether the gaps have been filled in in every case, at a time after the structures were no longer objects of use or reverence, so that the resulting enclosure could be put to a practical use. If the former were to prove to be the case, then the identification of these three monuments as henges would not stand, and they could at best be called proto-henges or hengiform earth-works. Even so, it is extremely likely that

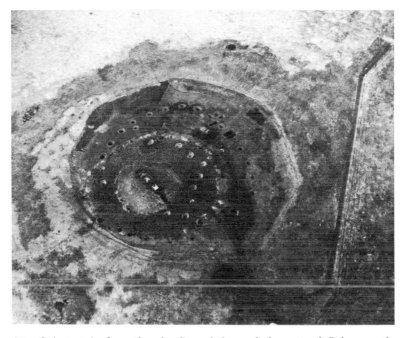

20   *Cairnpapple from the air. Stone-holes and the restored Cairn are the most conspicuous features*

Cononbridge, Henge (NH 543551), at the S. end of Cononbridge, Sheet 26 (A.9).   *Ross & Cromarty.*
   This is one of three small monuments about the identification of which there is certain room for doubt. At first sight they seem to be Class I henges; this one measures 75 ft. in diameter from crest to crest of the bank, the one at Contin (NH 443569) 70 ft., and the third, at Culbokie (NH 594577) 100 ft. But in each case the bank appears to run without interruption across the entrance causeway in the ditch. Only careful excavation could determine whether the banks were

they belong to some obscure phase of the transitional period early in the 2nd or even late in the 3rd millennium B.C.
Cairnpapple, Henge, Cairns, Burials (NS 987717), 1¼ miles ESE. of Torphi-chen, Sheet 65 (B.792 and by-road).
                    West Lothian.
   These structures, which crown the summit of isolated Cairnpapple Hill, form the most important assemblage of their kind, and are physically protected by the Ministry of Works (key in Tor-phichen when the gate is locked). The earliest monument on the site was a group of three huge boulders and an

arc of large stones, associated with a cremation cemetery of the late neolithic fashion. This was replaced by a henge monument (Class II) which contained an oval setting of stones; beaker burials were associated with this. In the third phase the henge was destroyed, and a kerbed cairn, 50 ft. in diameter, was built; a cist at its centre contained a food vessel inhumation. Later, the cairn was enlarged to a diameter of 100 ft., at which time two cinerary urn cremations were deposited in it. Last of all, four inhumation graves, possibly of Early Iron Age date, were inserted into the remains.

A microcosm of two thirds of local pre-history, Cairnpapple stands alone, as befits its lofty position, as a source from which confirmation and guidance can be directed upon research over a very wide field.

STONES AND CAIRNS

Settings of standing stones placed round cairns occur, as described above, at Clava and elsewhere; but it is well known that such circles are usually found with no visible feature within them. At Callanish, a small passage-grave forms part of the system which comprises a circle and avenues. Circles of stones form integral parts of some henge monuments. In rare cases, such as at Newbridge, Midlothian, what seem to be the survivors of a circle of standing stones are found round a cairn which is certainly not a chambered cairn. All this adds up to the conclusion that circles of standing stones may have had their origins in Late Neolithic times, and have lasted well into the succeeding period.

In addition to circles, stones stand in multiple rows and in single alignments as well as in pairs and singly. It has been observed in central Scotland that a pair of stones may often consist of one regular pillar and one stone of triangular outline. Standing stones vary, according to the material available, from ponderous and massive blocks, the height of which may hardly be twice their width, to soaring needles of such stone as flagstone. Excavations have occasionally been made at the feet of single or paired stones but these have provided singularly little information.

Round cairns of various kinds include straightforward mounds measuring between 25 ft. and 100 ft. in diameter, with a large majority about midway between the extremes, many of which have kerbs or peristaliths; and important minority groups such as ring and bell cairns presumably related to like classes of barrows. Most cairns of these kinds have been assigned to one part or another of the 2nd millennium B.C., a period during which burial customs changed from the large-scale magnificence of even a re-used chambered tomb to the humble though snug interments, often accompanied by no enduring grave goods, in small short cists, set in the ground upon which so much of the lives of the occupants must have been lived.

There is no well-defined limit to the period beyond which such burial customs may be said to have ceased altogether, and indeed some examples have been tentatively assigned to the 1st millennium B.C. Having no visible surface remains, the short cists and the cemeteries of cinerary urns which are unmarked by cairns or standing stones fall outside the scope of this Guide. It may be noted, however, that more than a further

21 *Round Cairn, Memsie*

millennium was to follow before the practice of raising visible and permanent memorials over even the most important dead was resumed, in the form of pagan and then Early Christian monoliths.

Memsie, Cairn (NJ 976620), 3 miles SSW. of Fraserburgh, Sheet 30 (A.981 B.9032).   *Aberdeenshire.*
This cairn, now under guardianship, is a splendid and well-preserved example of the larger round cairn. It is recorded that a beaker and a broken leaf-shaped sword were found within it.

East Finnercy, Cairn (NJ 766043), 2 miles ESE. of Echt, Sheet 38 (A.974 and by-road).   *Aberdeenshire.*
This cairn, excavated in 1952, was found to have been disturbed previously. No traces of any central burial remained, but it was adjudged to have been a normal Bronze Age cairn. The ground surface beneath the cairn was found to contain considerable quantities of Windmill Hill pottery, a leaf-shaped arrowhead and traces of hearths. It was presumed that this material represented the detritus of a neolithic settlement upon which the cairn had been built fortuitously.

Cullerlie, Stone Circle (NJ 785043), 3 miles E. by S. of Echt, Sheet 38 (A.974, B.9125 and by-road).   *Aberdeenshire.*
This monument appeared before excavation as eight rather squat, undressed boulders placed at approximately equal intervals round the circumference of a circle measuring 32 ft. in diameter. When cleared, these were found to enclose seven very small circular cairns showing signs of cremations, the largest of which occupied the central position

and the others the space between this and the upright stones. An earlier robbery had unfortunately cleared off any relics before the careful excavation of 1934, but the monument (in guardianship) is of interest in giving an indication of the unexpected variety and interest which may lie hidden beneath the sombre and forbidding exterior of such remains.

Dunchraigaig, Cairn (NR 833968), 2¾ miles N. by W. of Lochgilphead, Sheet 55 (A.816).   *Argyll, Mid.*
This cairn, lying in a little wood immediately W. of the road, was originally over 100 ft. in diameter and still stands to a height of 7 ft. A cist, 10 ft. long by 5 ft. wide, built of boulders rather than slabs and with a capstone 13 ft. long, lies in the SE. quadrant. Unaccompanied cremations and inhumations were found in it. A smaller cist high up in the body of the cairn near the centre contained a food vessel, as did a third.

Ballymeanoch, Standing Stones (NR 834964), 5¼ miles N. by W. of Lochgilphead, Sheet 55 (A.816). *Argyll, Mid.*
These stones are arranged in three groups, four in a line running N. and S. being the most conspicuous. Of these, one which is 12 ft. high and one other bear cup-and-ring markings. The second group, 130 ft. W. of the first, consists of two stones; while the third, 60 ft. NW. of these, comprises a single stone, now fallen, which bears cup-marks and is pierced by a hole.

A comparable setting of standing stones is situated 1 mile to the N. at Nether Largie (NR 828977).

Temple Wood, Stone Circle (NR 826979), 6½ miles NNW. of Lochgilphead, Sheet 55 (A.816 and by-road). *Argyll, Mid.*

This circle of 13, originally 20, earth-fast slabs measures 40 ft. in diameter within a slight and irregular bank. An empty cist formed of four slabs and measuring 5 ft. by 3 ft. lies in the middle of it. One slab of a pair originally marking an entrance survives in the SE. Little is known of such a monument, or of its affinities.

Nether Largie (South), Cairn (NR 828979), 6½ miles N. by W. of Lochgilphead, Sheet 55 (A.816 and by-road). *Argyll, Mid.*

This cairn, originally about 130 ft. in diameter, contains a segmented chamber 20 ft. long and up to 4 ft. wide with corbelled walls capped by immense slabs. No passage ever seems to have existed in this apparently degenerated form of Clyde-Carlingford tomb. Two secondary cists have been found in the cairn.

Nether Largie (Centre), Cairn (NR 830983), 6¾ miles N. by W. of Lochgilphead, Sheet 55 (A.816 and by-road). *Argyll, Mid.*

This cairn, measuring about 100 ft. in diameter and still retaining traces of a peristalith, covered two cists. One, in the NW. quadrant, is notable for having side slabs grooved to receive the end slabs. Both this cist and the other, in the S., were empty when opened in 1929.

Nether Largie (North), Cairn (NR 831985), 7 miles N. by W. of Lochgilphead, Sheet 55 (A.816 and by-road). *Argyll, Mid.*

This cairn, 70 ft. in diameter and 9 ft. high, within a low rubble bank, is locked up, and the key must be obtained from the Kilmartin Hotel. It has a central cist the underside of the capstone of which is carved with representations of bronze axes (as is a stone in the near-by cairn Ri Cruin—NR 825972) and cup-marks. Two axes are carved on the N. end-slab.

Kintraw, Cairns and Standing Stone (NM 830050), 10½ miles N. of Lochgilphead, Sheet 55 (A.816). *Argyll, Mid.*

Three small cairns and one larger one stand on level ground beside the road as this winds down to the broad flood-plain at the head of Loch Craignish. The large cairn, 48 ft. in diameter, and standing to a height of 8 ft. within the remains of a kerb, was excavated in 1959 and 1960. A post-hole in the old ground at the centre of the cairn was followed upwards as a space in the body of the cairn for a height of 3 ft. 4 in. A bipartite cist was found near the NW. border of the cairn, the larger compartment containing cremated bones and carbonised wood. The standing stone, situated 6 yds. SW. of the large cairn, attains a height of 13 ft.

Auchagallon, Stone Circle (NR 893346), 7½ miles W. of Brodick, Sheet 69 (B.880 and by-road). *Arran.*

This monument consists of a circular cairn which is surrounded by a circle of 15 standing stones. It is under guardianship.

Knockjargon, Cairn in Fort (NS 235473), 3 miles N. of Ardrossan, Sheet 63 (B.780). *Ayrshire.*

See **Knockjargon** fort.

Warth Hill, Cairn (ND 371698), 6 miles ESE. of Mey, Sheet 12 (A.836). *Caithness.*

This cairn, situated on the Warth Hill, the highest eminence in Canisbay parish, stands 350 yds. W. of and 100 ft. above the main road. Now somewhat spread, it originally measured 40 ft. in diameter within a double row of large blocks about 4 ft. apart, many individuals of which can still be seen. The cairn encased a central primary cist 3 ft. 6 in. long, 2 ft. 4 in. wide and 1 ft. 9 in. deep, covered by a single slab. This contained a crouched skeleton with no grave-goods. A secondary cist, 3 ft. to the SW. of the other, measured 4 ft. 6 in. in length, 2 ft. 3 in. in width and 1 ft. 8 in. in depth. This is reported to have contained an uncremated burial.

Ben Dorrery, Standing Stone (ND 066550), 9 miles SE. of Reay, Sheet 11 (A.836, by-road and moorland). *Caithness.*

This stone, one among several in the neighbourhood, stands a little above the 600 ft. contour on the E. flank of Ben Dorrery, 900 yds. W. of Dorrery Lodge. It attains a height of 5 ft. above present ground level, and measures 3 ft. in width by 1 ft. 2 in. in thickness.

Brouhster, Standing Stones (ND 048608), 6 miles SE. of Reay, Sheet 11 (A.836, by-roads and moorland). *Caithness.*

0   3   6

feet

0   1   2

metres

22   *Nether Largie North Cairn. Drawings of the Cup-marks and Axes which decorate the underside of the Cover of the Cist and the North End-slab*

This monument, which can be compared with another at Achavanich, stands on a moorland ridge between Loch Calder and the deserted township of Broubster. It now consists of only nine earthfast stones out of a possible 32, set about 12 ft. apart. They form part of the outline of a U measuring 140 ft. along the major axis and a maximum of 90 ft. transversely. The stone at the apex, in the NE., is the largest, standing to a height of 5 ft. 6 in. Like all the others, the broader faces of this stone are set at a right-angle to the line upon which they are laid out.

A single monolith 7 ft. high stands 130 ft. SW. of the first stone of the W. point of the U, but there is no reason to connect it with the setting.

Upper Dounreay, Stone Rows (ND 012659), 3¼ miles E. by N. of Reay, Sheet 12 (by-road and pasture land). *Caithness.*

This group of stone rows lies in a slight depression at the N. end of the Cnoc Freiceadain subsidiary of Shebster Hill. The slabs which now number about 100 seem to form the remnants of 13 rows, aligned WNW. and ESE. and originally containing perhaps 20 stones each. A cist-like setting of four slabs which lies just above them seems to provide a focus for at least some of the rows.

Loch of Yarrows, Standing Stones (ND 316432), 5½ miles SSW. of Wick, Sheet 11 (A.9, farm road and moorland). *Caithness.*

Two handsome stones of needle shape stand 18 ft. 6 in. apart on the crest of a ridge half a mile SE. of the Loch of Yarrows. They now attain heights of 8 ft. 6 in. and 6 ft. 6 in. respectively above the surface of the ground, but this was somewhat raised nearly 100 years ago when the ground in the vicinity of the stones was trenched in vain for burials. The stones both measure about 1 ft. 6 in. and 1 ft. axially on plan.

Garrywhin, Stone Rows (ND 313413), 7 miles SSW. of Wick, Sheet 11 (A.9, by-road and moorland). *Caithness.*

This monument lies at the E. foot of the hill upon which the Garrywhin fort is situated, and 200 yds. NNE. of the short horned cairn of the same name. It consists of a small cairn, about 18 ft. in diameter, from which six rows of earth-fast slabs radiate SW. down the slope.

The longest row measures 200 ft. in length. When planned in 1871, the average number of stones remaining in each row was eight, but since then a few have disappeared. If the cairn is in truth to be related to the rows (which is of course by no means certain), added interest and importance attaches to the report that it contained a cist in which were an inhumed burial and a vessel which was probably a beaker.

Mid Clyth, Stone Rows (ND 294384), 9 miles SSW. of Wick, Sheet 11 (A.9 and by-road). *Caithness.*

More than a dozen examples of stone rows have been recorded in Caithness and the adjacent part of Sutherland. This, the largest, situated on a south-facing hillside ponderously known as the Hill of Many Stanes, comprised 22 rows with an average of eight earthfast boulders in each when it was planned in 1871. In this example, as indeed in the majority, no other monument has been observed in the vicinity which can be thought to bear any relationship to the stones, and their date and function must at present remain uncertain. Other such structures, however, are found in the far SW., on Dartmoor, while a further comparison may be drawn with the alignments at Carnac, in Brittany. The avenues at Callanish, on the island of Lewis, may also be called to mind, even though the parallel is not close.

Achanarras, Cairn (ND 145552), 2¼ miles SSE. of Halkirk, Sheet 11 (by-road and moorland). *Caithness.*

This cairn now appears as a very low mound about 60 ft. in diameter which is surrounded by five prostrate blocks each about 6 ft. in length, probably all that remains of a once complete surrounding ring. There is no reason to suppose they were ever upstanding, although this might have been the case.

Dirlot, Stone Rows (ND 124488), 6¼ miles S. of Halkirk, Sheet 11 (by-roads, B.870 and by-road). *Caithness.*

Two small cairns, one measuring about 20 ft. and the other 15 ft. in diameter, stand on the crest of a low knoll 300 yds. SSW. of Dirlot. From these the fragmentary remains of possibly 20 rows of set stones radiate down the slope, each stone set with its major axis aligned with the row of which it forms a part. The more southerly group of rows is the better preserved; it includes rows with as many as 10 stones surviving out of a possible 20 over a distance of 100 ft.

Hill of Rangag, Standing Stone (ND 176448), 7 miles N. of Latheron, Sheet 11 (A.895). *Caithness.*

Conspicuous among several standing stones in the neighbourhood is the great stone of Rangag. It is a four-sided pillar about 2 ft. 9 in. square standing to a height of over 9 ft. above ground level, at a point only 30 yds. E. of the road.

Achavanich, Standing Stones (ND 188417), ¾ mile SE. of Achavanich, Sheet 11 (by-road). *Caithness.*

This setting of stones lies beside the by-road from Achavanich to Lybster ¼ mile S. of Loch Stemster. It takes the form of a truncated oval open to the SE., and from all appearances there are no reasons to suppose that it ever formed a complete oval. It measures 225 ft. on the long axis by a maximum of 100 ft. transversely. It may originally have comprised about 60 stones, but one third have weathered or have been removed. The stones are thick slabs of flagstone, protruding on average about 5 ft. above the ground, set at intervals of about 8 ft. with their broad faces towards each other, not along the line. A cist measuring 5 ft. by 3 ft. 9 in., formed by four slabs set on end into the ground, stands against the most northerly stone of the setting.

This monument, which can be compared only with the example at Broubster at present, should probably be assigned to the earlier part of the Bronze Age.

Clackmannan, Standing Stone (NS 9191), in the centre of the town, Sheet 58. *Clackmannanshire.*

The "clack-mannan" or stone of Manau now stands beside the Tolbooth in Clackmannan, having been rescued in 1833 from a recumbent position outside the old jail. Whether or not it is what it might be does not really matter, for it symbolises the object from which the name Clackmannan arises. The district Manau, Manau Guotodin or Manau of the Votadini, presumably including the country between Slamannan in modern SW. Stirlingshire and the little county of Clackmannan, comes on record in accounts dealing with the immediate post-Roman period, but its roots go back to the Votadini of the pre-Roman period.

Clochmaben Stone (NY 312666), ¾ mile SW. of Gretna, Sheet 85 (on the land of Old Gretna farm). *Dumfriesshire.*

The Clockmaben Stone stands on a very slight rise 300 yds. from the right bank of the channel of the River Sark, the border with Cumberland, at the head of the Solway Firth, and the same distance from the left bank of the Kirtle Water at a point 600 yds. from their confluence. It has been shown that in all likelihood this stone was a trysting place where justice could be administered and markets held, identifiable with *Maponi* in the British section of the *Ravenna Cosmography.* Although this was compiled in the 7th century, the place may well have been in use several centuries earlier, during the time when the Romans had a somewhat flexible system of frontier administration—in the 3rd century A.D.—and possibly long before that, in prehistoric times. The boulder, which measures 7 ft. in height and 18 ft. in girth, is clearly an erratic, but might none the less have been incorporated into a megalithic monument, as has been averred, although no clear evidence exists to demonstrate this.

Holmains Moor, Cairn (NY 076762), 2 miles SW. of Hightae, Sheet 85 (B.7020, farm road and moorland). *Dumfriesshire.*

This cairn, situated on the highest point of Holmains Moor at an elevation of 800 ft. O.D., measures 70 ft. in diameter. An excavation in the top has revealed part of a cist, but no record of the work exists.

Gubhill Rig, Cairn (NX 964933), 2¾ miles NNW. of Ae, Sheet 78 (by-road and forest track). *Dumfriesshire.*

Now within the Forest of Ae, this cairn measures about 90 ft. in diameter and 5 ft. in height.

Mossknowe, Cairn (NY 281693), ¾ mile S. of Kirkpatrick Fleming, Sheet 85 (B.6357 and by-road). *Dumfriesshire.*

This round cairn, 50 ft. in diameter, was excavated in 1908 by a Miss Bate. It was found to contain a cist which housed an inhumation with no surviving grave-goods. The cist was covered with two slabs, one on top of the other, the lower 7 ft. by 4 ft. and the upper 5 ft. 6 in. by 2 ft. 6 in.

A second cairn, 66 ft. in diameter and up to 7 ft. in height, lay 180 yds. to the SW.

Threip Moor, Cairn (NX 697950), 5¼ miles E. of Thornhill, Sheet 77 (by-road and moorland). *Dumfriesshire.*

This cairn standing on a ridge between the Capel Water and the Poldivan Lake measures 50 ft. in diameter and 6 ft. in height.

Burn, Cairn (NX 907984), 2¼ miles E. of Carronbridge, Sheet 78 (by-roads and footpath). *Dumfriesshire.*

This cairn lies in a field 400 yds. E. of Burn farmhouse on a bank above the Cample Water. It measures about 35 ft. in diameter and stands to a height of 5 ft.

Glengenny, Cairn (NS 813057), 3¼ miles SE. of Sanquhar, Sheet 78 (A.76, by-road and moorland). *Dumfriesshire.*

This cairn measures about 90 ft. in diameter and stands to a height of about 3 ft. It lies just above a good stretch of the mediaeval running earthwork known as the Deil's Dyke.

Airswood Moss, Cairn (NY 259933), 3¾ miles NW. of Bentpath, Sheet 79 (B.709 and moorland). *Dumfriesshire.*

This cairn measured about 50 ft. in diameter, but in 1828 at least 150 cart-loads of stones were removed from it to build an adjacent march dyke. During this operation a substantial central cist was revealed, and this now stands complete and uncovered with only one end-slab missing on a dry patch in Airswood Moss, a part of Bankhead Hill. This cist is aligned NE. and SW. One side is formed by a single slab 4 ft. long, the other two by two; the SW. end-slab is still *in situ*, as is the cover. The latter measures 4 ft. 3 in. by 2 ft. 10 in., and is 8 in. thick. The cist has now acquired the rural name of King Schaw's Grave.

Holywood, Stone Circle (NX 947794), 1 mile S. of Holywood, Sheet 84 (A.76, B.729). *Dumfriesshire.*

This circle stands in fields close to the NE. side of the road from New Bridge to Dunscore, ¼ mile from the left bank of the Cluden Water. Five stones remain earthfast out of 11, the highest standing to quite 6 ft. above ground level. The stones lie on the circumference of a circle 260 ft. in diameter, a size appropriate to such a monument as a henge.

Whiteholm Rig, Stone Circle (NY 217827), 5 miles E. of Lockerbie, Sheet 79 (A.709). *Dumfriesshire.*

This circle lies on the moor 200 yds. S. of the road connecting Lockerbie and Langholm. It measures 60 ft. in diameter, and seven of a probable 12 original stones remain. Four of these are still *in situ*, none protruding more than 2 ft. above the ground.

Whitcastles, Stone Circle (NY 224881), 6 miles NE. of Lockerbie, Sheet 79 (by-road and footpath). *Dumfriesshire.*

This circle of stones 160 ft. in diameter, standing on the open moor, consists of nine massive blocks, most if not all of which appear to have tumbled from what must at best have been a precarious stance in the unstable ground. Two of them are over 7 ft. long.

Dyke, Standing Stones (NT 084036), 1 mile S. of Moffat, Sheet 78 (A.701). *Dumfriesshire.*

Three squat massive blocks stand *in situ* in a wooden railing beside the newly cast section of the A.701 road between Moffat and the junction with the new A.74 road just N. of Beattock village. They stand 3 ft., 4 ft. and 5 ft. above ground respectively, and the broad faces, all some 3 ft. wide, do not conform either to part of the circumference of a circle or to a rectangular figure. It is possible that they may represent a megalithic monument the rest of which has perished. The situation on the spine of the ridge between the River Annan and the Evan Water (up which the main Roman road through Annandale runs) is a commanding one.

Pencraig Hill, Standing Stone (NT 581768), ¼ mile W. of East Linton, Sheet 67 (A.1). *East Lothian.*

This three-sided pillar stands in a field beside the Great North Road as this runs S. of W. on its way from East Linton to Edinburgh. It is 10 ft. high and the sides measure about 3 ft. in breadth just above ground level.

Kirklandhill, Standing Stone (NT 616776), 1¾ miles E. of East Linton, Sheet 67 (A.1, A.198). *East Lothian.*

This stone stands in the E. angle formed by the junction of the two roads. It is 11 ft. high and its four rather irregular flanks each measure about 1 ft. 9 in. in breadth at ground level. It belongs to the group of which the other members are noted here.

Whitekirk hill, Cairn (NT 595819), $\frac{1}{4}$ mile N. of Whitekirk, Sheet 67 (moorland). *East Lothian.*

This cairn stands on the summit of Whitekirk Hill which, although rising to only 200 ft. above sea level, is conspicuous in level country. The cairn measures 50 ft. in diameter and stands to a height of 6 ft. It is grass-grown, but boulders protruding through this indicate that it is formed of stone rather than of earth.

Tynemouth, Cairn (NT 637813), $2\frac{1}{4}$ miles E. of Whitekirk, Sheet 67 (farm roads and sea-shore). *East Lothian.*

This cairn stands on a pronounced rocky promontory protecting the N. side of the mouth of the River Tyne. It measures 60 ft. in diameter and rises to 10 ft. above the base.

Harestone Hill, Cairn (NT 567623), 4 miles SE. of Gifford, Sheet 67 (by-roads, farm road and moorland). *East Lothian.*

This cairn, known as Whitestone Cairn, stands at a height of 1650 ft. O.D. on the summit of one of the peaks of the Lammermuir Hills. It is circular, a little over 40 ft. in diameter, and today stands to a height of about 3 ft. above ground level. It has been robbed of stone for a sheepfold and a surveyor's cairn.

Penshiel Hill, Cairn (NT 637635), 7 miles ESE. of Gifford, Sheet 67 (B.6355 and moorland). *East Lothian.*

This interesting cairn stands at a height of a little over 1150 ft. O.D. on the NE. shoulder of Penshiel Hill. The cairn itself measures about 33 ft. in diameter at the base and has a flat top 23 ft. in diameter. It rises to a height of 4 ft. above the bottom of a broad surrounding ditch which is about 23 ft. wide. Outside this is a low bank about 7 ft. wide. The whole structure has the appearance of a bell cairn, a type which is uncommon but not unknown in the North.

Kingside Hill, Stone Circle (NT 627650), 6 miles SSE. of Gifford, Sheet 67 (B.6355). *East Lothian.*

This circle, which stands in open moorland on the NW. flank of Kingside Hill, consists of a circle about 40 ft. in diameter composed of 30 small boulders, the majority of which are set on edge. The centre of the cairn is occupied by a low mound about 10 ft. in diameter with a boulder nearly 2 ft. square protruding from the middle. This is probably a disc cairn, a type of monument known elsewhere in the region.

Mayshiel, Stone Circle (NT 617646), $5\frac{1}{2}$ miles ESE. of Gifford, Sheet 67 (B.6355). *East Lothian.*

This little setting of stones stands only 10 yds. from the S. side of the road. It consists of seven earthfast blocks which enclose a very slightly depressed area about 9 ft. in diameter. A very low bank surrounds the stones. Other remains in this vicinity can be compared to this structure, as can a well-known example at Kirkurd, in Peeblesshire.

Standingstone Farm, Standing Stone (NT 577736), 2 miles NNW. of Garvald, Sheet 67 (by-roads). *East Lothian.*

This handsome monolith stands in the stack-yard at Standingstone Farm, 400 yds. S. of another on Cairndinnis Farm. It attains a height above ground of 9 ft., and is almost square in section, showing a variation only between 2 ft. 3 in. and 2 ft. 8 in. in the measurements of the sides at ground level.

Cairndinnis Farm, Standing Stone (NT 578742), $2\frac{1}{4}$ miles NNW. of Garvald, Sheet 67 (by-roads). *East Lothian.*

This four-sided monolith is situated 300 yds. SSW. of Traprain Law. It is 8 ft. high and the sides vary in breadth from 2 ft. 6 in. to 1 ft. 3 in. This stone is known as the Loth Stone, on the supposition that it marks the grave of a fictitious eponymous monarch named Loth. It has been moved from its original position to the edge of the field to facilitate ploughing; at the time of its removal the ground about it was excavated, but nothing was found.

Spartleton, Cairn (NT 653655), $5\frac{1}{4}$ miles SE. of Garvald, Sheet 67 (by-road, B.6355 and moorland). *East Lothian.*

This cairn, magnificently sited on the summit of Spartleton, the principal feature of the Spartleton Edge ridge, measures 50 ft. in diameter. Some of the stones of which it was constructed have been placed in rows outside its perimeter in modern times, to indicate the points of the compass, and an observation cairn has been erected upon it, but otherwise the cairn does not appear to have been disturbed.

Yadlee, Stone Circle (NT 654673), $4\frac{1}{4}$ miles NNW. of Garvald, Sheet 67 (by-road and farm road). *East Lothian.*

This little circle stands above the right

bank of the West Burn 300 yds. S. by E. of Yadlee, on the NE. foot of Spartleton Edge. It consists of seven small stones, all but one still earthfast, which lie on the circumference of a circle 27 ft. in diameter. This little monument has not been excavated, but probing indicated stones beneath the turf inside it.

Priestlaw Hill, Cairn (NT 652623), 8 miles SE. of Garvald, Sheet 67 (B.6355 and track from Priestlaw). *East Lothian.*

This cairn is situated at a height of a little more than 1350 ft. above sea level on the summit of Priestlaw Hill. It measures 40 ft. in diameter and 5 ft. in height. It has been robbed of stone for the construction of a sheepfold and a cross-shaped mound of stones, but appears to be otherwise undisturbed.

Crystal Rig, Cairn (NT 665673), 5 miles SE. of Stenton, Sheet 67 (by-road and moorland). *East Lothian.*

This cairn, locally the Witches Cairn, stands near the summit of Crystal Rig at an elevation of 1045 ft. O.D. A surveyor's cairn built upon it out of its material may account for a spot level being marked at this point on the O.S. map. The cairn, which is otherwise undamaged, measures 60 ft. in diameter and 4 ft. in height.

Glassmount, Standing Stones (NT 244884), 2¾ miles SW. of Kirkcaldy, Sheet 66 (A.92 and by-road). *Fife.*

These two stones stand on rising ground 400 yds. SW. of North Glassmount farmhouse. They lie 19 ft. apart on an E. to W. axis. The W. stone is 6 ft. high and its profile is characterised by a triangular appearance in that while one side rises comparatively straight up towards the top, the other starts at a considerable angle to the vertical but, on reaching about half way up the total height of the stone, returns at a similar complementary angle to a narrow top. The E. stone, only a few inches shorter than its companion, is a four-sided monolith of regular appearance.

Lundin Links, Standing Stones (NO 404026), on the W. outskirts of Lundin Links, Sheet 59 (A.921). *Fife.*

These three spectacular stones are apparently all that remain of a setting which originally comprised at least one more stone and possibly others, forming a circle. The SE. stone is 13 ft. high, its broad S. and W. faces, each 5 ft. wide, giving it a massive silhouette. The S.

stone is 17 ft. high and the N. stone 18 ft., both of them tapering finely towards the top.

Norrie's Law, Cairn (NO 409073), 2¼ miles NNW. of Kirkton of Largo, Sheet 59 (by-road). *Fife.*

This ill-starred cairn is said originally to have measured about 53 ft. in diameter, to have had two kerbs, and to have been surrounded by a ditch 16 ft. wide. Cists containing bones and at least one food vessel were found in it. Today it is mutilated and uneven, a ragged mound spread to about 60 ft. in diameter within the fragmentary remains of the ditch. The cairn came to fame after the excavations of 1819 to 1822, during which a famous collection of what is in part at least Pictish silverware was recovered. "The precise facts connected with this remarkable discovery were never ascertained, owing to apprehensions of the interference of the Scottish Exchequer to reclaim the 'treasure trove'." The treasure, now in the national collections, includes a pin with the Pictish broken floriated rod incised upon it and a leaf-shaped plate 3½ in. long on which the double disc and Z-rod symbol, and a dog's head, are very beautifully represented.

Bogleys, Standing Stone (NT 295950), 1 mile N. of Dysart, Sheet 59 (A.92). *Fife.*

This stone, situated close to the W. side of the road, stands to a height of 6 ft. It is four-sided, and its girth increases towards the top so that it measures 8 ft. 6 in. at the base and 10 ft. 6 in. at the top.

Hare Law, Cairn (NT 187961), ¼ mile SE. of Lochore, Sheet 58 (farm track). *Fife.*

This cairn measures about 80 ft. in diameter, but its surface is ragged and reduced. This results from partly organised and quite unorganised attacks upon it in the years 1890 and 1891, before which the height was reported to have been in excess of 20 ft. The digging "brought to light the foundations of a wall surrounding the cairn"; and "on driving a broad trench" into the body of the monument a cist was revealed at a point 21 ft. from the perimeter. This contained a food vessel, teeth and bones. Another cist was encountered at the centre, its joints luted with clay. This contained teeth, bones and "an unmistakable strip of metal" which was oxidised beyond recovery. A third cist was found in a similar position to the first but several feet further N. This contained a food vessel with five lug handles and was otherwise crammed with bones, which weighed altogether 12 lb. The cist with the metal was probably the primary deposit; and the report suggests that it had been robbed previously.

Cairnfield, Cairn (NO 298112), 1 mile N. by W. of Ladybank, Sheet 59 (B. 9129). *Fife.*

This cairn is probably a bell barrow. The central mound measures 30 ft. in diameter, and both the ditch and the low external bank about 15 ft. in width. It is one of what originally must have been a considerable number in this part of the country which, being built of earth, were easily destroyed. Three such were despoiled in 1870 on the moor a short distance E. of Cairnfield. The only object recorded as having been found was an extended skeleton which was placed so near the top of the cairn in which it lay as to be recognisable as a secondary, perhaps modern, deposit.

Newton of Collessie, Standing Stone (NO 293133), ¼ mile E. of Collessie, Sheet 59. *Fife.*

This handsome stone has been broken, but still attains a height of 9 ft. above ground level. It has been sculptured, but nothing has been made of the worn remnants which can still be faintly perceived high up on its flatter faces.

Collessie, Cairn (NO 288131), 200 yds. SE. of Collessie Church, Sheet 59. *Fife.*

The remains of this cairn still occupy an area about 80 ft. in diameter, but they are worth beholding not just in their own right but for the relics which were somewhat prematurely removed from them in 1876 and 1877 and are now in the national collections. The report of the excavation, too, is worth reading, and not only for its archaeological content. The cairn originally measured 120 ft. in diameter and stood to a height of 14 ft. The results of the excavation began with the discovery of a deposit of burnt bones with a riveted dagger with a gold mounting. After this, and "when fully a thousand cart-loads of stones had been lifted and conveyed off the site, we began to realise the magnitude of the task we

had undertaken". When this part of the job had been completed, a slice had been cut out of the cairn measuring 24 ft. in width. A peristalith encountered during this great clearance may have belonged to an earlier version of the cairn. The ground beneath the cairn was found to be covered with charcoal and burnt bones. A cist found near the centre, on the original ground surface, contained a crouched burial and a beaker. A second beaker was "brought up" from 6 ft. into the natural, under circumstances which are not entirely convincing.

West Lomond, Cairn (NO 197066), 3½ miles W. of Falkland, Sheet 58 (by-road, farm road and moorland). *Fife.*

This large cairn which is conspicuously sited at a height of 1000 ft. above the plain ¼ mile below has been attacked and partly scattered by several unknown hands. It still stands to a height of 10 ft. and measures about 90 ft. in diameter.

Greenhill, Cairn (NO 345228), 1½ miles SW. of Balmerino, Sheet 54 (by-roads). *Fife.*

This circular cairn, 50 ft. in diameter and rising to a height of 5 ft., was excavated in 1899 and 1901. It was found to be contained within a kerb and to have a buried upright slab at the centre on the original ground level. Immediately W. of this was a cist which had been robbed. A pit covered with a slab was found 7 ft. N. of the cist; it contained a food vessel and an incense cup. Two more food vessels and some cremated bones, together with two small disc beads, were found in the E. quadrant of the cairn; 72 beads of a jet necklace lay a few feet S. of these; another food vessel and bones came from a pit under a stone in the W. quadrant; a fifth food vessel was found by itself close to this; and a sixth, and fragments of a seventh, food vessel came from the S. quadrant. The robbed primary burial, which might perhaps have contained a beaker, was by far the most imposing internal structure, the minor cists and pits being apparently of a rather informal nature. It is a matter for some regret that archaeological methods were not used in the eviscerating of this unusually important monument.

Nisabost, Standing Stone (NG 041973), 8¾ miles N. of Rodel, Sheet 18 (A.859 and moorland). *Harris.*

This stone stands to a height on 10 ft. 6 in. and measures 4 ft. 6 in. in breadth and up to 1 ft. 4 in. in thickness. At a distance of 8 ft. 6 in. to the W. two small earthfast slabs are placed at a right angle to the broad face of the stone, and the intervening space contains a quantity of small stones.

Orwell, Standing Stones (NO 149044), 1¾ miles E. of Milnathort, Sheet 58 (A.911). *Kinross.*

These stones stand just N. of the road a little to the W. of Orwell farmhouse. The W. stone stands to a height of 7 ft. 6 in., the E. stone, 48 ft. away, to 9 ft.

Dumglow, Cairn (NT 076965), 1¼ miles SW of Cleich, Sheet 58 (farm road and moorland). *Kinross.*

This cairn, standing on the summit of Dumglow at a height of 1243 ft. O.D., is within the precincts of the hill fort described below. It is 50 ft. in diameter and 5 ft. high. When opened in 1904 the upper levels of the cairn were found to have been permeated with "molten tar and the melted glass of whisky-bottles" as a result of successive bonfires having been ignited upon it on occasions of exceptional public rejoicing. Deeper, the cairn was found to be water-logged. At a depth of 6 ft. 7 in. below the centre of the top of the cairn the excavators found the remains of a hollowed tree-trunk 7 ft. long which may possibly have been a tree burial.

Redcastle, Standing Stone (NX 823653), 2⅒ miles N. of Dalbeattie, Sheet 84 (A.710 and farm road).
Stewartry of Kirkcudbright.

This block of red granite, standing to a height of over 8 ft. above ground level, is trapezoidal in section, diminishing upwards.

Clawbelly Hill, Cairns (NX 882610), 3 miles E. of Dalbeattie, Sheet 84 (A.745 and by-road). *Stewartry of Kirkcudbright.*

As in Dumfriesshire and the neighbouring parts of Ayrshire, groups of small cairns and less frequent circular stone foundations occur widely over the moors of the Stewartry. One of the more accessible examples of such groups lies close to the W. side of the by-road running up the valley of the Southwick Burn towards Southwick Halt on the Castle Douglas Branch of the Glasgow and South-Western Railway. The small cairns, varying from about 12 ft. to 15 ft.

in diameter, are of the class usually described as clearance cairns. No systematic study has been made of the construction of such cairns, and while many may be nothing more than piles of stones cleared from land which was required for scratch-ploughing, it is possible that some were first made, and others re-used, for sepulchral purposes.

Bargatton, Cairn (NX 689626), 1½ miles S. by E. of Laurieston, Sheet 84 (farm roads and fields).
Stewartry of Kirkcudbright.

This is a circular cairn 60 ft. in diameter and 8 ft. high which has had a considerable amount of stone removed from it.

Bargatton, Disc Cairn (NX 686626), 1 mile S. by E. of Laurieston, Sheet 84 (farm roads and fields).
Stewartry of Kirkcudbright.

Situated 175 yds. WSW. of a circular cairn (NX 689626), this monument is probably a disc cairn of a type not yet widely recognised in Scotland but at the same time not unknown. It consists of a circular bank 14 ft. thick and from 1 ft. to 2 ft. high which encloses an area 60 ft. in diameter. A low stony mound measuring 25 ft. by 20 ft. lies near the centre.

Lamford, Cairn (NX 528991), 4½ miles NW. of Carsphairn, Sheet 77 (A.713 and hill road). *Stewartry of Kirkcudbright.*

This cairn, lying beside the hill road running E. from the main road at Lamford, measures 48 ft. in diameter and nearly 6 ft. in height.

Blair Hill, Standing Stones (NX 404710), 3 miles N. of Minnigaff, Sheet 77 (by-road, footpath and moorland).
Stewartry of Kirkcudbright.

These two standing stones, one 6 ft. 8 in. and the other 7 ft. 4 in. in height, stand 14 ft. 6 in. apart, and the edge of a broken thin slab 3 ft. 9 in. long protrudes through the turf between and a little to the SE. of them. The stones stand in the SE. quadrant of an oval enclosure formed by a low rubble wall and measuring axially 30 ft. by 26 ft.

Stroanfeggan, Cairn (NX 640914), 6¼ miles N. by E. of St John's Town of Dalry, Sheet 77 (B.7000, B.729 and footpath). *Stewartry of Kirkcudbright.*

This cairn situated close to the left bank of the Stroanfeggan Burn measures about 75 ft. in diameter but has been severely quarried. An oblong cist was revealed at a point 25 ft. in from the E.

arc of the perimeter in 1910. This measured internally 3 ft. 5 in. in length, 2 ft. in width and 2 ft. 3 in. in depth beneath a cover stone 5 ft. long and 4 ft. wide. The sides were formed by four large slabs the joints between which were eked with smaller stones and luted with clay. It contained a plano-convex knife.

Dalarran Holm, Standing Stone (NX 638792), 1 mile NNE. of New Galloway, Sheet 77 (A.712 and A.713).

Stewartry of Kirkcudbright.

This stone stands on the flood plain of the Water of Ken, 100 yds. from the left bank of the river. It is a broad, thin whinstone slab 8 ft. 6 in. in height, the broad face measuring 3 ft. 8 in. at the base and 2 ft. at the top, and the thickness almost 1 ft.

Carlins Cairn, Cairn (NX 497884), 2¾ miles S. by E. of the head of Loch Doon, Sheet 77 (moorland).

Stewartry of Kirkcudbright.

This cairn stands on a ridge at the N. end of the Rhinns of Kells at a height of 2650 ft. above sea level. It measures 55 ft. in diameter and attains a height of 10 ft.

Mollance, Cairn (NX 780661), 2½ miles NNE. of Castle Douglas, Sheet 84 (A.75 and by-road).

Stewartry of Kirkcudbright.

This cairn, 50 ft. in diameter and 4 ft. high, was excavated in 1952. Built of greywacke boulders and topped by a pink granite capstone, it was found to contain an oval cist, 4 ft. in length by 2 ft. 6 in. in breadth, which contained sherds of a primary beaker burial and the food vessel of a secondary deposit. The finds are in the Dumfries Burgh Museum.

Cairntosh Hill, Cairn (NX 631583), 2¼ miles NE. of Gatehouse of Fleet, Sheet 83 (footpaths and moorland).

Stewartry of Kirkcudbright.

This cairn stands on the summit of Cairntosh Hill at a height of 1050 ft. above sea level. It measures 50 ft. in diameter and 8 ft. in height.

Cauldside Burn, Cairns, Stone Circles and Cup-and-Ring Markings (NX 5257) 3½ miles WNW. of Anwoth Church, Sheet 83 (farm road and moorland).

Stewartry of Kirkcudbright.

These monuments are situated on the head of the Cauldside Burn, on the lowest slopes of Cairnharrow Hill and Cambret Moor. The largest and best preserved

cairn measures 63 ft. in diameter and 10 ft. in height, and a cist is exposed in the summit. Immediately to the S. of it is a circle 70 ft. in diameter marked by 10 stones out of possibly originally twice as many.

The foundations of a second cairn, with a megalithic cist sunk in the ground within it, lie 150 yds. N. of the one already described, and the slight remains of another circle lie just S. of it.

The cup-and-ring markings occur on a large block of whinstone situated N. of the burn 400 yds. NNW. of the first cairn. One figure, measuring 2 ft. in diameter, comprises a cup surrounded by a ring from which a groove winds out through a spiral of 5½ turns. The other consists of a cup with three concentric rings.

Glenquicken, Stone Circle (NX 509582), 2¼ miles E. of Creetown, Sheet 83 (by-road and "Old Military Road").

Stewartry of Kirkcudbright.

This circle consists of 28 close-set low boulders placed with their broad faces on the line of the circumference. It measures 50 ft. in diameter and the centre is occupied by a granite boulder nearly 6 ft. high and of rectangular section.

A second monument of this kind, in which nine boulders form a circle 30 ft. in diameter and a boulder 5 ft. 6 in. high occupies the centre, lies beside the footpath 1½ miles to the SSE. (517560).

Garynahine, Stone Circle (NB 230303), 12 miles W. of Stornoway, Sheet 8 (A.858, B.8011). *Lewis.*

This monument, situated on an exposed hillside 1 mile S. of Garynahine, comprises the remains of a circle of upright slabs surrounding a ring of boulders which in turn encloses an upright slab at the centre. Five of a possible six slabs, the tallest 9 ft. high, remain of the outer circle; and the central slab is 2 ft. high.

Cnoc Fillibhir, Stone Circle (NB 225335), 12½ miles W. of Stornoway, Sheet 8 (A.858 and track). *Lewis.*

This monument comprises two concentric circles of tall upright slabs, the outer measuring 53 ft. and the inner 28 ft. in diameter. The outer circle contains eight upstanding stones, the highest reaching nearly 6 ft. above ground level, and the inner four slabs, the highest 7 ft.

Loch Roag, Cairn and Stone Circle (NB 222335), 12½ miles W. of Stornoway, Sheet 8 (A.858 and track). *Lewis.*

This monument consists of a circular setting of tall thin slabs with a diameter of 65 ft. surrounding a small cairn. Of the five slabs which remain standing, the tallest reaches 10 ft. 9 in. in height. The cairn, which is set a little E. of the centre of the circle and measures 28 ft. in diameter, has an excavated cavity near the centre.

Callanish, Standing Stones (NB 213330), 13 miles W. of Stornoway, Sheet 8 (A.858 and by-road). *Lewis.*
See **Callanish,** Chambered Cairn.

Clach an Trushal, Standing Stone (NB 375537), 13½ miles NNW. of Stornoway, Sheet 8 (A.857 and by-road). *Lewis.*

This stone is a monolith 19 ft. high, 6 ft. wide and 3 ft. 9 in. thick at the most. It stands near the 15th milestone on the road from Stornoway to Ness in the township of Ballantrushal.

Newbridge, Cairn (NT 123726), 2 miles W. of the Edinburgh City Boundary at Gogar, Sheet 65 (A.8 and by-road). *Midlothian.*

These remains are impressive in spite of their uninspiring surroundings on the edge of Newbridge village and within sound of the A.8 road. The cairn, now closely surrounded by a modern wall, is apparently made of earth, and measures 100 ft. in diameter. It now stands to a height of 10 ft. but it was opened in 1830, when at least a bronze rapier was recovered.

Three upright stones stand at distances from the centre of the cairn of respectively 100 ft. NW., 160 ft. SW. and 175 ft. E. The nearest is 7 ft. high, the next 6 ft. 6 in. and the last now only 4 ft. high. A fourth stone, 350 yds. E. of the cairn and standing to a height of 9 ft., probably has nothing to do with the central array.

In 1794 the monument was described as "a circular mound of earth surrounded with large unpolished stones at a considerable distance from each other". At the present time it is not known either how many stones have been removed since then or whether the three survivors formed part of a circle or not. If they did, it must have been eccentric to the cairn.

Caiy Stane, Standing Stone (NT 243684), ¼ mile W. of Fairmilehead, Sheet 66 (B.701). *Midlothian.*

This stone stands in a recess 54 ft. N. of the road. It measures 9 ft. in height, from 4 ft. 2 in. to 5 ft. 9 in. in breadth, and from 10 in. to 19 in. in thickness. Six small hollows on the E. face have been pronounced authentic cup-marks.

Caerketton Hill, Cairn (NT 237662), 1½ miles SW. of Fairmilehead, Sheet 66 (A.702 and footpath). *Midlothian.*

Caerketton Hill, the NE. feature of the Pentland Hills massif, commands extensive views northwards over Edinburgh, the Forth and Fife as well as over the plains to the east and west. This cairn, situated on the summit, has been larger than it now appears, but stone-robbing by dyke-builders has reduced it to an unknown degree. It still measures about 50 ft. in diameter and stands to a height of at least 5 ft., but its outline and surface are spoiled.

Carnethy Hill, Cairn (NT 203618), 4¼ miles SW. of Fairmilehead, Sheet 66 (A.702). *Midlothian.*

Among the peaks and summits of the Pentland Hills Carnethy Hill (1890 ft. O.D.) is topped only by its neighbour Scald Law (1898 ft. O.D.). The cairn on Carnethy summit is thus sited with flamboyance, to be visible from miles around in almost every direction. It measures 70 ft. in diameter and 8 ft. in height, and as far as can be judged the only interference with it has been of a superficial nature.

East Cairn Hill, Cairn (NT 122595), 5 miles NW. of West Linton, Sheet 65 (by-road and old drove road footpath). *Midlothian.*

This cairn is magnificently situated on the summit of the SW. extremity of the Pentland Hills and commands deep prospects right across the north Lanarkshire plains as well as in all other directions. It consists of a mound of stones measuring 55 ft. in diameter at the base and standing 8 ft. high. Some of the stones have been piled up to form a surveyor's cairn, but no other interferences are apparent.

Clach Mhor a Ché, Standing Stone (NF 770662), 9 miles W. by S. of Lochmaddy, Sheet 18 (A.867, A.865 and track). *North Uist.*

This stone, 8 ft. high, 4 ft. wide and

1 ft. 4 in. thick, stands 20 yds. from the shore of the tidal waters inside Kirkibost Island.

Bookan, Disc Barrow (HY 287137), 3½ miles NE. of Stromness, Sheet 6 (A.965, B.9055). *Orkney, Mainland island.*

This barrow, lying on the NE. shore of the Loch of Stenness, measures 100 ft. over all in diameter; the central mound accounts for half of this. The enclosing bank is spread to about 15 ft. in thickness and, like the mound, rises to a height of 3 ft. above the level of the ground outside.

Vola, Disc Barrow (HY 318141), 5¼ miles NE. of Stromness, Sheet 6 (A.965 and by-road). *Orkney, Mainland island.*

This oval structure measures externally 102 ft. from N. to S. by 85 ft. transversely. The central mound measures 60 ft. by 56 ft., and the enclosing bank an average of 18 ft. in width, both of them rising to a height of about 3 ft. above the general level of the ground in the vicinity.

Staney Hill, Standing Stone (HY 318156), 6 miles NE. of Stromness, Sheet 6 (A.965, A.986 and by-road). *Orkney, Mainland island.*

This stone stands on a rising ground close to the E. side of the road between Grimeston and Bimbister. It attains a height of 8 ft. above ground level. At the base it measures 3 ft. 9 in. in width and 13 in. in thickness, and it tapers gradually towards the pointed top.

Knowe of Smirrus, Cairn (HY 291215), 8 miles N. by E. of Stromness, Sheet 6 (A.967, B.9057, A.986). *Orkney, Mainland island.*

The parish of Birsay occupies the central part of the NW. lobe of Mainland, measuring over 10 miles in length from N. to S. and having a sea frontage 5 miles long on either side of Brough Head. This area is typical of Mainland in that it contains getting on for 200 round cairns and mounds of one sort or another, and that it is virtually impossible to walk over any stretch of the country without seeing some. Smaller than chambered cairns, the majority measure between 25 ft. and 50 ft. in diameter and stand only a foot or two in height, though a few are something more or less than this. In some a cist or possibly a chamber can be seen in part, and only too many have been dug into.

One, the Knowe of Smirrus, is considerably larger than the others, measuring about 100 ft. in diameter and standing to a height of 6 ft. It has been mutilated and despoiled, but the tattered remains of a stony structure which appear to be those of a part of a chamber or cist can be seen among the debris.

Knowes of Trotty, Cairns (HY 341175), 8 miles NE. of Stromness, Sheet 6 (A.965, A.986, by-road and farm road). *Orkney, Mainland island.*

The Knowes of Trotty, 11 in number, are mounds which are ranged along the foot of the steep W. slopes of the Ward of Redland, a ridge situated half way between the shores of Wide Firth and the Loch of Harray. Most if not all of them have been rifled, but only one is documented. This is the northernmost of the three largest, which lie in a row closer to the hill than the remainder. It is slightly oval on plan, measuring axially 61 ft. by 55 ft. It rises to a height of about 9 ft. above a "platform" which measures axially 93 ft. by 79 ft., and is 3 ft. high. The true character and purpose of this feature are matters of doubt at the present time.

The cairn was opened in 1858, and found to contain a short cist in which were cremated bones, four gold discs, and a number of beads and of irregularly-shaped pieces of amber. It is characteristic of Orkney in the Early Bronze Age—perhaps the middle of the 2nd millennium B.C.—that, although this is clearly the grave of a person of undeniable importance, no bronze was found among the grave goods.

Wheebin, Standing Stone (HY 253263), 10¼ miles N. of Stromness, Sheet 6 (A.967). *Orkney, Mainland island.*

Wheebin is the name of this stone which stands on the moor 300 yds. from the W. shore of the Loch of Boardhouse. It stands to a height of 12 ft., and while keeping an average thickness of a little over 1 ft. it varies in width from 5 ft. at ground level to 3 ft. 3 in. half way up, and thereafter continues to taper steadily.

Holland House, Standing Stone (HY 753529), ¼ mile N. of South Bay pier, Sheet 5 (by-road). *Orkney, North Ronaldsay island.*

This erect flagstone slab standing to a height of 13 ft. is only 4 in. thick at the base, but as much as 4 ft. wide. At a height of 6 ft. above ground level it is perforated by a small oval hole which, whether of natural origin or not, has in the past attracted seekers after symbolism. It is recorded that in 1794 "50 of the inhabitants assembled there on the first day of the year, and danced with moon light, with no other music than their own singing".

Too of Nugle, Cairn (HY 382335), 5 miles NW. of Brinyan pier, Sheet 6 (B.9065, B.9064, by-road and farm road).
Orkney, Rousay island.
This round cairn, 35 ft. in diameter and 5 ft. high, is made of gravel and rubble. Several large loose slabs lying upon it may possibly have once formed parts of a cist within it.

Burn of Mussetter, Standing Stone (HY 556329), 2 miles NNW. of Bay of Backaland pier, Sheet 5 (B.9063).
Orkney, Eday island.
This pointed slab rises to a height of 8 ft. 6 in. at a position on the highest part of a low ridge. It is only 5 in. thick, and it contracts as it rises from a width of 2 ft. at the base. It is said to have fallen and been re-erected.

Stone of Setter, Standing Stone (HY 564372), 4½ miles N. by W. of Bay of Backaland pier, Sheet 5 (B.9063 and by-road).
Orkney, Eday island.
This stone stands at a point 200 yds. N. of the N. end of Mill Loch, 100 yds. E. of the road. Furrowed by weathering, and of irregular form, it is 15 ft. high, up to 14 in. thick and 7 ft. wide.

Cutter's Tooer, Cairn (HY 672284), 1 mile E. of Whitehall pier, Sheet 5 (by-road and pasture land).
Orkney, Stronsay island.
This cairn stands conspicuously on the promontory Grice Ness at the N. of Mill Bay, where it serves as a landmark for fishermen. It measures 60 ft. in diameter and stands to a height of 3 ft. 6 in.

Woodend, Cairn (NT 121313), 3 miles S. of Broughton, Sheet 73 (A.701).
Peeblesshire.
This cairn stands in a little plantation on the opposite side of the road to Woodend cottage on the brink of an old bed of the River Tweed. It measures 60 ft. in diameter and stands 2 ft. in height. It has been robbed for stone and twice excavated, and the remains of a central cist can be seen near the centre. No trace

now remains of several other burials in somewhat informal cists which are said to have been found in the cairn.

Drumelzier, Cairn (NT 123326), 2 miles S. of Broughton, Sheet 73 (B.712 and by-road).
Peeblesshire.
Half this cairn has fallen away with the erosion of an old bank of the River Tweed but the remainder, which lies 190 yds. S. of the gamekeeper's cottage at Ford, can be seen in section from across the river by travellers on the A.701 road. The great interest of the cairn lies in the finds which came out of it during excavations in 1929 and 1930.

It is not very easy to be absolutely clear from the published report exactly what structural and funerary sequences the finds represent, but there is no doubt that the initial structure was a cairn with a kerb, 30 ft. in diameter, beneath the centre of which was a cremation pit. A sherd of secondary neolithic pottery found elsewhere in the cairn may belong to this initial period. At a later date the cairn seems to have been remade round a slightly different central point, this time with a cist at the centre, as at near-by Woodend cairn. A complete beaker of degenerate B form stood upright in this, and a fragment of another beaker, the neolithic sherd, a flint saw and 13 flakes of chert were also found in it. At later periods seven, and possibly nine, other cists were inserted into the cairn (cf. Woodend again). Sherds belonging to five cordonned and one unspecified urns, part of a jet armlet and part of a whetstone were also recovered, together with charcoal and the burnt kernel of a hazel nut. A slab of stone, one face of which is ornamented with pecked rings, was also brought out. This decoration, comprising a group of four double and one single rings, is of an unusual kind, to which the excavator could only cite one parallel, a slab in Berwickshire the location of which was not recorded.

This cairn, the Woodend cairn, and another just above Tweedsmuir that is associated with standing stones, throw an interesting light on the fairly early and long-lasting occupation of upper Tweeddale which is not reflected in occupation sites until the coming of the unenclosed platform settlements.

Harestanes, Stone Circle (NT 124443),

¾ mile S. of Blyth Bridge, Sheet 72 (A.72 and by-road).   *Peeblesshire.*

This little setting of four large boulders lies in a cottage garden at Kirkurd. The boulders are arranged on the circumference of a circle 10 ft. in diameter and two others, which are not earthfast, lie near them. Small erections of this kind also occur in North Wales.

Newbigging, Standing Stone and Cup-and-Ring Markings (NO 157356), 8¾ miles NNE. of Perth, Sheet 53 (A.93, by-road and woodland track). *Perthshire.*

This stone, re-erected in the 19th century, now stands to a height of 4 ft. 8 in. above ground level. It is remarkable for bearing several cup-and-ring markings and cup-marks on one face, many of them joined by gullies.

Monzie, Stone Circle (NN 882243), 2 miles NE. of Crieff, Sheet 58 (A.85, A.822 and private grounds). *Perthshire.*

The stone circle at Monzie consists of 10 boulders set with what broad faces they have facing inwards on the circumference of a circle 17 ft. in diameter. A primary cremation burial was found during excavations in 1938, and some sherds of a flat-rimmed vessel were recovered from a higher level. A large boulder, blazoned with cups and cup-and-ring markings lying 11 ft. SW. of the circle was found to be connected to this by a scatter of stones forming an informal causeway, reminiscent of the three larger similar phenomena at the ring cairn at Balnuaran of Clava. The association of Early Iron Age pottery with such a circle recalls the recumbent-stone circles of Aberdeenshire.

Craigneich, Standing Stone (NN 792179), 3 miles SSE. of Comrie, Sheet 57 (B.827 and by-road). *Perthshire.*

This is one of several standing stones which are situated in the upper part of the valley of the Machany Water. It measures 15 ft. 9 in. in girth at the base and stands to a height of 6 ft. 4 in.

Dowally, Standing Stones (NO 000479), 3¾ miles N. by W. of Dunkeld, Sheet 53 (A.9).   *Perthshire.*

The numerous standing stones of greater Strathtay are well represented by this pair situated perilously near the road. They stand 10 ft. apart, the N. stone reaching a height of 8 ft. 9 in. above ground level and the other 7 ft. 8 in.

Airlich, Stone Circle (NN 959386), 4¾

miles WSW. of Dunkeld, Sheet 53 (A.822 and moorland).   *Perthshire.*

This monument consists of a circle of nine stones set on a bank 25 ft. in diameter which encloses an inner circle now of eight smaller stones. None of the stones stands more than 3 ft. 6 in. in height, but the remains are nevertheless impressive.

Dunfallandy, Cairn (NN 947570), 1 mile S. of Pitlochry, Sheet 53 (by-road and field).   *Perthshire.*

This cairn, about 55 ft. in diameter, lies on the flood-plain of the River Tummel. It appears to be surrounded by a shallow ditch with a low bank outside it, and so to be a kind of bell barrow.

Croft Moraig, Stone Circle (NN 797472), 2 miles NE. of Kenmore, Sheet 51 (A.827).   *Perthshire.*

Excavations in 1965 revealed that the original Early Neolithic structure, a penannular setting of wooden posts, was very soon succeeded by the inner ring of standing stones with three stones to the SE., and by the enclosing bank about 185 ft in diameter one stone in which bears cup-marks. At about 2,000 B.C. the outer circle was added, with two stones 5 yds. to the E.

Machulm, Stone Circle (NN 682401), 3½ miles SW. of Fearnan, Sheet 51 (A.827).   *Perthshire.*

This circle consists of six massive stones standing on the circumference of a circle about 20 ft. in diameter on a mound about 40 ft. in diameter.

Kinnell, Stone Circle (NN 576327), ½ mile E. of Killin, Sheet 51 (private grounds).   *Perthshire.*

This circle of six stones erected each with a broad face on the line of the circumference of a circle 30 ft. in diameter stands close to Kinnell house at Killin, abode of the Macnabb. The stones vary in height from 4 ft. to 6 ft. 6 in.

Strathgroy, Cairn (NN 879653), 1½ miles E. of Blair Atholl, Sheet 43 (A.9, farm road and hill).   *Perthshire.*

This large round cairn measures 125 ft. in diameter and attains a maximum height of 18 ft. The remains of a peristalith can be detected as well as those of a cist, presumably secondary, which protrude through the top of the cairn near the centre.

Philip Law, Cairn (NT 727107), 7¼ miles SSE. of Jedburgh, Sheet 80 (A.68, by-road and footpath).   *Roxburghshire.*

This, one of the many circular cairns in the district, stands on the summit of Philip Law at a height of 1359 ft. O.D. It measures 42 ft. in diameter and 3 ft. 6 in. in height.

Eildon Mid Hill, Cairn (NT 547322), 1 mile S. of Melrose, Sheet 73 (B.6359). *Roxburghshire.*

The remains of this circular cairn measuring about 50 ft. in diameter lie on the SW. flank of Eildon Mid Hill, at an elevation of about 100 ft. below the summit on which a geographical indicator is mounted. The cairn is much robbed, now appearing merely as a low and irregular mound of stones from which a few boulders protrude to indicate the possible former presence of a burial cist. But it represents a class the majority of which are usually found far away from roads, and often covered with peat, grass or heather; and so is more worthy of a visit than might otherwise have been the case.

Whitfield, Saucer Barrows (NT 463168) 2½ miles NW. of Hawick, Sheet 79 (by-road and farm track). *Roxburghshire.*

These locally uncommon barrows, six in number, have all been ploughed to a mere annular groove except one, which can be recognised as a low cairn 28 ft. in diameter surrounded by a shallow ditch 4 ft. 6 in. wide which is itself circumscribed by a low bank 5 ft. 6 in. wide.

Smasha Hill, Cairn (NT 453171), 3¼ miles WNW. of Hawick, Sheet 79 (by-roads and moorland). *Roxburghshire.*

Typical of numerous cairns in the district, this one measures 32 ft. in diameter and is 2 ft. high, with part of a kerb of earthfast stones visible through the heather which covers it.

Burgh Hill, Stone Circle (NT 470062), 5 miles SSW. of Hawick, Sheet 79 (by-road and pasture land). *Roxburghshire.*

This oval "circle" measuring axially 54 ft. by 44 ft. comprises 25 stones of which 13 are still erect. They are all comparatively small slabs, and most of them have a broad face aligned on the perimeter of the setting.

Gray Coat, Cairn (NT 472051), 6 miles SSW. of Hawick, Sheet 79 (by-road and moorland). *Roxburghshire.*

• This cairn consists of a low mound about 20 ft. in diameter, now much disturbed, surrounded at distances of 5 ft., 10 ft. and 15 ft. respectively by three low banks. The resemblance of this plan to that of the cairn known as the Rounds of Tivla in Unst (which see) is striking.

Ninestone Rig, Stone Circle (NY 518973), 10 miles S. of Hawick, Sheet 79 (B.6399 and moorland). *Roxburghshire.*

This monument consists of eight earthfast stones, seven with a broad face on the line of the circumference of an oval measuring axially 23 ft. by 21 ft., and one fallen slab. All lean inwards, the largest attaining a height of 6 ft.

Russell's Cairn, Cairn (NT 855152), 8¼ miles SSE. of Town Yetholm, Sheet 81 (B.6401, by-road, track and moorland). *Roxburghshire.*

This is one of several cairns of different sizes which are situated on the ridge followed by a section of the border between Northumberland and Roxburghshire. It measures 55 ft. in diameter and 8 ft. in height, and may perfectly well be of Bronze Age date.

Nesbister Hill, Cairn (HU 403454), 5 miles NW. of Lerwick, Sheet 4 (A.970, A.971). *Shetland, Mainland island.*

This cairn, beautifully situated on the top of Nesbister Hill and commanding a magnificent view down Whiteness Voe to the Burra group and across to Foula, is circular on plan, measuring 26 ft. in diameter within a dilapidated masonry face. A cist measuring internally 4 ft. by 2 ft. 9 in. by 2 ft., formed by four thick slabs, is set at the centre, the coverstone lying half in it. The cairn is of interest in that the external masonry face of the cairn material can be seen to rise vertically through the two or three courses that still remain.

This is the best preserved of the circular stone-built cairns found in Shetland. They are probably related to the heel-shaped cairns; but very little work has been done among them, and even the distribution is unknown.

Busta, Standing Stone (HU 349674), 4½ miles NW. of Voe, Sheet 3 (A.970). *Shetland, Mainland island.*

This square-sectioned granite pillar stands uncompromisingly on the cliff-top 50 ft. above Busta Voe. Its height above ground is 10 ft. 6 in., and its sides vary between 4 ft. and 6 ft. in width. At 11·5 cubic feet to the ton, the part showing above ground weighs about 22 tons.

Haltadans, Cairn (HU 623924), 3 miles

E. of Ugasta pier, Sheet 1 (B.9088 and moorland). *Shetland, Fetlar island.*

This monument consists of a ring of stones measuring 37 ft. in diameter and now containing 22 earthfast and several loose slabs. The surviving set slabs are set edge to edge, and it is probable that a gap in the SW. is original. At a distance of 5 ft. inside and concentric with the stone ring is a low bank, with a gap 5 ft. wide in the SW. The centre of the space thus enclosed is occupied by two earth-fast boulders of rectangular section.

This interesting structure is closely comparable with three others which lie 550 yds. to the NW. and are called the Fiddler's Crus. Nothing is known about this class of cairn, but it has obvious affinities with ring cairns and hengiform barrows, and a general flavour of the Early Bronze Age.

The Rounds of Tivla, Cairn (HP 615107), 1¼ miles N. of Baltasound, Sheet 1 (moorland). *Shetland, Unst island.*

Among several cairns on Crussa Field, a prominent feature of central Unst, E. of the Loch of Cliff, are three which consist of sets of low concentric, stony banks with a central mound. In the best preserved the mound, of stones, now measures 13 ft. in diameter, as far as it appears above the turf. The three rings enclosing it measure respectively 30 ft., 40 ft. and 53 ft. in diameter, the inner apparently an earthen bank formed from a slight external quarry ditch, the others banks of stones lightly covered with earth produced from similar ditches. The outlandish aspect of these monuments is paralleled to some measure by the Halta-dans, on neighbouring Fetlar, but, surprisingly, also by an example almost identical in size which lies on Gray Coat hill, in Teviotdale, Roxburghshire.

Uyea Breck, Standing Stone (HP 605606), 1 mile E. of Uyeasound, Sheet 1 (by-road to Muness). *Shetland, Unst island.*

This monolith of schist, leaning a little to the NE. but still attaining a height of 10 ft. above ground level, stands 100 yds. S. of the road from Uyeasound to Muness. Its axial dimensions at the visible base are 2 ft. 10 in. and 1 ft. 3 in.

Beinn a'Charra, Standing Stone (NF 769321), 8 miles N. by W. of Lochboisdale, Sheet 22 (A.865 and moorland). *South Uist.*

This stone stands on the W. flank of the hill at a height of 200 ft. O.D. It attains a height of 17 ft. above ground level and its breadth near the ground is 5 ft., its thickness 2 ft.

Airthrey Castle, Standing Stone (NS 814964), 300 yds. SE. of Airthrey Castle, 2 miles NE. of Stirling, Sheet 57 (A.9 and private grounds). *Stirlingshire.*

This stone is a massive pillar of oblong section which stands to a height of 9 ft. above ground level. Another, originally about the same height, which stood ½ mile to the WNW., has quite recently been destroyed.

Hill of Airthrey, Cairn (NS 796981), ½ mile N. of Bridge of Allan, Sheet 57 (by-road). *Stirlingshire.*

This cairn is reported to have measured 78 ft. in diameter and 21 ft. in height before it was excavated in 1868; but as it now measures 60 ft. in diameter and only 7 ft. 6 in. in height these figures may be questionable. A central cist revealed by the excavation contained unctuous matter which included pieces of bone, among them recognisable pieces of skull, and was probably a cremation. In addition a beaker and part of another vessel of unspecified kind were recovered from a position above the cist, 2 ft. down from the top of the cairn.

Todholes, Cairn (NS 677870), 4 miles E. of Fintry, Sheet 57 (B.818). *Stirlingshire.*

This handsome cairn stands in isolation on a gently sloping moor above which it rises to a height of 8 ft. It measures 55 ft. in diameter within the fragmentary remains of a peristalith.

Waterhead, Standing Stones (NS 657839), 3 miles SE. of Fintry, Sheet 57 (B.822 and moorland). *Stirlingshire.*

These two stones are interesting in that they reflect the incidence of dissimilar pairs recorded further N. and E. The N. stone, now canted over at a severe angle, is 7 ft. 6 in. in height by 3 ft. in width and 2 ft. 6 in. in breadth. The S. stone is 5 ft. high; at the level of the ground it measures 2 ft. 8 in. in width, but half way up it expands on one side by another foot, only to taper again to a terminal width of 2 ft.

Cairnhall, Cairn (NS 554899), ½ mile NE. of Balfron, Sheet 57 (farm road). *Stirlingshire.*

This cairn occupies a considerable part of the farmyard, the farm buildings having been built round it. It measures 30 ft. in diameter, is 5 ft. high, and appears as a grass-covered stony mound.

Dumgoyach, Stone Alignment (NS 532807), 2 miles WNW. of Strathblane, Sheet 64 (A.81 and farm road).
Stirlingshire.

This little alignment straddles a ridge running S. from Dumgoyach hill and commanding a stretch of the valley of the Blane Water. It consists of five stones arranged in a line from NW. to SE. Three (the largest among them 5 ft. high) are earthfast, and the other two fallen. Only one other monument of this kind has yet been recorded in central Scotland, and this is now broken up for bottoming; the nearest extant examples occur further W., in Argyll.

Blochairn, Cairns (5775), 2 miles ENE. of Milngavie, Sheet 64 (A.81 and by-road).
Stirlingshire.

At one time at least five cairns were in existence in the vicinity of the Blochairn farms, as well as an earthen barrow, but all but two of them have been so wasted that their positions can hardly be determined.

At NS 577755 the largest of the remaining cairns forms a mound of boulders measuring about 60 ft. in diameter and rising to a height of about 3 ft.

At NS 579755 another round cairn, measuring 55 ft. in diameter, rises as much as 7 ft. above the ground outside; but it has a flat top, and its original proportions cannot be estimated.

Glen Loth, Standing Stone (NC 940150), 7 miles NNE. of Brora, Sheet 17 (A.9, by-road and moorland).
Sutherland.

This stone stands at the head of Glen Loth in cultivable open land. It is 11 ft. high, 5 ft. broad at a point 7 ft. above the ground, 2 ft. 9 in. broad at the base and 1 ft. 3 in. thick. Clearance cairns occur in the vicinity.

Learable Hill, Stone Rows (NC 8923), 9 miles WNW. of Helmsdale, Sheet 17 (A.897 and moorland).
Sutherland.

Several stone rows and numerous cairns occur on Learable Hill, Strath of Kildonan. They are aligned from SW. to NE. down the slope to the River Helmsdale. It is impossible to detect any definite relationship between the rows and any of the cairns, as sometimes seems to occur in examples farther to the

NE. A standing stone stands on the summit of the hill; a plain cross is carved on its W. face.

Other stone rows occur in the immediate neighbourhood.

Ospisdale, Standing Stone (NH 716895), 2 miles W. of Clashmore, Sheet 21 (A.9).
Sutherland.

This tall pillar stands a few yards E. of the entrance to Ospisdale House, but on the opposite side of the road. It attains a height of a little over 11 ft. above the ground and measures approximately 2 ft. by 1 ft. in breadth and depth.

Loch Loyal, Cairn (NC 621510), 4 miles SSE. of Tongue, Sheet 10 (A.836 and footpath).
Sutherland.

This cairn is situated at the head of the valley in which Loch Loyal lies, at a point ¼ mile E. of the road. It measures 50 ft. in diameter and stands to a height of 6 ft. It is kerbed by large contiguous earthfast boulders, set vertically. Despite a small informal excavation in the body of the cairn no slabs or boulders suggesting a chamber can be seen.

Earl Cairnie, Cairn (NT 158791), 2¼ miles NW. of Cramond Ferry, Sheet 65 (footpath between Cramond Ferry and South Queensferry).
West Lothian.

In 1791 this cairn was described as being about 160 ft. in diameter and 24 ft. in height, but now, after extensive robbing, it measures only 100 ft. in diameter and 15 ft. in height, still a most impressive monument. There remains, however, a stony mound at a distance of about 40 ft. from the edge of the ruin, and it is possible that this might represent an original perimeter.

Cairnpapple, Cairns (NS 987717), 1¼ miles ESE. of Torphichen, Sheet 65 (B.792 and by-road).
West Lothian.

See **Cairnpapple** Henge.

Torhousekie, Stone Circle (NX 383565), 3¼ miles W. by N. of Wigtown, Sheet 82 (B.733).
Wigtownshire.

This circle stands as close to the S. side of the road between Wigtown and Kirkcowan as does an enigmatic double-walled circular structure to the N. of it some 500 yds. farther W. The circle consists of 19 granite boulders set on end on the circumference of a circle about 60 ft. to 65 ft. in diameter. Three upright boulders stand in a line near the centre of the circle. The low arc of rubble adjoining these to the NW. may be of later date than the boulders.

Crows, Standing Stone (NX 365556), 4 miles SE. of Kirkcowan, Sheet 83 (B.733, B.7052). *Wigtownshire.*

This stone stands close to the E. side of the road 300 yds. N. of Crows farmhouse. It measures 5 ft. in height and 4 ft. in breadth, and is perforated right through at a point 14 in. from the curved top. The hole is formed by the connection of two opposing bowl-shaped depressions about 9 in. wide and as many deep by a channel 4 in. long.

Shennanton, Cairn (NX 336631), 1¼ miles NNE. of Kirkcowan, Sheet 82 (B.735 and A.75). *Wigtownshire.*

This cairn, one of the many large round cairns still to be seen in varying stages of decay throughout Wigtownshire, lies in a field at a point about 400 yds. N. of the A.75 road. Its diameter is about 60 ft. but its height has been severely reduced by robbing stones for building purposes.

Lingdowie, Cairns (NX 1466), 2 miles NW. of New Luce, Sheet 82 (farm road and moorland). *Wigtownshire.*

These cairns lie E. of the source of the Lingdowie Burn. The one to the E. still appears as a pile of stones some 60 ft. in diameter and 4 ft. high. The one to the W. measures about 75 ft. in diameter and attains an elevation of 10 ft.

Cairnerzean Fell, Cairns (NX 1366), 2½ miles NW. of New Luce, Sheet 82 (farm road and moorland). *Wigtownshire.*

These cairns lie W. of the source of the Lingdowie Burn. The one to the N. measures 55 ft. in diameter and is 6 ft. high, the one to the S. is about the same size but has been more severely pillaged.

Milton of Larg, Cairn (NX 166638), 4½ miles N. by W. of Glenluce, Sheet 82 (by-road). *Wigtownshire.*

This cairn standing beside the by-road joining New Luce and the A.75 road E. of Stranraer measures about 70 ft. in diameter and stands to a height of 6 ft.

Mid Gleniron, Cairn (NX 187611), 2¼ miles N. by W. of Glenluce, Sheet 82 (by-road and farm road). *Wigtownshire.*

The road up to Mid Gleniron farmhouse is bordered by two chambered cairns, which see, and this round cairn which measures 56 ft. in diameter and stands to a height of 9 ft.

Long Tom, Standing Stone (NX 081718), 2¼ miles NE. of Cairnryan, Sheet 76 (moorland). *Wigtownshire.*

This elegant standing stone attains a height of 6 ft. above ground level. It measures 2 ft. 2 in. in both directions at the base, and diminishes to an edge at the top.

CUP-AND-RING MARKINGS

The ornamentation of rock-faces, standing stones, cist slabs and other structural and ceremonial places with motifs of a special kind, broadly known as cup-and-ring markings, is widespread throughout parts of Scotland, England and Ireland. The designs, which usually appear to have been made with a pick or a driven punch, are very often well preserved. They include a majority of simple cup-like depressions and a large minority of such depressions surrounded by one or more continuous or broken circular grooves; and in addition to these all sorts of bizarre and sometimes freakish patterns occur. In some cases a single "symbol" is found, in others groups, and in a few places large expanses of outcropping rock-faces are covered with the patterns. They are found on the upper faces of flat stones and boulders and exposures of rock, but also on the flanks and even on downward-facing facets. They are found on standing stones and on portable slabs propped up in tombs. It is thus quite clear that they were not intended to hold any liquid, such as blood, although they could perfectly well have been filled with coloured matter such as raddle, or painted.

There need be no doubt that their manufacture entailed laborious and often protracted operations. Their occurrence on standing stones and cist covers and among funerary deposits as well as on what now seem to be merely convenient expanses of rock, insist at once both that the carvings must have been significant and important to those by and for whom they were made, and that the places where they occur must likewise have had a character above the merely practical.

It has long been noticed that there is a broad likeness, and a contemporaneousness, between the cup-and-ring markings and the decorations on certain chambered tombs, especially in Ireland. It has likewise been observed that closely similar ornamentations occur in northern Spain in broadly contemporary contexts. These coincidences, combined with other factors, have led to the suggestion that in some cases at least the basic symbol of the cup-and-ring may be related to the labyrinth design, so widespread throughout the Mediterranean world at that time, or to a formalised conception of a source of heat, such as the sun; and that they may have been produced in connection with the activities of the copper-prospectors, miners, smelters and smiths of the first half of the 2nd millennium B.C.

23 *Achnabreck. The exposed rock surface is decorated over a wide area with Cup-and-ring markings*

Stronach Wood, Cup-and-Ring Markings (NS 003366), ¾ mile WNW. of Brodick, Sheet 69 (pasture land). *Arran.*

These markings occur on an exposed rock face on the hill 100 yds. above the highest part of Stronach Wood. They consist chiefly of several groups of double penannular rings with gullies issuing downwards from them, but in addition there are simple cups and at least three triple rings, two with radial gutters. The key-hole pattern to which the majority conform recalls the group at Kilmichael Glassary.

Achnabreck, Cup-and-Ring Markings (NR 856906), 1¾ miles N. of Lochgilphead, Sheet 55 (A.816, farm road and field). *Argyll, Mid.*

One of the largest groups of cup-and-ring markings known occurs on two contiguous exposed rock faces ¼ mile N. of Achnabreck. The markings comprise cups, varying in diameter from 1 in. to 5 in., and cups with from one to seven rings. One on the upper face, a cup with seven rings, measures 3 ft. in diameter. Most of the cup-and-ring markings have a radial groove, some of them have two. A double spiral marking occurs on the upper rock face. Almost all the markings are comparatively shallow.

Cairnbaan, Cup-and-Ring Markings (NR 838910), 2½ miles NW. of Lochgilphead, Sheet 55 (A.816, B.841 and footpath). *Argyll, Mid.*

These fine markings, now protected by a railing, comprise several large cup-and-ring motifs with up to four rings and with radial grooves, together with several smaller examples and cups by themselves. Gullies joining several of the individual markings also occur.

Kilmichael Glassary, Cup-and-Ring Markings (NR 858935), in Kilmichael Glassary Village, Sheet 55. *Argyll, Mid.*

These markings comprise a compact group of deep and large cups, many paired to give the appearance of a dumbbell and several outlined with grooves of keyhole or horseshoe shape.

Baluacraig, Cup-and-Ring Markings (NR 831970), 6 miles N. by W. of Lochgilphead, Sheet 55 (A.816). *Argyll, Mid.*

Contiguous exposed rock faces, now protected by a railing, bear a great number of cups and of cups with one or two rings, the majority of which are in an exceptionally good state of preservation.

Ballygowan, Cup-and-Ring Markings (NR 816978), 6½ miles NNW. of

Lochgilphead, Sheet 55 (A.816, by-road and footpath). *Argyll, Mid.*

This group of cup-and-ring markings, which includes several horseshoe-shaped examples, is under guardianship.

High Banks, Cup-and-Ring Markings (NX 710490), 2 miles SE. of Kirkcudbright, Sheet 84 (by-roads, farm road and pasture land).
Stewartry of Kirkcudbright.

Several groups of cup-and-ring markings occur on an exposure of rock nearly 100 ft. long ¼ mile SE. of High Banks farmhouse. The most remarkable feature of the carvings is the close massing of great numbers of simple cup-marks around cup-and-ring markings. A feature of the latter is the wide spacing of the outer rings. Several other groups of such markings occur in the vicinity.

Newlaw Hill, Cup-and-Ring Markings (NX 735490), 1¼ miles NW. of Dundrennan, Sheet 84 (by-road and pasture land). *Stewartry of Kirkcudbright.*

This group of markings is carved on the sloping face of a smooth outcrop about 200 yds. S. of the by-road opposite the entrance to Auchengool house. The largest element is a figure nearly 2 ft. in diameter comprising a cup with five concentric rings all of which are traversed by a radial groove. The surface all round this is pitted with small almost contiguous cups. The "cups" of two of the other figures are very large and deep, and have either been worn by natural processes since first being carved or have been deliberately mutilated. These two figures, and two more, all essentially cups with concentric rings, are surrounded by groups of small individual cups.

Cauldside Burn, Cup-and-Ring Markings (NX 5257), 3¼ miles WNW. of Anwoth Church, Sheet 83 (farm road and moorland). *Stewartry of Kirkcudbright.*

See **Cauldside Burn,** Cairns.

Cardoness House, Cup-and-Ring Markings (NX 565535), 3 miles SW. of Gatehouse of Fleet, Sheet 83 (A.75).
Stewartry of Kirkcudbright.

Two cup-and-ring marked slabs collected locally are kept in the garden of Cardoness House. One has three cup-marks two of which are surrounded by four and one by five concentric pen-annular rings. The other has several different markings, the most conspicuous

being a cup with six concentric pen-annular rings. The breaks in the rings are bordered by parallel grooves which run free from the marking right across the slab to merge with a group of several large cups each with a single ring. Among other features on this stone is a cup with three concentric rings the space between the outer pair of which is occupied by small cups placed at equal distances apart.

Mossyard, Cup-and-Ring Markings (NX 546515), 4 miles SW. of Gatehouse of Fleet, Sheet 83 (A.75 and farm road).
Stewartry of Kirkcudbright.

A natural rock outcropping in a field near the shore 700 yds. SW. of Mossyard farmhouse bears a single cup with five concentric rings, the whole of which figure lies in one sector of a nearly circular double groove measuring about twice the diameter of the largest ring.

Lower Laggan Cottage, Cup-and-Ring Markings (NX 545526), 4½ miles SW. of Gatehouse of Fleet, Sheet 83 (A.75.).
Stewartry of Kirkcudbright.

A thin slab of whinstone, found near by and set up in the garden of Lower Laggan Cottage, bears 17 cups of which 12 have a narrow, neat groove set close outside the lip. Several channels run between the various marks.

Tormain Hill, Cup-and-Ring Markings (NT 129697), 3¼ miles SW. of Ratho, Sheet 65 (B7030.). *Midlothian.*

Several cup-and-ring markings have been found on outcropping rock surfaces on the highest point of Tormain Hill, a low ridge which stands within a tricorn plantation 1 mile N. of Hatton House. They occur on at least eight outcrops in one area measuring about 15 yds. by 7 yds. They include plain cups, cups with rings, concentric circles and gutters, arranged singly or in various combinations.

Newbigging, Cup-and-Ring Markings (NO 157356), 8¾ miles NNE. of Perth, Sheet 53 (A.93, by-road and woodland track). *Perthshire.*

See **Newbigging,** Standing Stone.

Croft Moraig, Cup-and-Ring Markings (NN 797472), 2 miles NE. of Kenmore, Sheet 51 (A.827). *Perthshire.*

See **Croft Moraig,** Stone Circle.

Braes of Taymouth, Cup-and-Ring Markings (NN 793447), 1¼ miles ESE.

of Kenmore, Sheet 51 (A.827 and by-road). *Perthshire.*

The region of upper Strathtay between Logierait and Fearnan is one of the few for which a comprehensive study of cup-and-ring markings and allied patterns has been published. It has been demonstrated that in general the plain cup markings tend to occur chiefly along the lower levels of the valley, while cups with rings, and other devices, occur most frequently at the higher levels. Two of the latter, carved on natural boulders, survive on the boulder-strewn hillside E. of Tombuie Cottage. These include among other motifs several gapped circles which coincide with the Galician category supposed to have been introduced from Spain and Portugal into parts of Ireland in which copper and gold occurred in comparative plenty in Early Bronze Age times. In due course the gapped circles were to some extent assimilated into the art-forms used by the builders of passage graves, and the Braes of Taymouth carvings seem to reflect this combined tradition. The distribution suggests that the cup-and-ring carvers entered Strathtay from the W., as did the builders of local chambered tombs, while food-vessels seem to have arrived from the E.

Glenlochay, Cup-and-Ring Markings (NN 532358), 3¼ miles NW. of Killin, Sheet 51 (A.827 and by-road).
Perthshire.

These markings are carved in an elongated glaciated boss of micaceous schist situated between the Glenlochay road and the River Lochay immediately below the old farmhouse of Duncroisk. The surface of the rock is marked spasmodically over a total distance of over 60 ft. The markings include cups alone, numerous cups with a single ring, and some with two rings, and they form one of the best displays in the country. Other cup-marked rocks have been noted in the vicinity.

King's Park, Stirling, Cup-and-Ring Marking (NS 783930), in the S. part of the park, Sheet 57. *Stirlingshire.*

This single cup-and-ring marking is carved on the surface of the rock which

24 *Drumtroddan. Several of the Cup-and-ring markings are connected*

forms the table on which most of the King's Park is situated. It has been cleared of turf for many years, and although restricted search has been made for others near at hand, only an extensive and probably unwelcome deturfing operation could give assurance that no other examples exist near by, as they might be expected to do. The cup measures 1½ in. in diameter, the ring 5 in. in diameter and 1 in. in width. Both are very shallow, but the remains of a second ring, 4 in. outside the first, are even more slight and are indeed barely visible in strong light. It is interesting to note that in an area of sandy ground a few hundred yards to the S. several Bronze Age burials have been recorded, including at least one with a beaker.

North Balfern, Cup-and-Ring Markings (NX 433510), 2¼ miles N. of Sorbie,
Sheet 83 (A.746 and farm road).
Wigtownshire.

These markings are carved on an exposed rock 200 yds. WNW. of North Balfern farmhouse. They occur in two main groups, and vary from cups with five rings to simple cups.

Drumtroddan, Cup-and-Ring Markings (NX 362444), 1½ miles ENE. of Port William, Sheet 83 (A.714 and footpath). *Wigtownshire.*

These markings, now under guardianship, are situated on a flat exposed rockface on which they form several groups. They comprise cups, cups with concentric rings both with and without radial grooves, and connecting channels. Two other inscribed rock-faces, also under guardianship, are situated near by at Big Balcraig and Clachan.

HOMESTEADS

The monuments listed in this section represent a few of the unknown but large number, most of which probably date from one time or another in the 1st millennium B.C., a few possibly somewhat earlier. In the north and west, the homesteads—the dwellings of families, large or small, rather than of communities—have stone walls. The brochs and certain duns, representing the more substantial and the better known structures of this class in the region, are described separately below, but some others can be included here.

The homestead locally known as a wag (possibly from the Gaelic *uaigh*, a cave) is found in parts of Caithness and Sutherland. Briefly, a wag comprises a round stone-walled house with an attached above-ground oblong chamber—a plan which may proclaim relationship with some of the souterrains of later periods.

In the western and northern isles the aisled round-house and the wheel-house occur in quite unknown but probably large numbers. The plan of the former is very close to that of the southern all-timber house. It is circular, typically about 30 ft. in diameter, within a stone wall, and contains a ring of about a dozen stone pillars and a central hearth. In the wheel-house, the pillars are attached to the wall.

In the eastern and southern parts of the country two types of home-steads are now known from which a species of flat-rimmed pottery, at present the earliest known Iron Age pottery in Scotland, has been recovered. In one of these, in Perthshire, the unenclosed circular house is recognised by traces of two thin virtually concentric stone walls, the space between which must have been filled with insulating material; a ring of post-holes sited very close inside the inner wall; and a central hearth. In the other example, in Tweeddale, the only difference is that the double wall is made of wattle screens instead of stone.

The other timber homesteads of the south and east consist of from one to four circular timber-framed houses enclosed within a fence or a bank or a wall. One type of house, possibly as early as the ones already described, is represented now only by a ring of post-holes with a central post, the hearth lying between the two. Such structures leave no traces on the surface of the ground; but houses of two other principal types do. These—the ring-groove and the ring-ditch houses—date from the last two or three centuries B.C. The plan of the ring-groove house comprises

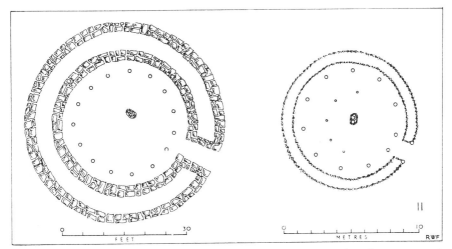

25 *Plans of two houses from which Flat-rimmed Pottery has been recovered.
I, Dalrulzion, Perthshire* (after Thorneycroft); *II, Green Knowe, Peeblesshire.
The faces of the wall of I are founded upon narrow stone walls, those of II consist
of wattle screens. The ring of posts supporting the roof is close to the inner face of
the wall in each example, while the internal diameters of the houses are similar*

one (or two) circular settings of post-holes together with one (or two)
narrow penannular trenches in which wattle or split-timber walls were
seated. The plan of the ring-ditch house includes a broad and very
shallow ditch.

It has been established, at least in the southern part of the country,
that circular houses represented by raised rings formed by a ruined wall
date from no earlier than the 1st century A.D.

Langwell, Homestead (ND 102218),
1 mile WSW. of Berriedale, Sheet 17
(A.9 and footpath). *Caithness.*
This monument is included as a typical
example of one class among the numerous remains found in the N. and NE. part
of the mainland about which hardly
anything is known. It consists of the
foundation of a circular wall 6 ft. thick
and 27 ft. in internal diameter which has
two contiguous entrances. One of these
gives access to the house from outside,
the other gives access from the house to a
contiguous galleried structure. The latter
is oblong on plan, measuring about 48 ft.
by about 14 ft. within a wall of similar
character to that of the house. It has
rounded corners which in fact form
rounded short ends, and is divided internally into two roughly equal parts by a
cross wall fitted with a doorway 3 ft.

wide. Three upright pillars of stone are
set on either side of the long axis of the
inner chamber, dividing it into a central
passage, or nave, and two side aisles. The
roof, some 6 ft. above floor level, was
constructed of large thin slabs balanced
at one end on the pillars and the other
on the head of the wall; the nave was
similarly bridged between the rows of
pillars. This type of structure strongly
resembles a certain type of souterrain on
plan. A confused assemblage of small
finds was recovered from this monument,
including saddle and rotary querns, a
small piece of corroded iron—but no
pottery.
Forse, Homestead (ND 204352), 1 mile
NNE. of Latheron, Sheet 11 (A.9 and
farm road). *Caithness.*
It is probable, though by no means
certain, that the earliest feature at the

wag at Forse was a circular enclosure measuring 45 ft. in diameter within a wall 4 ft. thick. The identity of this is doubtful, and its dating a matter of conjecture. It could possibly have been comparable to the circle assigned to the earliest Iron Age phase at Jarlshof.

At Forse the ruins of several other buildings, some perhaps contemporary with the circular enclosure and others possibly later, have accumulated on the site. It is possible, too, that the circular enclosure was situated within an oval yard measuring about 125 ft. by about 100 ft. along the major axes within a turf bank. Various small finds broadly datable to the Iron Age have been dug out of this homestead.

Scotstarvit, Homestead (NO 361109), 2½ miles SW. of Cupar, Sheet 59 (A.92 and by-road). *Fife.*

This little homestead became famous as a result of excavations carried out in it by Gerhard Bersu in 1946 and 1947. It consists of an oval enclosure measuring about 110 ft. by 90 ft. within a much-decayed bank, with a central house. Bersu discovered that certainly three successive timber-framed houses had stood on much the same site within the enclosure, two definitely and the third probably very similar in plan. Briefly, the frame of the house comprised three concentric rings, the outer a trench, the median a shallow trench punctuated by post-holes, and the inner a ring of eight post-holes. A pre-Roman Iron Age date was suggested for all the houses.

Greencraig, Homestead (NO 324215), 5¼ miles NNW. of Cupar, Sheet 53 (A.913, A.914 and by-road). *Fife.*

This homestead, lying at the foot of the hill upon which the large Greencraig fort is situated, was excavated by Bersu in 1947. Rectangular on plan, it measures 65 ft. by 55 ft. within a low stony mound. A single circular house was found within it, the wall of which was formed by a low turf-and-stone bank out of which posts rose to support the ends of the rafters. The house measured 32 ft. in diameter internally, and contained an inner ring of post-holes. No finds were recorded, but it seems probable that the homestead may date from after the pre-Roman Iron Age, judging by the rectangular plan of the enclosure and the solid base of the wall of the house.

Green Knowe, Unenclosed Platform Settlement (NT 212434), 3 miles NW. of Peebles, Sheet 73 (A.72 or A.703, and by-road). *Peeblesshire.*

The first unenclosed platform settlement to have been recorded was eventually the first to be excavated, as it represented a typical example of the class. It lies on the E. face of Green Knowe, on the farm of Harehope, at a height of 900 ft. O.D., facing two contiguous settlements of a similar nature which sprawl across the NW. foot of White Meldon hill on the opposite side

26 *Reconstruction of an Unenclosed Platform Settlement*

of the Meldon Burn. It consists of nine platforms, the fourth from the N. end being the excavated one. When the floor of the platform was cleared, the post-holes of a circular timber-framed house 26 ft. in internal diameter were revealed. The only material found on the floor consisted of about 50 pieces of rather inferior pottery. A score of these, however, could be fitted together to form a large part of the wall of a tall, situlate vessel with a flat rim, datable to the closing stages of the transitional period between the Bronze Age and the Iron Age—perhaps the 4th century B.C., perhaps a little earlier.

Unenclosed platform settlements in Tweeddale and Clydesdale are described and illustrated in the *Inventories* of Peeblesshire and Lanarkshire, while others as far north as Aberdeenshire and the Great Glen, Invernessshire, are recorded in Feachem, 1973.

Ford, Drumelzier, Small Settlement (NT 123327), 1 mile SW. of Drumelzier, Sheet 72 (B.712 and by-road).
Peeblesshire.

This interesting small settlement was first recorded when excavations at the near-by cairn were begun in 1929. It lies behind the game-keeper's cottage at Ford, between a large fold and a small stand of conifers. It is typical of a small group of similar monuments which occurs in the neighbourhood, being circular on plan and measuring 110 ft. in diameter within a ruinous stony rampart. The interior contains the remains of three timber-framed houses of the broad-ring-ditch type.

The settlement stands 200 yds. E. of the old ford across the River Tweed which, although it once took the main road to Edinburgh, is not now passable to ordinary cars.

Glenachan Rig, Palisaded Homestead (NT 106328), 2 miles SSW. of Broughton, Sheet 72 (A.701 and by-road).
Peeblesshire.

This little homestead was excavated in 1959, when it was found to consist of an enclosure formed by a fence or palisade sunk in a continuous trench and measuring 108 ft. by 84 ft., with an inturned entrance in the NE. This enclosure contains the surface traces of two narrow-ring-ditch timber-framed houses, one of which was entirely excavated. A third

such house lies 100 yds. N. of the main settlement. The penannular narrow, shallow ditch surrounded a platform near the margin of which was a ring of post-holes 21 ft. in diameter. The interior contained a central post, and a fire-pit. The finds comprised only rubbing stones. The plan of the house was compared with those of Late Bronze Age/Early Iron Age houses found elsewhere, and the suggestion was put forward that, locally, such houses might at least reflect a Late Bronze Age tradition, if not actually belonging to that period.

Parkgatestone Hill, Small Settlement (NT 083353), 2¼ miles WSW. of Broughton, Sheet 72 (A.701 and by-road).
Peeblesshire.

This small settlement stands on a ridge dividing the Biggar Water and the Kilbucho Burn, in good agricultural land. It is bounded by a single bank with the remains of an external ditch which has been encroached upon by the plough. It measures 160 ft. in internal diameter and contains the surface traces of four timber-framed houses of the ring-ditch type. Only one of these is reasonably well preserved, as the interior has both been cultivated and used as a dump for stones. This is a good example of the small settlements of the Biggar Gap area.

Dalrulzion, Homestead (NO 1257), 8 miles NNW. of Blairgowrie, Sheet 53 (A.93 and footpath).
Perthshire.

Great but as yet unknown numbers of annular and penannular banks, and small cairns, are found in association and separately in that part of Perthshire which lies between lower Strathtummel and Strathisla and contains Strathardle and Glenshee. Hardly any work has been done on any of them, but it is possible to work out from what published plans there are of a few at Dalrulzion that some at least of the homesteads consisted of houses measuring about 28 ft. in diameter within a wall composed at the base of two skins, each about 3 ft. thick, placed about 5 ft. apart. The skins are made of stones, the faces set in the ground and the interstices filled with rubble. The space between the faces may have been filled with earth or sods. A setting of post-holes is placed about 2 ft. in from the inner face of the wall. The marked similarity between such a house and the one found on a platform in an

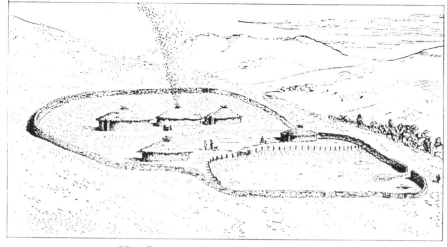

27   *Reconstruction of a Scooped Settlement*

Unenclosed Platform Settlement at Green Knowe, Harehope, is striking. The finds in one of the houses at Dalrulzion included saddle querns and pottery which is datable to the earlier part of the local Iron Age.

The remains of a settlement of similar houses from which "flat-rimmed" pottery was recovered lie among the sand dunes at Forvie, Aberdeenshire (*Aberdeen University Review*, XXXV, No. 109 (1953), 150–71).

Shoulder Hill, Homestead (NT 825233), 2 miles ESE. of Morebattle, Sheet 74 (B.6401, by-road and moorland).
Roxburghshire.

The remains of this palisaded homestead consist of the surface traces of three timber-framed houses in the form of arcs of narrow, shallow grooving, and those of about half of the palisade forming the enclosure in which they lie.

Mowhaugh, Scooped Settlement (NT 816208), 3¾ miles SE. of Morebattle, Sheet 74 (B.6401, by-road and pasture land).
Roxburghshire

This example of a scooped settlement is included as a representative of the type although it has not yet been established whether homesteads and settlements of this class belong to the truly prehistoric period, as seems most probable, or to the early part of our era. It consists of an enclosure quarried out of the hillside, measuring axially 150 ft. by 100 ft. within the ruin of a stony bank.

It contains several floors, some or all of them stances for timber-framed buildings, and a courtyard.

Greenbrough Hill, Homestead (NT 813169), 5½ miles SSE. of Morebattle, Sheet 80 (by-road, footpath and moorland).
Roxburghshire.

This all-timber homestead consists of the surface traces of a subrectangular enclosure, formed by a single fence and now appearing as a narrow and shallow groove surrounding an area 95 ft. long from NE. to SW. by 75 ft. transversely, in which are the penannular grooves of two timber-framed houses.

Gray Coat, Homestead (NT 471052), 6 miles SSW. of Hawick, Sheet 79 (by-road and moorland).
Roxburghshire.

See **Gray Coat,** Settlement and Homestead.

Kilpheder, Aisled Round-house (NF 735205), 3¾ miles W. by N. of Lochboisdale, Sheet 31 (A.865, by-road and machar land).
South Uist.

Among the few examples of the unknown number of such structures to have been excavated, this aisled round-house in the Kilpheder machar is one of the most easily accessible and best preserved. It exhibits the principal characteristics of its kind, first among them being the well-built circular outer wall which holds back the sand and earth from an area 29 ft. in diameter. Within this is a series of 11 oblong dry-stone pillars disposed radially, standing free of the wall and leaving in the centre of the house an open area 18 ft. in diameter which contains a hearth. It is at once apparent that this is a stone version of a timber house such as is found elsewhere in the country. Finds from this and other aisled round-houses show that they were occupied early in the 1st millennium A.D., and it is not impossible that they may date from a period a little earlier than this.

West Plean, Homestead (NS 810876), 3 miles SSE. of Stirling, Sheet 57 (A.80 and by-road). *Stirlingshire.*

Very little remains of this unobtrusive monument on the surface, but a series of excavations concluded in 1955 revealed it as one of the more important Early Iron Age sites in North Britain. The homestead was found to consist of an enclosure 90 ft. in diameter bounded by a ditch and containing two successive timber-framed houses. The earlier, the centre post of which was also the point from which the circular ditch had been laid out, was represented by a ring of 11 post-holes 23 ft. in diameter. The remains of the later house, centred a little N. of the other, comprised a circular foundation trench 38 ft. in diameter which had contained a small post every 3 ft.; and an inner ring of 11 or 12 posts to support the rafters. This house also had a porch. In addition to these structures, a conjectured rectangular timber building and certain other features were revealed. The excavator showed that the earlier house reflected late Bronze Age traditions, and that the later one was of Early Iron Age date, possibly being occupied as late as the beginning of the 1st century A.D. Since this work was done, excavations in the Lowlands and in Northumberland have established repetitions of this sequence.

Keir Hill of Gargunnock, Homestead (NS 706942), 5 miles W. of Stirling, Sheet 57 (A.811). *Stirlingshire.*

A small but conspicuous promontory knoll stands between two streams in the S. part of Gargunnock village. Excavations carried out on the top of the knoll in 1958 revealed settings of post-holes, traces of walling, a hearth and a palisade trench, all of which represented parts of possibly several phases of the occupation of the site by a timber-framed homestead or a series of such. The havoc wrought by disturbances of the soil in historic times had served to blur the outlines, but the small finds suggested occupation in pre-Roman times as well as in the 1st century A.D. Nothing can be seen on the surface of the ground to indicate where the house stood, but the actual site is worth a visit. The name Keir, an English form of the British *caer*, implying a stronghold, was given indiscriminately both to places where fortifications existed and to conspicuous natural features which may never have been inhabited; and its use here is thus of no archaeological significance.

HILL-FORTS AND SETTLEMENTS

The word "fort" is unsatisfactory in this context, but it has been found difficult to replace. It has a military connotation which is false in that it implies an aggressive or defensive stronghold manned entirely by armed men, whereas most if not all of the native hill-forts were rather defended villages or, in rare cases, towns. While it is not yet possible to pronounce on every example, there would appear to be a strong probability that the very great majority, if not indeed all, were built to defend the occupants against comparable neighbouring communities, whether those occupants were established settlers or new arrivals. They were not the bastions of an occupying power, such as were the Roman forts. It has long been recognised that whereas some hill-forts contain the surface traces of dwellings, others do not, and it was at one time assumed that the apparently empty ones had contained only the tents and temporary quarters of soldiers. Now, however, that it is understood that certain types of timber-framed domestic dwellings leave no surface traces when they have been long ruined, the apparent lack of them is no longer a source of confusion.

The distinction between hill-forts and settlements is slight. Ideally, the hill-fort as defined occupies a conspicuous eminence or promontory, the flanks of which provide a degree of natural defence and an assurance to the watchful against surprise attack. At the same time the defences are strong enough to repel any expectable raid. The settlement, on the other hand, if it is not placed on such a site as that just described, may lie on sloping or even level ground, possibly dominated from adjacent heights; and its defences may be less formidable. With certain exceptions, therefore, it is as well to think of both types as belonging to one broad class of structure, serving one purpose.

Although they are of course in a ruinous condition, the present appearance of these monuments may suggest to the imaginative observer a basis upon which a tentative reconstruction can be made. The process of natural decay has played an important part in obliterating detail, but perhaps a greater degree of spoliation has resulted from the systematic pillage of stones and rubble from the ruins for use as building material and other purposes. Difficulties to which these conditions give rise include, first, that of deciding how the walls or ramparts originally appeared, depending of course on the original method and materials employed. In the simplest form, the defence was a palisade or stockade, a heavy timber fence set firmly in a trench, the individual upright timbers probably united with rails, and possibly made more impenetrable by the use of interwoven slats or stems. Stockades consisting of a single line of posts, or of a double line spaced 6 ft. apart, or of a pair set as much as 15 ft. apart, are known. In some examples a single or double inner stockade is accompanied by an outer one lying at a distance of up to 50 ft. or so outside it. It has been supposed that the space between was used for enclosing beasts at certain times, such as the autumn gathering-in or a time of uncertainty.

Such palisades or stockades are today represented on the surface merely by narrow, shallow grooves, caused by the settling of the packing stones when the timber rotted or after it had been removed. The gates may have been of a removable hurdle type, or have been grudgingly swung on extensions of the main upper and lower members; or have been hinged by setting the bottom of one of the vertical side members in a hollowed stone and enclosing the top in a loop protruding from the gate-post. Both single leaf and double gates were probably used.

In the case of the simple stone wall, often the successor to the wooden fence, there is evidence that in some examples the structural method adopted was to build inner and outer faces of carefully laid blocks and

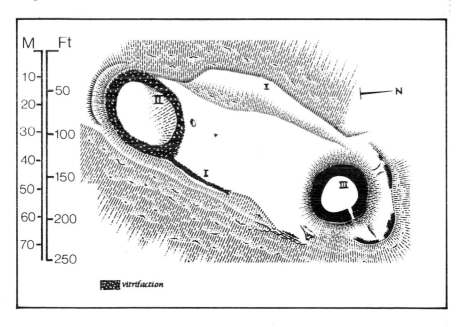

28 *Plan of hill-fort and dun, Dun Skeig* (see p. 108)

to fill the intervening space with rubble or stones. In general, such a wall may have been anything from 8 ft. to 14 ft. thick and about as much high, with or without a parapet. Walls packed with stones were often built round a skeleton of stout timbers. In Scotland, only a very few such ramparts or walls have been properly examined by excavation, but what records there are show that the timbers have usually been found represented only by the sockets in which they originally lay. The use of such a framework enabled the builders to produce an unmortared timber-laced wall of the most imposing strength, anything between 10 ft. and 40 ft. in thickness. Gate towers of wood were fitted to the entrances, and the form of structure resulting from such a method of building may not be difficult to visualise. The battered outer face of the wall might rise to a height of 15 ft. or more, over a parapet, and the great gates stand recessed between the towers.

The houses contained in hill-forts and settlements varied from the circular timber-framed kind found in homesteads to a lean-to terrace form recently revealed and expounded in the far north by Mr J. R. C. Hamilton, but doubtless present over a much wider field. It was indeed foreseen nearly two centuries ago by Williams, who wrote: "Immediately on the inside of this wall, there are ruins of vitrified buildings. I imagine these inner works have been a range of habitations, reared against or under the shade of the outer wall" in his report on the stone-walled fort on Knock Farril.

Williams' mention of vitrifaction suitably introduces the fact that it so happened, over the whole period during which timber-laced walls and ramparts of a great many differing kinds were being employed, that an unspecified number of them were set on fire. This resulted in the generation of tremendous heat within the wall which melted the stone in varying degrees and so formed solid fused masses. It has long been recognised that in a number of examples vitrified masses are only found in the vicinity of the gates; in many cases, however, vitrifaction extends either all round the wall or round parts of it. And it has generally been thought that the burning of the gate, or the deliberate firing of the wall from outside, must both be the result of hostile attack. While the former may seem at least probable, the latter does not necessarily appear very likely. Now, however, the ignition of the wall following upon the accidental or deliberate burning of the internal lean-to houses can also be adduced. Such buildings were bound to the inner face of the wall by timbers, and they may have covered most of its length and have risen to two or even three storeys in height. If these started to blaze the whole wall might easily be set alight. Dr Euan MacKie has demonstrated that hill-forts with timber-framed walls first appeared in Scotland in the 8th century B.C., before the introduction of the manufacture and use of iron, both techniques probably being introduced from the Continent.

The familiar undulations caused by eroded ramparts which contained little or no stonework and by their accompanying ditches are visible in many parts of the country. Such ramparts, generally from one to three in number, form perhaps the best-known class of fort and settlement. They have suffered from decay, the removal of what stonework there might have been and from deliberate levelling to allow the ground to be ploughed, but before all this destruction they were often formidable. The ditches of even a small example may have been 10 ft. deep and twice as wide; the ramparts kerbed or faced with stone or timber and topped with such an obstacle as a parapet or a row of close-set posts forming a kind of *chevaux de frise*.

Hill-forts and settlements of several recognisable distinct kinds occur from place to place throughout the country. Hardly any have been excavated even to a limited extent, and virtually none to a degree which approaches completion. The few excavations which have taken place, however, together with ever-increasing field surveys, can be combined to show that the distinctions in lay-out and in structural method tend to define local groupings, and that variations occur between the several peoples, or tribes, who inhabited definable geographical regions.

There is hardly any part of the country east and south of the central Highland massif in which it is not possible to see the site of a hill-fort or settlement. To the west and north of the massif the picture is different, because of the difference in the nature of the countryside. For here the inhospitable though picturesque hills and moors occupy nearly all the available space, leaving only coastal strips and narrow valleys from which the hardy settler could wrest an austere and reluctant livelihood. In consequence, the family unit is represented in this region almost to the exclusion of the larger communal group.

Forts and settlements in Scotland vary in extent from as little as 1 acre to as many as 40. Only the two largest, Traprain Law and Eildon Hill North, could truly be described as cities upon hills, sheltering inhabitants working upon manufacture and industry as well as those who attended to the fields and pastures outside, though doubtless small-scale 'cottage industries' were carried on in the smaller examples.

Hill-forts and settlements were widespread throughout the regions mentioned by the end of the 1st millennium B.C. From the beginnings in the 8th century B.C. they were built in increasing numbers and in a great variety of designs. Some were to fall out of use as social circumstances demanded, others to endure, with modifications, it might be for several centuries. In some districts at least there is reason to suppose that a considerable number were still occupied at the beginning of our era. Many were re-occupied, and some partly reconstructed, later, but that is not at present relevant.

Knockargetty Hill, Fort (NJ 455030), 2½ miles N. of Dinnet, Sheet 37 (B.9119, A.9/4, by-road and woodland).
Aberdeenshire.

This unfinished fort lies on a ridge in open woodland which overlooks the Muir of Dinnet from the N. It is oval, measuring about 800 ft. by 390 ft. within a single line marked out partly by a slight terrace and partly by an equally slight trench. Work was begun on piling up a rampart on either side of the entrances in the E. and W., but had not got very far before the project was abandoned.

Mortlich, Fort (NJ 535017), 2 miles N. of Aboyne, Sheet 37 (A.93, farm roads and moorland). *Aberdeenshire.*

The remains of this fort occupy the termination of an isolated ridge from which the entire length of upper and middle Strathdee can be observed from a height of 1248 ft. above sea level and 800 ft. above the river at Aboyne. It consists of a ruined wall enclosing an area measuring 200 ft. by 145 ft. It has been robbed partly to build field boundaries and partly, no doubt, to eke out stone quarried for the purpose of building the large modern cairn which occupies the exact summit of the hill within the fort. This was surmounted by a cemented cone of stones in which a heavy cross of wrought iron was implanted. The whole has been cast down, presumably by natural forces. Lying among the ruin is a slab inscribed

CHARLES 10th MARQUIS OF HUNTLY.

DIED 18th SEPTEMBER 1863.

ERECTED BY MARY ANTOINETTA HIS WIDOW AND THE TENANTRY OF ABOYNE.

Barra Hill, Fort (NJ 803257), 1 mile S. of Old Meldrum, Sheet 38 (A.981 and farm road). *Aberdeenshire.*

This fort bears certain resemblances to the Barmekin of Echt. The innermost line of defence is a ruined wall which encloses an area measuring 400 ft. in length by 320 ft. in width, with a single entrance in the E. Two ramparts and ditches lying outside this are equipped with three entrances, two of which are still flanked with the remains of walls. It

is clear that the innermost enclosure with one entrance is almost certainly a later structure than the somewhat larger enclosure with three entrances formed by the ramparts and ditches.

The interior has long been under the plough, the effects of which have also caused some damage to the N. sector of the defences. It is featureless except for a huge erratic boulder which must have been placed on the hill in glacial times.

Barmekin of Echt, Fort (NJ 725070), 1¼ miles NW. of Echt, Sheet 38 (B.977, farm road and moorland). *Aberdeenshire.*

The Barmekin of Echt, like the Brown Caterthun, is distinguished in having an unusual number of ramparts and an inordinate number of entrances. The outermost defences are three ramparts which enclose an area measuring about 500 ft. in diameter. They are pierced by five entrances, the entrance passages being lined with the remains of flanking walls which continue inwards for up to as much as 90 ft. The ramparts bend very slightly in at each side of the entrances.

Some 10 ft. within the enclosure thus formed is a fourth line, a ruined wall which encloses an area 450 ft. in diameter. It runs without interruption across three of the entrances in the outer system, although one of the remaining pair is partly blocked. The innermost defence, a heavy ruinous wall placed between 10 ft. and 40 ft. within the one just described, encloses an area 370 ft. in diameter. The two entrances in this conform with those in the wall immediately outside it. There is no doubt that at least two, and possibly three structural phases are represented by these remains.

Mither Tap of Bennachie, Fort (NJ 683224), 2¼ miles SSE. of Oyne, Sheet 38 (A.979, by-road and footpath).
Aberdeenshire.

The Mither Tap (1698 ft. O.D.) is the highest and the most easterly of the several summits of the Bennachie conmontation which borders Garioch on the S. and the middle part of Strathdon on the N. No part of the country E. of the Mither Tap attains to even half its height, so that the view it commands is extensive.

The Tap is in fact a tor, composed of a coarse, in places almost pegmatitic, granite with red felspar phenocrysts. The ruined walls of the fort mingle with the fragmented tor to produce enormous masses of tumbled blocks and boulders among which it is not at first easy to pick out the plan. The outermost wall, about 15 ft. thick, runs round the bottom of the tor nearly 100 ft. below the summit; several stretches of its faces can be distinguished, and there are suggestions of a parapet in one place. A second wall encircles the interior of the enclosure thus formed about half way up towards the summit. Traces of circular stone foundations, probably though not necessarily of later date than the fort, lie between the walls and above the inner wall.

Pittodrie, Fort (NJ 694244), 3½ miles SE. of Oyne, Sheet 38 (A.979, by-road and private grounds). *Aberdeenshire.*

This little fort occupies an unobtrusive nose at the NE. extremity of the Bennachie conmontation. It consists of a wall enclosing an area measuring 80 ft. by 65 ft., with an entrance in the S. This is surrounded at a slightly lower level by a rampart with an external ditch, the entrance gap in which conforms with that in the wall. There is a gap 60 ft. long in the NE. arc of the rampart, but the ditch is continuous. Both are breached in the E. by a bay in the rocky hillside which comes in as far as the wall. There is no reason to suppose that both systems of defence are not contemporary, though nothing to prove that they were.

Dunnideer, Fort (NJ 613281), 1 mile W. of Insch, Sheet 37 (by-road and footpath). *Aberdeenshire.*

The Hill of Dunnideer rises only to a height of 876 ft. above sea level, but there is no higher ground between it and the coast at Newburgh, 25 miles to the E., so that it is conspicuous from afar. The summit of the hill is occupied by a ruinous mediaeval tower built largely from the remains of an oblong and highly vitrified fort in which it stands. This measures 220 ft. by 90 ft. internally, and a depression near the W. end probably represents the site of a well. Slight traces of outer works lie close to this, especially in the N. and E.

Considerably lower down the flanks of the hill an incomplete rampart appears for the most part as a marker trench, but in the vicinity of the entrances, in the E. and W., as a rudimentary bank cast up from an external quarry ditch. A similar incomplete rampart, represented entirely by marker trenching, lies outside this. The remains must represent at least two main structural phases, if not more; but at the present time no evidence exists to indicate whether the vitrified fort preceded the half-finished outworks, or *vice versa.*

Barmkyn of North Keig, Fort (NJ 599200), 5¼ miles SSW. of Insch, Sheet 37 (B.992, farm road and pasture land). *Aberdeenshire.*

This stone fort crowns the broad flat summit of an isolated hill which overlooks the Howe of Alford from the N. It consists of an almost circular enclosure measuring 115 ft. by 110 ft. within two ruined walls, the inner the more ruinous. The slight remains of a cairn 25 ft. in diameter are the only feature visible in the interior.

Cairnmore, Fort (NJ 503248), 1½ miles S. of Rhynie, Sheet 37 (by-roads and farm roads). *Aberdeenshire.*

This stone fort occupies the termination of a broad spur protruding N. from the Correen Hills to overlook the plain between Rhynie and Insch. It consists of an enclosure measuring 170 ft. by 150 ft. within two ruined walls, with an entrance in the SE. The gently domed interior is now featureless.

Tap o' Noth, Fort (NJ 485293), 1½ miles NW. of Rhynie, Sheet 37 (A.941 and moorland track). *Aberdeenshire.*

The Tap o' Noth is a conical eminence which rises from the W. end of the Hill of Noth to attain a height of 1851 ft. above sea level, and of 1300 ft. above the Water of Bogie at Rhynie. It is visible from the sea 30 miles to the E. The fort which crowns this superb site—the second highest fort in Scotland—consists of a single wall which may originally have been 20 ft. thick or more. It is now heavily vitrified, and overgrown with grass and heather. The interior measures about 335 ft. by about 105 ft. A depression about 90 ft. from the S. end probably represents the site of a well. A second wall consisting mainly of a row of huge detached boulders lies low down the N. and E. flanks of the hill. Outside and to the S. of the fort platforms similar to those upon which timber-framed houses were built have been noticed.

Craighill, Fort and Broch (NO 432358), 3 miles NE. of Dundee, Sheet 54 (B.978 and by-road). *Angus.*

The remains of this multivallate fort are very denuded, and the main interest and importance of the site lie in the presence of a broch, secondary to the fort. This was excavated in 1957, when it was found to measure 35 ft. in diameter within a wall 15 ft. thick, with the entrance in the E. Lying as it does between the brochs at Liff (Hurley Hawkin) and Drumsturdy, it represents the latest discovery among the ten Tay-Tweed brochs.

Laws Hill, Drumsturdy, Fort and Broch (NO 493349), 1¾ miles NNW. of Monifieth, Sheet 54 (B.961). *Angus.*

The remains on the Laws of Monifieth acquired a certain fame more than 100 years ago, when an account based on a detailed examination was published. The fort is oval, measuring about 400 ft. by 200 ft. within the ruin of a wall 30 ft. thick. The faces of the wall are built of large, carefully laid blocks, and the interior is of rubble. Considerable quantities of vitrified stone have been noticed in the core. An outer wall of the same character but not so thick covers either end of the fort, and a third is added at the SW. end. The broch, now very much reduced by robbing and overgrown with rank vegetation, has a wall 16 ft. thick and an interior 35 ft. in diameter. This is the easternmost of the three brochs of the Tay-Tweed group which lie just N. of the Tay estuary.

Denoon Law, Fort (NO 355444), 2½ miles SW. of Glamis, Sheet 54 (by-roads). *Angus.*

The grass-grown remains of this fort are wasted by Time but not much mutilated by Man. Its plan is somewhat trapezoid, as dictated by the shape of the hill, the interior measuring axially a maximum of 370 ft. in length by 220 ft. in width, within a massive and lofty mound which stands to a height of 14 ft. from the inside and is spread to 50 ft. in width. The easiest approaches to the fort, from NW. and NE., are covered by the denuded remains of three very much

slighter ramparts, and it must be questioned whether all are contemporary or whether the fort occupies an older site. On the face of it, the former alternative may seem the more probable. No vitrified material has been found, but the size and proportion of the main ruin leave little room for doubt that it must contain the remains of a timber-laced wall, which could be 30 ft. thick, or more.

Turin Hill, Fort and Duns (NO 514534), 3½ miles NE. of Forfar, Sheet 54 (B.9133 and farm road). *Angus.*

Turin Hill commands extensive views across central Strathmore as well as to the E. The fort which crowns its long summit ridge appears to have been reconstructed at least once in its period of use, having begun as an oval enclosure measuring about 900 ft. by 400 ft. within two ramparts. Whether these were finished or not is doubtful; but at any rate a new and much smaller structure was eventually built within them, measuring 500 ft. by 130 ft. (cf. Finavon) within a single stone wall. It is quite possible that this wall is timber-laced, and that the fort it forms belongs among the monuments of that class.

After the forts were disused, a circular dun about 90 ft. in diameter within a wall 12 ft. thick was built partly upon the N. sector of the wall of the later fort, if surface appearances are interpreted correctly. What may be a second, similar structure lies 150 yds. to the W., and a third the same distance to the E.

Finavon, Fort (NO 506556), 4 miles NE. of Forfar, Sheet 54 (A.94 or B.9134 and farm road). *Angus.*

This elongated, heavily vitrified timber-laced fort with a well in it measures about 500 ft. by a maximum of 120 ft. internally. Excavations carried out between 1933 and 1935 by Childe showed that the wall was about 20 ft. thick, and that it stood 12 ft. internally and 16 ft. externally beneath the grass-grown rubble. It had been built on a course laid out regardless of the variations in the contours of the hill. Further excavations, by MacKie, in 1966, established a date of 8th to 6th centuries B.C. for what were probably floor-timbers.

White Caterthun, Fort (NO 548660), 5 miles NW. of Brechin, Sheet 44 (byroads). *Angus.*

The hill on which this fort stands is

29 *White Caterthun Fort. Both the ruined stone walls and the earthworks are conspicuous*

only 35 ft. higher than its neighbour, the Brown Caterthun, 1 mile to the NE. The fort is almost oval on plan, measuring about 500 ft. by 220 ft. within the most imposing ruined wall in Britain. This may originally have measured as much as 40 ft. in thickness, and now appears as a tremendous pile of boulders and blocks with an entrance in the SE. Close outside this ruin is another, probably representing a wall about 20 ft. thick. The combined tumble from the two walls spreads over a width of 100 ft. The interior contains a well, probably contemporary with the fort, and a recent rectangular turf enclosure.

Immediately outside the ruined walls a low rampart with an internal quarry ditch encircles the hill-top, while at distances varying between 100 ft. and 230 ft. outside this there are the remains of two ramparts, with traces of two more, probably incomplete, to NW. of them.

It is possible that more than one period is represented by these various defences, but no evidence exists to show which was the earlier, the stone fort or the outworks. The walls are probably timber-laced. Up to the present time they have remained remarkably free from stone-robbing, and it is quite probable that the lowest courses of the wall may, as at Finavon, be standing to a considerable

height beneath the security of the tumbled mass fallen from the upper levels. While the remains of these walls are notable because of their volume, it must be remembered that in many another case only the removal of stone by the cart-load, so often recorded, has reduced massive ruins which might even have rivalled this favoured monument.

Brown Caterthun, Fort (NO 555668), 5 miles NW. of Brechin, Sheet 44 (by-roads). *Angus.*

The remains of this fort cannot be compared closely with those of any other, even though some smaller and less complex structures in southern Aberdeenshire show some parallel features. No less than six lines of defence corrugate the gentle flanks of the hill. The innermost is a very ruinous stone wall enclosing an area measuring as little as 260 ft. in length by 200 ft. in width, with a single entrance in the N. which does, in fact, lie right on the summit of the hill. Outside this, at distances ranging from as little as 60 ft. to as much as 180 ft., there runs a heavy rampart which might also originally have been a wall. This is spread to a thickness of about 25 ft., and contains several stretches of large boulders along its outer face. It has nine entrances.

Two ramparts with a median ditch fit

closely outside this wall and are probably contemporary with it. They also have nine entrances. Beyond them comes a rampart with no apparent ditch which has a pronounced, unaccountable kink in the E. This has eight entrances. Also with eight entrances, conforming reasonably closely with those in the line just described, is the outermost defence of all, a rampart with an external quarry ditch. This encloses all the other works in an area measuring 1000 ft. by 900 ft.

With nothing to build upon, the problems raised by these defences defy interpretation, although it may be safe to suggest that perhaps at least three separate structural phases are involved.

Caisteal na Sithe, Fort (NR 962691), 1½ miles SSW. of Kames, Sheet 62 (A.886, by-road and moorland).   *Argyll, Cowal.*

This fort occupies the summit of a rocky ridge to the shape of which it conforms. It measures 260 ft. in length by about half as much in width within a dry-stone wall.

Dunadd, Fort (NR 837936), 3¾ miles NNW. of Lochgilphead, Sheet 55 (A.816 and farm road).   *Argyll, Mid.*

This fort occupies a small, isolated rocky hill on the E. of Moine Mhor, the mossy flood plain of the River Add. The several different levels and terraces of the rock have been edged by walls to form the fort, and the uppermost division measures about 100 ft. in length by 45 ft. in maximum width. A short distance outside the entrance of this several items have been wrought in the living rock, chief among them the likeness of a boar, incised in a style which is indisputably Pictish. The fort may have been built in Early Iron Age times; if, however, current opinion about such carvings is anywhere near correct, this work must have been done no earlier than the middle of the 7th century A.D. and no later than the end of the 9th, and preferably during the period embraced by the late 7th and the early 8th century. It is recorded in the *Annals of Ulster* that Dunadd was besieged by Picts in A.D. 683 and 736, but whether the boar dates from one of these actions or was there before either, when Dunadd was a Pictish fortification, remains a question which probably cannot be solved.

On either side of the boar are a basin and the "imprint" of a right foot. An Ogam inscription which has not yet been read is carved N. of the foot.

Duntroon, Fort (NR 803959), 6 miles NW. of Lochgilphead, Sheet 55 (A.816, by-road and private grounds).   *Argyll, Mid.*

This fort, situated a little way from the NW. shore of Loch Crinan, consists of an oval enclosure measuring 140 ft. by 90 ft. within a timber-laced wall about 10 ft. thick, parts of which are vitrified. This lies within an outer enclosure formed by a similar but narrower wall and measuring 300 ft. in length by 180 ft. in width, which is further defended on the SW. by two outer walls. The relics recovered during excavations in 1904 included 36 saddle querns and no rotaries, various stones and pebbles worn by use and other Early Iron Age objects.

Slockavullin, Fort (NR 815980), 1¼ miles WSW. of Kilmartin, Sheet 55 (A.83, by-road and farm land).   *Argyll, Mid.*

This fort, situated on a rocky knoll ¼ mile W. of what Christison described as "the cheerfully situated hamlet" of Slockavullin, is oval on plan, measuring 114 ft. by 50 ft. within a now ruinous wall originally about 12 ft. thick. This represents one of the local types of defensive enclosure.

Dun a Chogaidh, Fort (NR 745876), ½ mile NE. of Tayvallich, Sheet 55 (hillside).   *Argyll, Knapdale.*

The ruin of this fort is splendidly situated to overlook Loch Sween and the Sound of Jura, and commands impressive long prospects in all directions in clear weather. It consists of a dry-stone wall originally about 12 ft. thick enclosing an area about 150 ft. long by 75 ft. wide. The entrance is in the SW.

Dun Skeig, Fort and Dun (NR 757571), 10 miles SW. of Tarbert, Sheet 62 (A.83, farm road and hill).   *Argyll, Kintyre.*

The hill upon which these remains stand rises steeply to a height of 469 ft. from a point near the SE. shore of the mouth of West Loch Tarbert and commands magnificent and extensive views. The fort is oval on plan, measuring 90 ft. by 65 ft. within a heavily vitrified wall. The dun, 50 yds. NE. of the fort, measures about 45 ft. in diameter within a wall about 13 ft. thick. The entrance, in the E., is checked for a door.

Carradale, Fort (NR 815364), 1¼ miles

S. of Carradale, Sheet 68 (footpath and moorland). *Argyll, Kintyre.*

This vitrified fort occupies the central part of Carradale Point, a narrow peninsula which may be isolated at high water. It is of oval form, measuring about 190 ft. by 75 ft. within a wall among the debris of which are large masses of vitrifaction. Traces of outer defences can be seen both N. and S. of the fort.

Benderloch, Forts and Dun (NM 903382), 5¾ miles NE. of Oban, Sheet 49 (A.85, A.828 and private grounds). *Argyll, Lorn.*

These structures have been the subject of a considerable amount of comment, and have even acquired the spurious Latin name of Berigonium as well as the more lofty-sounding Gaelic Dun Mac-Sniochan. They occupy a rocky ridge at the head of Ardmucknish Bay, and the earliest of them consists of a timber-laced wall which surrounds the entire summit of the ridge to measure about 700 ft. in length by a maximum width of 100 ft. This structure was superseded by a small subrectangular, now vitrified fort about 170 ft. long by 60 ft. wide, and by a circular and probably vitrified dun measuring about 60 ft. in diameter. Relics recovered from an unspecified part of these works include a Romano-British enamelled fibula and other objects which point to occupation in both the pre-Roman and Roman Iron Age.

Loch nan Gobhar, Fort (NM 970633), 2¼ miles W. of Corran, Sheet 41 (A.861 and moorland). *Argyll, North.*

This vitrified fort occupies a ridge rising from the N. shore of the loch under the towering flanks of Meall Dearg Choire nam Muc. It measures 250 ft. in length by up to 30 ft. in width within the ruin of a wall in which massive vitrifaction has been recorded, especially near the W. extremity. Access to the fort is gained up the E. flank of the ridge.

Portencross, Fort and Dun (NS 171491), 2 miles WNW. of West Kilbride, Sheet 63 (B.7048). *Ayrshire.*

The ruins of this fort are badly decayed, but are of interest partly because they exhibit vitrifaction and partly because of the presence of a secondary structure. They occupy the precipitous tail of a ridge named Auld Hill, where they appear as a grass-grown mass bordering a subrectangular area 100 ft. by 50 ft. in extent. Immediately to the S. the ridge is crossed by two ditches cut through the rock, and farther S. still a small dun, measuring about 45 ft. by 27 ft. within a thick wall, crowns the actual summit of the site. It is probable that the dun is the later structure, and that it has cut off part of the precincts of the earlier fort.

Dow Hill, Fort (NX 192962), ¾ mile SE. of Girvan, Sheet 76 (A.714). *Ayrshire.*

The remains of this fort are denuded and robbed, but the original structure, or structures, is of considerable interest. The summit of the hill is enclosed by a ruinous stone wall of a thickness which might be established by excavation but certainly cannot be established from surface indications. Christison described it as being 50 ft. in diameter within a wall spread to as much as 30 ft. in width, but gave no estimate of the original dimensions. It seems quite possible, nevertheless, that these remains represent a dun; and if so, it is also possible that this was a secondary feature, the first being a fort with a main enclosure measuring about 130 ft. in length by a maximum of about 50 ft. in width. At all events, arcs of five decayed ramparts cross the E. instep of the hill, and the innermost of these could well have been the inner rampart of a fort.

Hollowshean, Fort (NS 244063), 1 mile S. of Kirkoswald, Sheet 76 (by-road). *Ayrshire.*

As at Kildoon, this fort consists of an enclosure placed at the end of a ridge, the neck of which is cut off by outworks. The enclosure measures about 240 ft. in length by about 150 ft. in width, within a ruinous rampart which may represent a robbed stone wall. The three outer ramparts crossing the neck beyond this are of slighter appearance. It is possible that the main rampart was a timber-laced wall, but only excavation could determine this.

Kildoon, Fort (NS 298074), 1½ miles S. of Maybole, Sheet 76 (by-road). *Ayrshire.*

Kildoon Hill is a basalt ridge crowned by a monument to Sir C. Fergusson of Kilkerran which has destroyed part of the defences of the fort. The latter consists of the remains of a vitrified timber-laced rampart which encloses an area measuring about 150 ft. by, at the greatest, 100 ft. The approach from the W. is defended by two ramparts, each with an external rock-cut ditch.

The Knock, Fort (NS 202268), 1½ miles N. of Largs, Sheet 63 (A.78 and by-road). *Ayrshire.*

The Knock overlooks Largs Bay from a height of 712 ft. The summit is surrounded by a rampart enclosing an area measuring 165 ft. by 95 ft., from the ruin of which enough vitrified material has been found to indicate that it had been a timber-laced wall. Beneath this, on the flanks of the hill, a shallow rock-cut ditch can be seen in the S., NW. and N., bordered in places by a low rampart or upcast mound on the outer lip.

Knockjargon, Fort and Cairn (NS 235473), 3 miles N. of Ardrossan, Sheet 63 (B.780). *Ayrshire.*

These structures crown one of the hills from which the land falls steadily to the Firth of Clyde, commanding extensive views across to Arran and beyond. The cairn, measuring about 50 ft. in diameter, is on the summit (758 ft.) within the two walls of the fort which enclose an area measuring 150 ft. by 100 ft. An outer line of defence consisting of a ditch with an upcast mound along parts of the outer lip covers the S. approach.

Carwinning, Fort (NS 286528), 2 miles N. by W. of Dalry, Sheet 63 (B.784). *Ayrshire.*

This stone-walled fort, now in an extremely wasted condition, occupies a splendid situation on the W. side of the valley of the Picton Burn, the flank of which is here particularly steep. Like the Harpercroft fort, it consists of a central enclosure about 300 ft. in diameter which lies within the remains of an outer wall placed at a distance of about 100 ft. from it. An additional feature here is a small central enclosure about 100 ft. in diameter formed by a stony mound. This might be intrusive, and might represent the robbed remains of a dun.

Hadyard Hill, Fort (NX 259989), 1¾ miles SSW. of Dailly, Sheet 76 (by-road). *Ayrshire.*

Hadyard Hill commands an extensive prospect to the W., NW. and N. over the valley of the Water of Girvan towards the Firth of Clyde. The fort which crowns it is oval, measuring 270 ft. by 230 ft. within two ramparts which are not quite concentric. These are on the whole slight, never rising more than 4 ft. in height or spreading to a greater width than 24 ft., and in places all traces of them are absent. There is even a question whether they did in fact ever exist in the NNW., or whether the fort was either unfinished or completed by a fence.

Harpercroft, Fort (NS 360325), 1¼ miles SSW. of Dundonald, Sheet 70 (B.730 and by-road). *Ayrshire.*

This fort, crowning a subsidiary summit of the Dundonald range, consists of an inner ring, formed by a ruinous stone wall and measuring about 300 ft. in diameter, situated within an outer one which lies about 300 ft. outside it. Both are now low stony banks spread to a maximum width of about 20 ft. The plan is unusual, if one period only is, as seems probable, represented; but it may be compared with the fort at Carwinning, 13 miles to the NW.

Wardlaw, Fort (NS 359327), 1 mile SSW. of Dundonald, Sheet 70 (B.730 and by-road). *Ayrshire.*

The remains of this fort crown the highest summit of the Dundonald range which consists of an oval plateau measuring 340 ft. in length from NE. to SW. by 200 ft. transversely. Parts of the rim of this are bordered by the remains of a stony grass-covered rampart which stands to a height of 5 ft. at best, and is spread to as much as 20 ft. in width. Its main interest lies in its proximity to the fort named Harpercroft (from the land upon which they both lie) which is situated less than ¼ mile to the SSE.

Little Conval, Fort (NJ 295393), 2 miles W. of Dufftown, Sheet 28 (B.9009 and moorland). *Banff.*

Situated at a height of a little over 1800 ft. O.D., this fort occupies a gentle-sided eminence on the watershed between Strathspey and Glenrinnes. The innermost element of the defences, which were not as much as half finished when work upon them was abandoned, consists for the most part of a band of stones spread to a width of about 10 ft., but in the N. and NE. merely of a marker trench. This embryo wall, which encloses an area measuring 680 ft. in length by 400 ft. in width, is accompanied at a varying distance outside by a second line consisting entirely of a marker trench. A third line starts off 75 ft. outside the N. arc of the second as a marker trench; but after running for 200 yds. it is suddenly replaced by a wall 6 ft. thick faced with very large slabs. This, instead of keeping in conformity with the inner lines, sheers off down the E. flank of the hill to end up 70 yds. outside the second marker trench among a group of shapeless enclosures which may be contemporary with the fort. A fourth line comprises a bank 110 yds. long covering the N. approach. The interior of the fort is remarkable only for the profusion of cloud-berries which may be gathered there in the season.

Edinshall, Fort, Broch and Settlement (NT 772603), 2¼ miles NW. of Preston, Sheet 67 (B.6355 and farm road).
Berwickshire.

These most interesting structures, lying on the NE. flank of Cockburn Law, are most easily reached along the farm road past Cockburn farm. The first structure on the site is one which could be unequivocally described as a hill-fort if it did not lie on a sloping site with almost no natural defensive features. It must originally have measured about 440 ft. in length by 240 ft. in width within two ramparts with external ditches; the entrance was in the W. The next structures to be built, the broch and its outworks, probably date from the beginning of the 2nd century A.D., although the circumstances in which such

an event could have occurred are by no means obvious.

This broch, alone among the ten Tay-Tweed brochs, is situated in the territory of the Votadini, a people who were undoubtedly to some extent in treaty with the Roman power. The brochs at Torwoodlee and Bow, in central Tweeddale, are presumed to have been erected by Pictish immigrants to a countryside which had fallen under the severe disfavour of the Romans and been to some extent depopulated. In the first 40 years of the 2nd century A.D., during the gap between the 1st and 2nd century occupations, there might well have been an opportunity for such colonisation in Selgovia. But no such circumstances are presumed to have occurred in Votadinian territory. Nevertheless, the broch is there, distinguished from others only by measuring 55 ft. in diameter. The wall is 17 ft. thick, and contains three sets of chambers in addition to the guardrooms on either side of the entrance passage.

The broch lies within a ruinous subrectangular enclosure which may be contemporary with it or may belong to the last structure on the site, an open settlement. This covers the W. half of the fort, having overridden and obliterated the NW. sector of the defences. The settlement phase is represented by lengths of walling and by circular stone foundations.

30 *Edinshall Fort, Broch and Settlement*

The chronology of the remains may be summed up as first, in the late 1st millennium B.C. or early 1st A.D., the fort; then the broch, probably at the beginning of the 2nd century A.D.; and finally the settlement, from the later 2nd century A.D. onwards.

Marygold Hill Plantation, Fort and Settlement (NT 806605), 2 miles NNW. of Preston, Sheet, 67 (A.6112, B.6438).
Berwickshire.

Several earthworks and enclosures survive in various states of decay on the high ground N. of Preston, the most interesting—situated ¼ mile NW. of Marygold farmhouse—being flanked on either side by another. This consists of an oval fort measuring 320 ft. by 255 ft. within twin ramparts with a median ditch. It has been re-used as an open settlement, and several circular stone foundations and linear banks lie both within and outside it. Several sherds of local late Iron Age pottery were recently recovered from the roots of a fallen tree within the fort.

Coldingham Loch, Fort and Settlement (NT 899688), 1¾ miles N. of Coldingham, Sheet 67 (B.6438 and farm road).   *Berwickshire.*

These monuments occupy a rocky knoll 1 mile SW. of St Abb's Head, 200 yds. from the cliff-top at the SE. end of a Measured Mile. The fort is D-shaped on plan, measuring 220 ft. along the chord, which is defined by the brink of the steep N. side of the knoll, by 180 ft. transversely. The arc is formed by two ramparts with a median ditch, with an entrance in the S. The settlement, measuring 170 ft. by 120 ft. within the grassgrown ruin of a wall, lies entirely within the fort. It contains several foundations of circular stone-built houses, and more of these lie between the settlement wall and the fort ramparts as well as on and outside the latter. This is an example of the open settlements which grew up at disused forts in the 2nd and succeeding centuries A.D. There are four other small settlements in the vicinity.

Earn's Heugh, Forts and Settlement (NT 892691), 2 miles NNW. of Coldingham, Sheet 67 (by-road). *Berwickshire.*

These interesting remains are situated on the summit of Tun Law, a hill a little over 500 ft. in height which has been partly washed away by the sea. Parts of the earthworks have fallen away with the erosion of the 500 ft. precipice, Earn's Heugh. They comprise two now D-shaped but probably once oval or circular enclosures and a later settlement. The E. enclosure, which appears to be the earlier of the two, measures 220 ft. by 120 ft. within the remains of a single rampart with an external ditch and having an entrance in the W. This was succeeded by the larger W. enclosure which partly overrides it. More than half this is now missing, but it must originally have measured about 260 ft. in diameter within two ramparts with a median ditch, with an entrance in the W.

The settlement measured about 180 ft. in diameter within a single rampart without a ditch, and was placed entirely within the fort, as is so often the case. Several circular stone foundations lie against the inner face of the settlement wall or rampart, while certain minor banks probably belonging to this period also occur outside or over the earthworks.

The W. fort and the settlement repeat the now well-established pattern of the settlement with stone-built houses developing at a pre-Roman Iron Age site after this had become disused. Relics dated between A.D. 150 and 400 came from the houses during some excavations in 1931.

Dean Castles, Fort (NT 808702), 2 miles ESE. of Cockburnspath, Sheet 67 (A.1107 and by-road). *Berwickshire.*

This is an example of one of the small promontory forts, the date of which is often uncertain. It consists of the extremity of a very steep-sided tongue of land which is cut off by two ramparts with external ditches.

Habchester, Fort (NT 944588), 2 miles SE. of Ayton, Sheet 67 (A.1 and by-road). *Berwickshire.*

This fort is a typical bi-vallate oval structure measuring 380 ft. by 270 ft. within two bold ramparts with external ditches. The SW. sector has been obliterated by ploughing, but at the surviving entrance, in the NE., the ramparts can be seen to join round the head of the inner ditch. The NW. sector of the defences is represented by the crest of a natural steep scarp, and it is probable that in its original state the fort would have been bounded on this side by only the inner rampart. An interesting feature is a ragged zone of small quarries which accompanies the inner foot of the remaining portion of the inner rampart, giving the impression that it was a source from which material was extracted to top this rampart up, possibly as a secondary development.

Addinston, Fort (NT 523536), 1 mile E. of Carfraemill, Sheet 66 (A.697).
Berwickshire.

The remains of this fort are conspicuous to travellers on the A.68 road immediately S. of the junction with A.697 at Carfraemill, as they cut the skyline above Addinston farmhouse. They consist of an oval enclosure measuring axially about 280 ft. by 160 ft. within two massive ramparts with external ditches, the outer of which has an upcast mound along parts of its course. In the NW. both ramparts stand over 15 ft. in height. Several circular grass-grown, stony foundations lie inside the fort, but the most conspicuous, which measures 42 ft. in diameter, may be suspected of being of a later date than the rest, possibly even a fold.

Longcroft, Fort and Settlement (NT 532543), 1¼ miles ENE. of Carfraemill, Sheet 66 (A.68 and farm road).
Berwickshire.

These remains crown the nose of a steep-sided ridge which forms the watershed between two burns. They are of a complex nature, and reveal two or three successive periods of construction. The earliest is a fort defended by two heavy ramparts with a median ditch which enclose an area measuring 320 ft. by 200 ft. Within these, and secondary to them, are two concentric ramparts without ditches, the inner of which encloses an area measuring 230 ft. by 180 ft. These two may or may not be contemporary. Inside, several enclosures and circular stone foundations testify to a late occupation, probably from the 2nd or 3rd centuries A.D., while a rectangular one is probably later still.

Blackchester, Fort and Settlement (NT 508504), 2 miles NNW. of Lauder, Sheet 66 (A.68). *Berwickshire.*

Although situated in a plantation, these structures are fairly well preserved. The fort consists of a pair of concentric ramparts with external ditches which enclose an area nearly 400 ft. in diameter with entrances in the ENE. and SW. The settlement, 300 ft. in diameter, is formed by a grass-grown stony bank which lies inside the fort. It contains traces of several circular stone houses, mostly disposed along the rear of the N. sector of the inner rampart, and there is room for many more.

Haerfaulds, Fort and Settlement (NT 574500), 1¼ miles NNW. of Cambridge, Sheet 74 (hill walk). *Berwickshire.*

These most impressive ruins stand on open moorland on the brink of a steep descent S. of some 200 ft. to the Blythe Water. The fort is sub-oval, measuring about 380 ft. by 240 ft. within a ruined wall spread to a thickness of about 15 ft. Nothing is known about the structural method used in building this wall, or of its original measurements, but the massive character of the ruin—despite the fact that it has been severely robbed and mutilated—suggests that it must have been at least 10 ft. thick, and possibly of timber-laced construction.

The settlement is represented by numbers of circular stone foundations which have been built in and around the inner margin of the ruin of the wall, and are associated in places with linear walls no more than 3 ft. thick. These may perfectly well belong to the series already noted which developed locally during Roman–British times, but the fort is somewhat less easy to place. Several other not dissimilar structures are recorded in the eastern Lowlands, and in north Northumberland, however, among which this may well belong.

Barone Hill, Fort (NS 069630), 1¼ miles SW. of Rothesay, Sheet 63 (B.878 and pasture land). *Bute.*

This oval fort measures 200 ft. by 145 ft. within two now ruinous and much robbed dry-stone walls. The inner is alleged to have contained vitrified material, but no confirmation of this is on record.

Dunagoil, Fort (NS 085530), 7¼ miles S. of Rothesay, Sheet 63 (A.844, by-road and pasture land). *Bute.*

This fort occupies a narrow and abrupt ridge which rises 100 ft. above the shore 1 mile NW. of Garroch Head. The fort is defended partly by the steep flanks of the ridge and partly by a heavily vitrified wall. Two entrances, both fitted with bar-holes, are reported to have been seen during clearances of debris. Relics recovered from the fort and its immediate vicinity include artifacts of lignite and steatite, pottery, an iron La Tène brooch and evidence of the industrial use of iron and bronze.

St John's Point, Fort (ND 310752), 2 miles NE. of Mey, Sheet 7 (A.836, by-road and footpath). *Caithness.*

This, the most northerly promontory fort on the mainland of Britain, is formed by a ditch with a stony rampart some 10 ft. high on the inner lip, and a slight upcast mound on the outer lip. This crosses the landward end of the headland from cliff to cliff for a distance of about 600 ft. The entrance lies about 50 ft. from the W. extremity. The area thus cut off measures about 10 acres in extent.

Promontory forts of this kind occur all along the N. coast as far as Durness. No evidence has yet been obtained from any of them from which an estimation of the date of their original construction can be extracted, but comparisons with similar works elsewhere suggest that they may well have been made in the Iron Age, even though possibly re-used by Vikings or later mediaeval overlords.

Holborn Head, Fort (ND 108715), 1½ miles N. by W. of Thurso, Sheet 12 (A.822 and pasture land). *Caithness.*

This fort is formed by a broad wall which cuts off the precipitous headland. Its defensive power is increased by awesome fissures and chasms in the ground just outside it which form a grotesque set of ditches at the remote bottom of which, some 50 ft. or more below, the water surges and breaks. The entrance through the wall is aligned with a gap in these.

Shurrery, Fort (ND 053577), 7 miles SE. of Reay, Sheet 12 (by-roads and moorland). *Caithness.*

This structure, once known as Cnoc na Ratha, is situated a little over a mile to the N. of and more than 300 ft. lower down than the fort on Ben Freiceadain. It consists of a wall of stone slabs about 7 ft. thick surrounding an area measuring 300 ft. by 230 ft. The two entrances both have the lining of slabs which is characteristic of hill-forts in the NE., and there is no reason to suppose that this is anything other than such a fort. A secondary circular enclosure about 30 ft. in diameter formed by a now ruinous and grass-grown wall about 7 ft. thick impinges on to the SE. sector of the outer face of the fort wall.

Ben Freiceadain, Fort (ND 059558), 8 miles SE. of Reay, Sheet 12 (by-roads and moorland). *Caithness.*

The northernmost hill-fort of any size on the mainland of Britain occupies a splendid situation on the summit of Ben Freiceadain, with unlimited prospects over Caithness and Orkney to the N. and E. and a broad panorama of the Sutherland hills to the W. over broken country and to the S. over an expanse of level bog. It is known as Buaile Oscar. The fort measures 900 ft. in length by 470 ft. in width within a single wall about 12 ft. thick. The entrance, in the WNW., has been lined with large slabs set on end in the manner characteristic of forts in the NE. A ruinous chambered cairn of unknown type occupying the exact summit of the hill is of course about 2000 years older than the fort, which is probably of Early Iron Age date.

Garrywhin, Fort (ND 314414), 6¼ miles SSW. of Wick, Sheet 12 (A.9, by-road and moorland). *Caithness.*

The Garrywhin fort occupies an area 590 ft. in length by up to 200 ft. in width of a ridge situated between Warehouse Hill and Loch Watenan, surrounded by boggy tracts on all sides except the N. It is formed by a single stone wall 8 ft. thick and 450 yds. long, the entrances in which are lined with stone slabs set on edge. The remains of these at the N. entrance form the most impressive example of this phenomenon among all the forts in the far NE. of Scotland.

Castle Craig, Fort (NS 911976), on the N. outskirts of Tillycoultry, Sheet 58. *Clackmannanshire.*

This fort occupies a promontory on the S. face of the Ochil range, overlooking the upper part of the Firth of Forth across the plain of western Clackmannanshire. It has been nibbled by a quarry from the S. A deep rock-cut ditch with a stone wall along the inner lip and the remains of a stony rampart on the outer cuts off an area of the tip of the promontory measuring 300 ft. in width by at least 200 ft., and probably originally more, in length. The interior contains an exactly circular enclosure measuring 82 ft. in diameter within the remains of a very well built stone wall 12 ft. thick.

Whether or not the two structural features are contemporary cannot be decided from the surface remains which do not coincide at any point, but the probability is that the circular enclosure is an intruder, and may be of post-Roman date.

Dun Cholla, Fort (NR 377914), 2 miles SSW. of Scalascaig, Sheet 61 (A.870, A.869).   *Colonsay.*

This fort is formed by a wall 10 ft. or more in maximum thickness which encloses the rocky surface of a plateau, the only easy approach to which is in the NE. The entrance, in this sector, is 5 ft. wide. An interesting feature is the presence of a circular stony foundation 25 ft. in diameter which appears to overlie part of the ruined NW. arc of the wall and which contains a ring of six postholes. Such a structure would not be out of place elsewhere in the earliest centuries of the 1st millennium A.D. It may be noted that surface traces of other round houses with stony walls have been observed in Colonsay although they are uncommon elsewhere in the vicinity.

Ward Law, Fort (NY 024667), 6½ miles SSE. of Dumfries, Sheet 84 (by-road, B.725 and farm-land).   *Dumfriesshire.*

This fort crowns the terminal feature of the ridge running SSE. from Dumfries between the River Nith and the Lochar Moss. It measures 210 ft. by 180 ft. within two much worn ramparts, and has been planted with trees. Its interest lies in its situation, commanding the narrowing Solway Firth, and in the presence of a Roman Fort, now ploughed out almost to obliteration, only a few yards to the N.

Kirkmichael Fell, Fort (NY 014893), 8 miles NNE. of Dumfries, Sheet 84 (A.701, farm road and moorland).
                                   Dumfriesshire.

This locally characteristic fort, standing on a shelf on the S. flank of Kirkmichael Fell, measures about 225 ft. in diameter within a single massive rampart with a wide external ditch. The entrance is in the SW.

Brieryshaw Hill, Fort (NY 370917), 4½ miles N. of Langholm, Sheet 79 (A.7 and hill).   *Dumfriesshire.*

This typical Dumfriesshire fort stands on a nose protruding from the SE. flank of Stake Hill. It is formed by two heavy ramparts with a median ditch which enclose a circular area measuring 190 ft. in diameter. The inner rampart is spread to a thickness of about 25 ft., the outer to about 30 ft., and the ditch between them measures about 30 ft. in width and 7 ft. in depth. This, in essence, is one of the types occurring most frequently in the county—a comparatively small and often circular enclosure with proportionately heavy ramparts and a broad ditch. The ramparts often have enough stones showing near the crests to suggest that they were originally capped by a parapet.

Bailiehill, Fort (NY 256905), 9 miles NW. of Langholm, Sheet 79 (B.709 and by-road).   *Dumfriesshire.*

This fort is one of the many which occur in the stretch of Eskdale above Langholm. It lies on a hill beside the by-road which follows the valley of the Water of Milk from Annandale to Eskdale, reaching the latter at the point where the Black and White Esks come together. It is almost certainly a work of two main structural periods, the inner enclosure probably being the later. This is almost circular, measuring about 150 ft. in diameter within a stony bank which is probably a ruined wall. This is spread to a maximum thickness of 20 ft., and stands 5 ft. high.

The enclosure thus formed lies within a larger one measuring 360 ft. by 160 ft. within two massive ramparts with a median ditch. This work probably represents the original fort, and the walled enclosure may be an example of similar structures which, where found farther E., have long been assumed to belong to the immediate post-Roman period.

Castle O'er, Fort (NY 242928), 10½ miles NW. of Langholm, Sheet 79 (B.709, by-road and forest tracks).
                                   Dumfriesshire.

This locally large fort is now completely swallowed up by a forest of conifers, and although not planted itself is to a certain extent blurred and defaced by the tussocks into which the grass which covers it has coagulated. A visit is nevertheless worth while, and the lay-out can be best appreciated from the summit of the rocky knoll which is included in the defended area.

The fort recalls that on Bonchester Hill, in that the inner part, occupying the rocky summit, is surrounded at a considerable distance by an outer line of ramparts. The summit of the knoll is girt by the remains of a rampart or wall which encloses an area measuring about 300 ft. by 150 ft.; and the base of the knoll is in turn defended by a rampart thrown up from an internal quarry ditch. This combined work, measuring over all about 500 ft. by 350 ft., lies within the outer pair of ramparts with a median ditch which enclose an area measuring 800 ft. in length which includes a well.

Over Cassock, Fort (NT 231044), 15 miles NNW. of Langholm, Sheet 79 (B.709). *Dumfriesshire.*

This fort or settlement lies on a low promontory beside the left bank of the Barr Burn 1 mile N. of the Eskdalemuir Observatory in one of the wettest parts of the country. It takes the form of two contiguous enclosures, the lower occupying the tip of the promontory and measuring about 115 ft. by 80 ft. along the axes and the other—acting as a bailey to the first—about 260 ft. by 220 ft. This work is the uppermost of the forts, settlements and other enclosures in Eskdale, lying 3½ miles above the Roman forts at Raeburnfoot.

Woody Castle, Fort (NY 073837), 1 mile NW. of Lochmaben, Sheet 78 (by-road and farm road). *Dumfriesshire.*

Woody Castle, situated on a low eminence in cultivated ground, represents the type of the Dumfriesshire circular fort which often goes by the name of birren. It measures 200 ft. in diameter within a massive rampart spread to a width of 35 ft., surrounded by a ditch measuring 45 ft. in width where best preserved.

Corncockle Plantation, Fort (NY 090861), 2¼ miles N. of Lochmaben, Sheet 78 (B.7020 and by-road). *Dumfriesshire.*

Although now in an ageing plantation of conifers, this fort is of interest in that it is formed by a massive stony rampart with a broad external ditch, a locally widespread type. The interior is oval, measuring 160 ft. by 130 ft. along the axes, and the entrance is in the E.

One of the best preserved mediaeval homestead moats in the county is situated a few hundred yards SE. of the fort on Gotterbie Moor.

Burnswark, Fort (NY 185785), 3½ miles SE. of Lockerbie, Sheet 85 (A.74, farm road). *Dumfriesshire.*

The hill named after the fort is a conspicuous table which dominates most of Annandale and is visible from as far N. as the head of the valley at a point on the A.701 road 4¾ miles NNW. of Moffat to the B.5299 road across the central Cumberland plateau SW. of Carlisle. The fort shows a development from an oval enclosure measuring about 900 ft. by 650 ft. to an irregularly shaped defended area 1650 ft. in length and 17 acres in extent. Great interest attaches to this place because of the presence of a small Roman siege camp on both the NW. and the SE. flanks of the hill, and of a fortlet datable to the 2nd century A.D. in the corner of the SE. camp. The fortlet predates the siege camps; and as the former can be assigned to the time of the second Roman incursion into the north in about A.D. 140, it is assumed that the siege camps were used in a punitive expedition after the uprisings of A.D. 155, when the near-by Roman fort at Birrens was destroyed. The fort must have been demobilised in the 1st century A.D., but the presence of the fortlet might suggest that it was still occupied in the first half of the 2nd century. There can be no doubt that occupation ceased after the siege. It has been suggested that this fort, in which excavations in 1966 by Mr George Jobey disclosed an original palisade dated to the 7th or 6th century B.C., might have been the principal centre or *oppidum* of the Novantae.

Broomhill Bank Hill, Fort (NY 131911), 6 miles N. of Lockerbie, Sheet 78 (A.74, farm road and hill). *Dumfriesshire.*

This fort, splendidly situated on the summit of Broomhill Bank Hill, commands extensive prospects in all directions. Its oval interior measures 190 ft. by 170 ft. within defences consisting of a rampart on either side of a broad ditch. There are two entrances. This fort is characteristic of many in the district.

Broom Hill, Fort (NY 154916), 6 miles N. by E. of Lockerbie, Sheet 79 (B.723 and farm road). *Dumfriesshire.*

This fort is another typical example of a type widely spread in Dumfriesshire. Virtually circular, with a diameter of 170 ft., where best preserved the defences consist of a very heavy and massive rampart with a ditch 27 ft. wide outside it. The entrance is in the W.

Range Castle, Fort (NY 086764), 1¼ miles SSW. of Hightae, Sheet 85 (B.7020 and footpath). *Dumfriesshire.*

This fort situated on a ridge on the W. side of Annandale consists of a largely rock-cut ditch with accompanying banks surrounding an area measuring about 300 ft. in diameter and including a rocky boss. The latter is defended by the remains of walls, the smallest, highest, innermost enclosure measuring about 80 ft. in diameter.

Barrs Hill, Fort (NY 015834), 1 mile NE. of Amisfield Town, Sheet 78 (farm land). *Dumfriesshire.*

Barrs Hill commands an extensive panorama over Nithsdale and Annandale. The fort is oval, measuring 270 ft. by 210 ft. within a now ruinous massive rampart with a broad external ditch outside which are two more ramparts with a median ditch and, in the N. and W., sections of a fourth. The entrance is in the E.

Friars Carse, Fort (NX 918852), 3 miles NW. of Holywood, Sheet 78 (A.76 and footptath). *Dumfriesshire.*

This oval fort crowns a knoll on the right bank of the River Nith. It measures 200 ft. by 140 ft. within defences formed to N. and E. by the river bank and to S. and W. by a pair of ramparts with a median ditch. The entrance is in the E. The interior contains a stone circle erected in or about 1827.

Tynron Doon, Fort (NX 820939), 1¾ miles W. by S. of Penpont, Sheet 78 (A.702, by-road and hill). *Dumfriesshire.*

The hill upon which this fort stands rises abruptly to a height of 947 ft. above sea level in a bend of the Shinnel Water 3 miles W. of its confluence with the River Nith. The remains, which are as spectacular as the situation, are complex, and have not yet been thoroughly analysed. They consist first of a central enclosure measuring about 150 ft. in length by 130 ft. in width within a ruinous stone wall and, outside this, three massive ramparts the outer scarps of which rise to between 14 ft. and 20 ft. above the ditches. The work presents many problems, the elucidation of which will be a useful as well as an interesting task.

Shancastle Doon, Fort (NX 815908), 2¼ miles E. of Moniaive, Sheet 78 (A.702 and hill). *Dumfriesshire.*

Shancastle Doon is a dilapidated fort which is magnificently situated on the E. extremity of the watershed between the Shinnel and Cairn Waters at the point where a road joins the two valleys. It has been an all-stone structure the wall of which included some very large blocks, but despite the mass of debris its precise form could only be established by excavation.

Dalwhat, Fort (NX 728940), 3¾ miles NW. of Moniaive, Sheet 77 (by-road and hill). *Dumfriesshire.*

This fort occupies a ridge overlooking the lower part of the valley of the Dalwhat Water from the NW., and in consequence the NW. sector of its defences was originally the strongest and is now the best preserved. Here the remains of three ramparts, their external ditches now levelled into the form of terraces, can be discerned. The interior measures about 270 ft. in length by 160 ft. in width.

Mullach, Fort (NX 929870), 1 mile NW. of Dalswinton, Sheet 78 (farm land and moorland). *Dumfriesshire.*

This fort occupies a splendid situation overlooking central Nithsdale from a height of 800 ft. O.D. It is oval in shape, measuring 300 ft. by 260 ft. within two concentric walls about 100 ft. apart. The remains of these are massive, and the presence of considerable quantities of vitrifaction proclaim that they were of timber-laced construction. The Dalswinton Roman fort lies 1 mile to the S.

Morton Mains Hill, Settlement (NS 892006), 2¼ miles NE. of Carronbridge, Sheet 78 (A.702, farm road and pasture land). *Dumfriesshire.*

The remains of this palisaded settlement are of the greatest interest, showing as they do the same sequence of events as do those of the settlement on Hayhope Knowe in Roxburghshire. The earliest phase of construction is represented by a twin palisade with a single outlier, traces of both of which can be seen on the surface surrounding the hilltop on all sides except to the E., where the ground falls steeply to a reservoir formed in the Kettleton Burn. The enclosure thus formed measures 280 ft. in length by 200 ft. in width.

The second phase is shown by the

beginnings of a rampart, laid out so that the outlying palisade of the first phase forms an inner revetment to it—as at Hayhope and Braidwood. The rampart appears as several disjointed stretches of a low mound cast up from an external quarry ditch, a work which was abandoned before completion. No surface traces of houses or other internal structures can be detected in the coarse grass and patches of rushes which cover the interior.

Kemp's Castle, Fort (NS 770089), 1 mile SW. of Sanquhar, Sheet 71 (by-road). *Dumfriesshire.*

This fort occupies an attenuated promontory at the confluence of the Euchan Water and the Barr Burn. Approach from the W. is first cut by a broad ditch with a rampart on the inner lip; after a gap of 66 ft., a second ditch, 42 ft. wide and with upcast mounds on the lips, runs across the promontory from N. to S. Both these defences have entrances at the S. end. Immediately within the inner ditch there are traces of walls which may originally have run all round the rest of the promontory. Vitrifaction has been observed in these remains.

Beattock Hill, Fort (NT 065021), 1 mile W. of Beattock, Sheet 78 (by-road and moorland). *Dumfriesshire.*

Several monuments are situated in the coarse pasture on Beattock Hill upon which a herd of hill cattle accompanied by a bull ranges freely. One of the most interesting is the stone fort which occupies the summit, ¼ mile N. of the by-road from Beattock to Kinnelhead. It consists of a massive but now ruinous stone wall enclosing an area measuring 210 ft. by 100 ft. along the axes. The entrance, in the S., is protected by a length of rampart or wall with external quarry ditch, and another covers the N. extremity.

White Hill, Fort (NT 075117), 4 miles N. of Moffat, Sheet 78 (by-road). *Dumfriesshire.*

This fort is situated on a low ridge in the middle of the uppermost part of Annandale where this is bordered by the steep hillsides which end in the Devil's Beef Tub 1 mile to the NE. It is visible to passengers in vehicles driving along the pass between Annandale and Tweeddale. It is a structure of two phases; the outer and probably earlier work consists of a pair of ramparts with a median ditch, enclosing an area measuring axially 230 ft. in length by 180 ft. and with an entrance in the E. The inner work, lying entirely within the enclosure thus formed, consists of a now ruinous wall surrounding an area measuring 170 ft. in length by 125 ft. in width, with an entrance in the ESE.

Tail Burn, Fort (NT 186146), 9 miles NE. of Moffat, Sheet 79 (A.708). *Dumfriesshire.*

The Tail Burn descends steeply from the flanks of White Coomb (2696 ft. O.D.) to join the Moffat Water, including in its course a waterfall known as the Grey Mare's Tail. The remains of this work lie on the left bank of the burn, and more than half of the defences as well as of the interior have been swept away by the action of the water. Originally the fort must have been subrectangular or D-shaped on plan, measuring about 120 ft. along the axes within a stony rampart with an external quarry ditch.

Dumbarton Rock, Fort (NS 400745), in the S. outskirts of Dumbarton town, Sheet 63 & 64. *Dunbartonshire.*

Although no remains of a prehistoric fort have been recorded on the steep flanks and lofty summit of Dumbarton Rock, it is reasonably certain that here, as at the comparable site in Stirling, such a fort once existed. The importance of the site, together with its striking physical appearance, warrant its mention here and reward a visit. The name derives from the dun of the British, and it is considered that the capital or *oppidum* of the Strathclyde Britons, earlier the Damnonii, was here. That such a precipitous situation can support a reasonably large defended area is shown by the present buildings which encumber all the surface of the upper part of the rock, while a closely comparable site on which the ruins of a prehistoric fort are still preserved can be seen at North Berwick.

Sheep Hill, Fort (NS 435744), 1 mile WNW. of Bowling, Sheet 64 (A.82). *Dunbartonshire.*

This fort occupies a rocky hill-top on the massif which borders the Firth of Clyde to the N. near its junction with the river proper, and commands long prospects in all directions. The main defence, a thick but now ruinous wall, encloses an area 300 ft. by 150 ft. in extent. The wall

31   *Dumbarton Rock, from the south shore of the Clyde Estuary not far from the Roman Fort at Whitemoss*

was a timber-laced structure, as is witnessed by several exposures of vitrified material along its course. A vitrified wall around the summit was shown by excavation in the 1960s to be earlier than the main defence and than an outer wall on the S. This small vitrified fort may have affinities with the scatter in Renfrewshire and Ayrshire, and with the group in E. Stirlingshire, all in Damnonian territory.

North Berwick Law, Fort (NT555842), ½ mile S. of North Berwick, Sheet 67 (B.1347).   *East Lothian.*

This fort occupies one of the most dramatic sites in the country. North Berwick Law rises steeply, in some aspects precipitously, to an elevation of 500 ft. from the plain below, and only the S. flank moderates eventually to a more gradual slope. The remains of the fort are for the most part scanty, as much of the material of the dry-built stone walls has very naturally toppled down the hill. An area measuring about 500 ft. by about 300 ft. was enclosed by a wall running on a level of some 50 ft. below the summit. The terrace immediately below this on the SW. was likeways enclosed. The gentler slope, nevertheless covered in outcrops and crags, which intervenes between the second wall and the foot of the hill is enclosed by a third wall, several other stretches of which can be detected round the other sides of the hill. In this lowest enclosure it is still possible to see the striking remains of numerous circular platforms upon which houses once stood, and several examples of the lowest courses of the stone walls of these.

The S. toe of the hill, including the S. part of the lowest enclosure, has been removed by a quarry which is now dead. While the ground was being cleared before the removal of the stone, middens were exposed and several relics of an Iron Age occupation were recovered.

Kaeheughs, Fort (NT 518763), 1½ miles N. of Haddington, Sheet 66 (A.1 and farm road).   *East Lothian.*

This fort, situated at the E. end of the Garleton Hills, ¼ mile W. of Barley Mains farmhouse, is bordered to the N. by a cliff which has been quarried so that the E. part of the fort is no longer in existence. The remainder consists of an enclosure, now 460 ft. in length by 230 ft. in width, formed by a substantial stony rampart which is covered by two others at wide intervals. The interior contains slight hollows which might represent stances for timber-framed houses.

The Chesters, Drem, Fort (NT 507782), 1 mile S. of Drem, Sheet 66 (B.1377 and by-road).   *East Lothian.*

This fort has long roused interest and speculation by the fact that, although on plan it would seem to belong among the larger and better preserved hill-forts in the country, it nevertheless stands on a very low ridge immediately under the lee of a precipitous scarp 50 ft. high from which even a most elementary missile could be directed into the interior.

32   *Traprain Law*, oppidum *of the Votadini. Digging on the slopes on the right produced relics indicating occupation extending for about 1000 years from the middle of the 1st millennium* B.C.

Apart from this anomaly, the fort represents a type of multivallate work, the innermost defended zone of which is bordered by a whole series of ramparts and ditches, and there is reason to believe that the existing visible remains may represent parts of more than one phase on construction. The innermost enclosure measures 380 ft. by 150 ft. within a ruinous rampart appearing for the most part as a mere scarp. This is surrounded by another rampart, and thereafter by traces of up to six others. The external measurement of the whole structure is 900 ft. by 500 ft.

The interior contains the surface traces of several circular stony foundations which vary in size. Certain of them overlie the ruined defences, an indication that they represent a period of occupation subsequent to the time when the ramparts were in use and probably dating from the 2nd or later centuries A.D.

Traprain Law, *Oppidum* Hill-fort (NT 581746), 2 miles SE. of East Linton, Sheet 67 (A.1 and by-road). *East Lothian.*

Traprain Law bulks "like a harpooned whale" on the East Lothian plain N. of the Lammermuir massif. It rises 500 ft. from the ground below, the N., E. and S. flanks falling steeply, but only the latter at all precipitously, the W. face sloping gently enough to have accommodated a great many timber-framed buildings. The sequence of prehistoric and proto-historic events that must have taken place on this conspicuous and majestic landmark was first revealed after a party of workmen had been employed to dig up a considerable area of the principal terrace on the W. slope, during the first quarter of the present century. The relics thus obtained included the spectacular hoard of Roman silver which has been published separately, together with a great mass of native material which indicates that the hill was in occupation for a period of about 1000 years, from the middle of the 1st millennium B.C.

During this time several sets of defensive works succeeded each other to enclose different amounts of the surface of the hill. No remains of the earliest are apparent, but it can be safely assumed that one or more palisaded enclosures were formed on the W. slope and on the summit before the first ramparts and walls appeared. The length of the occupation has had the effect of blurring and obscuring the earlier versions of these more substantial works, but it is possible to follow part of what may have been the first of them, a scarp strewn with occasional grass-covered stones and boulders which borders the summit area on the N. This would have enclosed an area of about 10 acres, comparable to the so-called minor *oppida* of Tweeddale, among them the earliest phase of the *oppidum* of the Selgovae on Eildon Hill North (q.v.). The next structural development, it is suggested, took in a further 10 acres of the gentle slope immediately N. of the enclosure just described. This can be traced by the rather tenuous ruins of a rampart bordering the true summit to the W. and NW., and by extensions of the same nature which run along the brink of the descent to the N.

The third major reconstruction is deemed to have taken in the terraces and slopes on the W. face of the hill, enlarging the enclosed area to 30 acres and so producing the second largest hill-fort or *oppidum* in Scotland—indeed in the whole of North Britain, except Stanwick, in the North Riding of Yorkshire. Yet another enlargement followed, in which the N. face of the hill was also incorporated, and the size of the *oppidum* reached 40 acres, comparable to the Eildon Hill *oppidum* at its largest.

The 40-acre capital of the Votadini must have been a veritable town, containing numerous inhabitants employed upon industries such as metal-working as well as on agriculture, stock-breeding, and trading with the south, probably by way of the east coast sea route. It has been inferred that the Votadini were in treaty with the Romans, for as far as can be seen at the present time, the successive later reconstructions took place after Pictish, rather than Roman, destructive expeditions. The 40-acre wall or rampart may have been built in the 1st century A.D., shortly before the local arrival of the Romans in the 80s; and it may have been reconstructed at least twice, after such events as the Pictish raids of 197 and 297.

The final form of the *oppidum* is represented by the most impressive remains on the hill today. A stone-faced, turf-cored wall, 3500 ft. in length and 12 ft. in thickness, was laid out to relinquish the N. face of the hill and so to reduce the area enclosed to 30 acres again. As this wall overlies almost all the other

ramparts at one place or another it is naturally the first object to strike the eye of the visitor, and parts of it are in a good enough state of preservation to reward examination.

It has been suggested that the town defended by the last wall began in locally sub-Roman times, in the last half of the 4th century A.D., and that it lasted perhaps until the Saxons came.

The long and virtually continuous occupation of the *oppidum* on Traprain Law, its degree of sophistication when compared to the bucolic settlements all round about, and its more than local standing, make it by far the most important place in the late prehistory and early proto-history of Scotland, and of a wider area including north-eastern England; while, by reason of the supposed accommodation the Votadini had made with the Romans, it has a unique place as a "free" British town in Roman times. The only *oppidum* of comparable size, that on Eildon Hill North, appears to have been deserted during the period of the Roman occupation, and never to have been used again; and the same probably applies to all the few other *oppida* which have been recorded in the north. There can be no doubt that here, if nowhere else in North Britain, excavations on a generous scale carried out over a considerable period would be vastly rewarding, with reference to a thousand most interesting and formative years.

Blackcastle Hill, Fort (NT 712718), 1½ miles SSW. of Innerwick, Sheet 67 (by-road). *East Lothian.*

Unfinished forts occur rather rarely from place to place all over the country. In many cases their nature is perfectly clear, but in others the work of construction has gone so far that it is difficult to be sure that missing stretches of ramparts and ditches or walls have not been obliterated by later circumstances rather than never completed. In this example, however, the case is quite clear. The inner element consists of a stony rampart enclosing an area measuring 170 ft. by 150 ft. This contains two circular stony foundations which are referred to below; slight quarries along the inner foot of the rampart; and an arc 50 ft. in length of a ditch 12 ft. wide and 1 ft. deep which lies 20 ft. in from the rampart.

At a distance of 22 ft. outside the rampart four short stretches of an outer rampart and ditch have been begun. They vary in length from 17 ft. to 50 ft. It is clear that they represent an unfinished scheme directed towards strengthening the original rather small defended area. The arc of ditch in the interior is not so easy to account for, and only excavation could show whether it was anything more than what it appears.

The stone foundations of circular buildings most probably belong to a period long after the attempt at reinforcing the original enclosure had been abandoned, as the latter is most likely to have taken place during Early Iron Age times, while the foundations are unlikely to belong to any period earlier than the 2nd century A.D., and may be considerably later.

Kidlaw, Fort (NT 512642), 2¾ miles SW. of Gifford, Sheet 66 (by-roads).
East Lothian.

The remains of this splendid circular fort, situated on a spur 300 yds. E. of the farmhouse, reveal inconsistencies indicating that most of what now appears represents a reconstruction. The fort measures about 370 ft. in diameter within three ramparts with external ditches. The inconsistency appears in the SE., where a disused and almost obliterated stretch of an older rampart lies between the innermost and the second of the existing fort. Entrances break the W. and E. arcs of all the ramparts.

Homesteads probably of the Roman period or later occupy parts of the interior.

Stobshiel, Fort (NT 497638), 3½ miles SW. of Gifford, Sheet 66 (B.6355 and by-roads). *East Lothian.*

This promontory fort is couched in an angle of the Birns Water on a small plateau isolated by the burn on the E. and N. and by a steep-sided natural gully on the SW. The interior is triangular, measuring axially 250 ft. by 190 ft. within a stony rampart with an entrance in the NW. and a possible second one in the NE. An outer rampart, lying some 50 ft. outside the inner one, has an external ditch the S. arc of which is 30 ft. wide. At this point, too, the outer rampart is 30 ft. thick, and 15 ft. high. The uneven interior contains no recognisable traces of dwellings.

Witches Knowe, Fort (NT 519635), 3 miles SSW. of Gifford, Sheet 66 (by-roads). *East Lothian.*

This fort occupies a knoll separated from the Lammermuir Hill massif to the S. by a narrow and steep-sided gully like a marginal meltwater channel. It measures 340 ft. by 130 ft. within the remains of three ramparts. The innermost is a wall 12 ft. thick, the outer pair ramparts with external ditches. The interior is covered with heather and nothing can be seen in it. There are two entrances, in the SE. and SW., at each of which the median rampart is produced to form a baffle.

The Castles, Dumbadam Burn, Fort (NT 531642), 2½ miles S. of Gifford, Sheet 66 (by-roads). *East Lothian.*

The remains of this multivallate semi-promontory fort occupy an eminence embraced by a curve of the Dumbadam Burn. The fort is oval, measuring 300 ft. by 150 ft. within a denuded rampart which is accompanied where the ground is level by an external ditch and by scarps where these already exist. There is an entrance at each end. Another major line of defence follows the inner one at a distance of up to 100 ft. outside it, and this in turn is covered to the W. by a third bank and to the N. by a fourth which sweeps round W. to cover the third as well. The interior, which contains no surface remains, has been ploughed. The nature of several contiguous depressions which occur in the space between the SW. arcs of the third and fourth ramparts is obscure.

Harelaw, Fort (NT 546632), 3 miles S. by E. of Gifford, Sheet 66 (by-road and moorland). *East Lothian.*

This substantial fort occupies the rocky summit of a spur running NE. off the main massif of the Lammermuir Hills between two burns. The ground falls steeply at the N. of the site, which is at an elevation of 1250 ft. O.D., giving extensive views over the East Lothian plain. The summit area is bordered by the massive ruins of a timber-laced stone wall about 12 ft. thick, which has been severely mutilated in the N. by stone-robbing perpetrated to provide stones for the modern wall, some 4 ft. thick at the base, which misleadingly encircles the summit. It is probable that the interior originally measured about 200 ft. by 100 ft. in extent. The remains of outworks survive on the NW. and SE. and especially on the SW., where the only easy approach to the fort can be made. Here two ramparts with external ditches cut off all access, and allow only a narrow pathway to extend from the hillside to the entrance of the fort, on the W.

Park Burn, Fort (NT 571652), 2¾ miles SE. of Gifford, Sheet 67 (B.6355 and by-road). *East Lothian.*

The remains of this fort, though damaged by the action of the plough, are quite well preserved in places. They consist of three ramparts with external ditches which defend an area measuring 190 ft. by 160 ft. The innermost rampart is spread to a greatest width of 20 ft., but hardly stands to more than 1 ft. in height. This can be traced all round the enclosure, but the others only appear on the vulnerable SW. side, where the outermost, for some reason the best preserved, stands to a height of 6 ft. above the ground inside it and to 10 ft. above the exterior. This rampart exhibits traces of a line of walling along its crest which is a characteristic of several forts in the south-eastern area.

Black Castle, Fort (NT 580662), 3 miles SE. of Gifford, Sheet 67 (B.6355). *East Lothian.*

This fort is almost circular, measuring about 380 ft. by 340 ft. within two ramparts with a median ditch. The inner rampart is imposing, spread to a thickness of 20 ft. and standing to as much as 10 ft. above the bottom of the ditch. It is topped with the remains of what may be a contemporary wall, as at other monuments in the district. The outer rampart is slighter than the inner. Entrances in the W. and S. arcs are clearly marked by causeways in the ditch, even if tumbled stones may appear to block them.

Green Castle, Fort (NT 582657), 3¼ miles SE. of Gifford, Sheet 67 (B.6355). *East Lothian.*

This triangular fort rests on the steep right bank of the Newlands Burn and is protected a short distance away to the N. by a minor watercourse. It consists of an enclosure measuring axially 225 ft. by 190 ft. within a rampart which borders a natural plateau and so has a steep outer scarp. Another rampart of a less substantial nature provides further cover outside this. The entrance is in the W. apex, and apart from a hollow inside

this the interior is featureless. Despite its rather unusual situation, there is no reason to suspect that this is not a fort or settlement of the pre-Roman Iron Age.

White Castle, Fort (NT 613686), 2 miles SE. of Garvald, Sheet 67 (by-road). *East Lothian.*

This fort occupies a steep-flanked promontory beside the by-road which joins Garvald to the B.6355 road by way of the upper reaches of the valley of the Whiteadder Water. It occupies a promontory which is easily approachable only from the S. The interior of the fort is oval, measuring 230 ft. by 180 ft. within three lines of defence, the innermost of which is a rampart now represented for the most part by a mere scarp—which does, however, rise to as much as 8 ft. in height in the E. This rampart appears to have no ditch. The median rampart lies up to 50 ft. outside the innermost, and the outermost another 30 ft. beyond this. There are indications here, as at neighbouring and comparable forts, that the ramparts were topped with a stone wall or parapet.

Friar's Nose, Fort (NT 664632), 8¼ miles ESE. of Gifford, Sheet 67 (A.6355). *East Lothian.*

The well-preserved remains of this multivallate fort lie on a promontory between the Whiteadder Water and the Killmade Burn, which forms part of the boundary between East Lothian and Berwickshire. On the W., where four ramparts survive, the innermost and the third are the most substantial, while on the NW. the lines of the ramparts are somewhat confused. It seems certain that the existing remains represent works of two different periods, the later of the two amounting to a complete reform and probably doubling of the earlier defences. Two stony rings at the foot of the innermost rampart near the principal entrance, in the NW., probably represent dwellings erected during a reoccupation of the site in Roman or post-Roman times.

Garvald Mains, Fort (NT 583698), ¾ mile S. of Garvald, Sheet 67 (by-road). *East Lothian.*

This fort lies on a small flat, broad plateau near the right bank of the Papana Water, protected to S. and W. by steep slopes. It is almost circular on plan, measuring 280 ft. by 240 ft. within a broad heavy rampart which is crowned by the ruin of a thick stone wall. The entrance, in the SE., leads in to a grassy space in which there are no visible surface remains.

The Hopes, Fort (NT 570636), 3½ miles SE. of Garvald, Sheet 67 (by-roads, farm road and footpath). *East Lothian.*

The remains of this large and complex monument occupy the termination of a ridge and are thus raised up above the neighbouring ground except to the W. They probably represent works of at least two phases of construction, but interpretation is not now easy. Starting outside from the NW., the first obstacles encountered are two long but unfinished ramparts with external ditches. They rest at either end on the steep E., S. and SW. flank of the ridge, and form an arc 1000 ft. in length with a gap in the middle. At the NE. they are prevented from reaching the actual brink of the natural descent by a bank and ditch which border this. This feature continues NE. along the crest of the descent for a distance of 200 ft., whereupon it joins with another exactly similar work which runs off to N. and S. for some distance before dying out. This system of outer ditches probably represents an unconventional version of the defensive cross-dyke seen at several forts in Tweeddale and elsewhere.

Inside the two unfinished arcs of rampart and ditch, at distances of between 60 ft. and 140 ft. from them, another similar stretch of low rampart and ditch runs N. from the natural declivity for 300 ft., to stop at one side of an entrance. And although another apparently similar defence resumes on the opposite side of the gap, it does not run quite on the line of the section just described. It belongs to a set of three ramparts which are not otherwise accompanied by a ditch and which form a trivallate enclosure about 350 ft. by 250 ft. in extent. The question arises whether the last-named enclosed area represents an original work to which a beginning had been made to add the outer ones, or whether it was a secondary work begun after the incompleted ramparts and ditches had been abandoned. No clue to the matter of the sequence is provided either by the juxtaposition of the various remains or by their surface appearance.

The Chesters, Fort (NT 660739), 2½ miles E. of Stenton, Sheet 67 (B.6370 and by-roads). *East Lothian.*

This large example of the circular bivallate fort has been robbed of any stonework that may ever have existed and been under the plough, but the remains are still impressive. It measures about 350 ft. in diameter within two massive ramparts with external ditches. The inner rampart is now spread to a width of as much as 60 ft. but is still 7 ft. high, while the outer is 45 ft. wide and 5 ft. high. The original entrance is in the ESE., and another in the W. may also be authentic.

An Sgurr, Fort (NM 462846), 1½ miles W. by N. of Galmisdale, Sheet 39 (moorland). *Eigg.*

This fort occupies the summit of a sheer-sided table of pitchstone which rises 400 ft. above its base on all sides except the W. Here, where approach is possible up a steep and rocky ascent, it has been barred by a wall 10 ft. thick and 250 ft. long which connects the brinks of the N. and S. precipices. The resulting enclosure measures about 1320 ft. in length and about 300 ft. in width, an area of more than 9 acres.

Craigluscar Hill, Fort (NT 060910), 2¾ miles NW. of Dunfermline, Sheet 58 (A.907 and by-road). *Fife.*

The remains of this interesting fort were excavated to some extent in 1944 and 1945. The innermost of the three lines of defence was found to be a stone-faced, rubble-cored wall 12 ft. thick. The median rampart consisted of two parallel double rows of large laid stones separated by a space 3 ft. wide filled with clean loam, and was considered to have been a twin palisade. The outer rampart, placed only on the N. flank of the fort where approach is the easiest, was a decayed version of the innermost. The entrance in the inner rampart, 9 ft. in width, was narrowed to 6 ft. by a setting of four posts which must have held the gate structure, while that in the outer (median) rampart was closed from inside by a gate supported on two posts. The fort, which measures 175 ft. by 110 ft. in extent, was considered to be of pre-Roman date.

Dunearn Hill, Fort (NT 211872), 1¼ mile NW. of Burntisland, Sheet 58 (A.909). *Fife.*

The remains of this fort occupy the summit of Dunearn Hill which dominates the pass into the hinterland of Fife from the N. shore of the Firth of Forth at Burntisland. It commands broad views S. over the Forth, and itself forms a conspicuous feature of the northward view from Hanover Street, in Edinburgh. The remains represent structures of two periods. The earlier is a fort measuring about 400 ft. by 130 ft. within the ruin of a heavy stone wall. The entrance, in the E., is protected by a long hornwork of slighter but still very stout proportions. The second period is represented by an almost circular enclosure measuring 120 ft. in diameter within a wall about 12 ft. thick. The similarity of the structure of the fort to others in the neighbourhood such as Cockleroy is striking; and the circular enclosure is demonstrably secondary to it because parts of the wall of the former overlie the ruin of the latter.

East Lomond, Fort (NO 244062), 1 mile SW. of Falkland, Sheet 59 (A.912 and farm road). *Fife.*

Although situated at the little more than average height of 1394 ft. above sea level, this fort is conspicuous because of the isolation of the steep summit upon which it stands, and can be seen from great distances S. of the Firth of Forth as well as N. of the Tay estuary. The remains may represent those of two structural periods, but the actual summit area is so small that they may as well all belong together. The interior measures 200 ft. by 100 ft. within a ruined wall. Several other ramparts are represented by both long and short stretches on the slopes below this, while to the S., on the only easy line of approach, a final heavy bank and ditch afford a serious obstacle.

Although it appears to be of standard Early Iron Age construction, the fort contained evidence that it was occupied to some extent at a very much later date than this. Hollow glass beads and a mould for casting ingots have been picked up among the debris of the wall, and a slab with an incised bull (see under Pictish Symbol Stones) was found within the fort in 1920.

Greencraig, Fort (NO 323215), 5¼ miles NNW. of Cupar, Sheet 59 (A.913, A.914 and by-road). *Fife.*

The remains of this fort bear a certain resemblance to their neighbour on Norman's Law, 1½ miles to the SW. They are more decayed, however, and can only be followed with some difficulty. The fort is formed by two stony ramparts or walls which enclose an irregular oval measuring about 600 ft. by 330 ft. A secondary structure crowning the summit of the hill consists of an oval enclosure 100 ft. long by 85 ft. wide within a ruined stone wall. This now appears to be only about 6 ft. thick, and at that is hardly comparable to the otherwise similar works at such places as Norman's Law.

Norman's Law, Fort (NO 305203), 5¼ miles NNW. of Cupar, Sheet 59 (A.913 and farm road). *Fife.*

Norman's Law, the highest summit of the E. tail of the Ochil range, commands magnificent views of the Firth of Tay and the Howe of Fife. The fort which crowns its summit is of great interest, revealing as it does a sequence of differing structures, some of them well preserved. One of these is a heavy stone wall which includes all the rather uneven summit of the hill, measuring about 700 ft. by 250 ft. in extent. Another is a wall which takes in all the south-west foot of the hill to enclose an area which, including the one already described, measures 1000 ft. from NE. to SW. by 550 ft. transversely. The question here is, which came first; is the summit fort the earlier, and the SW. annexe a later addition, or is the latter in fact an original unitary structure and the summit fort a later work? The contours of the hill do suggest that the former alternative may be the more likely, but at present there is no real evidence either way.

There need be no doubt, however, about the latest important structure on the hill. This is an oval enclosure measuring 170 ft. by 100 ft. within a wall 12 ft. thick. Here again is one of the structures which occur so widely throughout southern and central Scotland, which may be of post-Roman date. A rash of circular stony foundations which occurs both within and upon the ruined ramparts of the fort may, on analogy with others elsewhere, belong to the Roman Iron Age, representing the change from fortified to open settlements.

Denork, Fort (NO 455137), 3¼ miles WSW. of St Andrews, Sheet 59 (by-road). *Fife.*

This stone fort is situated close to Denork house and within ½ mile of the broch at Drumcarrow. It consists of a stone wall about 12 ft. thick which encloses an area measuring 450 ft. in length by 150 ft. in width. It has been built on the very brink of the precipitous flanks of a low knoll, so that the lowest courses of the outer face are very often some feet down this. It falls naturally into the class of such large stone forts which is spread over Fife and West Lothian. At one time it was considered to be of post-Roman date, but there is now better reason to suppose that it is pre-Roman.

Clatchard Craig, Fort (NO 244178), ½ mile SE. of Newburgh, Sheet 59 (A.913 and quarry road).   *Fife.*

Clatchard Craig rises from the NE. foot of Ormiston Hill to a height of 300 ft. O.D., commanding a pass through the Ochils from the S. to the S. shore of the Tay estuary. The fort is large and well defended, the existing remains representing at least three main structural phases. The latest of these, a subrectangular enclosure measuring 230 ft. in length by perhaps half as much in width, has now been almost entirely blasted away by the quarry which is consuming the hill from the NE. It was recently partially excavated, and it is understood that relics of Early Christian date were recovered from within it.

This enclosure stands within another, oval in form, which measures 330 ft. by something over 200 ft. in extent, and is formed by a heavy rampart. Outside this again there is a series of four ramparts, with several minor additions and supplementary features. The innermost of the four ramparts may have been a timber-laced structure, as what have been described as deposits of charred wood are recorded as having been found among its debris.

While the smallest enclosure, on the summit, is undoubtedly the latest structure to have been built on the hill, and may well date from the period of the relics found within it, the order in which the other two phases were constructed has not been established. The likelihood is, however, that the rampart forming the enclosure measuring 330 ft. in length was later reinforced by the multiple outworks, all this in pre-Roman times.

Black Cairn Hill, Fort (NO 234172), ¾ mile S. of Newburgh, Sheet 58 (farm road and moorland).   *Fife.*

The simple and denuded remains of this fort consist of a ruined stone wall, originally about 10 ft. thick, which encloses the oval top of the hill that measures 400 ft. in length by 320 ft. in width. The site is free of all near rivals and commands extensive views in all directions. The fort corresponds to several other such structures in the district, and is presumably of Early Iron Age date.

Craig Phadrig, Fort (NH 640453), 1½ miles W. of Inverness, Sheet 26 (A.9 and by-road).   *Inverness-shire.*

This famous fort forms a flat crown to the afforested hill which overlooks the narrows at the E. end of the Beauly Firth from the SW. It consists of an inner, heavily vitrified wall spread to a thickness of about 30 ft. which encloses an area measuring 245 ft. in length by 75 ft. in width. An outer wall, also heavily vitrified, lies at distances varying between 45 ft. and 75 ft. outside this.

Excavations in 1971-72 disclosed that the two ramparts date from about 500 B.C., but also brought to light a hanging bowl of about the 7th century A.D.

Cabrich, Fort (NH 534428), 9¼ miles W. of Inverness, Sheet 26 (A.9, by-road and footpath).   *Inverness-shire.*

The remains of this fort occupy a rocky table which rises from the scrub and mangled conifers on the serrated NE. flank of Phoineas Hill. The highest part of the site, measuring 185 ft. by 125 ft., is bordered by the ruin of a wall among which vitrified masses can be seen. To the NE. of this enclosure the surface of the table extends for a distance of 440 ft. with an average width of 130 ft.; it is bordered by the remains of a wall. At a point 100 ft. NE. of the upper enclosure the table is crossed from NW. to SE. by a pair of feeble stony mounds with a quarry ditch between them.

Ashie Moor, Fort (NH 600316), 9¼ miles SSW. of Inverness, Sheet 26 (A.862).   *Inverness-shire.*

This fort occupies a low rock outcrop on the generally barren expanse of Ashie Moor. It is oval on plan, measuring 125 ft. by 110 ft. within a ruined stone wall originally some 10 ft. thick. An outer wall runs at varying distances from this to enclose it in an area measuring 300 ft. by 150 ft. in extent. Both walls have entrances in the SW.

Strone Point, Fort (NH 530286), 1½ miles ESE. of Drumnadrochit, Sheet 26 (A.82 and footpath). *Inverness-shire.*

Strone Point is occupied by the ruins of mediaeval Urquhart Castle which lie on the very head of the land beyond a moat contemporary with them. Among the ruins, to the S. of the best preserved block, vitrified material protrudes through the turf on the flanks of a rocky boss. This has formed part of one of the small stone-walled forts characteristic of Loch Ness district; and part of the upper stone of a rotary quern which lies in the castle gatehouse might possibly belong to the occupation of the fort rather than to that of the castle.

Dun Scriben, Fort (NH 491235), 4 miles S. by W. of Drumnadrochit, Sheet 26 (A.82 and farm road). *Inverness-shire.*

This small fort stands on the brink of the steep hillside which borders the central part of Loch Ness on the W. It consists of a ruinous wall enclosing a roughly subrectangular area measuring about 60 ft. in either direction.

Inverfarigaig, Fort (NH 526238), 8 miles SSW. of Dores, Sheet 26 (A.862 and by-road). *Inverness-shire.*

This fort occupies one of the most spectacular situations possible on the top of a rock which stands up like a tooth above the mouth of the River Farigaig and commands long vistas over the waters of Loch Ness and northwards into Ross and Cromarty. The site is best observed from the by-road which branches SW. off the A.862 road 4½ miles SSW. of Dores (Sheet 28) to pass Bochruben and Ballaggan on its way to Inverfarigaig village, rather than from the shore road. The fort itself must also be approached from this road, through Dirichurachan.

The remains consist of a ruinous wall spread to a thickness of about 15 ft. which enclose the high NE. part of the summit area. The interior measures 80 ft. by 43 ft.; a depression near the W. apex may have served as a well. Several patches of vitrifaction can be seen among the debris of the wall.

Glen Nevis, Fort (NN 126702), 3¾ miles SE. of Fort William, Sheet 41 (by-road). *Inverness-shire.*

This vitrified fort named Dun Dear-dail stands at a height of 1127 ft. above sea level on the brink of the steep W. side of Glen Nevis at a point 2½ miles W. of the summit of Ben Nevis. It can be reached perfectly well from the road at the bottom of the glen by way of a slope which rises 1100 ft. in 800 yds., but it is more easily approached from the opposite side over a gradual ascent from Blarmachfoldach, 700 ft. lower down.

The fort measures 150 ft. by 90 ft. within a massive vitrified ruin some 50 ft. thick in places. The entrance is in the NW. The interior, which slopes down from the NE., contains a cross-wall which is probably later than the fort. Traces of outer defences which may, however, be contemporary with it can be seen to the W. and S. on the rocky slopes outside the fort.

Arisaig, Fort (NM 693839), 2½ miles ESE. of Arisaig, Sheet 40 (A.830 and footpath). *Inverness-shire.*

This fort has suffered more than most from an extraordinary nomenclature, including Arka Unskel, Ard Ghaunsgoik and Ard Ghamhgail. The last version of these three now appears on the O.S. map. It stands on a promontory on the N. side of Loch nan Uamh, and is divided by a natural depression. The part to landward measures about 50 ft. in either direction within a heavily vitrified wall, the outer part only about 24 ft.

Eilean nan Gobhar, Fort (NM 694794), 4¾ miles SE. of Arisaig, Sheet 40 (boat from Inverailort). *Inverness-shire*

This fort is situated on a small but high rocky island in the mouth of Loch Ailort. It is in two parts, the one measuring internally 175 ft. by 70 ft. and the other 75 ft. by 25 ft., both within walls showing considerable vitrifaction.

Am Baghan Burblach, Fort (NG 832199), 1 mile ENE. of Glenelg, Sheet 33 (by-roads and moorland). *Inverness-shire.*

The remains of this fort lie a short distance above the road on the N. side of Glen More. They consist of a wall 11 ft. thick forming an enclosure measuring 170 ft. by 100 ft. with an entrance at either end. The interior contains a circular enclosure 40 ft. in diameter, a ruined cottage and other foundations, all of which are probably of comparatively recent date.

Dun Chliabhain, Fort (NH 476460), 3 miles W. of Beauly, Sheet 26 (A.9, A.831, by-road and moorland). *Inverness-shire.*

This fort, lying in the felled part of Farley Wood, occupies a steep-sided rocky boss typical as the site of a fort in this district. It measures 77 ft. by 48 ft. within a stone wall up to 12 ft. thick, with an entrance in the E. An outer wall covers this in the NE.

Tighnaleac, Fort (NH 457452), 4¼ miles W. by S. of Beauly, Sheet 26 (A.9, A.831, farm road and moorland).

Inverness-shire.

This is one of a group of forts situated on the hills overlooking the lower reaches of the River Beauly from the W. It stands on a crag the N. and W. flanks of which are precipitous while the others slope more gently down to marshy ground. It is oval on plan, measuring 70 ft. by 63 ft. within a ruined stone wall originally between 15 ft. and 18 ft. thick, with an entrance in the SE. An outer wall 15 ft. thick covers approach from the S. and E.

Avielochan, Fort (NH 905171), 2½ miles N. of Aviemore, Sheet 36 (A.9 and quarry road). *Inverness-shire.*

This once strong stone-walled fort occupies a rocky promontory on the W. side of Strathspey above Loch Vaa. The E. part of the rock is being quarried, and its surface is clothed with a virtually impenetrable juniper jungle; but it is nevertheless a place of great interest and a certain wild beauty. The approach from the foot of Beinn Ghuilbin takes the form of a narrow neck which is traversed by a high fence for restricting the movements of deer; immediately beyond this the first of a series of ruinous walls formed of massive boulders is encountered. The next line of defence is a wall, now mostly represented by a terrace, which girdles the promontory at a level of some 20 ft. below the summit level; and the last line to be encountered is a ruinous wall enclosing an area of juniper-choked summit which measures about 220 ft. in length by 80 ft. in width.

Laggan, Fort (NN 582930), 6 miles NNW. of Dalwhinnie, Sheet 35 (A.889, A.86 and woodland footpaths).

Inverness-shire.

The uppermost fort in Strathspey occupies a superb situation on the nose of a long promontory ridge which divides the main valley from Strathmashie. The flanks of the promontory fall steeply from the summit (1484 ft. O.D.) to the

flood-plain 600 ft. below, and approach is only reasonably easy along the spine from the SW. The fort conforms in shape to the crag, measuring 460 ft. by 260 ft. within a wall which, as it hugs the uneven contours of the outcrops, varies in width from 13 ft. to 23 ft. In places the faces are exposed to a height of as much as 9 ft., revealing that the wall is built of great numbers of rather small coursed stones.

Cairnton, Fort (NO 633723), 1¼ miles SW. of Fettercairn, Sheet 45 (B.966).

Kincardineshire.

This vitrified fort, sometimes called Green Cairn and sometimes Finella's Castle, occupies a broad shelf with no particular defensive qualities near Balbegno, whence it overlooks from the N. the N. part of Strathmore and the floodplain of the River North Esk. It lies close to the S. side of the road and has been under the plough, so that all that now remains is a stony mound representing part of the rampart or wall. Vitrified masses can be seen among the debris and dragged into the interior by cultivation. The fort may have measured about 150 ft. by 50 ft. internally.

Benarty, Fort (NT 154979), 3½ miles SE. of Kinross, Sheet 58 (A.90, by-road and moorland). *Kinross.*

Benarty rises steeply, precipitously in places, to a height of more than 1000 ft. from the S. flood-plain of Loch Leven, and the opposite side of the hill rises by no means gently. Its rocky and irregular summit is bordered on the N. by cliffs, so that a fort shaped like a distorted D on plan has been formed by appending an arc of walling to a section of these. The walling is 450 yds. long, and encloses about 5 acres. Its remains are rather scanty, but they include several stretches of gargantuan stonework, including boulders up to 9 ft. in length.

Dummiefarline, Fort (NT 088968), 1 mile S. by W. of Cleish, Sheet 58 (farm road and moorland). *Kinross.*

This fort occupies a rocky eminence on the Cleish Hills 1 mile E. of Dumglow and 300 ft. lower down. It is formed by a stone wall 10 ft. thick and now no longer traceable throughout the whole of its length. It encloses an area measuring about 210 ft. in length by 70 ft. in maximum breadth. The interior contains an arc of walling which may belong to a secondary structure such, for example, as that at Dunearn Hill. Traces of vitrified material have been reported from this piece of walling.

Dumglow, Fort (NO 076965), 1½ miles SW. of Cleish, Sheet 58 (farm road and moorland). *Kinross.*

This fort occupies an upland promontory which forms the apex of the little Cleish Hills range. The hilltop is bordered to N., W. and S. by steep cliffs, and it is only against approach from the E. that defences have been drawn. These and the cliff-tops contain an area measuring 500 ft. by 400 ft. The defences consist of four low stony ramparts placed only 12 ft. apart which are pierced by an entrance near each end.

The Moyle, Fort (NX 848575), 2¼ miles SSE. of Dalbeattie, Sheet 84 (A.710 and forest track). *Stewartry of Kirkcudbright.*

This fort consists of an enclosure measuring axially 930 ft. by 500 ft. within the massive ruin of a stone wall about 10 ft. thick, and is thus the largest in Galloway. A small enclosure measuring 120 ft. by 90 ft., defined for the most part by a scarp representing a denuded rampart, lies within the fort, and it is reasonably certain that the S. arc of the wall of the latter overlies it. In recent years this has had the distinction of being the only hill-fort in Scotland on the telephone, as a result of the establishment within it of a forestry look-out tower.

Mark Moat, Fort (NX 815540), ¼ mile NW. of Rockliffe, Sheet 84 (footpath). *Stewartry of Kirkcudbright.*

Although now in a very denuded state, this fort is interesting both for having been found to be formed by a vitrified timber-laced rampart and on account of the relics recovered from it. It consists of an enclosure which occupies the summit of a conspicuous eminence on the NE. side of Rough Firth, and which measures 270 ft. in length by from 105 ft. to 55 ft. in width. Relics found in the fort during an excavation in 1913 include a sherd of *terra sigillata* and a fragment of a *mortarium* which suggest that the earliest occupation was carried on into the Roman period; and a great mass of moulds for brooches and other articles of early mediaeval date.

Barcloy, Fort (NX 854524), 1 mile SSE. of Rockliffe, Sheet 84 (footpath). *Stewartry of Kirkcudbright.*

This fort occupies a bold promontory on the E. side of the mouth of the Urr Water. It consists of an oval enclosure measuring axially 140 ft. by 95 ft. within the substantial ruin of a stone wall about 10 ft. thick, faced with large squared blocks laid in courses. This is defended from approach from the landward side by a broad and necessarily rock-cut ditch with a rampart on the outer lip. Pottery of early mediaeval date now in Dumfries Burgh Museum has been found in the fort.

Castlegower, Fort (NX 792589), 2¾ miles SE. of Castle Douglas, Sheet 84 (B.736, B.727, farm road and pasture land). *Stewartry of Kirkcudbright.*

This fort, occupying a rocky eminence about 80 ft. high in broken country, consists of an oval enclosure measuring axially 125 ft. by 50 ft. within a ruinous wall in the debris of which masses of vitrifaction occur. Several outworks far down the flanks of the knoll cover the principal enclosure. The work belongs to the class exemplified by Trusty's Hill.

Dunguile, Fort (NX 773572), 3¼ miles S. by E. of Castle Douglas, Sheet 84 (B.736, B.727, by-road and hill). *Stewartry of Kirkcudbright.*

This fort occupies the summit of a hill 1 mile S. of Gelston. It measures 590 ft. in length by 510 ft. in width within three widely spaced and now very ruinous walls. Most of the interior has been under cultivation, but the few depressions still visible indicate that it was once appointed with timber-framed houses.

Little Merkland, Settlement (NX 689738), 2½ miles N. of Parton, Sheet 84 (by-road and farm road). *Stewartry of Kirkcudbright.*

This earthwork may provisionally be considered as an Early Iron Age settlement on the analogy of similar structures farther E. It consists of two low ramparts with a broad median ditch which enclose an oval area measuring axially about 100 ft. by 60 ft. No surface traces of any kind are visible on the surface within the enclosure.

Drummore, Fort (NX 687456), 3¼ miles S. of Kirkcudbright, Sheet 84 (A.711, by-road and hill). *Stewartry of Kirkcudbright.*

This fort, occupying a conspicuous hill on the E. of Kirkcudbright Bay, is oval on plan, measuring 210 ft. in length by 160 ft. in width within a stony rampart or wall which has a hornwork covering the entrance, in the NE. This is surrounded by two other ramparts with a median ditch, which may be strictly contemporary with it or, perhaps more likely, modifications designed to add strength.

Dungarry, Fort (NX 757536), 5 miles NE. of Kirkcudbright, Sheet 84 (B.727, farm road and moorland).
Stewartry of Kirkcudbright.

Dungarry fort consists principally of two stone walls enclosing the summit area of a rocky eminence measuring 210 ft. by 125 ft. in extent. The inner wall probably measures 12 ft. in thickness, the outer about 6 ft. The entrance, in the E., is covered by a hornwork, while an annexe encloses a shelf to the NE.

A fort which may be compared, if not equated, with this one stands 1¼ miles S. by E. of it on Suie Hill (NX 765508).

Suie Hill, Fort (NX 765508), 2 miles W. by S. of Auchencairn, Sheet 84 (by-roads and moorland).
Stewartry of Kirkcudbright.

See **Dungarry** fort.

Kirkcarswell, Fort (NX 752497), 1¼ miles N. of Dundrennan, Sheet 84 (by-road and moorland).
Stewartry of Kirkcudbright.

This fort, representative of several in the district but in a better state of preservation than many, consists of an area 220 ft. long by 80 ft. wide defended by two concentric ramparts with a median rock-cut ditch. The S. end is further defended by outworks. The entrance is in the W.

Twynholm, Fort (NX 658539), ½ mile SW. of Twynholm, Sheet 84 (by-road).
Stewartry of Kirkcudbright.

This fort, which has been called Campbeltown Mote, occupies a low rocky eminence the summit of which, measuring about 90 ft. in length by 50 ft. in width, has been fortified by a wall. Further defences are provided by outworks lower down the flanks of the knoll, especially at the N. and S. ends where approach is easiest. The fort belongs to the class typified by the famous example on Trusty's Hill.

Edgarton, Fort (NX 673630), 1¼ miles SSW. of Laurieston, Sheet 84 (A.762 and farm road). *Stewartry of Kirkcudbright.*

This fort occupies the summit and flanks of a prominent knoll. The summit, measuring about 75 ft. in length and 45 ft. in width, has been defended by a now much mutilated wall among the debris of which vitrifaction has been found. Outside this, several outer works comprising banks and ditches add to the defensive strength of the fort and complete the strong resemblance, both in structure and situation, to Trusty's Hill.

Barstobric Hill, Fort (NX 687607), 6 miles N. of Kirkcudbright, Sheet 84 (A.711, A.762, farm road and hill).
Stewartry of Kirkcudbright.

This fort crowns a conspicuous rocky hill, also known as Queen's Hill, which commands the countryside all round to such an extent that it was chosen as the site for a pyramid 35 ft. high commemorating a former proprietor, James Beaumont Neilson, inventor of the hot-blast. The fort in which this monument stands is formed by a now ruinous wall, originally some 10 ft. thick, which encloses an area measuring 850 ft. in length from N. to S. by 375 ft. transversely, and thus recalls The Moyle, distant 10 miles to the ESE.

Barnheugh, Fort (NX 599475), 2 miles WSW. of Borgue, Sheet 83 (by-road and pasture land). *Stewartry of Kirkcudbright.*

This fort occupies an eminence overlooking Wigtown Bay from the E. The principal enclosure, somewhere between oval and subrectangular in shape, measures about 120 ft. by 75 ft. within a ruinous wall, and the remains of dual outworks cover it at either end. A locally unusual feature is the presence of three circular stony foundations, two within the main enclosure and one between this and the outworks. The resemblance of the plan to that of Trusty's Hill is striking.

Borness Batteries, Fort (NX 619446), 2¼ miles S. by W. of Borgue, Sheet 83 (by-road and farm land).
Stewartry of Kirkcudbright.

A great many of the promontories round the coasts of Galloway have been defended by walls or earthworks on the landward side, their steep seaward flanks affording sufficient protection against approach from other directions. The erosion of the cliffs has often resulted in the interiors of such forts appearing today in the most bizarre and attenuated shapes, and it is often quite impossible to judge how much ground was originally enclosed. The period when these forts were constructed is likewise often a matter of speculation, and there is no doubt that some were reoccupied. In the Isle of Man similar works have been found to contain rectangular houses of early mediaeval date, attributable to the Vikings, while others there, in Galloway and in Ulster contain visible remains of later mediaeval structures. Nevertheless it can be assumed that some if not all these promontory forts originated in the Early Iron Age, and a selected few are accordingly described in this *Guide*.

Borness Batteries is typical of many, the area enclosed by the cliffs and by the ramparts being kite-shaped on plan with maximum measurements of about 190 ft. in length and 160 ft. in width. The landward defences comprise two ramparts with external ditches and a third, lesser, rampart on the outer lip of the outer ditch.

Trusty's Hill, Fort (NX 588561), ½ mile W. of Gatehouse of Fleet, Sheet 83 (A.75 and footpath).
Stewartry of Kirkcudbright.

This little vitrified fort is one of a class of similar structures which abound in the district. Almost subrectangular on plan, it measures internally 90 ft. by 60 ft. within a wall in which vitrifaction occurs. The entrance, in the SE., lies between two outcrops. Outworks including stretches of ramparts and ditches occur outside the main wall lower down the flanks of the knoll upon which the fort stands.

The more southerly of the two outcrops at the entrance is carved with three Pictish symbols—a double disc and Z-rod, a so-called lacustrine monster with what looks like a dagger pointing at its belly, and an attractive figure composed of a circle from which two long curled horns protrude and which contains simplified human features. This latter symbol, which is not known elsewhere, bears a fanciful resemblance to the Torrs Chamfrein.

Glengappock, Fort (NX 750704), 2¼ miles W. of Kirkpatrick Durham, Sheet 84 (by-road and footpath).
Stewartry of Kirkcudbright.

The innermost feature of this fort is a very denuded enclosure measuring about 100 ft. by 60 ft. within an intermittent scarp representing a ruined rampart

which recalls the similar structure in the Moyle fort. This enclosure may have been the earliest structure on the hill, and have been mutilated and partly obliterated during the construction and occupation of the later work the main feature of which is a stone wall enclosing an area measuring 160 ft. by 125 ft. This is further defended to the S. by a precipice, and in all other directions by two ramparts thrown up from internal ditches.

Margley, Fort (NX 770733), 2¼ miles NW. of Kirkpatrick Durham, Sheet 84 (by-road, B.794 and farm land).
Stewartry of Kirkcudbright.

This little circular fort, superficially recalling some of the raths of Ireland, measures about 100 ft. in diameter within a low mound spread to as much as 18 ft. in width outside which is a shallow ditch measuring about as much in width with an outer mound, measuring about the same as the inner one, on its outer lip.

Stroanfeggan, Fort (NX 637921), 6¾ miles N. by E. of St John's Town of Dalry, Sheet 77 (B.7000, B.729 and moorland).   *Stewartry of Kirkcudbright.*

This fort occupies a prominence which dominates the passes running N. and E. from the confluence of the Water of Ken and the Stroanfeggan Burn. The principal enclosure measures about 140 ft. by 125 ft. within a ruinous wall spread to a thickness of up to 25 ft. This is covered by other walls to the NE., NW. and SW., and the general appearance of the fort recalls that of members of the Trusty's Hill group.

Candybank, Fort (NT 065411), 2½ miles NE. of Biggar, Sheet 72 (A.702).
Lanarkshire.

This fort is oval, measuring 280 ft. by 190 ft. within the remains of three ramparts, only the inner one of which is now at all well preserved. It contains several well-marked quarried platforms with crescentic scarps at the rear which measure from 20 ft. to 40 ft. in internal diameter and are stances for timber-framed houses. Five of these can be clearly distinguished, while faint traces of others can be traced in the disturbed interior which has space for at least twice as many, if not more.

Quothquan Law, Fort (NS 987384), 3½ miles W. of Biggar, Sheet 72 (A.73 and by-road).   *Lanarkshire.*

As far as can be discovered this large and well-preserved fort was first noted by O. G. S. Crawford when flying up Clydesdale in the year 1939. The hill stands in a bend in the River Clyde which here turns N. at the start of the great loop ending at Hyndford Bridge. The country round about is fairly open, and the hill, and the defences on it, can be seen for miles. The original fort occupying the summit of the hill measured 400 ft. by 250 ft. within a single rampart. It was later enlarged by taking in the W. face of the hill, the defended area thus being increased by an additional space measuring 300 ft. by 200 ft. In the latter, but not in the former, area the surface traces of at least 14 timber-framed houses can be distinguished, with room for more than twice as many. Unlike many in this district, but very like some others such as those in the Hownam Law minor *oppidum*, they appear simply as saucer-like depressions in the fine pasture with which the hill is clothed.

Park Knowe, Fort (NS 970367), 1 mile S. of Thankerton, Sheet 72 (A.73).

Lanarkshire.

This fort occupies a detached hill which forms the N. toe of Tinto. It is oval on plan, measuring 200 ft. by 170 ft. within two now ruinous stone walls, and thus bears a striking similarity to the rather smaller fort which used to stand on Cairngryfe Hill, 3½ miles to the NW. In 1939, when the latter began to be menaced by the ultimately fatal programme of quarrying for road-metal, a workman found a jet ring, a Donside terret, a hollow hemisphere of lead and a bronze object of uncertain use in one of the ramparts. Cairngryfe fort was planned by both Christison and Childe, and it is clear that, as at Park Knowe, the walls were joined at several places by cross-walls of a less substantial nature than the main ones. The interior of the Park Knowe fort is featureless.

For some reason the earliest editions of the O.S. maps marked this structure as "Remains of supposed Druids' Temple", while the Statistical Account of Scotland identifies it as a Sheriff's Court.

Chester Hill, Fort (NS 952396), 1½ miles NW. of Thankerton, Sheet 72 (A.73 and by-road). *Lanarkshire.*

This fort lies within a plantation on a hill which overlooks from a height of 200 ft. the natural through-route cutting off a large bend in the River Clyde between Thankerton and Hyndford Bridge. It is formed by two massive concentric ramparts with a median ditch, which enclose an area 280 ft. in diameter. The inner rampart is now in general about 20 ft. thick, 5 ft. high above the interior and 8 ft. above the bottom of the ditch, while the outer rampart is somewhat smaller, though by no means a mere upcast mound. The gaps in the ramparts at both the entrances, one in the W. and the other in the SE., are slightly staggered, which is an unusual feature locally.

Cow Castle, Large Settlement and Small Settlement (NT 042331), 1¼ miles ESE. of Culter, Sheet 72 (A.702 and by-road). *Lanarkshire.*

These interesting remains occupy the SW. end of an isolated ridge which was certainly bordered on the N. by a marsh, if not a sheet of water, at some time probably in the Iron Age or later, as a crannog was found there, and destroyed, when drainage operations were being carried on in the 19th century. The larger and earlier settlement is D-shaped on plan, conforming to the shape of the available ground, and measures 230 ft. by 160 ft. within a single heavy rampart with an external ditch where the exigencies of the contours allow. The smaller, secondary, structure is also D-shaped, measuring 140 ft. by 100 ft. It lies right on top of the other, providing a classic example of sequence in earthworks. These two are the principal works on the site, although several subsidiary minor stretches of rampart and of ditch also occur. Traces of timber-framed houses are evident both within the smaller settlement and, outside the limits of this, in the larger. Whether the single one placed in the latter position really belonged to the earlier settlement or whether it represents expansion from the smaller is not evident. It appears to be of the same kind as those unequivocally within the smaller structure. The latter compares in size and appearance with several others, most of them a little farther to the E., in Peebles, but one only 70 yds. away, on the other end of the ridge.

Nisbet, Fort (NT 035321), 1½ miles SE. of Culter, Sheet 72 (A.702 and by-road).

Lanarkshire.

This fort straddles the broad back of a ridge which divides the Culter Water from the Nesbit Burn. Like others in the district, it appears to exhibit two structural phases. The smaller of these is formed by a ruinous stone wall which encloses an area measuring 200 ft. by 115 ft. The whole of the NW. sector of the wall has been cleanly removed for use elsewhere, and several other stretches have been robbed and otherwise wasted. An entrance in the NE. is certainly, and another in the SE. probably, original. The larger element, which surrounds the smaller, consists of a heavy rampart with an external ditch, enclosing a space 255 ft. by 165 ft. in extent. The outer lip of the ditch is occasionally accompanied by an upcast mound. The only entrance is in the NE., conforming with one of those in the inner wall, but a gap has been broken through the N. arc in recent times. Slight and rather uncertain traces of a single platform such as might have supported a timber-framed house can be seen on a rocky outcrop which rises within the interior of the fort, but there are no other internal features except some amorphous foundations and enclosures which appear to be of no great age.

Devonshaw Hill, Fort (NS 953284), 2¼ miles SW. of Lamington, Sheet 72 (A.702). *Lanarkshire.*

The rocky promontory upon which this fort stands dominates a steep drop of 300 ft. to the W., at the bottom of which lies the flood-plain of the River Clyde, but the approaches from all other directions are reasonably gentle. The fort is oval, measuring 200 ft. by 150 ft. within a single rampart which was laid out so as to gain considerable advantage from the steep, rocky flanks of the site. Slighter outworks cross these where the natural gradient was deemed insufficient.

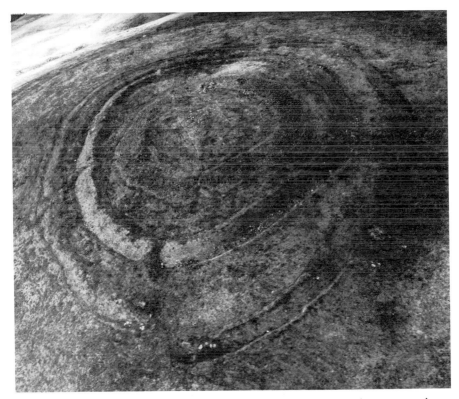

33   *Arbory Hill Fort, in Upper Clydesdale, is among the best preserved of such monuments*

At either end of the fort an entrance leads into a hollow, while traces of six timber-framed houses are visible in the interior. A little banked enclosure lies immediately NE. of the fort on the hillside which begins to rise gradually to the extensive higher ground beyond. It is formed by a low mound, is almost circular, and contains a single crescentic scarp which probably represents the site of another timber-framed house.

Arbory Hill, Fort (NS 944238), 1 mile ENE. of Abington, Sheet 72 (A.74 and by-road). *Lanarkshire.*

The very well preserved remains of this spectacular structure crown Arbory Hill (1407 ft. O.D.), a promontory which thrusts out W. from the higher mass to the E. to overlook a stretch of the Clyde valley at the point where the Roman road down Clydesdale descends the valley of the Raggengill Burn. As at Black Hill across the way, and certain other forts in the vicinity, the remains consist of a walled enclosure lying inside a set of ramparts and ditches which may well not be of one build with it. The walled enclosure measures 140 ft. in diameter, and has an entrance in the E. and another in the SW. The pair of ramparts, each with an external ditch, enclose an area measuring 270 ft. by 220 ft., and each rampart, where best preserved, rises to as much as 10 ft. above its ditch. The rampart system has five entrances. While the E. entrance of the walled enclosure matches one in the ramparts, its SW. entrance does not, but leads only into the space between the two systems. The interior contains what may be surface remains of timber-framed houses, together with an enigmatic pile of stones and a rectangular foundation.

Black Hill, Fort (NS 908239), 1½ miles W. of Abington, Sheet 72 (A.74). *Lanarkshire.*

This fort stands on the SE. extremity of Black Hill on a subsidiary swelling about 100 ft. lower than and ½ mile SE. of the main summit, overlooking a broad crook in the Duneaton Water. The remains, which are apparently those of two separate periods of construction, consist of a now ruinous stone wall enclosing an area about 120 ft. in diameter which lies within, but not concentric with, a single rampart with an external ditch. The area enclosed by this measures

about 200 ft. in diameter. The rampart and ditch have a regular entrance in the NW., and a broad gap, in which another original entrance might once have existed, in the NE. The wall, however, only has an entrance in the NE. While the doubtful nature of the second entrance in the outer line of defence precludes certainty, it seems very likely that the wall may be a secondary feature representing a reconstruction of the fort.

Crawford, Settlement (NS 944215), 1 mile NW. of Crawford, Sheet 72 (A.74 and by-road). *Lanarkshire.*

This is the southernmost of three earthworks which lie on the lower slopes of the massif known as Castle Hill which is bordered to S. and W. by the River Clyde, just below Crawford. It occupies an isolated knoll which is separated from a part of Castle Hill called Richie Ferry by a marginal meltwater channel. It consists of an enclosure 280 ft. long by 140 ft. wide formed by a single rampart, and having four entrances. It is notable for containing the surface traces of eight broad-ring-groove timber-frame houses which, like the four entrances, recall the Braidwood settlement, in Midlothian. The surface traces of several of the houses are very clearly marked, as good examples of their class as exist. Two small enclosures lie close to the W. end of the settlement, the better preserved of the two containing possible sites of more timber-framed houses—as at Devonshaw Hill fort, near by.

Crawford, Fort (NS 952219), 1 mile NNW. of Crawford, Sheet 72 (A.74 and by-road). *Lanarkshire.*

Like the settlement ½ mile to the W., this fort occupies the surface of a knoll separated from the main mass of Castle Hill by a meltwater channel. It is oval on plan, measuring 360 ft. by 130 ft. within the denuded remains of a stony rampart which is accompanied only on the SW. by an external ditch. A rather slight outer rampart develops on the outer lip of this to run thence NW., N. and NE. and die out at the entrance, in the NE. Nothing can be seen in the interior, which in the season is partly covered in bracken.

Bodsberry Hill, Fort (NS 963169), 2¼ miles S. of Crawford, Sheet 78 (A.74). *Lanarkshire.*

This, the uppermost fort in Clydesdale,

crowns the steep-sided Bodsberry Hill to overlook from a height of 400 ft. a considerable stretch of the valley, and the approaches to the Dalveen Pass to the W. The main defence is a broad, stone-faced rampart enclosing an area 330 ft. in length by 280 ft. in width, with four entrances all of which appear to be original, as the rampart turns in slightly on either side of them. Extra defences have been provided outside the NW. and SE. sectors, covering the entrances, but the steepness of the flanks of the hill sufficed in the case of the other two. An additional rampart, however, crosses the face of the hill on the very brink of the steep descent to the NW. For this reason it was necessary to quarry the material from inside, instead of from outside, the rampart, a rare but not unparalleled occurrence. Although the interior of the fort is diversified only by slight and problematical traces of a few timber-framed houses, and a well, the situation is such that it well repays a visit on a fine day.

Rudha na Berie, Fort (NB 235474), 15 miles NW. of Stornoway, Sheet 8 (A.857, A.858 and farm tracks).   *Lewis.*

This promontory fort, occupying a rocky peninsula which measures 690 ft. in length by 300 ft. in breadth, is formed by a wall, spread to a thickness of up to 23 ft., which stretches from the N. side to within 12 ft. of the S. side. Placed at a waist in the headland, this is 102 ft. long, and is accompanied on the landward side by a ditch with a low bank on either side. The date of such a structure is quite uncertain, and there is at present no knowledge of whether internal ruined buildings are contemporary or later.

Arthur's Seat, Fort (NT 275728), in The King's Park, Edinburgh, Sheet 66.
                                                    Midlothian.

Arthur's Seat is strictly the name of the highest peak of the leonine hill which occupies most of The King's Park. The subsidiary summit, the Crow Hill, S. of the Seat, is however also included in the fort which must have measured some 20 acres in extent and about 1200 ft. by 1100 ft. along the major axes. Three parts of the perimeter are bordered only by the steep flanks of the hill, although some defences may well originally have followed some at least of this line. The only easy approach, that from the E., is

blocked by the ruins of two formidable stone walls, the best preserved parts of which lie S. of the path leading to the peak, on the flank of the Crow Hill. Immediately S. of the path, and W. of this region, later enclosures have obscured the lines of the walls and penetrated into the erstwhile interior of the fort. No traces of dwellings can be distinguished in the interior, but this has all been under the plough, so that any remains of either timber-framed or stone-built houses that might ever have existed in it have been obliterated. If it was an occupied site, then it must rank as a locally major *oppidum*, the fourth largest in Scotland.

Dunsapie, Fort (NT 282731), in The King's Park, Edinburgh, Sheet 66.
                                                    Midlothian.

The remains of this fort crown the rocky hill which borders the E. side of Dunsapie Loch. The walls have been most severely robbed of stone, but sufficient remains to show that originally the summit of the hill was bordered by a wall and the E. flank by another. Whether they were contemporary might be determined by excavation, but there is no reason to suppose that they were not. The summit area measures about 350 ft. in length by a maximum width of 200 ft., being bordered on the W. and N. by precipitous crags and on the other sides by the spread remains of the inner wall. The outer wall is visible below the steep crags bordering the W. margin of the summit, running thence S. and E. round the prolonged E. toe of the hill, where the entrance lies. It runs NW. from this, rising up the margin of the toe of the hill until, at a point 200 ft. SE. of the NE. angle of the summit enclosure, it fades away as its line is replaced by steep crags. Several platforms in the E. part of the interior lying between the outer and inner walls suggest stances for Early Iron Age timber-framed houses.

Braidwood, Settlement (NT 193596), 10 miles SSW. of Edinburgh, Sheet 66 (A.702).   *Midlothian.*

The remains of this settlement crown a low hill which forms part of the Pentland massif. Two structural phases are represented, the first an all-timber settlement enclosed by a single palisade which is accompanied at a distance of some 45 ft. outside it by another single palisade. These two were joined at the entrances by connecting fences, and the space between them may have been used for enclosing cattle. The second structural phase saw the replacement of the fences by two banks with quarry-ditches. The inner bank was apparently piled up against the outer palisade, using this for a kind of revetment, and as a result its quarry-ditch lies inside it, an unusual but not unique occurrence. The outer bank, which likewise has an internal quarry-ditch, is almost ploughed away.

Within the enclosure can be seen short sections of the original inner palisade and more than a dozen depressed rings or ovals which represent the sites of timber-framed houses. Some, perhaps almost all, of these belong to the later period of occupation, several of them palpably overlying the palisade of the earlier period; others may represent traces of the original houses. The total occupation of the settlement may have extended over a considerable period, beginning at some time during the pre-Roman Iron Age and possibly ceasing in the 1st or 2nd century A.D. The main Roman road from the Solway to the Forth passes very close to the settlement.

It was at this settlement that timber-framed houses of the type later classified as Ring-ditch houses were first investigated by excavation.

Castle Law, Fort (NT 229638), 3 miles SW. of Fairmilehead, Sheet 66 (A.702).
Midlothian.

The fort at Castle Law is an interesting though now denuded monument which has been shown by excavations to have gone through a series of structural modifications of a now familiar nature. One of the plans illustrating the excavations of 1931–2 shows the single palisade trench of the earliest structure that was succeeded by a single rampart which was reinforced internally with timber beams at least in the vicinity of the gate. The course of the rampart differed slightly from that of the palisade, so that on one side of the entrance in the former the palisade was found outside it, and on the other, inside it.

In the third phase a pair of ramparts and ditches was added outside the singleton, to produce a standard multi-vallate fort of the period immediately before the local arrival of the Roman armies in A.D. 79 or 80.

An interesting feature at Castle Law is a well-preserved souterrain which was constructed in the ditch between the two ramparts of the final phase. This, like its few other companions in the eastern Lowlands, dates from the period not very long after the Roman occupation ceased locally, perhaps the 3rd century A.D.

Lawhead, Fort (NT 216622), 4 miles SW. of Fairmilehead, Sheet 66 (A.702).
Midlothian.

The remains of this fort are slight but interesting. They lie on a ridge protruding from the SE. flank of Turnhouse Hill, where they bear witness to the occupation of this area in Early Iron Age times, as does the settlement at Braidwood, 2 miles to the SW.

The defences consist of a bank with an external ditch which is best preserved in the W. and N., though traceable in the other sectors too, on the opposite side of the stone field-boundary which bisects the site. The interior contains the surface traces of at least two out of what must originally have been a considerably greater number of timber-framed houses of the ring-ditch type.

Dalmahoy Hill, Fort (NT 135669), 2 miles W. of Balerno, Sheet 65 (A.70).
Midlothian.

The remains of this fort occupy the twin eminence to that upon which the Kaimes Hill fort stands. They represent at least two structural periods, the earlier of which is very difficult to interpret. Briefly, the craggy and uneven hill was enclosed by a system of stone walls which defended an area measuring 1200 ft. in length by a maximum of about 400 ft. in width, bordered to the NW. by the precipitous face of the hill. The second phase structure is an oval enclosure, on the very summit of the hill, which measures 140 ft. by 85 ft., almost identical with the similar secondary enclosure at the Craigie Hill fort 5½ miles to the N. This enclosure must occupy the same ground as did the central feature of the fort.

While there is no reason to suppose that the earlier works are not of pre-Roman Iron Age date, the period at which the later enclosure was built has not yet been established. There is reason to believe that it may be of post-Roman date, as it belongs to a class of such monuments which are almost always found to overlie pre-Roman forts and which have, in some cases, produced relics of early mediaeval (Dark Age) date. A gold stud-cap $\frac{1}{6}$ in. in diameter was picked up in the Dalmahoy secondary enclosure, as were several fragments of moulds, all of which can be assigned to that late period. Only excavation could answer the problem satisfactorily.

Kaimes Hill, Fort (NT 130665), 2 miles W. of Balerno, Sheet 65 (A.70).
Midlothian.

The remains of this large and important fort have been robbed and mutilated in the past, and today are fast being blown up and consumed by a quarry. In 1940, when quarrying began to make serious inroads upon the remains, a small excavation was carried out with the intention of determining something of the structural history of the place. The results were interpreted to show that the original structure was an enclosure measuring 550 ft. by 220 ft. within a stone wall 10 ft. thick. Such a work would be comparable to the forts on Cockleroy and Bowden Hill, 8 miles to the NW.

This inner, original enclosure was eventually strengthened by outworks which also took in as much again of the NE. part of the hill, the resulting enclosure measuring 1000 ft. by 400 ft. It is clear that the later works were modified at one time or another, as there are two entrances only 50 yds. apart in the E. sector, which are unlikely to belong to one period. A third phase of occupation is represented by numerous circular stony foundations of houses, situated indiscriminately all over the interior and ignoring the original wall, but apparently all within the outermost lines of defence. These presumably marked the final occupation of the fort, during the later part of the Roman period.

Longfaugh, Fort (NT 404617), 1½ miles S. of Pathhead, Sheet 66 (A.68 and by-road). *Midlothian.*

The conspicuous remains of this circular fort stand in open woodland in an elevated position on the ridge W. of Longfaugh farmhouse. The defences originally consisted of a pair of heavy concentric ramparts apparently constructed of earth heaped up from the ditch between them and faced with stone

or timber. The fort stands very close to the line of the Roman main route to Inveresk from the S., but neither the track of this section of the road nor the precise location of a near-by Roman post have yet been established. Evidence that the latter did exist is provided by the presence of building stones with Roman carving on them which are built into the fabric of an adjacent souterrain of the post-Roman period.

Crichton, Fort (NT 384618), 1¼ miles SSW. of Pathhead, Sheet 66 (B.6367).
Midlothian.

This fort, situated on an insignificant knoll at the W. end of the village of Crichton, represents one of the simpler classes of Early Iron Age forts. The defence consists of a single heavy rampart, now in a denuded condition, which even so stands to as much as 3 ft. above the interior which measures 300 ft. by 190 ft. in extent. This rampart, like so many others, must originally have been faced and revetted by either stone or timber, or both.

Middle Hill, Settlement (NT 444519), 4½ miles N. of Stow, Sheet 66 (A.7 and by-road). *Midlothian.*

The little structure on Middle Hill, 1 mile NW. of Middleton, is here listed as a settlement because of its outward appearance, although no traces of houses are visible on the surface of the interior. It is circular on plan, measuring only 85 ft. in diameter within a pair of low ramparts with a broad, shallow median ditch. Entrances break the E. and NW. arcs. The appearance and proportions of the ramparts recall those of the palisaded settlement at Harehope, and it is quite possible that Middle Hill is another such Early Iron Age habitation.

Hodge Cairn, Fort (NT 409514), 4¾ miles NNW. of Stow, Sheet 66 (A.7 and by-road). *Midlothian.*

The fort called Hodge Cairn is the southernmost of the group of three which lie in the angle between the Heriot and Gala Waters. It has been planted with trees which have been felled comparatively recently, and may be replanted. It is oval on plan, measuring 400 ft. by 250 ft. within two concentric ramparts some 40 ft. apart, with a median ditch. The remains are conspicuous from the A.7 road, as the inner rampart stands to a height of as much as 15 ft. above the ditch. The entrance is in the NE. No internal features are visible on the surface.

Halltree Rings, Fort (NT 400519), 5¼ miles NNW. of Stow, Sheet 66 (A.7, B.709). *Midlothian.*

The fort Halltree Rings crowns a summit 1100 ft. above sea level in the angle between the Heriot and Gala Waters, less than a mile E. of the large fort Corsehope Rings. It is circular on plan, measuring 260 ft. in diameter within a single heavy rampart with an external quarry ditch, the entrance being in the W. At best the rampart rises 10 ft. above the ditch. No traces of buildings are visible on the ground in the interior, which has been ploughed, but it is very likely that the post-holes of timber-framed houses exist beneath the turf.

Corsehope Rings, Fort (NT 392519), 6 miles NW. of Stow, Sheet 66 (A.7, B.709). *Midlothian.*

The defences which acquired the name Corsehope Rings cover a considerable area even though individually their surface remains are comparatively insignificant. Four principal lines are involved, each consisting of a slight rampart with an intermittent external ditch. Together they form a band at the least 100 ft. broad, enclosing an area measuring 420 ft. in length by 270 ft. in width. Three entrances, all of which may be original, break through the defences, but the one in the NE. sector differs from the other two in being oblique. The interior has been ploughed, but it is still possible to distinguish a score or so of ring-ditch house sites on the surface.

The slight nature of the ramparts, contrasting with their considerable length, has given rise to the conjecture that they might originally have held palisades, as at the Harehope settlement, though no exploration has been attempted. This fort is the largest example in which surface traces of ring-ditch houses have been recorded, in contrast to the ring-groove types which can be seen in greater numbers at such places as Cademuir Hill.

Heriot Station, Fort (NT 406547), 7 miles NNW. of Stow, Sheet 66 (A.7). *Midlothian.*

This oval fort is crossed by a field wall and has been both robbed of stone and levelled by the plough, but enough remains to show that it originally measured about 250 ft. by 200 ft. within two ramparts 36 ft. apart, with a median ditch. It is the uppermost fort in the valley of the Gala Water, and forms one of an interesting group comprising several forts and settlements of the Early Iron Age, presumably of the Selgovae.

Burghead, Fort (NJ 109691), in Burghead, 8 miles NE. of Forres, Sheet 28 (B.9089). *Moray.*

The remains of this fort, after which the broad rocky headland upon which it stands is named, are still impressive, but until comparatively recently they must have been magnificent. For it was not until 1808 that certain improvements were begun under the direction of a Mr James Young which "unfortunately necessitated, or seemed to necessitate, the destruction of these fortifications" which were, as was afterwards discovered, the only examples of a timber-laced wall nailed at the joints yet to have been discovered in Scotland. Fortunately, if ironically, the fort had been planned with detail and with what may seem to be more care than mere duty required, by General W. Roy in the 1740s, at the request of the Duke of Cumberland. From this admirable survey it is clear that the outermost element of the massive fortifications was a set of three ramparts each about 800 ft. in length which ran obliquely across the neck of the headland to cut off an area measuring at the greatest about 1000 ft. in length and 600 ft. in width. The combined width of the three ramparts as they lay was about 180 ft., and they were all pierced by an entrance sited about half way along. All these were swept away by the Young reforms, graphically described on p. 445 of *P.S.A.S.*, XXV, in a stirring passage a footnote to which reads "A contract for the removal of 20,000 cubic yards of rampart is in my possession".

The area cut off by the three ramparts was surrounded on the other margins by a wall and bisected longitudinally from ESE. to WNW. by another, the division formed to the SSW. of the latter wall being elevated several feet above the somewhat larger division to the NNE. Holes were dug in various parts of the walls in 1861 and again in 1890. The report of the latter operation makes it clear that at one point the wall measured

24 ft. in width at the base and that the existing remains stood to as much as 17 ft. in height. It was therefore deduced that originally the height must have been at least 20 ft. The outer face of the wall, one or two slabs and about 3 ft. in thickness, presented a solid face to an observer standing outside; but the inner face, about 3 ft. 6 in. in thickness, was penetrated at intervals of 3 ft. both horizontally and vertically, by the ends of transverse beams some 6 in. or 9 in. square which ran into the core of the wall but were not taken out through the outer face. These transverse timbers were connected horizontally (but not vertically) by planks from 2 in. to 3 in. thick and about 10 in. to 12 in. wide, and made of oak. At the points of contact between the planks and the beams, iron "bolts", at least 8 in. long and about 1 in. thick and with square heads, had been thrust through to increase the stability of the structure.

Today, the principal part of the remainder of this sad ruin is the wall dividing the two inner compartments. This runs along an open space between the encroaching town and the sea, and offers the observer a microcosm of what there must have been a century and a half ago.

The plan of the fort as delineated by General Roy may suggest a work of more than one period, but this is by no means unlikely. Whether or not it might have been the case, the remains represent those of works of kinds not easy to parallel in Scotland. Promontory forts are normally either small or defended by more moderate obstacles, but here there is evidence of a work which, compared to other known examples, is of mighty proportions. Walls as thick as this, or even thicker may occur in inland hill-forts, usually of types which stand alone or have, at the most, a single outer work. The fort at Burghead was greater than any of these, and must have had a status at the nature of which it is now only possible to guess.

Two other suitably remarkable circumstances occur at Burghead. One is a well of sufficiently unusual proportions which, according to General Roy, was situated right on the line of the great wall bordering the NNE. division on the ESE., about 30 yds. SSW. of the entrance.

This suggests that the well was made at a time when the rampart was out of use; and although no authoritative demonstration has as yet been made to give a convincing estimate of its date, there may be a likelihood that it belongs in a later rather than an earlier mediaeval context. It comprises a rectangular chamber about 16 ft. square and 12 ft. high, with well-rounded angles, cut out of rock at the base of a crag and opening on to a half-bowl shaped slope at a depth of some 20 ft. below the present general level of the ground above. The floor is bordered by a ledge surrounding a basin 10 ft. square and 4 ft. deep, again with rounded corners. When found, during the improvements, the chamber roof was broken and the entrance ill-defined; and the archway now forming the latter was then constructed.

The other remarkable objects at Burghead are the several carved stone slabs, decorated in early and later Pictish styles, as well as in a Viking form. The justly famous representations of bulls are illustrated on p. 192. Here it is only necessary to speculate on what relation they bore, if any, to what phase of occupation of the fort. This is bound up with the questions—did the Romans, either on their excursion in the 1st century A.D. or during another, in the 2nd or 3rd century, reach Burghead; and was it then a great central capital, a Pictish *oppidum*; and did the Roman army sack it, even though subsequently departing without consolidating their victory? Excavations in 1966, while failing to find any of the iron 'bolts' reported earlier, examined a section of walling in which the timbers did not penetrate the wall, and were dated to the 4th or 5th century A.D. It could be that in the early historical Pictish period, a major stronghold was established here on the already fortified promontory—even possibly the place where Columba visited the Pictish king Bruide in the 6th century.

Doune of Relugas, Fort (NJ 003495), 6 miles SSW. of Forres, Sheet 27 (A.940, B.9007 and private grounds). *Moray.*

This little vitrified fort occupies a steep-sided hill immediately S. of the confluence of the Rivers Findhorn and Divie. The summit area, measuring 160 ft. by 100 ft. in extent, is girt by the remains of a wall which has been largely obliterated by the formation of a terrace and by a dry-stone dyke. At several places, however, especially near the entrance in the E., masses of vitrified stones and boulders can be seen.

The flanks of the hill fall steeply from the summit in all directions for about 50 ft., and the S. and E. slopes continue on very steeply down to the river. The less formidable approaches from the N. and W. are barred by a ditch dug near the base of the hill and a rampart on its outer lip. The latter is composed partly of soil from the ditch and partly of natural ground, so that in the W. it rises to a height of as much as 25 ft. from the ground outside.

Knock of Alves, Fort (NJ 163629), 3¼ miles W. of Elgin, Sheet 28 (A.96).
Moray.

The Knock of Alves rises from the plain between Forres and Elgin at a distance of 5 miles SE. of Burghead. It is crowned by a mausoleum and a tower named the York Tower which stand within the uppermost and innermost enclosure of the fort. This measures 125 ft. by 75 ft. within the fragmentary remains of a wall; and it in turn stands within a walled enclosure measuring 415 ft. by 75 ft., outside which is a possibly contemporary second wall now mostly obliterated by the access-road leading up the hill. Outside all these two ramparts, about 18 ft. apart, run round the lower slopes of the hill. The passage of time, the building of the mausoleum and the tower, the encroachment of quarries and the planting of conifers have all conspired to deface and mutilate, though not yet entirely destroy, this very interesting monument.

Caisteal an Duin Bhain, Fort (NM 422786), ½ mile S. of Port Mor pier, Sheet 39 (moorland). *Muck.*

This fort occupies an elevated table which rises from 15 ft. to 30 ft. above the general ground level on the SW. of Port Mor. It measures 130 ft. by 95 ft. within a wall up to 9 ft. thick. The entrance is in the NNE. Foundations of one or two probably mediaeval rectangular buildings can be distinguished within the fort, but nothing is known of their date.

Dun Evan, Fort (NH 827475), 2 miles SW. of Cawdor, Sheet 27 (by-roads and footpath). *Nairn.*

The Doune of Cawdor, as this fort is also known, occupies an isolated crag dominating others in a stretch of uneven ground and commands extensive views which include the whole of lower Strathnairn. The summit of the crag is crowned by a ruined wall which encloses an oval area measuring 195 ft. by 85 ft. in which the only recognisable feature is the depression marking the site of a well. The wall appears as a partly grass-grown mass of debris spread to a width of 25 ft. Several stretches of outer walls are to be found lower down the flanks of the crag, conspicuous among them the tumbled masses of a wall situated immediately NW. of the entrance (in the NE.); the debris here stands to a height of 14 ft. above the lowest courses of some facing stones which are exposed near the base of the mass. Vitrifaction has been recorded at this fort in the past, and while none has been reported in recent years the character of some of the ruins suggest that timber lacing may very well have been used.

Castle Finlay, Fort (NH 888514), 3 miles S. of Nairn, Sheet 27 (B.9090, by-road and woodland track). *Nairn.*

This fort squats on a very insignificant ridge on the NW. flank of the Hill of Urchany. The innermost feature is an enclosure 120 ft. long by 60 ft. wide, formed by a heavy ruinous wall among the debris of which lumps of vitrifaction can be found. The weakness of the site demands outer defences, and these exist in the form of a discontinuous rampart formed from the upcast of an internal ditch, as at the Doune of Relugas.

Dunearn, Fort (NH 933406), 10 miles SSE. of Nairn, Sheet 27 (A.939 and by-road). *Nairn.*

This fort occupies a wooded hill named Doune near the right bank of the River Findhorn ¼ mile S. of Bridge of Dulsie. Its shape, which conforms to that of the hill, is that of an S, and it measures medially about 900 ft. in length by a maximum of 160 ft. in width. It is formed by two walls, both now very ruinous; the inner reveals patches of vitrifaction, notably in the SE. sector, the outer for the most part now a mere scarp. The interior was under the plough until 1906, and is featureless.

Caisteal Odair, Fort (NF 731766), 12¼ miles WNW. of Lochmaddy, Sheet 18

(A.865 and moorland). *North Uist.*

This promontory fort occupies a headland at the extreme NW. of North Uist which is bounded by sheer cliffs except to the SE. where a wall 360 ft. long and 9 ft. thick on the average cuts off approach. The entrance, which curves through the wall, measures 15 ft. in length and about 5 ft. in width. The remains of several circular stone foundations lie inside the fortified area, but nothing is known about their connection with the fort.

Northshield Rings, Fort (NT 257493), 1½ miles NNE. of Eddleston, Sheet 73 (A.703). *Peeblesshire.*

This well-preserved fort lies on the spine of a ridge dominating the valley of the Eddleston water from the NE. The innermost of three ramparts and ditches, enclosing an area measuring 240 ft. by 210 ft., has three entrances, one of which, being 50 ft. wide, is probably incomplete. The two outer ramparts and ditches, which are concentric with each other but not with the innermost system, also have three entrances. It is clear that two structural periods are represented, though not obvious in which order they occurred.

Cademuir Hill, Fort (NT 230375), 2 miles SW. of Peebles, Sheet 73 (A.72 and by-road). *Peeblesshire.*

This well-known fort crowning the elongated SW. ridge of Cademuir Hill commands extensive views up and down the valley of the River Tweed and that of the Manor Water, the substantial ruin of its single stone wall enclosing an area about 8 acres in extent. The entrances, in the NE. and SW. sectors, are well marked. The interior contains the surface traces of between 30 and 40 timber-framed houses, with room for as many more, and there can be no doubt that in the early part of the Iron Age, to which it belongs, the fort had a status of more than immediately local significance. Structures of comparable size are recorded at a distance of 6 miles to the SW. (Henry's Brae) and 20 miles to the E. (Eildon Hill North). The occupation of this minor *oppidum* probably came to an end very shortly after the arrival of the Romans in the vicinity in A.D. 80, for there are no traces of stone-built houses or other secondary structures in the fort.

Cademuir Hill, Fort (NT 224370), 2½ miles SW. of Peebles, Sheet 73 (A.72 and by-roads). *Peeblesshire.*

This small, stone-built fort occupies a minor summit of the long ridge upon the highest point of which the ruinous minor *oppidum* of the same name is situated. Like the small, stone-built fort on Dreva Craig, its outer defences include a *chevaux de frise*, a setting of upright, earthfast boulders embedded in a natural slope immediately E. of the fort. The plan of the main structure is irregular, consisting of an enclosure measuring about 230 ft. by 150 ft., bounded by the massive ruins of a very substantial drystone wall, and several subsidiary enclosures which bud off this. Nothing positive is known about the date of this fort. It is situated less than ½ mile from its larger neighbour which, from the evidence of its general character and of the surface traces of timber-framed houses with which its interior is so plentifully studded, belongs to the Early Iron Age. It is, however, at present impossible to say whether the smaller fort belongs in the later Iron Age, or to some period in sub-Roman or even later times.

White Meldon, Fort (NT 219427), 2¼ miles NW. of Peebles, Sheet 73 (A.72 and by-road). *Peeblesshire.*

The wasted remains of this once impressive fort occupy the summit of the White Meldon (1401 ft. O.D.), where they enfold a now denuded circular cairn, a very few of the kerb stones of which protrude through the ruined mass. The main enclosure measures about 700 ft. in length by about 500 ft. in width, within two ruinous ramparts. Although these are almost entirely obliterated in places, the presence of a lobe protruding S. from the general course of the ruins can still be interpreted as evidence of at least one reconstruction of the defences. The interior contains the most notable surface traces of large timber-framed houses.

Harehope, Palisaded Settlement (NT 203448), 4 miles NW. of Peebles, Sheet 73 (A.72 and by-road). *Peeblesshire.*

This settlement appears on the surface as an asymmetrical, multivallate sub-rectangular earthwork with broadly rounded corners, and was thought to be classifiable only as an earthwork of uncertain age. It was excavated in 1960, and found in fact to be two successive settlements, each enclosed by a pair of low banks with broad and shallow median ditches. The banks were the seatings of continuous palisades, and the entrance of at least the later of the two settlements had been flanked with little wooden towers. Inside, the remains of three successive timber-framed houses were discovered, although no traces had been visible on the surface, as this had been under the plough. The earliest house was of a type believed to show Late Bronze Age affinities, the next was similar to houses at the Hayhope Knowe settlement, and the last was generally comparable to a house of the pre-Roman Iron Age excavated at West Plean, Stirlingshire.

Harehope Rings, Fort (NT 196445), 4 miles NW. of Peebles, Sheet 72 (A.72 and by-road). *Peeblesshire.*

This fort, situated near the extremity of a blunt ridge protruding from the SE. flank of Harehope Hill at an elevation of 1300 ft. above sea level, is conspicuous from the by-road running through the Meldon valley from Eddleston to Lyne. It is circular, about 190 ft. in diameter, within two ramparts with a median ditch. There are two entrances, at each of which the outer and inner ramparts join round the heads of the ditch. Surface traces of a dozen timber-framed houses can be seen in the interior, two of the most distinct showing sections of the foundation trenches of the walls as well as the platforms. An additional outer defence is provided by a bank and ditch which traverse the ridge at the point where this meets the main hillside, at a distance of about 50 yds. from the fort

Henderland Hill, Fort (NT 149459), 1½ miles SW. of Romannobridge, Sheet 72 (A.701). *Peeblesshire.*

The ramparts of this fort are conspicuous from the highway, as they cut the crest of Henderland Hill at a distance of 400 yds. to the SE. The fort is oval, measuring 220 ft. by 140 ft. within the remains of two ramparts with external ditches. The silhouette seen from the road coincides with a section where the inner rampart rises to a height of 12 ft. above its ditch and the outer to 9 ft. above this and to 6 ft. above its own ditch. Although the fort has suffered mutilation both from the encroaching plough and from bonfires being lit within it on occasions of private and public rejoicing, it is still possible to detect within it the sites of a few timber-framed houses of the Early Iron Age type. At a later date in its history, when in a state of disuse, a walled enclosure was built in the E. part of the interior.

Whiteside Hill, Fort (NT 168461), 1¼ miles SE. of Romannobridge, Sheet 72 (A.701, B.7059). *Peeblesshire.*

This fort is one of the best-preserved and most conspicuous in the Lowlands. It crowns Whiteside Hill (1200 ft. O.D.), a spur forming part of the E. side of the valley of the Lyne Water, and commands extensive views up and down this as well as over the flatter country to the SW. The remains are those of a series of constructions and reconstructions, beginning with an almost circular fort measuring 240 ft. in diameter within a single rampart and ditch. The next phase saw this surrounded by an additional pair of ramparts and ditches, and in the third the size of the fort was reduced and the defence formed by a now ruinous wall enclosing an area of only about 200 ft. in diameter. Yet a fourth phase, reducing again, is represented by another ruinous wall which encloses only 140 ft. by 85 ft., and is comparable to the late stone-walled enclosure at Henderland Hill fort. During one or more of the earlier phases timber-framed houses stood on the platforms which can be seen in the interior.

Additional outworks were built to protect the N. and S. sectors of the defences which faced the easiest approaches to the fort, while the slight remains of an advanced rampart and ditch bar access to the fort from the adjacent higher hill, Drum Maw.

Ladyurd Rings, Fort (NT 152424), 2 miles SE. of Blyth Bridge, Sheet 72 (A.72). *Peeblesshire.*

The remains of this fort stand on high ground commanding the confluence of the Tarth Water with the Lyne Water. They consist of two very heavy ramparts, both still standing in places to a height of 6 ft. above the ground outside them, although a good deal of the outer has been removed by ploughing. They enclose an area about 180 ft. in diameter which is featureless, as it has been under cultivation. This rather unassuming work is typical of a small local class.

Langlaw Hill, Fort (NT 100382), 1½ miles NW. of Broughton, Sheet 72 (A.701). *Peeblesshire.*

This fort occupies a conspicuous summit which stands 500 ft. above the valley of the Broughton Burn and commands considerable prospects in all directions, including the whole of the Biggar Gap. The remains consist of defences drawn round a rocky boss which crowns the hill; a slight, and possibly unfinished, rampart and ditch which lie some 150 ft. outside this; and a bank-and-ditch obstacle which crosses the easiest approach to the site, from the N. At one point the latter runs so close to the slight rampart and ditch that it appears most unlikely that they belonged to one structural phase. It is probable that the inner defences and the cross-dyke represent one scheme, and the slight ring another, possibly earlier. A final occupation phase may be indicated by a stone-walled enclosure, the slight remains of which occupy less than all the surface of the central rocky boss.

Helm End, Fort and Settlement (NT 110353), at Broughton, Sheet 72 (A.701). *Peeblesshire.*

These remains occupy a prominent position on the NE. extremity of the ridge which divides the Biggar and Holms Waters, commanding the E. half of the Biggar Gap as well as a stretch of the N.–S. route through upper Tweeddale and the valley of the Broughton Burn. They now lie half within a newly replanted forest and half in pasture land, but it is still possible to distinguish the remains of the two ramparts which form the oval fort, 340 ft. in length by 270 ft. in width. In addition to these, a bank with a ditch on the far side of it crosses the spine of the ridge SW. of the fort to provide additional protection on the easiest line of approach. The settlement, measuring 225 ft. by 160 ft. within a stone wall, lies inside the fort, and although now in a very dilapidated condition, still contains the visible foundations of at least five stone-walled circular houses. This is another example of the intrusion of such a settlement into a disused Early Iron Age hill-fort which is remarked below at Chester Rig.

Chester Rig, Fort and Settlement (NT 099320), 3 miles SSW. of Broughton, Sheet 72 (A.701 and by-road). *Peeblesshire.*

These structures stand on a slight eminence protruding from the face of Blakehope Head in a commanding position on the south side of the Holms Water valley. The fort is formed by a pair of ramparts with a median ditch which contain an area 180 ft. in diameter. Closely fitted within this is a stone-walled settlement containing traces of the foundations of eight stone-built houses, three of which are very well preserved. It is reasonably certain that the settlement is intrusive, on analogy with similar structures elsewhere.

Dreva Craig, Fort (NT 126353), 1 mile SE. of Broughton, Sheet 72 (A.701 and by-road). *Peeblesshire.*

This fort occupies a magnificent situation overlooking the bend of the River Tweed at Drumelzier from immediately above its confluence with the Biggar Burn; it thus commands the eastern mouth of the Biggar Gap, the valley 7 miles in length which affords easy communication between the upper reaches of the Rivers Clyde and Tweed. The craig is girt by two ruinous stone walls, the inner enclosing an area measuring about 190 ft. by 140 ft. The fort has long been famous for having a *chevaux de frise,* an area immediately outside the SW. arc of the outer wall in which great numbers of boulders have been set in the ground to protrude like teeth, to the discomfort of enemies attempting to rush the fort. It is quite possible that a similar barrier lay outside the fort to the NE. as well; but, if so, it has been partly extracted and partly incorporated into the buildings and enclosures of a secondary settlement which now occupies the ground. A similar settlement lies on the NW. face of the hill, below the fort. The interior of the fort contains several small circular stone foundations, but short of excavation there is no way of telling whether they are contemporary with it or of later, perhaps settlement, date.

Henry's Brae, Fort (NT 139339, ¼ mile NE. of Drumelzier, Sheet 72 (B.712). *Peeblesshire.*

This fort, as long as its fellow on Cademuir Hill (800 ft.) but not so wide, occupies a ridge immediately adjacent to Tinnis Hill. The single stone wall has been almost entirely removed towards the NE. extremity, but forms a massive ruin along the margin of the higher, SW., end of the ridge. Here a fold built out of the debris has caused a certain amount of damage, but it is still possible to detect the surface traces of about 30 timber-framed houses. There is room for at least as many more in the rest of the area enclosed, some of which has been under the plough.

Tinnis Castle, Fort (NT 141344), $\frac{1}{2}$ mile NE. of Drumelzier, Sheet 72 (B.712). *Peeblesshire.*

This fort occupies a prominent ridge which stands off the lower slope of Venlaw. The ruins of a mediaeval castle lie within it, and the construction, occupation and destruction of this have caused a certain amount of damage to the fort. The oval central enclosure, measuring internally about 200 ft. by 85 ft., is defended by a now ruinous stone wall which was probably timber-laced, as lumps of vitrifaction have been recovered from the debris. Outside this, two more ramparts and several minor defences add strength to the fort. No other timber-laced walls have been recorded in Tweeddale, though others may exist.

Kerr's Knowe, Fort (NT 182384), $\frac{1}{2}$ mile N. of Stobo, Sheet 72 (B.712). *Peeblesshire.*

This fort, situated on the summit of an isolated hill which has recently been cleared of timber, and so may be re-planted, has the distinction of having no fewer than six ramparts, the innermost of stone, and possible originally a wall. The interior measures 300 ft. by 175 ft., the entrance being in the W. All the ramparts curve slightly in at the entrance, showing that the whole work is probably all of one build. This is the only structure in the county so well defended.

White Hill, Fort (NT 055338), 2$\frac{1}{4}$ miles SE. of Biggar, Sheet 72 (B.7016 and by-road). *Peeblesshire.*

This fort, which crowns White Hill at a height of 1300 ft. above sea level, aroused the contempt of Christison, who wrote in 1886 that "the rampart has a rude character, as it slavishly follows all the inequalities of the ground". This peculiarity, and the meagre stature of the work upon which Christison made caustic comment, is due to the fact that the rampart, and two others outside it, are unfinished. It is possible to detect within the area enclosed an earlier fortification made entirely of wood. Two palisade trenches, themselves surrounded by the embryo inner rampart, enclose an area measuring 400 ft. in length by 240 ft. in width, and it was to replace these that the new ramparts were started, but never completed. This is one of the clearest and largest examples of this sequence of events to have been recorded anywhere.

Mitchelhill Rings, Fort (NT 062341). 2$\frac{1}{2}$ miles SE. of Biggar, Sheet 72 (A.702 and by-road). *Peeblesshire.*

This fort stands on the NE. extremity of the ridge of which the highest part, called White Hill, is crowned by the unfinished fort listed above under that name. Although it has been severely robbed of stone, its still impressive remains consist of a ruinous stone wall, enclosing an area measuring about 170 ft. in diameter, which lies within a substantial rampart with an external ditch on the outer lip of which some traces of an upcast mound remain. There is a question whether all these works belong together or whether the wall is either primary or intrusive. Several other forts exhibiting the same problem are to be found in the vicinity, and the consensus of opinion derived from a study of the whole group suggests that the inner element, in this case the stone wall, is more likely to be a secondary feature than a primary one.

Muirburn Castle, Fort (NT 090412), 5 miles NE. of Biggar, Sheet 72 (A.72). *Peeblesshire.*

Although the remains of this fort are now in an advanced stage of obliteration and decay, it is included because it is so clearly visible by travellers on both the A.72 and the A.701 roads in the vicinity of their point of junction. It crowns a conical, isolated summit, the flanks of which are nevertheless rather gentle. In the last 100 or 150 years the defences have been severely robbed, and the fort has been planted with trees which have almost all since been felled. It is, however, still possible to distinguish two concentric ramparts which enclose an area about 250 ft. in diameter. The interior can still show some signs of the platforms upon which timber-framed houses were built. A second structural phase is now represented by the last vestiges of a stone wall which ran at varying distances inside the inner rampart. Small enclosures of a later date encroach upon the E. and SE. sectors of the ruined ramparts.

Caerlee Hill, Large Settlement (NT 324367), ¼ mile W. of Innerleithen, Sheet 73 (A.72). *Peeblesshire.*

This settlement, which has been mutilated by quarrying, crowns a hill immediately W. of Innerleithen which commands extensive views both up and down the adjacent stretches of the valley of the River Tweed. It consists of a small inner enclosure measuring 200 ft. by 150 ft. but now half obliterated by the quarries, formed by a denuded rampart or wall and containing traces of six timber-framed houses. There could have been twice that number originally. This inner portion stands freely within an outer enclosure, formed by two heavy ramparts, the inner of which, and probably the outer too, was furnished with an external ditch. The outer enclosure measures 360 ft. by 275 ft. Excavations made in the 19th century somewhere within the W. part of the settlement produced several penannular bronze bracelets with expanded terminals. As far as can be judged in the present state of knowledge, these Late Bronze Age articles are unlikely to have belonged to the builders of the settlement.

Moncrieffe Hill, Fort (NO 136200), 2½ miles SSE. of Perth, Sheet 53, 58 (A.90 and woodland path). *Perthshire.*

This fort occupies the central summit of the ridge which divides the lower reaches of the Rivers Tay and Earn. It consists of an enclosure formed within two ruined walls and measuring 560 ft. by 330 ft., similar in appearance to the larger element in the fort on Dumyat. Like this, too, it has a dun-like structure measuring about 160 ft. by 120 ft. within a ruined wall originally about 12 ft. thick which seems to overlie a sector of the inner wall of the larger enclosure. It may, indeed, have been built at a time after the large fort had been abandoned, possibly in fully post-Roman times. The presence both within and outside the smaller enclosure of circular stone foundations of houses suggests an occupation in later Roman times at the earliest.

Forgandenny, Fort (NO 100155), 2½ miles SW. of Bridge of Earn, Sheet 58 (by-roads and footpath). *Perthshire.*

This fort occupies a slight eminence protruding from the NE. flank of Culteuchar Hill ¾ mile SW. of Ecclesiamagirdle, on the gloomy N. slopes of the Ochils about which the compiler of the first Ordnance Survey Gazetteer gleaned so apt a verse:

*The lasses o' Exmagirdle
   May very well be dun;
For frae Michaelmas till Whitsunday
   They never see the sun.*

The fort was excavated in 1891, when the walls were found to contain the sockets of beams preserved entire. No further details were recorded of this vitally interesting structure. The inner of the two walls encloses an area measuring 180 ft. by 80 ft., but the plan is confused by the presence of a length of straight wall which pierces the E. end of the fort near the entrance and runs through the inner wall for some distance into the centre. In this it recalls to a lesser degree the through-wall at Knock Farril. Several outworks defend the easiest approach from the hillside to the S.

Abernethy, Fort (NO 183153), 3½ miles ESE. of Bridge of Earn, Sheet 58 (A.90, A.913, by-road and moorland). *Perthshire.*

Castle Law, Abernethy, looks out over the confluence of the Rivers Earn and Tay from a distance of 2 miles SW. of the Roman fort at Carpow. It was excavated between 1896 and 1898, when it was found to consist of a main enclosure measuring 136 ft. by 51 ft. which was covered on the W. by an outer wall up to 18 ft. thick. The inner wall, varying in thickness from 18 ft. to 25 ft., and still standing to a height of as much as 7 ft., was found to contain sockets for horizontal timbers running both from front to back and longitudinally within the wall. A rock-cut well was found in the interior. This fort was the nucleus of Childe's Abernethy complex. The discovery in this and other forts with timber-laced walls of such objects as La Tène Ic brooches led him to suppose that such forts must be assignable to a date well back in the second half of the 1st millennium B.C. if, for the sake of argument, the owners of the brooches and the builders of the forts were one and if, as one of the principal techniques of archaeology would have it, the brooches could be used for dating purposes.

Dun Mor, Fort (NN 906304), 6 miles NNE. of Crieff, Sheet 52 (A.85, A.822, B.8063, farm road and moorland). *Perthshire.*

This fort stands at a height of 1500 ft. O.D. overlooking the mouth of the Sma' Glen and lower Strathalmond, at a distance of 1½ miles NNW. of the Roman fort at Fendoch. It measures about 150 ft. by 90 ft. within two ruinous walls, the entrance being in the NW. It has been cited as a fort with timber-laced walls, but this claim cannot be substantiated by external evidence alone, as the walls are both narrow and low in appearance and so entirely without traces of structural details that it may even be questioned whether they were ever completed. It is not impossible that the stones were merely piled in preparation for building, as in the case of examples farther N., such as Little Conval.

Dundurn, Fort (NN 707233), 4 miles W. of Comrie, Sheet 51 (A.85 and farm road). *Perthshire.*

This famous fort occupies an isolated rocky knoll which rises from the floodplain of the River Earn at a point 1 mile downstream from the foot of Loch Earn. It consists of a series of ruined walls which form defended compounds and courtyards all over the flanks of the knoll, the uppermost measuring about 70 ft. in diameter.

The fort is presumed to be the place referred to in the *Annals of Ulster* as being under siege in the year 683, and to have been a principal Pictish stronghold. If this was in fact the case, then it may possibly have served such a purpose for something above 800 years prior to that date.

Rossie Law, Fort (NN 997124), 1¾ miles SW. of Dunning, Sheet 58 (B.8062, farm road and moorland). *Perthshire.*

This fort is the largest of those which occupy peaks on the N. face of the Ochil range overlooking lower Strathearn from the S. It is formed by a single wall which measures 14 ft. in thickness in places and which encloses an area 600 ft. in length by 500 ft. in width. Very slight traces of platforms or scoops which can be distinguished in parts of the interior might represent traces of the sites of timber-framed buildings.

Machany, Fort (NN 902158), 3¼ miles NW. of Auchterarder, Sheet 58 (by-road). *Perthshire.*

This fort occupies a low ridge ¼ mile N. of Machany, close to the right bank of the Machany Water. It consists of an oval enclosure measuring 170 ft. by 115 ft. within a wall now reduced to a stony mound about 15 ft. thick in which several masses of vitrified matter can be seen. Apart from being in trees, the conditions and situation of this fort are comparable to those of the Cairnton vitrified fort at the N. end of Strathmore.

Evelick, Fort (NO 199257), 3 miles SE. of Balbeggie, Sheet 53 (A.94, by-road and farm road). *Perthshire.*

This is one of the forts on the SW. extremity of the Sidlaw Hills. It is oval on plan, measuring about 250 ft. by 200 ft. within defences which are stronger towards the easy approach from the N. but now entirely absent in the S. where the site is bordered by an extremely steep slope to a burn. In the NW. and N. there are up to five ramparts and ditches, all pierced by the entrance causeway.

Dunsinane (Dunsinnan), Fort (NO 214316), 3 miles NE. of Balbeggie, Sheet 53 (B.953 and by-road). *Perthshire.*

This fort occupies the conspicuous summit of Dunsinane Hill, 12 miles ESE. of Birnam Wood with which it is inter-visible. It was somewhat spoiled by excavations in 1854. The central enclosure measures about 180 ft. by 100 ft. within a bold ruined rampart which might have been a timber-laced wall; it is strengthened by the remains of three lesser ramparts. The excavators found a small bi-lobed souterrain inside the fort, and some vitrified stone. They gave the impression that the main wall was the source of this, the wall "prepared by an ancient people, who had advanced so far in refinement as to have felt the importance of uniting in considerable bodies, to defend themselves against their powerful enemies". The fort may probably be numbered among the timber-laced structures.

Barry Hill, Fort (NO 262504), 1½ miles NE. of Alyth, Sheet 53 (B.954). *Perthshire.*

The remains of this fort comprise chiefly a massive tumbled stone wall among the ruins of which lumps of vitrified matter occur, indicating that it was a timber-laced structure. The interior measures about 200 ft. in length by 120 ft. in width. Several subsidiary ramparts lie outside this, and the possibility exists that the main wall was a secondary work. A well-like hollow lies outside the W. arc of the main wall but within the protection of an outer rampart.

Inchtuthill, Fort (NO 115393), 1¾ miles E. by S. of Caputh, Sheet 53 (A.984 and farm roads). *Perthshire.*

This fort occupies a promontory at the SW. extremity of the plateau formed by the shifting of the bed of the River Tay and occupied for the most part by its ephemeral neighbours, the Roman fort and camp. It is remarkable for having provided some of the earliest evidence for all-timber defences in Scotland. This consisted of a palisade trench running across the tail of the promontory accompanied by a ditch, both elements being found when a trench was dug into the fort in 1901. The area demarcated by the palisade and the rim of the promontory measured about 200 ft. by 100 ft. along the principal axes. This was more than doubled at some time after the Romans had abandoned their ambitious works on the main part of the plateau, when as many as five ramparts and ditches were thrown across the neck of the promontory. The defended area now measured about 250 ft. athwart the promontory and 150 ft. along it. The defences occupied a space some 300 ft. in width by 200 ft. in length. Great numbers of the blocks of Gourdie stone used by the Romans to face their rampart were taken and used in this remarkable work. A hole was made in the middle of the enclosure in 1901, revealing what appeared to be part of the paved floor of a circular house.

Duncan's Camp, Fort (NO 046394), 1¾ miles SSE. of Birnam, Sheet 53 (A.9 and private grounds). *Perthshire.*

This fort stands on high ground from which it commands uninterrupted views across Stormont and middle Strathtay to the far side of Strathmore. It is formed on a natural plateau measuring 200 ft. by 90 ft. at the maxima. Only slight traces of defences now survive, in the shape of two ramparts and ditches which cover the entrance in the N.

Castle Dow, Fort (NN 929513), 4¼ miles ENE. of Aberfeldy, Sheet 52 (A.827, B.898 and moorland). *Perthshire.*

This fort is placed on a steep-faced hill dominating the bend in the River Tay at Grandtully. It consists of a main enclosure measuring about 300 ft. by 215 ft. within a thick ruined wall, with two additional walls, in a much more ruinous state, forming a kind of annexe.

Dun Mac Tual, Fort (NN 778474), 1¼ miles N. by E. of Kenmore, Sheet 51 (forest paths). *Perthshire.*

Dun Mac Tual is now shrouded in the conifers of the Drummond Hill plantation, but the bold rocky knoll upon which it stands is still elevated above the nearest trees. It consists of a central enclosure formed by a wall which includes an area of the summit of the knoll measuring about 300 ft. by 210 ft. along the axes. This is protected on the W. by two outer walls, while an extension or annexe runs off to the N. This is perhaps the best preserved of the forts of this kind which are found within a comparatively small area.

Bareyra, Fort (NN 608333), 2 miles E. of Killin, Sheet 51 (by-road). *Perthshire.*

This fort stands in sparse woodland on a steep-flanked eminence ½ mile from the S. shore of Loch Tay, commanding the through route between the hills and the loch. It is shaped according to the somewhat subrectangular knoll upon which it stands, measuring about 350 ft. in length by 150 ft. in width within a heavy stone wall which incorporates outcrops where convenient. Although first noted by Pennant towards the end of the 18th century, it appears to have remained unnoticed thereafter until 1938.

Bochastle, Fort (NN 601075), 1½ miles W. of Callander, Sheet 57 (A.84, A.821 and moorland). *Perthshire.*

This fort is situated 250 ft. above and ¾ mile SW. of the Roman fort which once stood near the right bank of the River Teith, a little above the present town of Callander. It is protected on the E. by a precipitous slope and in other directions by four impressive, heavy ruinous walls, the silhouette of which can be seen from afar. The area enclosed measures about 180 ft. from N. to S. by about 150 ft. transversely. A depression near the centre probably marks the site of a well.

Craigmarloch Wood, Fort (NS 344718), 1¾ miles NW. of Kilmacolm, Sheet 63 (A.761). *Renfrewshire.*

This fort stands in open woodland on a hill which separates the houses of East and West Kilbride. It is a flattened oval on plan, measuring 160 ft. by 85 ft. within the ruin of a stone wall originally about 10 ft. thick. On either side of the entrance, in the WNW., small masses of vitrified matter have been observed, implying that in this sector at least the wall was laced with timber. An annexe 130 ft. in length and 60 ft. in breadth lies against the N. side of the fort, and traces of outer works lie to the S. Excavation showed that the fort was preceded by a palisade of the 8th century B.C.

Walls Hill, Fort (NS 411588), 1¼ miles SE. of Howwood, Sheet 64 (by-road and farm road). *Renfrewshire.*

This fort crowns a steep-sided rocky table measuring 1600 ft. in length by 700 ft. in greatest width, and the remains of the fort wall, which can be traced here and there round much of the perimeter, enclose an area of a little more than 18 acres. This puts it well into the *oppidum* class, locally, for apart from Traprain Law and Eildon Hill North, such an acreage is exceeded only by Hownam Law and the somewhat questionable Arthur's Seat, and approached only by Burnswark. As at the Seat, however, there are no surface traces of dwellings on Walls Hill; but excavations have revealed two Early Iron Age occupations, with circular timber-framed houses. If this fort is what it seems, therefore, it must be an *oppidum*—if not *the oppidum*—of the Damnonii.

Duncarnock, Fort (NS 500559), 2½ miles W. of Newton Mearns, Sheet 64 (by-road, B.769, by-road). *Renfrewshire.*

Although now only just S. of the obliterating conurbations SW. of Glasgow, it is still possible to realise what pleasant and extensive views this hill once commanded to N. and E. as well as to S. and W. Its summit consists of a broad ridge at the N. extremity of which a rocky knoll rises rather suddenly. The fort comprises a wall, originally about 10 ft. thick, which takes in the whole feature, and the suggestion of a partial inner defence round the knoll. The fort measures 630 ft. in length by 330 ft. in breadth, the summit of the knoll 110 ft. by 80 ft. A piece of pre-Roman native pottery has been picked up in the fort.

Dunwan, Fort (NS 547489), 2½ miles SW. of Eaglesham, Sheet 64 (B.764 and moorland). *Renfrewshire.*

This fort occupies an isolated hill rising from near the N. limit of an extensive tract of hilly marshland. It is triangular on plan, measuring 260 ft. by 160 ft. within a single wall or rampart originally at least 12 ft. thick. The interior contains surface traces of two circular timber-framed houses. Traces of an outer line of defence can be followed round the lowest slopes of the hill.

Kessock, Fort (NH 663491), 2 miles N. of Inverness, Sheet 26 (Kessock Vehicular Ferry and forest footpaths). *Ross & Cromarty.*

The Ord of Kessock attains a height of 633 ft. above sea level on the N. side of the narrows at the junction between the Beauly and Moray Firths, matching Craig Phadrig 2½ miles to the SE. The pair of them are seen to the best advantage from the straight stretch of the A.9 road immediately N. of Beauly, 7 miles to the W. The whole of the summit of the Ord, which measures about 900 ft. by 230 ft., has been surrounded by a stone wall. As the hill is now planted with conifers just reaching their prime, it is difficult to get a comprehensive view of the fort, while several long stretches of the wall have disappeared over rock-faces and low cliffs in the N. and E. sectors. The entrance is in the S., and one stretch of the wall to the NE. of this is represented by low but massive vitrifaction adhering to the living rock, indicating that the wall was timber-laced. The entrance is protected by outer walls which now take the form of broad mounds of tumbled blocks and boulders about 30 ft. apart.

Knock Farril, Fort (NH 505585), 1¼ miles E. of Strathpeffer, Sheet 26 (footpath). *Ross & Cromarty.*

Knock Farril was one of the forts which attracted the attention of John Williams of the Honourable Board of Annexed Estates in the 1770s, and has never ceased to occupy an important place in the study of vitrified forts. Its plan is enigmatic, for although the main enclosure measures a conventional 425 ft. by up to 125 ft., it is transfixed by a heavy vitrified wall which protrudes at either end, in one case double. There are also outworks of a conventional kind at either end. The great size of all the remains, and the blurring of outlines and details, render almost all questions about this fort unanswerable as yet.

Cnoc an Duin, Fort (NH 696769), 9 miles NE. of Evanton, Sheet 21 (A.9, A.836 to Strathrory, then moorland footpath). *Ross & Cromarty.*

This fort is situated on an eminence forming part of the N. side of Strathrory 1½ miles W. of Scotsburn House. It is a splendid example of an unfinished fort, several others of which occur in E. Scotland. The wall which was to enclose an area measuring about 730 ft. in length by about 250 ft. transversely has been only a little more than half completed, and the W. end reveals some interesting constructional information. Outside, two unfinished lines of ramparts with external quarry ditches lie on the flanks of the hill in deep heather. The interior is flat and barren for the most part, enlivened only by a stone-lined well of unknown date.

Gairloch, Fort (NG 802753), S. end of Gairloch, Sheet 19 (A.832).

Ross & Cromarty.

This little fort occupies a small promontory named An Dun on the E. shore of Loch Gairloch. Although several contiguous enclosures have been described as occupying the site, it seems certain that in fact only one of them is authentic. This is bordered on the E. by natural fissures which have been quarried until they form deep ditches with a causeway 7 ft. wide between them. The enclosure, lying W. of this on the promontory proper, is formed by the grass-grown remains of a wall which stand to a general height of 2 ft.; it measures about 65 ft. in either direction. A large mass of vitrified matter flanks the entrance on the S. Beyond the fort the tip of the promontory is cut off from the rest by a natural gully, but there is no evidence available to suggest that this too was a defended area, even though this may seem to have been a probability.

Creagan Fhamhair, Gairloch, Fort (NG 823726), 2¾ miles SSE. of Gairloch, Sheet 19 (A.832 and moorland).

Ross & Cromarty.

This fort stands on the rocky hill round the S. and W. parts of the foot of which the River Kerry bends W. and N. 1 mile before debouching into Loch Kerry. To W. and N. the site is flanked by cliffs 50 ft. high forming natural defences which are completed to E. and S. by a wall, so that together they enclose an area measuring about 100 ft. in either direction. The wall was at least 6 ft. thick, and until robbed in recent years stood as high. The entrance is in the SW.

Dun Lagaidh, Fort and Broch (NH 143914), 1¾ miles SSE. of Ullapool, Sheet 20 (boat). *Ross & Cromarty.*

This fort, situated opposite Ullapool on the SW. shore of Loch Broom, measures 300 ft. by 120 ft. within a wall about 12 ft. thick along parts of which vitrified material can be seen. The entrance, in the E., is further defended by ditches and banks. The E. part of the interior is occupied by a secondary broch; the lower courses of the wall of this are so encumbered with debris that its dimensions cannot easily be established, but at the lowest point possible they were found to be a wall thickness of about 12 ft. and an internal diameter of 36 ft. MacKie has shown that the fort, dating from about the 7th century B.C., was reoccupied in mediaeval times.

Dun Canna, Fort (NC 112008), 4 miles N. of Ullapool, Sheet 15 (A.835 and footpaths). *Ross & Cromarty.*

This fort stands on the shore a mile N. of the mouth of the River Kanaird, looking W. over the bay towards the Summer Isles. The main defence is a massive wall, heavily vitrified, which amply defends a narrow promontory. The attenuated W. extremity of the latter is occupied by a separate, also heavily vitrified, wall which encloses an area measuring about 140 ft. in length by 40 ft. in width. It is certainly possible that the latter is a separate and later work than the former, though difficult to prove.

Inverpolly, Fort (NC 066155), 4½ miles SSW. of Lochinver, Sheet 15 (by-road and moorland). *Ross & Cromarty.*

The coast between Lochinver and Achiltibuie is archaeologically unexplored, and what now appears as an isolated monument may in fact be one of several works of one kind or another. This small vitrified fort occupies an oval promontory which is almost insulated at high tide and which is best approached by boat, owing to the intransigent nature of the ground behind it. The main enclosure wall is heavily and generally

34   *Eildon Hill North*, oppidum *of the Selgovae. The Romans built their forts and supply depots at the foot of the hill, at Newstead*

vitrified—at present the most northerly example of such a phenomenon on the W. coast.

Eildon Hill North, *Oppidum* Hill-fort (NT 555328), 1 mile SE. of Melrose, Sheet 73 (footpath).   *Roxburghshire.*

This hill-fort, the *oppidum* of the Selgovae, is only matched in area in Scotland by Traprain Law, the *oppidum* of the Votadini. Unlike the latter, however, its life appears to have ended on the arrival of the Roman armies in Tweeddale in A.D. 79. Nevertheless, three structural periods can be recognised, the earliest a fort formed by a now almost invisible single wall or rampart enclosing the summit of the hill for a length of about 600 ft. and a width of about 170 ft. This was superseded by a minor *oppidum* 9 acres in extent which took in the flanks of the hill N. and NE. of the earlier work as well as the area already covered by this. Finally, the place was fundamentally reconstructed within two heavy ramparts to include about 40 acres and so to form a hill-top town some 1500 ft. in diameter. Numerous platforms, about 300 of which

are easily visible, testify to the former presence of timber-framed houses.

A little W. of the summit of the hill a penannular shallow ditch represents the last visible trace of a Roman signal-station of the 1st century A.D., presumably erected in connection with the great fort and supply base situated at that time at the NW. foot of the hill.

Little Trowpenny, Fort (NT 631256) ¾ mile N. of Ancrum, Sheet 74 (A.68).   *Roxburghshire.*

This interesting promontory fort occupies the end of a steep-flanked spur just above and E. of the A.68 road. Its almost circular interior, about 200 ft. in diameter, is defended by the remains of a stone wall about 12 ft. thick, with an entrance in the E. Beyond this the saddle of the spur is crossed by three additional ruined walls, the outer pair of which have been severely robbed, and mutilated by cultivation. The design and appearance of this fort are perfectly consistent with a date in the pre-Roman Iron Age.

Castle Hill, Ancrum, Fort (NT 624249), ¼ mile NW. of Ancrum, Sheet 74 (A.68, B.6400).   *Roxburghshire.*

The substantial remains of this fort crown one end of an isolated mound situated in a crook of the Ale Water $\frac{1}{2}$ mile SW. of Little Trowpenny fort, described above. The central enclosure is oval, measuring 200 ft. by 165 ft. within the remains of a stone wall about 10 ft. thick. It is protected on the NW. and N. by an outer ruinous wall, but this is brought to a sudden termination in the NE. by one of two walls which run out from the central enclosure to border each side of the ridge which runs off to the NE. Two outer walls crossing the ridge also join at their ends to these flanking walls, the whole system providing a rather stronger version of the defences at Little Trowpenny. Their appearance suggests, however, that they may represent a reconstruction; and as no very close parallel to this design is known among the local pre-Roman Iron Age monuments, they have been considered to be of later date.

Ringleyhall, Fort (NT 667312), 4 miles SW. of Kelso, Sheet 74 (A.699).
Roxburghshire.

This fort, situated on the steep right bank of the River Tweed, now consists of a rampart enclosing an area measuring about 190 ft. in diameter surrounded in part by the remains of two others. The entrance is in the SE.

Hownam Law, Fort (NT 796220), 2½ miles SE. of Morebattle, Sheet 74 (by-road, farm roads and moorland).
Roxburghshire.

This minor *oppidum*, situated between its fellows on Yeavering Bell, in Northumberland, and Eildon Hill North (q.v.), is formed like them by a single wall about 10 ft. thick. It contains surface traces of at least 155 timber-framed houses in the form of shallow platforms or saucer-like depressions, according to the degree of natural slope upon which they were constructed. The fort covers an area of 22 acres; a small embanked enclosure lying in the NE. corner is probably of later date.

Hownam Rings, Fort (NT 790194), 3¾ miles S. by E. of Morebattle, Sheet 80 (by-road and footpath). *Roxburghshire.*

This fort has become one of the most important in Britain by reason of an excavation carried out in 1948 during which a long sequence of occupations,

each accompanied by a reconstruction, was revealed. These consisted of, first, a settlement defended by a single palisade; then a reconstruction in the same form; then a conversion to a stone wall some 10 ft. thick; then a remodelling of the defences in the form of three ramparts with external ditches; and finally, after the defences were abandoned, an open settlement of circular stone-walled houses and a subrectangular homestead with one or more similar houses, a type of structure now well known in Northumberland.

The results of this break-through to an understanding of the sequence of structural techniques covering more than half a millennium cannot be over-estimated.

Hayhope Knowe, Settlement (NT 860176), 6¾ miles SE. of Morebattle, Sheet 80 (B.6401, by-roads, green road and moorland). *Roxburghshire.*

Hayhope Knowe, the first place at which surface traces of palisades and timber-framed houses were recognised on the surface by the use of air-photographs, was excavated in 1949. It consists of an oval enclosure formed by twin palisades, traces of which are clear among the short coarse pasture, measuring 285 ft. by 165 ft. and containing at least 14 timber-framed houses the annular grooves representing parts of several of which are also clearly visible. The settlement was surrounded at a distance varying between 20 ft. and 40 ft. by an outlying palisade, presumably to form a corral for cattle; but this was mostly obliterated by a bank and ditch, begun to strengthen the defences but abandoned before completion.

Loddan Hill, Fort (NT 755111), 8¼ miles S. of Morebattle, Sheet 80 (by-road and moorland). *Roxburghshire.*

This is an example of the bivallate, virtually circular, forts which contain surface traces of timber-framed houses. It measures 225 ft. in diameter almost exactly, within the denuded remains of two ramparts, and contains traces of at least five houses in the form of penannular rings of grooving.

Burnt Humbleton, Fort (NT 852280), 2 miles ESE. of Kirk Yetholm, Sheet 74 (by-road, farm track and moorland). *Roxburghshire.*

The most conspicuous feature of this fort is a walled enclosure measuring 160 ft. by 100 ft. which crowns the hill. This oval enclosure, however, stands within the ruin of a wall which forms an enclosure measuring about 300 ft. in length by 190 ft. in width and which may be an earlier structure. If this diagnosis is correct, then the smaller work may be comparable to others such as the one at Dalmahoy (q.v.), and may possibly date from the early centuries A.D.

Steer Rig, Settlement (NT 859254), 3 miles SE. of Kirk Yetholm, Sheet 74 (by-road, farm track and moorland).

Roxburghshire.

This settlement, cut by the fence which here borders Northumberland and Roxburghshire, consists of the traces of parts of a palisaded enclosure measuring about 200 ft. in length by 150 ft. in width in which are the surface traces of at least five ring-groove timber-framed houses.

Peniel Heugh, Fort (NT 654263), 3½ miles N. of Jedburgh, Sheet 74 (A.68, B.6400 and farm road). *Roxburghshire.*

The forts on Peniel Heugh, a conspicuous hill topped by a Waterloo monument, are of great interest in that they exhibit a sequence of completely contrasting structural techniques. The earlier fort is an oval bivallate structure formed by two rubble ramparts, the remains of which are now slight. The later is a kidney-shaped fort formed by a single wall, some of the lower courses of which, particularly in the NE. sector, are still well preserved.

Shaw Craigs, Fort (NT 673095), 7 miles S. by E. of Jedburgh, Sheet 80 (A.68, by-road and pasture land).

Roxburghshire.

This fort, and its small neighbour on Hophills Nob (NT 707094), are visible to the traveller reaching Carter Bar from the S. The Shaw Craigs fort comprises the remains of three structural phases. The first, formed by a single rampart and measuring about 700 ft. in length, was succeeded in the second phase by a trivallate fort 865 ft. long. The final phase is represented by a ruined wall enclosing an area 280 ft. long by 160 ft. wide.

Woden Law, Fort (NT 768125), 8¾ miles SE. of Jedburgh, Sheet 80 (by-roads and green Roman road).

Roxburghshire.

35   *Woden Law Fort and Roman Siegeworks. The Roman road known as Dere Street descends the gully just beyond the fort*

This multivallate fort reveals three structural phases; first a single stone wall, then this with a pair of ramparts added to create defence in depth, and lastly another single wall, the innermost of the present four visible lines of defence. But the fort is of especial interest in that it is invested by the banks and ditches of Roman siege-works. One system of these comprises two banks between three ditches situated close outside the fort, while other, independent, siege lines consisting of a bank with a ditch on either side, lie at varying distances beyond. The siege-works are considered to have been made as training exercises by the Roman army, presumably by troops billeted in the near-by temporary camps at Pennymuir.

Kaim Law, Fort (NT 512131), 1 mile SE. of Hawick, Sheet 79 (B.6399 and by-road). *Roxburghshire.*

This fort represents the elongated ridge-forts of Teviotdale, measuring 360 ft. in length by 90 ft. in width. The defences at the narrow ends consist of two ruinous ramparts with external ditches, but no surface traces remain along the crests of the long sides. The interior contains surface traces of at least five ring-ditch timber-framed houses measuring, on average, about 25 ft. in diameter.

Bonchester Hill, Fort (NT 595117), 5½ miles E. of Hawick, Sheet 80 (A.6088 and pasture land). *Roxburghshire.*

The remains of this fort form a complex of ruinous walls, ramparts and ditches which represent several structural phases and modifications. An early occupation is attested by the recovery during excavations of a ring-headed pin and part of a La Tène Ic brooch, and a later one by the presence of foundations of several circular stone-walled houses probably dating from the 2nd century A.D.

Rubers Law, Fort (NT 580155), 6 miles E. of Hawick, Sheet 80 (A.698, A.6088, by-road and moorland). *Roxburghshire.*

This fort crowning a spectacular igneous peak is a work of at least two structural periods. The earlier is represented principally by a wall or rampart most of which can be followed as it forms an enclosure measuring about 900 ft. in length from N. to S. by about 600 ft. transversely at a level considerably below that of the summit of the hill. The later work, a walled enclosure, includes only the summit of the hill and measures axially about 300 ft. by 200 ft. It is of great interest in that some of the blocks lying in the ruin of the wall are re-used Roman stones, identifiable by their having one face etched with diamond broaching. This implies that the enclosure of the second period must have been built in part from the ruin of some such building as a signal-station, at some time later than about the year A.D. 200.

Southdean Law, Fort and Settlement (NT 635094), 9 miles ESE. of Hawick, Sheet 80 (A.698, A.6088 and pasture land). *Roxburghshire.*

This bivallate Early Iron Age fort presents a classic demonstration of such a structure being succeeded early in the 1st millennium A.D. by an open settlement of stone-walled houses. It measures 290 ft. by 150 ft. within the two ramparts, but the NE. half of the interior and the same sector of the ramparts have been overlain and obliterated by the later structures.

Tamshiel Rig, Settlement (NT 643062), 10 miles SE. of Hawick, Sheet 80 (A.698, A.6088 and moorland). *Roxburghshire.*

This settlement originally consisted of an Early Iron Age bivallate enclosure measuring axially about 250 ft. by 175 ft., probably comparable to the settlement at Harehope (q.v.). This was in due course replaced by a walled settlement 140 ft. long and 125 ft. wide, containing several circular stone-walled houses and dating from the early centuries A.D. It is of outstanding interest in that it stands at the head of a D-shaped system of fields belonging to the later phase of occupation which are, at present, the only representatives of such phenomena in North Britain.

White Knowe, Settlement (NT 494079), 4 miles S. of Hawick, Sheet 79 (B.6399 and footpath). *Roxburghshire.*

This settlement, in the Stobs estate which has been used as a military training area, is of great interest in that it comprises at least 11 ring-groove timber-framed houses within the remains of two very slight banks with a median ditch. The settlement may represent a completed example of the kind of work that was being carried out at Hayhope Knowe (q.v.) when the circumstances prevailing caused it to be abandoned.

Penchrise Pen, Fort (NT 490062), 5 miles S. of Hawick, Sheet 79 (by-road and pasture land). *Roxburghshire.*

This fort, crowning a steep-sided peak in ground that has been used as a military training area and may not be innocent of explosives, is a trivallate structure with two annexes. One of these, to the W., contains surface traces of at least four ring-groove timber-framed houses.

Gray Coat, Settlement and Homestead (NT 471049, NT 471052), 6 miles SSW. of Hawick, Sheet 79 (by-road and moorland). *Roxburghshire.*

The larger of these two monuments, situated on the summit of the ridge called Gray Coat, consists of an almost sub-rectangular enclosure formed by the low, pillaged ruin of a wall and measuring 350 ft. in length by 200 ft. in width. It contains surface traces of at least eight ring-groove timber-framed houses of which three appear as double rings.

The homestead, lying about 300 yds. N. of the settlement, is formed by the surface traces of a twin palisade, the elements of which unite in a curve on either side of the entrance. It measures 154 ft. in length by 123 ft. in width, and contains the surface trace of a ring-groove house 50 ft. in diameter.

Highchesters, Fort (NT 450135), 3 miles W. of Hawick, Sheet 79 (A.7, B.711 and pasture land). *Roxburghshire.*

This fort is an example of the sub-rectangular ridge-forts of Teviotdale. It measures axially 220 ft. by 160 ft. within the remains of three ramparts which are better preserved at the narrower ends of the fort, athwart the ridge.

Kemp's Castle, Settlements (NT 438165), 4 miles WNW. of Hawick, Sheet 79 (A.7, B.711, by-road and moorland). *Roxburghshire.*

The remains of two settlements comprise, first, an oval palisaded settlement measuring 300 ft. by 150 ft. within a very slight intermittent mound which probably represents the course of a palisade and which contains surface traces of at least four ring-groove houses. This settlement is partly overlain at the NE. by a smaller one, formed within a bank with an external ditch and containing at least five similar houses, one of them oval.

Carby Hill, Fort (NY 490844), 2 miles S. of Newcastleton, Sheet 79 (B.6357 and by-road). *Roxburghshire.*

This fort, crowning the conspicuous summit of Carby Hill, consists of an oval enclosure measuring 285 ft. by 225 ft. within the massive ruin of a stone wall which must originally have measured 10 ft. or 12 ft. in thickness. The inner edge of the tumble is followed by the ruin of a comparatively recent dry-stone dyke, the builders of which were probably responsible for a good deal of the ruination of the remains of the wall.

It is possible, however, that the fort wall was reduced at a much earlier date. The interior contains six circular stone foundations, a type which normally occurs in this part of the country either in small, possibly walled, settlements or in ruined forts, and which has been shown to date from no earlier than the 2nd century A.D. or later. Carby Hill fort might just possibly represent an unusually large example of this kind of late settlement; but it is also possible that it originally contained timber-framed houses of which no surface trace remains in the coarse grass and rushes which clothe the interior, and that it dates from pre-Roman times.

Torwoodlee, Fort and Broch (NT 475381), 2 miles NW. of Galashiels, Sheet 73 (A.72). *Selkirkshire.*

This fort, which lies in a plantation and has suffered mutilation from quarrying, is a very ruinous bivallate structure measuring about 450 ft. by 350 ft. internally. It is probable that when the Roman armies arrived in Tweeddale in A.D. 80 the occupants of this, as of other forts in the territory of the Selgovae, were despoiled of their stronghold, and its defences reduced.

When the Roman occupation ceased in A.D. 100, it would seem that a group of enterprising Picts entered the district, for one of the 10 brochs known to be situated in the Tay-Tweed area was built partly on the ruin of the inner rampart of the fort and partly within the interior. A considerable amount of Roman pottery and glass dating from the 1st century A.D. was found by excavators both on the broch floor and under its wall. This material must have been gleaned from the then abandoned Roman base at Newstead, 6 miles to the E.

The life of the broch must have been as brief as that of its builders, for when the Romans returned for the second occupation, in A.D. 140, one of their first acts was to knock it down and put as much as possible of the stone from its walls into its ditch. It is reasonable to suppose that the same timetable of erection, occupation and demolition should be applied to the neighbouring broch at Bow, Midlothian (q.v.).

The Rink, Fort (NT 480327), 2¼ miles S. of Galashiels, Sheet 73 (A.7, B.7060).
Selkirkshire.

The striking remains of this fort lie for the most part in a walled plantation on a ridge a few hundred yards NW. of The Rink farmhouse, to which they gave its name (Rings). The earliest work on the site appears to have been an oval fort or settlement measuring some 500 ft. by 300 ft. within a single rampart, which is now represented only by a ploughed-out fragment lying W. of the plantation wall. The next structural phase was an almost circular enclosure about 200 ft. in diameter, formed by two heavy concentric ramparts, with a median ditch. The ruin of a massive stone wall lies on the inner rampart, but it is impossible to tell whether this is a contemporary feature or whether it represents a third structural phase. Surface finds indicate occupation in pre-Roman and in early Roman-British times. The ruinous foundations of several rectangular buildings which lie immediately E. of the fort are probably of comparatively recent date.

Clickhimin, Fort, Broch, etc. (HU 465408), in the W. outskirts of Lerwick, Sheet 4 (A.970). *Shetland, Mainland island.*

The early settlement at Clickhimin, the fort, the broch and the later dwellings which have all occupied the site at one time or another have recently been excavated under the direction of Mr J. R. C. Hamilton. The ruins, preserved and placed under guardianship by the Ministry of Works, form as informative and impressive a group as Jarlshof and contain interest comparable to Mousa. As at these other two places, the Official Guide alone can do justice to the series of diverse problems which excavation and research have discovered and have answered. It may be remarked here, however, that the Clickhimin "block-house" is at the present time the best

preserved and most easily understood of these rare and interesting monuments.

Ness of Burgi, Fort (HU 388084), 1½ miles S. of Sumburgh airport, Sheet 4 (by-road and pasture land).
Shetland, Mainland island.

This fort is one of the "block-house" structures which have only been thoroughly explored and understood recently, during the excavations at Clickhimin. The fort on Ness of Burgi consists of inner "block-house" defence as well as a formidable set of outworks. The latter comprise two ditches, cutting off the tip of the Ness, with a substantial ruined wall, about 21 ft. in thickness and 7 ft. in height, between them. The piece of land cut off by these heavy works now measures little more than 100 ft. in either direction. The "block-house" is situated along the inner lip of the inner ditch, now stretching over a distance of as much as 74 ft. but originally running a little farther to the SW. where falls of the cliff have pruned the wall. It is 20 ft. thick. It is pierced at approximately the middle by a passage which is aligned with a gap in the wall between the ditches; the passage is checked for a door and fitted with a bar-hole.

On either side of the passage a cell occupies the thickness of the wall, while a third such is broken open by the fall at the SW. extremity. The entrances to the cells still have several massive lintels *in situ*, as does the outer section of the passage beyond the door-checks.

It has been found at Clickhimin that the "block-house", for long so puzzling an object, was in fact a fortified gatehouse against the inner face of which lean-to houses, up to three storeys in height, were built. They were tied to the face of the wall, which indeed formed one of their own, by heavy beams thrust into prepared sockets. It was also found that the "block-house" fort was succeeded by the broch, and must thus be earlier, if only by a little, than the latter structure.

Loch of Huxter, Fort (HU 558620), 1½ miles E. of Symbister, Sheet 3 (by-roads and moorland). *Shetland, Whalsay island.*

This well preserved example of the "block-house" fort occupies a small island joined to the shore of Loch Huxter by a man-made causeway, a position closely comparable to that

36　*Ness of Burgi "Blockhouse" Fort. The entrance passage from the interior*

selected by the builders of the similar structure at the Loch of Clickhimin. The "block-house" measures 41 ft. in length by 11 ft. in width, the same as at Clickhimin, but here the wall attached to either end of the "block-house" and forming an enclosed garth or fort is in a good state of preservation. The area thus defined measures about 70 ft. in diameter.

Burgi Geos, Fort (HP 477034), 5 miles NE. of Gutcher, Sheet 1 (3½ miles of moorland NW. from Dalsetter, or by sea).　*Shetland, Yell island.*

This "block-house" fort occupies a position similar to but twice as high as and much more remote than the Ness of Burgi. The outer defence is a wall of large independent set stones which from afar give the impression of a rather coarse *chevaux de frise.* Behind this, the tail of the promontory is defended by a "block-house" wall about 35 ft. long and 13 ft. thick.

South Haven, Promontory Fort (HY 223723), 300 yds. SSW. of North Haven pier, Sheet 4 (by "Good Shepherd" from Grutness).　*Shetland, Fair Isle.*

This fort occupies a promontory separating the South Haven from Mavers Geo which measures 175 ft. in length by an average width of 32 ft. The long E. and W. flanks, meeting at the S., fall precipitously through 70 ft. to the shore below, but the narrow N. neck has been defended by three rubble ramparts with quarry ditches. While this fort could be of prehistoric origin, it could equally be early mediaeval.

Dun Gerashader, Fort (NG 489453), 1 mile NNE. of Portree, Sheet 23 (A.855).　*Skye.*

This fort stands on a flat-topped ridge near the left bank of the River Chracaig. Oval on plan, it measures 170 ft. by 100 ft. within a wall up to 14 ft. thick in the S., from which direction approach is easiest. The entrance is in the E. At least two lines of boulders cross the S. approach, at distances of 60 ft. and 80 ft. respectively from the S. arc of the fort wall, and two other possible lines lie nearer in. These form an obstacle akin to a *chevaux de frise.*

Dun Cruinn, Fort (NG 412516), 6½ miles NW. of Portree, Sheet 23 (A.850, footpath and moorland).　*Skye.*

This fort occupies a flat-topped rocky hill the summit of which measures 300 ft. in length by 80 ft. in maximum width. This was originally surrounded by a dry-stone wall most of which has now fallen away. An earthen rampart quarried from an internal ditch borders the foot of the NE. and SE. flanks of the hill at a distance varying from 35 ft. to 80 ft. from the wall of the fort. The entrance is in the SW.

The ruin of what may be a small dun, measuring about 40 ft. by 30 ft. within a ruined and overgrown wall, occupies the S. end of the summit plateau, while banks, circles and a ditch also lie upon it.

Dun Skudiburgh, Fort and Dun (NG 374647), 1¾ miles NW. of Uig, Sheet 23 (A.855, farm road and moorland). *Skye.*

This fort occupies a conspicuous rocky ridge near the shore 1 mile N. of Uig Bay. It is oval on plan, measuring axially 150 ft. by 120 ft. within a ruinous wall about 10 ft. thick. It is covered on the E. by a similar wall 320 ft. long and on the N. by two walls, the outer of which stops short of the long wall to leave an entrance gap.

A small drop-shaped dun measuring internally 34 ft. by 24 ft. lies on the E. arc of the ruined wall of the fort near the probable position of the entrance in the latter. The wall of the dun varies between 9 ft. and 12 ft. in thickness.

Dumyat, Fort (NS 832973), 2¼ miles E. of Bridge of Allan, Sheet 57 (A.9, by-road and moorland). *Stirlingshire.*

This fort occupies the W. shoulder of Dumyat (earlier Dun Myat, and pronounced with the accent on the "y"), from which a descent of one in one falls to the Carse of Forth 1000 ft. below. To S. and E. the defended area is bordered by sheer rock faces, but to N. and W. it is enclosed by the ruins of two heavy stone walls. The interior measures axially 320 ft. by 180 ft. Slight outworks lie outside the main defences to the W. The actual summit of the site is occupied by an oval enclosure measuring about 85 ft. by 50 ft. with the ruin of a stone wall which must originally have been about 12 ft. thick. This is one of the places where the question arises whether the two defensive structures are contemporary, or whether the smaller enclosure is a late-comer, built in a ruined and disused fort. The latter may seem to be the more likely if analogies such as Dunearn Hill or Craigie Hill may be cited.

Abbey Craig, Fort (NS 809956), 1 mile NE. of Stirling, Sheet 57 (A.9, A.997 and footpath). *Stirlingshire.*

The remains of this fort have been mutilated almost into oblivion by the erection within them of a memorial tower and out-buildings during the 19th century. The area of the fort is bounded to the W. by a precipice, but was defended on the E. by a heavy stone wall which, judging by the presence among its debris of lumps of vitrified material, was a timber-laced structure. The interior measures about 175 ft. by about 125 ft.

Sauchie Craig, Fort (NS 763893), 3 miles SW. of Stirling, Sheet 57 (by-road and moorland). *Stirlingshire.*

This fort occupies a rise on the crest of the precipice which overlooks the Bannock Burn reservoir from the E. It consists of an oval enclosure 215 ft. long by 110 ft. wide defined in part by the cliff and in part by the ruin of a stone wall. Two ramparts with a median ditch lie outside this to bar approach from the gentle slopes to the E. The entrance is in the E., and the interior is featureless.

Braes, Fort (NS 797847), 1¼ miles NNW. of Dunipace, Sheet 57 (A.80 and farm road). *Stirlingshire.*

This little stone fort, noted in 1793 as a Danish observatory, stands on the top of an isolated hill just behind the farmhouse. It consists of an oval enclosure measuring 150 ft. by 85 ft. within a ruined wall among the debris of which lumps of vitrified material have been found. Minor works defend the ends. Small vitrified forts of such a size and character occur throughout the territory of the Damnonii in south-western Scotland.

Langlands, Fort (NS 822854), 3 miles NW. of Larbert, Sheet 57 (A.9 and by-road). *Stirlingshire.*

This fort occupies the end of a ridge in an otherwise level stretch of country. It is very ruinous, but can still be recognised as consisting of a circular enclosure about 75 ft. in diameter formed by an almost completely robbed wall about 12 ft. thick. This structure lies within a rampart enclosing an area about 145 ft. in length by 120 ft. in width. The remains are so far gone that it is even more difficult than usual to decide whether the smaller work is contemporary with the larger or a later intrusion.

Myot Hill, Fort (NS 781825), 2 miles W. of Denny, Sheet 57 (B.818 and by-road). *Stirlingshire.*

The slight remains of this fort crown

isolated Myot Hill the N., W. and S. flanks of which are so steep that no defences existed, or have survived, along their crests. The summit is therefore cut off only by the remains of a single rampart which crosses the approach from the E. from N. to S. to define an area measuring 215 ft. in length by 140 ft. in breadth.

Meikle Reive, Fort (NS 639789), 1 mile NE. of Lennoxtown, Sheet 64 (B.822 and moorland). *Stirlingshire.*

This fort occupies a little promontory at the foot of the steep NW. face of the Kilsyth Hills. It consists of an enclosure measuring 145 ft. by 120 ft. within a ruined wall originally measuring 12 ft. thick. This structure may overlie a rampart belonging to an earlier period of construction which includes several outer ramparts and ditches barring access from the N.

Dun Creich, Fort (NH 651882), 3½ miles SE. of Bonar Bridge, Sheet 21 (A.9 and farm road). *Sutherland.*

This fort occupies a magnificent site on a peninsula which rises 370 ft. above the estuary waters which link the Kyle of Sutherland with the Dornoch Firth. But the peninsula is so heavily afforested at the present time, and the remains of the fort so overwhelmed with vegetation, that in summer it is difficult to follow the course of the walls or to see anything of the view.

The summit of the hill is enclosed by a rampart. The area thus defined measures 260 ft. by 220 ft., but the highest part of it is further defended by a rampart enclosing a space 170 ft. long by 100 ft. wide. A mediaeval ruin is situated in this, and it is not impossible that the two are closely connected. A patch of vitrifaction of a massive nature is exposed outside and beneath the W. arc of the inner rampart. Although the circumstances are obscure, it may be thought probable that this should be attributed to an earlier wall, robbed and overlain by the inner rampart already described.

Duchary Rock, Fort (NC 850050), 3¼ miles W. by N. of Brora, Sheet 17 (A.9, by-roads and peat-track). *Sutherland.*

This fort occupies a rocky boss on the E. flank of the massif between Dunrobin Glen and Strathbrora, overlooking Loch Brora from the S. and the mouth of the river from the W. The site is magnificent,

and very strong. Its flanks fall precipitously to the E., and low cliffs provide natural strength on all other sides except the NW. It is in this quarter that the wall forming the fort is best preserved, appearing as a great band of tumbled blocks, many of them very large. Stretches of both the inner and outer faces indicate that the wall is 12 ft. thick. The entrance is lined with erect slabs, a characteristic common and exclusive to the forts of the NE. of which this is the southernmost representative. The rest of the perimeter of the fort is marked either by the crest of the precipice to the E. or by lengths of ruined walling. The E. sector, which is 12 ft. thick, is pierced by a narrow but apparently valid entrance only 4 ft. wide. The interior, measuring 780 ft. by 180 ft., contains peat, some of which has been cut, and is featureless.

Ben Griam Beg, Fort (NC 831412), 3½ miles W. by S. of Forsinard, Sheet 10 (moorland). *Sutherland.*

The highest hill-fort in Scotland crowns the peaked summit of Ben Griam Beg (1903·ft. O.D.). The next highest fort, going S., is on Carrock Fell, in Cumberland (2170 ft. O.D.), the highest in Britain on Ingleborough, in Yorkshire (2370 ft. O.D.).

The remains consist of a stone wall about 6 ft. thick which encloses an area measuring 500 ft. by 200 ft. at the top of the hill, with an entrance in the N. Below this, however, on the S. flank of the hill there lie the remains of other linear walls and of walled enclosures which, if they are contemporary with the fort and of Early Iron Age date, may represent an expansion of the true fort into a much larger defended and occupied area.

Portskerra, Fort (NC 866661), 1 mile NW. of Portskerra, Sheet 10 (by-road and pasture land). *Sutherland.*

Several promontory forts of various shapes and sizes occur along the N. coasts of Caithness and Sutherland W. of Holborn Head. One such occupies the westernmost narrow promontory in the bay between the headlands Rubha na Cloiche and Rubha Brha, NW. of Portskerra. The E. and W. flanks of the promontory rise some 80 ft. sheer from the shore, and access to the grassy plateau 250 ft. long by 100 ft. wide can only be had along a narrow ridge 50 ft.

long and often only 2 ft. wide. The plateau is bordered by a bank, presumably both defensive and protective in character.

Culkein, Fort (NC 041340), 8 miles NW. of Lochinver, Sheet 15 (A.837, B.869, by-roads and moorland).
Sutherland.

The high rocky point known as the headland of the fort, Rubh 'an Dunain, protrudes NE. from the shore-line between the Bay of Culkein and the Point of Stoer. It has been made into a promontory fort by a wall 40 ft. long and 7 ft. thick, built of very large blocks, which crosses it from NW. to SE. at a point about 100 ft. from the extreme tip. The enclosed area is divided into two by a chasm which is crossed by a narrow natural bridge of rock.

Craigie Hill, Fort (NT 153757), 1½ miles W. of Cramond Bridge, Sheet 65 (A.90 and by-road). *West Lothian.*

This fort straddles the abrupt ridge called Craigie Hill at a point immediately N. of the cutting through which the by-road passes between Cramond Bridge and Kirkliston. It is a large fort for the district, measuring 730 ft. in length by about 180 ft. in width. The long E. side is now marked only by the precipitous face of the hill and the rest of the perimeter by three substantial walls, now very ruinous. The main points of interest are first, the presence within the fort of several circular stony foundations varying from 20 ft. to 28 ft. in diameter, and secondly an oval enclosure situated in the N. extremity of the fort. This measures internally 148 ft. by 90 ft., almost identical to the similar enclosure on Dalmahoy Hill, 5½ miles to the S. The enclosure lies over the line of the three walls of the fort, and is undoubtedly secondary to it, probably being built at a time when these had long been disused and could be used as quarries. It belongs to a class of monument known as Defensive Enclosures, for which there is reason to believe that a late, even post-Roman, date might be applicable.

Cockleroy, Fort (NS 989745), 1½ miles S. of Linlithgow, Sheet 65 (by-roads). *West Lothian.*

This fort crowns a most conspicuous, rugged and precipitous hill with a heavy ruinous wall enclosing an area 410 ft. in length by 200 ft. in width. The entrance is in the SE. The NW. end of the fort is further protected by an outer wall. The similarity of this structure to the one on Bowden Hill, ¾ mile to the W., is striking.

Bowden Hill, Fort (NS 977745), 1¼ miles SW. of Linlithgow, Sheet 65 (A.706 and farm road). *West Lothian.*

Like the fort on Cockleroy, ¾ mile to the E., this was formed by a single stone wall which ran round the perimeter of the summit of the hill and took the best advantage of natural defensive features. It enclosed a very similar area to that of its twin, and there is every reason to suppose that the two were contemporary, unlike many other pairs of juxtaposed forts. The Bowden Hill fort has been severely robbed, but parts of the wall still remain impressive.

Doon of May, Fort (NX 295515), 9 miles W. by S. of Wigtown, Sheet 82 (B.7005). *Wigtownshire.*

This fort now lies buried in trees and scrub, but these will not last for ever, and were not there in 1911 when the whole fort was visible. It consists of a single massive and heavily vitrified wall enclosing an area measuring 140 ft. by about 100 ft. No trace has been observed of any hornworks or other outworks as are common in such small vitrified forts in the vicinity, as that on Trusty's Hill.

North Balfern, Fort (NX 436509), 2¼ miles N. of Sorbie, Sheet 83 (A.746 and farm road). *Wigtownshire.*

The remains of this fort crown the W. extremity of a low hill overlooking Wigtown Bay from the W. Oval on plan, the fort measures 190 ft. by 135 ft. within the ruins of two dry-stone walls. A somewhat dubious report of the discovery of vitrified material in the fort has never been substantiated.

Burrow Head, Fort (NX 454341), 2 miles SW. of Isle of Whithorn, Sheet 83 (farm road and pasture land). *Wigtownshire.*

The promontory forts sited round the Whithorn peninsula are well exemplified by three on Burrow Head of which this one is perhaps the best. The "interior" is now merely an attenuated triangle of level ground bordered by eroded cliffs except to the N., where is is defended by the remains of a series of ramparts and ditches some among which are of considerable size.

Barsalloch Point, Fort (NX 347413),

1½ miles SSE. of Port William, Sheet 82 (A.747). *Wigtownshire.*

This little promontory fort, now under guardianship, is formed by two ramparts with a broad and deep median ditch which enclose the tip of a low headland on the landward side of the road. Before the work was protected, a stretch of one of the interminable field-boundaries that are to be seen all round the coasts of SW. Scotland and NW. Ulster was constructed partly over the defences.

Fell of Barhullion, Fort (NX 374418), 2½ miles ESE. of Port William, Sheet 83 (A.714, B.7021, farm road and pasture land). *Wigtownshire.*

This fort occupies what, though only a little above 400 ft. above sea level, is perhaps the most commanding situation in the Whithorn peninsula. It is an oval structure measuring about 140 ft. by 60 ft. within two walls. The debris of the inner wall is particularly massive, while that of the outer is such as might be expected to result from the decay of a wall about 8 ft. thick. The suggestion has been made that the inner wall may contain either chambers of galleries, although no steps have been taken towards the necessarily laborious task of proving it. Though this would be most unusual in a hill-fort in this district, it is by no means beyond the bounds of possibility when the proximity of the subrectangular or D-shaped galleried duns of Argyll is taken into account, and in particular the exotic at Castle Haven, 14 miles to the ENE.

An outer defence formed by a scanty band of earthfast blocks may originally have been another wall from which most of the material has been robbed, although the possibility exists that it might have been a *chevaux de frise.*

Bennan of Garvilland, Fort (NX 215627), 3¼ miles NE. of Glenluce, Sheet 82 (by-road and moorland). *Wigtownshire.*

This fort, constructed on a large rocky eminence, measures 300 ft. by 200 ft. within two ruined stone walls which in places were originally 12 ft. thick. The entrance, in the SW., is covered by a third wall of similar character.

Knock Fell, Fort (NX 255557), 3½ miles ESE. of Glenluce, Sheet 82 (A.747, by-road, farm road and hill). *Wigtownshire.*

Like its neighbour, the Bennan of Garvilland, this fort is a comparatively large walled enclosure. It measures about 570 ft. by 300 ft. within a main, now ruinous, wall originally up to 13 ft. thick and the remains of a second, probably about 8 ft. thick. The highest point in the interior is girt by traces of an independent wall, but it is impossible to say whether this represents a partition or an earlier, smaller, work.

Laigh Sinniness, Fort (NX 216522), 3¼ miles S. by E. of Glenluce, Sheet 82 (A.747 and farm road). *Wigtownshire.*

This interesting promontory fort is defended by a massive dry-stone wall originally perhaps 15 ft. thick and now spread over a width of as much as 40 ft. This is accompanied at a distance of some 40 ft. on the landward side by a rampart with an external ditch. The interior of the fort now measures about 70 ft. along either axis.

Cruise Back Fell, Fort (NX 179623), 3 miles N. by W. of Glenluce, Sheet 82 (by-road and moorland). *Wigtownshire.*

This ruinous stone fort consists of an oval enclosure formed on a small rocky plateau by a heavy stone wall and measuring internally about 50 ft. by 40 ft. It is joined on the S. by what can be described as an annexe, a subsidiary enclosure measuring about 80 ft. in length.

Cairn Pat, Fort (NX 044564), 3 miles SSW. of Stranraer, Sheet 82 (A.77 and farm land). *Wigtownshire.*

The fort called Cairn Pat crowns the most conspicuous hill in the stretch of country lying between Port Patrick and Luce Bay. It consists of an enclosure measuring 450 ft. by 410 ft. within two very ruinous walls, covered on the W. by two now very faint ramparts with external ditches.

Caspin, Fort (NX 005733), 3 miles NNW. of Kirkcolm, Sheet 76 (A.718, by-road and pasture land). *Wigtownshire.*

This fort occupies a promontory near Milleur Point at the mouth of Loch Ryan which is cut off from the mainland by a natural gully. It has been defended for the most part by the natural precipitous nature of its flanks, but the landward margin, over the natural gully, is bordered by the ruin of a dry-stone wall some 8 ft. thick. This is the northernmost of the numerous promontory forts of several kinds which occur on the coasts of the N. and S. limbs of W. Wigtownshire.

Kemp's Walk, Fort (NW 974598), 3¾ miles NNW. of Portpatrick, Sheet 82 (A.764 and farm road). *Wigtownshire.*

This fort occupies a large promontory set back from the shore of Larbrax (or Broadsea) Bay. The interior measures about 300 ft. in length by 170 ft. in greatest width, and has probably originally been defended by a continuous wall or rampart with an outer one to the N., E. and S. of it. The main defences lie to the N. or landward of the fort; here the inner and second ramparts are accompanied by external ditches and are strengthened by the presence of a third rampart and ditch. These all break for an entrance placed towards the E. end of the promontory, but the third or outer rampart and ditch are not continued E. of this. This large fort is perhaps not typical of the Galloway promontory forts, but mere absence of erosion of the cliffs might to some extent at least be the cause of its apparently extraordinary size.

Kirklauchlane, Fort (NX 035506), 3¼ miles SE. of Portpatrick, Sheet 82 (A.77, B.7042, by-road and farm track).
Wigtownshire.

This promontory fort, one of many on the coasts of the Rhinns and Mull of Galloway, is defended at the landward

side by three ramparts with external ditches which still present arresting profiles. The innermost rampart rises to as much as 8 ft. 6 in. above the bottom of its ditch, the outermost 2 ft. 6 in. The defended area now measures 180 ft. in length by a maximum of 85 ft. in breadth.

Portankill, Fort (NX 142323), 2¾ miles S. of Drummore, Sheet 82 (B.7041, by-road and moorland). *Wigtownshire.*

This fort consists of an almost circular enclosure about 40 ft. in diameter situated on the tip of a promontory and defended on the landward side by a rampart with three external ditches. Very slight indications suggest that the rampart probably continued all round the enclosure.

Dunman, Fort (NX 096335), 3 miles SW. of Drummore, Sheet 82 (B.7041, by-roads and moorland). *Wigtownshire.*

This fort, measuring internally about 300 ft. along each axis, crowns a flat-topped eminence the SW. flank of which falls precipitously through 400 ft. to the sea shore. The NW. flank is unassailable too, while to the NE. and SE. the site is bordered by natural gullies. The defences along the inner crests of these consist of a now ruinous massive wall originally between 8 ft. and 12 ft. in thickness. No evidence of the date of this structure exists, but it is most probably a work of the Early Iron Age.

BROCHS

The broch, a very special form of circular dwelling, is peculiar to quite a short period round about the turn of the pre-Christian and Christian eras. Only a handful of exceptionally situated brochs—a dozen or so out of a total of between 500 and 600—have been recorded outside the northern part of the mainland and the western and northern isles. The broch, more perhaps than any other individual monument, has been recognised as having been used exclusively, and probably invented, by an element among the prehistoric northern Picts.

The most famous of the better preserved examples, on the little island of Mousa (Shetland), has been patched up and repaired more than once during its long life, and its silhouette is familiar. It is impossible to be sure how typical its height is of brochs in general; for it is a fact that in several instances ruined brochs situated in remote places appear to have formed only quite modest mounds of debris, not enough to represent the tumble of a wall 40 ft. or 50 ft. high.

The broch wall is a dry-stone structure, circular on plan, usually about 15 ft. thick and from 30 ft. to 40 ft. in internal diameter. The single entrance, some 5 ft. or 6 ft. high, checked for a door and fitted with bar-holes, often has a communicating mural chamber. The wall contains other chambers and one or more staircases leading to tiers of galleries, the purpose of which was structural.

Dr Euan MacKie has recently improved our knowledge of brochs and their development and character by a programme of excavations the main conclusions from which are given in the work cited in the bibliography. Excavations in several brochs have revealed traces of timber-framed lean-to houses, and brochs which survive to a sufficient height retain traces of ledges on which either a roof or a floor could be supported.

The distribution of brochs scarcely overlaps with those of duns and hill-forts, and the broch may be considered to be the homestead of its area. Most brochs lie on land suitable for farming and grazing, a certain number necessarily situated close to the sea where such land only exists in narrow coastal strips.

Despite its striking appearance, the broch is no more than an extreme form of a defended homestead, the occupants of which may be likened to the tender meat of a crustacean secure within the hard shell. If all brochs had been as high as Mousa, it seems probable that mention might have been made of such a marvel by classical writers. While the absence of such reference provides no evidence that they were definitely not, it may give a limited measure of support to the supposition that the average height might have been little more than 20 ft.

Hurley Hawkin, Broch (NO 333328), 4 miles WNW. of Dundee, Sheet 53 (A.923 and by-road). *Angus.*

The ruins of this structure, one of the ten Tay-Tweed brochs, stand on high ground overlooking the Firth of Tay from the N. Until recently very little was known about it, but since 1958 several brief sessions of excavation have revealed post-holes in the floor, which measures 40 ft. in diameter within a wall 17 ft. thick, together with numerous relics, including rotary querns, whorls, loom-weights and sherds. A most interesting discovery was made in 1960, when a souterrain, of proto-historical or early mediaeval date, was discovered in the filled-in ditch of the broch.

Craighill, Broch (NO 432458), 3 miles NE. of Dundee, Sheet 54 (B.978 and by-road). *Angus.*

See **Craighill** Fort.

Laws Hill, Drumsturdy, Broch (NO 493349), 1¼ miles NNW. of Monifieth, Sheet 54 (B.961). *Angus.*

See **Laws Hill, Drumsturdy** Fort.

Craigie, Broch (NS 427327), 3¼ miles S. of Kilmarnock, Sheet 70 (A.77, by-road). *Ayrshire.*

This broch, known as Camp Castle, occupies a rocky ridge with steep N. and S. side. The W. arc of the wall has been removed by quarrying, but the rest remains as a grass-grown mound. When excavated in 1961 this was found to contain a wall 15 ft. thick, and the courtyard surrounded by this to measure 30 ft. in diameter. Part of a mural chamber was exposed. At present this broch stands in isolation on the distribution map.

Dun Cuier, Broch (NF 664034), 3 miles N. of Castlebay, Sheet 31 (A.888 and moorland). *Barra.*

This broch, standing on a rocky boss in the NW. part of Barra, is one of the very few to have been excavated in modern times. The interior measures 29 ft. in diameter within a wall 16 ft. thick, constructed in the form of two skins of approximately equal thickness, separated for much of their course by a narrow gallery. The entrance is in the E. A scarcement runs round the inner face of the wall at a height of 4 ft. 6 in. above foundation level. A few of the small finds recovered from the broch, including a saddle quern and other stone objects, are typical of the main broch period at the turn of the eras. At Dun Cuier, however, evidence of later occupations was found both in structural additions and in small finds, some of them suggesting a period early in the 7th century A.D.

Edinshall, Broch (NT 772603), 2½ miles NW. of Preston, Sheet 67 (B.6355 and farm road). *Berwickshire.*

See **Edinshall** Fort.

Westerdale, Broch (ND 133510), 5 miles S. of Halkirk, Sheet 11 (by-road, B.870 and pasture land). *Caithness.*

The remains of this broch are typical of several in NE. Scotland in that they appear as a large and uneven mound which does in fact include both outworks and secondary structures as well as a ruined broch. They lie on the right bank of the Thurso River ½ mile S. of Westerdale, where they are cut off from approach from other directions by a ditch which today is wet when the river rises and originally may have been permanently full of water. A walled causeway 6 ft. wide leads across it into the enclosure in which the broch stands. The wall of the broch measures 12 ft. in thickness, the interior about 28 ft. in diameter.

Ousdale, Broch (ND 072188), 4 miles SW. of Berriedale, Sheet 17 (A.9 and moorland). *Caithness.*

This broch stands on the right bank of the Ousdale Burn midway between the modern road and the sea, 350 ft. above the latter and 300 ft. below the former. It is defended on the E. by the steep descent to the burn, and on other sides by a wall 8 ft. thick. The wall of the broch is 14 ft. thick, the courtyard a little less than twice this figure in diameter. The entrance, in the SW., is checked for two doors, and a mural cell opening off the SE. flank of the passage between them may have fulfilled the alleged purpose of a guard chamber. This remote ruin is well preserved, and many interesting features of construction can be observed in it.

Bruan, Broch (ND 310394), 7½ miles SSW. of Wick, Sheet 11 (A.9).
Caithness.

Great numbers of brochs lie on the fertile valley and coastal land between Wick and the Ord of Caithness, the majority having been robbed to build, amongst other structures, the numerous now ruinous cruck-framed houses of the district. Bruan is such a broch. It lies between the road and the sea, a turf-covered stony mound some 10 ft. in height, standing in the middle of an enclosure formed by a ditch with a wall on its inner lip which is best preserved in the W.

Keiss, Broch (ND 353611), immediately N. of Keiss Harbour, Sheet 12 (links). *Caithness.*

There are well over 100 brochs in Caithness, although a close approximation cannot be made at present because of certain doubtful identifications of stony mounds that might be either cairns or brochs. Among them all are several which have been excavated, albeit very badly, including some in the close vicinity of Keiss at the N. end of the long sweep of dunes and links bordering Sinclair's Bay.

This broch, the first N. of Keiss Harbour, shows evidence of reconstruction and of re-use. Its wall is 12 ft. thick, its courtyard 35 ft. in diameter. The original entrance, in the SE., has been ruined; a secondary entrance, broken through the outer skin of the wall from the back of a mural cell, has been blocked. As at the neighbouring broch 700 yds. to the NW., close to the side of the A.9 road and named the Road broch, the faces of the wall have been buttressed and relined in places, and the interior contains secondary enclosures while others sprawl outside. The remains of what might have been part of a primary outwork survive a short distance to the NE.

Skirza, Broch (ND 394684), 2¾ miles S. of Duncansby, Sheet 12 (A.9 and by-road). *Caithness.*

This broch occupies the neck of a narrow promontory which is flanked by precipitous cliffs except to the W. where approach is cut off by a broad ditch. The wall of the broch, 14 ft. thick, encloses a courtyard 22 ft. in diameter. The entrance, from the E.—the seaward end of the promontory—is checked for a door. Secondary structures can be distinguished both inside and outside the broch.

Drumcarrow, Broch (NO 459133), 3½ miles SW. of St Andrews, Sheet 59 (B.939 and by-road). *Fife.*

This monument was originally recorded as a fort and later debased to a "Cairn (supposed)", but it is in fact a large and reasonably well preserved broch. It belongs among the ten Tay–Tweed brochs, and like the other large example at Edinshall it stands alone, so far as is known, in contrast to the groupings N. of the Tay and elsewhere. It occupies what is now recognised as a typical broch situation, an elevated position in good farming land.

Castle Spynie, Broch (NH 542421), 8 miles W. of Inverness, Sheet 26 (A.9 and by-road to Crockanord). *Inverness-shire.*

This broch and the one at Struy are the most southerly outliers of the main broch concentrations to have been recorded near or on the E. coast, the next being the three on the N. side of the Tay estuary. From this it seems clear that the territory in between must have been effectively closed to broch-builders during the period round about the turn of the era and into the 1st and 2nd centuries A.D. Castle Spynie occupies a rocky knoll which towers high into the air when viewed from the S. shore of the Beauly Firth, but which can be approached easily over gently rising ground from the S. and W. The ruin is encumbered with unkempt trees and scrub and luxurious bracken, but nevertheless contains several interesting details including a cleared entrance passage in the SW. The wall is 14 ft. thick, the interior 36 ft. in diameter. The broch is defended by outworks, the N. section of which includes a wall composed of gigantic boulders.

Dun Telve, Broch (NG 829173), 1½ miles SE. of Glenelg, Sheet 33 (by-road). *Inverness-shire.*

This broch and its neighbour Dun Troddan are, after Mousa in Shetland, the best preserved examples of their class, and both are under guardianship. The wall of Dun Telve measures 13 ft. 6 in. in thickness at the base at the entrance, and the courtyard 32 ft. in diameter. The wall now stands to a maximum height of 33 ft. 6 in., even though Thomas Pennant noted that "in 1722 some Goth purloined from the top seven feet and a half, under the pretence of applying the material to certain public buildings". All the usual appurtenances of a broch are seen here to great advantage, including galleries and two scarcements. The broch was cleared of debris in 1914, and although many relics were recovered (most of them now in the national collection), there is nothing in the report to show whether the floor was subjected to anything more delicate than shovelling and brushing.

Dun Troddan, Broch (NG 834073), 1¾ miles SE. of Glenelg, Sheet 33 (by road). *Inverness-shire.*

This broch is somewhat less well preserved than its neighbour Dun Telve, but is nevertheless the third best among all brochs. The wall, which rises to a maximum height of 25 ft., is 13 ft. 6 in. thick at the entrance, and the courtyard 28 ft. in diameter. All the usual broch features occur—entrance passage, mural cells, scarcement, stairs and three galleries. The inside was cleared during sporadic operations ending in 1920. Evidence of several layers of occupation was recorded, culminating in a hearth on the original ground level which was adjudged to have been contemporary with the broch. Also deemed to be of the original period was a ring of 10 post-holes placed at a mean distance of 6 ft. from the inner face of the wall. This may have taken the main supports of a lean-to gallery, or galleries.

Bragor, Broch (NB 286474), 12½ miles NW. of Stornoway, Sheet 8 (A.857, A.858). *Lewis.*

The comparatively well preserved remains of this broch occupy a low tongue on the NE. shore of Loch an Duna. The wall, which stands to a maximum height of 14 ft., measures 12 ft. in thickness and the courtyard 30 ft. in diameter. The scarcement, corbelled out from the inner face to a width of 1 ft., is situated at a height of 9 ft. 6 in. above the ground at the entrance.

Dun Carloway, Broch (NB 189412), 15½ miles WNW. of Stornoway, Sheet 8

37   *Dun Troddan, like its neighbour Dun Telve lower down Glenelg, stands over 20 ft. in height in parts*

(A.858, B.8010, B.8012 and A.858).

Lewis.

The remains of this broch are now under guardianship, but before such protection was offered they suffered severely from the activities of stone robbers. Nevertheless it is one of the best preserved among brochs, and a small part of the wall still attains an elevation of 30 ft. above the ground. The wall measures about 11 ft. in thickness and the courtyard 25 ft. in diameter. The entrance passage, with its fittings and cell, is in good condition, while one of the mural chambers entered at ground level gives access to a stair leading to the galleries. The internal structure of the broch wall is as clearly demonstrated here as at any other example, the slabs bonding the two skins and forming the floors of the galleries being freely exposed, and the tapering galleries themselves seen to great advantage. The scarcement, 7 ft. above the ground, is formed by the corbelling of the lower part of the wall; above it the inner face rises vertically.

Bow, Broch (NT 461416), 1¾ miles S. of Stow, Sheet 73 (A.7).   *Midlothian.*

The broch known as Bow Castle stands on level ground on the brink of a steep descent SW. to the valley of the Gala Water, and is easily reached by a tractor-track leading up the hill from the main road at a point 400 yds. E. of Bow farmhouse. It is one of the 10 Tay–Tweed brochs, and is situated only 2 miles N. of its fellow at Torwoodlee. The ruin of the wall is surmounted by a tall modern cairn built out of the debris. The broch was originally formed by a wall 15 ft. thick which enclosed a court 31 ft. in diameter, with the entrance in the NE. The structure was excavated in 1890, when pottery—including some Roman pieces—was discovered. In 1922 a Selkirk antiquarian found an enamelled Roman–British bronze brooch in the form of a cock among the ruins of the wall. This and the other small finds are now in the national collections.

Dun Nan Gall, Broch (NM 433431), 9 miles SW. of Tobermory, Sheet 47 (A.848, by-road, B.8073 and sea shore).

Mull.

This broch, situated on a low rocky headland on the NE. of Loch Tuath, measures 35 ft. in diameter within a wall 11 ft. thick. The entrance, in the E., is checked for a door and fitted with a bar-hole. A doorway in the S. arc of the inner face of the wall leads to a stair-lobby, and another mural cell can be distinguished in the NE. sector. The scarcement remains entire, and traces of an upper gallery still exist above it.

Netlater, Broch (HY 323173), 7 miles NNE. of Stromness, Sheet 6 (A.965,

38   *Dun Carloway Broch, though fragmentary, still towers above later dwellings*

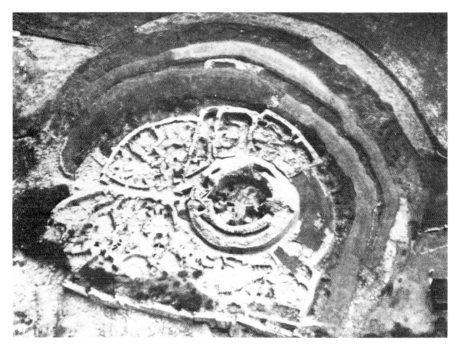

39   *Gurness Broch from the air. The outworks and later buildings lie round the ruined Tower*

A.986).   *Orkney, Mainland island.*

The remains of this broch that were partly cleared many years ago lie on low ground 200 yds. S. of the Manse of Harray. The wall, 12 ft. thick, encloses a court 33 ft. in diameter. The entrance is in the E., and three mural chambers lie in the wall at the cardinal points, that to the S. leading in to the internal stair. Secondary buildings occur both within and outside the broch, but the well, in the SW. sector of the interior, is probably an original feature.

Oxtro, Broch (HY 253267), 11 miles N. of Stromness, Sheet 6 (A.967).

Orkney, Mainland island.

The remains of this broch, opened in 1871, lie on cultivated ground 200 yds. W. of the Loch of Boardhouse. The passing interest of the name is that it is sometimes written Haughster, but pronounced the same in both cases. Though now neglected and ruinous, more than half the outline of the wall can be traced and the positions of two mural chambers noted. The proportions of the wall and

the interior are near to one extreme of the allowable in a broch—the wall is 13 ft. thick, the interior 45 ft. in diameter. The two chambers lie one in the E. and the other in the S. part of the wall. A well placed centrally in the court has a drain leading out W. through a long breach in the wall where the entrance originally existed. A considerable and varied collection of relics, embracing something like the whole of the 1st millennium A.D., is now in the national collection.

Gurness, Broch (HY 383267), 13½ miles NE. of Stromness, Sheet 6 (A.967, B.9057 and farm road).

Orkney, Mainland island.

This broch, under guardianship, stands about 15 ft. above highwater mark, and the action of the sea has removed parts of the outworks. The site has had several occupations, each leaving its mark in new or modified constructions.

The broch was the first building on the chosen ground, standing eccentrically within a wall, only small sections of which are now visible. The wall is surrounded by a rock-cut ditch contemporary with it, and two other ramparts and ditches lying outside this probably belong to the same system.

The broch itself appears on plan to be very like Dun Cuier, in that the wall was built in two thick concentric skins touching for some of their course but separated by a narrow gully over the rest. The wall is about 14 ft. thick, the interior 34 ft. in diameter. The interior contains a well.

At a date subsequent to that of the disuse of the broch great numbers of subsidiary structures were built between it and the inner ditch, engulfing the wall and replacing it by buttresses. These buildings include various kinds, from cellular houses almost if not quite contemporary at least with the latter part of the broch's active life down as far as Viking times.

St Mary's, Broch (HY 470013), at W. end of St Mary's, Sheet 6 (A.961 from Kirkwall). *Orkney, Mainland island.*

This broch stands at the N. end of the Loch of Ayre at St Mary's, the first village on Mainland N. of the Churchill Barriers. The broch was excavated in 1901 and 1902, when it was found to measure 30 ft. in diameter within a wall 14 ft. thick. The entrance, in the E., is checked for two doors; and a cell, now broken, leads into it from the N. Later buildings were found within and outside the broch.

Mid Howe, Broch (HY 371307), 4½ miles WNW. of Brinyan pier, Sheet 6 (B.9064 and by-road).

Orkney, Rousay island.

This broch and the attendant later buildings were excavated between 1930 and 1933 at considerable private expense, and then handed over to the nation. The broch measures 30 ft. in diameter within a wall 15 ft. thick still standing to a height of 14 ft., which can be seen to be composed at the lower levels of two virtually separate skins, as at Dun Cuier. It stands near the shore, within the precincts of an enclosure formed by a thick wall with a quarry ditch on either side. The outer face of the wall is steep if not sheer, the inner face considerably battered. It still stands to a height of 7 ft. on the outside, and its width varies from 13 ft. 6 in. to as much as 19 ft. The broch

contains many of the usual features, but particularly well displayed—door-checks, bar-holes, guard-cell, galleries and staircase.

The later buildings occupy all the space between the broch and the wall as well as the courtyard, and the best preserved details of their arrangements are of some interest.

Burrian, Broch (HY 762513), 1 mile SE. of South Bay pier, Sheet 5 (pastureland). *Orkney, North Ronaldsay island.*

This broch, placed on a cliff close to the sea near the S. extremity of North Ronaldsay, was "extensively explored" in 1870. The wall, measuring 15 ft. in thickness at the base, encloses an area 32 ft. in diameter. A scarcement 5 in. deep runs round the inner face at a height of about 3 ft. above the floor. For 4 ft. 2 in. above this the inner face rises with a slight intake, but thereafter it abruptly reduces its diameter by 4 in. and then proceeds to rise vertically. The entrance is in the SE., and a mural chamber lies in the NE. arc of the wall. The promontory on which the broch stands is defended by the remains of four ramparts. There is a well in the N. part of the interior.

The NW. arc of the outer face of the broch wall was buttressed. This work might have been done during one of the secondary occupations of which the excavators found abundant traces. The broch had first been turned into a sort of wheel-house with septal divisions, and then reoccupied at least by squatters at a much later date. These last people left behind them the phalanx of an ox incised with the crescent and V-rod and another symbol—if, as seems certain, the article is authentic. There was also found a pebble with five- and six-pointed stars incised on it, the former adorned in the *cloisons* with a goose of undeniably Pictish appearance and several other devices.

Coldoch, Broch (NS 697982), 7½ miles W. of Stirling, Sheet 57 (A.873, B.8031). *Perthshire.*

This, the westernmost member of the Tay–Tweed group of 10 brochs, stands in the grounds of Coldoch House on the N. side of the Blairdrummond Moss. The wall measures about 18 ft. in thickness and the courtyard about 28 ft., so that it represents one of the low-ratio brochs

40   *Mousa Broch. The "windows" in the inner face
of the wall above the entrance*

rather than one of those with a wall
which is thin in proportion to the space
enclosed. The wall, built of small stones,
now stands about 4 ft. high within the
broch and somewhat more outside. The
passage is checked for a door, and the
N. section of the bar-hole is still *in situ*.
Three mural cells and one stair-lobby
open into the interior. Two small
recesses occur low down on the inner face
of the wall.

Dun Lagaidh, Broch (NH 143914), 1¾
miles SSE. of Ullapool, Sheet 20 (boat).
Ross & Cromarty.
See **Dun Lagaidh** Fort.
Rhiroy, Broch (NH 149901), 2¾ miles
SE. of Ullapool, Sheet 20 (boat).
Ross & Cromarty.
This broch is distant a little less than
1 mile from another at Dun Lagaidh, but
further examples do not occur in the
vicinity. One-third of its wall has fallen

41   *The recent excavations at Clickhimin have cleared the three principal structures —the outer wall, the "Blockhouse" Fort and the Broch, the entrances in all of which are here seen in line*

over the edge of the rocky bluff upon which it stands, but the rest remains to a maximum height of 9 ft. 6 in. over accumulated debris about 4 ft. deep. The wall is about 14 ft. thick, the internal diameter about 38 ft.

Caisteal Grugaig, Broch (NG 866251), 1 mile SW. of Ardelve pier, Sheet 33 (ferry and footpath).   *Ross & Cromarty.*

This broch is well preserved from ground level to a maximum height of 13 ft. It displays several features of broch structure with admirable clarity—the entrance, in the NE., with door-check and bar-hole and chamber; a large mural chamber in the NW. sector and a small one in the SE.; and close to this a stair-lobby with several treads of the stair and a fragment of a gallery. The natural floor is on a slope, so that the scarcement, which is level, lies at heights varying between 2 ft. 4 in. and 7 ft. above it. The lintel above the outer end of the entrance passage is triangular.

Torwoodlee, Broch (NT 475381), 2 miles NW. of Galashiels, Sheet 73 (A.72 and farm road).   *Selkirkshire.*

See **Torwoodlee** Fort.

Mousa, Broch (HU 457236), 11 miles S. of Lerwick, Sheet 4 (A.970, by-road and boat).   *Shetland, Mousa island.*

The broch of Mousa is so famous, so well documented and in some ways so controversial, that only the briefest summary is required here. It stands near the W. coast of Mousa, an island made of flagstone (schistose slate) lying on bed and providing as ready a natural supply to the broch-builders 20 centuries ago as to those responsible for paving the streets of Lerwick in our own.

The wall measures 50 ft. in external diameter at the base, 40 ft. at the summit which is now 43 ft. 6 in. above the rock surface. The external profile follows an ogee curve which is said to have been formed to some extent by the settling of the stones, although it is not explained how this would effect the complex and delicate internal stairs and galleries within the thickness of the wall. The basal internal diameter of the wall is no more than 20 ft., showing a ratio of 4 to 3 with the thickness of the wall. In this the broch is exceptional, the average being 2 to 1. It is possible, if not probable, that the great height is equally exceptional to a degree which is nicely expressed by the ratio.

Despite a certain amount of later occupation and the beneficent attentions of many restorers, much can be learned from the broch. Its doorways, its staircases, its galleries, its scarcements, even its secondary buildings—all are bigger, more grandly conceived and better preserved than at any other comparable structure. No other monument is better worth a visit, no other Official Guide so worth the money.

Clickhimin, Broch (HU 465408), in the W. outskirts of Lerwick, Sheet 4 (A.970).
Shetland, Mainland island.
See **Clickhimin** Fort.

Burland, Broch (HU 445360), 3 miles SSW. of Lerwick, Sheet 4 (A.970 and moorland). *Shetland, Mainland island.*

This broch occupies a narrow headland which protrudes due W. of Bard Head, Bressay. The cliffs on three sides fall precipitously for 50 ft. to the rocky shore, and the only approach to the site, from the N., is cut off by three cross-walls with external ditches. The broch wall measures 15 ft. in thickness, the courtyard 35 ft. in diameter. The entrance, remarkably, is in the SW., where it now opens only a few uncertain feet from the brink of the cliff. Various later walls and piles of debris indicate secondary occupation.

Jarlshof, Broch (HU 397096), ¼ mile S. of Sumburgh airport, Sheet 4.
Shetland, Mainland island.
See **Jarlshof** Early Settlements.

Sae Breck, Broch (HU 210780), 4½ miles E. by N. of Hillswick Sheet 3 (A.970, B.9078).
Shetland, Mainland island.

This broch stands on the hill now named Sae Breck which, because it commands a good prospect of part of the Atlantic Ocean and of St Magnus Bay, was recently crowned by a wooden hut from which hostile or suspicious moves could be supervised. The hut stands in the ruin of the broch. The latter appears as a stony mound, the N. and S. sectors of which can be seen to be formed by stretches of a wall some 15 ft. thick surrounding an area 25 ft. in diameter. The entrance was probably in the E. Two mural chambers survive among each principal part of the debris; upwards of 120 sherds of pottery were recovered from the one near the hut. The broch lies within a garth formed by a wall about 10 ft. thick and measuring about 120 ft. in length by about 110 ft. in breadth.

The earlier sherds among the collection already referred to compare closely with the earliest of that class from Jarlshof, representing a type the manufacture of which seems to have been established in the more northerly districts of the Shetland mainland in the 1st century B.C./A.D.

Burra Ness, Broch (HU 556956), 2¼ miles S. by E. of Gutcher, Sheet 1 (farm road and moorland). *Shetland, Yell island.*

The impressive remains of this broch stand on the NE. nose of Burra Ness, facing across Uyea Sound to Unst and Fetlar. The wall is 15 ft. thick, the interior 27 ft. in diameter, and the scarcement can be seen on the inner face at a height of 12 ft. above the floor. It is hard to believe that in 1774 the broch was "in the midst of a field of corn", reaching to the edge of the shore; but the ploughing of the ground incidental to this has probably led to the obliteration of a set of outworks.

Hoga Ness, Broch (HP 557005), 2 miles E. of Uyeasound, Sheet 1 (A.968).
Shetland, Unst island

This broch, occupying the SW. tip of Unst near the Belmont ferry terminal, is more interesting for the remains of its outworks than for those of the tower itself, for the latter is now for the most part a grass-grown mound of debris. The headland upon which it stands is cut off from approach from the N. and E. by two ditches separated by a mound standing up to a height of 11 ft. above the bottom of the inner ditch. The inner lip of this ditch is defended by a wall 12 ft. thick, faced with well-laid blocks and filled with coarse rubble.

A short sector of the broch wall exposed in the SW. part of the annular mound of debris showed a thickness of 15 ft., and it may be deduced from this that the courtyard measured about 30 ft. in diameter.

Dun Ard an t'-Sabhail, Broch (NG 318333), 2 miles N. by W. of Talisker, Sheet 32 (footpath and moorland). *Skye.*

This broch, one of several which are to be found on the Isle of Skye, stands on a hill overlooking Fiskavaig from the SW. It is virtually circular with a diameter of about 35 ft., within a wall which varies slightly in thickness up to about 12 ft. The entrance passage is furnished with a cell or guard-chamber, but there is no sign of door-checks. Traces of galleries can be detected in the ruined wall. The broch is protected to the SE. by outworks.

Dun Fiadhairt, Broch (NG 230506), 2½ miles NW. of Dunvegan, Sheet 23

(A.850, hill road and moorland). *Skye.*

This broch, cleared of much of its debris in 1914, measures 31 ft. within a wall up to 12 ft. thick. The entrance, in the W., is checked for a door and fitted with two communicating cells. Another cell lies in the NW. sector of the wall, and the stair-lobby in the N., while a gallery occupies the E. and S. sectors.

Boreraig, Broch (NG 195531), 5 miles NW. of Dunvegan, Sheet 23 (A.850, B.884, by-road and moorland). *Skye.*

This prominent ruin, one of several well-preserved brochs in NW. Skye, measures 35 ft. in diameter within a wall with a maximum thickness of 13 ft. The entrance, in the W., has been despoiled of facing stones, and it is difficult to determine whether a cell in the wall just S. of it originally communicated with it or not. A gallery can be traced round most of the rest of the wall. The wall stands to as much as 9 ft. in height outside, and a section of a scarcement survives at a height of 7 ft. in the SW. arc. The broch stands within an enclosure shaped somewhat like a parallelogram formed by a wall 4 ft. thick.

Dun Hallin, Broch (NG 257593), 2¼ miles N. by W. of Lusta, Sheet 23 (by-road and moorland). *Skye.*

This broch lies within an enclosure of irregular shape formed by a wall some 6 ft. thick and measuring 150 ft. by 130 ft. along the main axes. The broch itself measures 36 ft. in diameter within a wall up to 11 ft. thick and now 12 ft. high. The entrance, in the SE., is damaged, but two cells and a stair-lobby can be seen in the wall.

Struanmore, Broch (NG 339386), 1 mile W. of Bracadale, Sheet 23 (A.863 and moorland). *Skye.*

This, one of the best preserved brochs in Skye, measures 36 ft. in diameter within a wall 14 ft. thick. The entrance, in the E., is checked for a door but not fitted with a communicating cell. Inside, however, a cell exists in the wall a short distance N. of the entrance, and a cell combined with a stair-lobby lies in a similar position just S. of it. A long gallery is entered from a portal in the W. arc. The wall stands to a height of 12 ft.

Dun Suledale, Broch (NG 374526), 8½ miles NW. of Portree, Sheet 23 (A.850 and moorland). *Skye.*

This broch, like the one called Dun

Hallin, lies within an enclosure formed by a wall some 6 ft. thick and, in this case, measuring about 140 ft. in length by 100 ft. in width. The broch, which stands conspicuously on a rocky plateau, measures 42 ft. in diameter within a wall up to 12 ft. 6 in. thick. The entrance, in the W., is checked for a door and has a communicating cell or guard chamber. In addition, two cells and a gallery can be traced in the thickness of the wall.

Tor Wood, Broch (NS 833849), 2 miles NW. of Larbert, Sheet 57 (A.9).

Stirlingshire.

This broch is most easily reached from the NE. by a woodland path leading from the by-road which leaves A.9 opposite the point where this passes the NW. apex of Glenbervie golf course. The broch presents a pleasing appearance, as a result of the clearance of the interior (35 ft. in diameter) just 100 years ago. Little or none of the outer face of the wall is visible, but the inner is free for a height of 8 ft. above the slight debris which now covers the actual floor. The thickness of the wall—20 ft.—can be seen at the entrance, in the cleared passage of which the door-checks and bar-holes are exposed. The inner face of the wall is pierced by a stair-lobby and by 12 small recesses like aumbries, while the scarcement can be followed all round at the level of the lintels of the entrance passage and the stair-lobby.

The broch stands on the brink of a low cliff, but to N., E. and S. it is protected by two ruinous walls. The finds from the excavation, some in the national collection and some in Falkirk Burgh Museum, are perhaps more interesting for what they do not include—that is to say, any Roman relics.

Dunrobin, Broch (NC 870013), 2½ miles E. by N. of Golspie, Sheet 17 (A.9). *Sutherland.*

This broch, one among many in SE. Sutherland, is situated on a bank overlooking the sea just S. of the newly reformed road bridge over the track of the Highland Railway. It stands within the remains of outworks which are themselves defaced by the ruins of secondary structures. Various details proper to a broch can be discerned—the door-checks, bar-hole and chamber in the entrance passage (18 ft. long) and the stair-lobby, scarcement and chambers opening from the inner face of the wall into the interior, 30 ft. in diameter. Secondary walls and excavations encumber the interior.

Cinn Trolla, Broch (NC 929081), 3 miles NNE. of Brora, Sheet 17 (A.9).
Sutherland.

This broch stands beside the Highland Railway track less than ¼ mile from the shore. Excavations revealed that the entrance passage was altogether 18 ft. long, 7 ft. high and about 3 ft. wide, checked twice for doors and provided with a cell or "guard-chamber" 7 ft. in diameter and 11 ft. high. The interior of the broch measures 31 ft. in diameter. Another chamber and a stair-lobby can be seen in the wall, while a well 7 ft. deep with steps leading into it was found in the SE. quadrant close to the wall. A scarcement runs round the inner face 8 ft. from the floor from which, when clear, the wall rises to as much as 15 ft.

Castle Cole, Broch (NC 795133), 9 miles NW. of Brora, Sheet 17 (by-roads and moor road). *Sutherland.*

The great numbers of brochs which were built in the valleys and on the good farming lands of SE. Sutherland constitute the extension of the equally wide distribution in the equivalent fertile regions of Caithness. Among them, this broch is situated on a rocky eminence on the left bank of the Black Water. It is a small broch, the wall measuring 13 ft. in thickness and the interior only 21 ft. in diameter. It is well enough preserved to contain several discernible items of detail, including double door-checks in the entrance passage and at least seven wall recesses like the so called aumbries of Torwood broch. An outwork protects the broch from approach from the N. and E., while the steepness of the flanks of the site serves the same purpose in the other directions.

Kilphedir, Broch (NC 995187), 3 miles NW. of Helmsdale, Sheet 17 (A.897 and footpath). *Sutherland.*

This broch appears from afar as a great flat-topped pile of stones standing in an enclosure formed by a ditch some 23 ft. wide and 9 ft. deep with a rampart 14 ft. thick on its inner lip. A slight upcast mound follows parts of the outer lip, and E. of the entrance, in the N., there is a short stretch of outer ditch. The broch itself measures 32 ft. within a wall

15 ft. thick. One mural chamber opens into the interior at a point opposite the entrance.

Dun Viden, Broch (NC 726518), 6 miles S. of Bettyhill, Sheet 10 (A.836, B.871). *Sutherland.*

Strathnaver, the broad and fertile valley joining Bettyhill and Altnaharra, contains great quantities of ruinous monuments—chambered cairns, cairns, cairn-fields, standing stones, enclosures, so-called hut-circles and brochs. The only comprehensive account available at the time of writing is the relevant part of the *Inventory* of Sutherland, but there are reasons to believe that further research might lead to the re-identification of some of the monuments and the discovery of even more.

The broch Dun Viden stands on a knoll rising 75 ft. above the rich flood-plain of the River Naver, only easily approachable from the E. where the position is defended by a strong stony rampart up to 12 ft. in height which is itself covered by a lesser one. The broch wall measures 15 ft. in thickness, the internal diameter is 30 ft.—a normal ratio.

Dun na Maigh, Broch (NC 552531), 4 miles SW. of Tongue, Sheet 10 (A.838).
Sutherland.

This broch stands on a rocky eminence overlooking the fertile land at the head of the Kyle of Tongue. It is protected by outworks on the N. and S. The entrance passage, in the E., is 16 ft. long, the interior about 28 ft. in diameter. The faces of the wall stand well above the ruins, but if cleared off would possibly appear for as much as 15 ft. Details of chambers and lintels can be recognised in spite of the encumbrance of debris.

Dundornadilla, Broch (NH 455449), 9 miles NW. of Altnaharra, Sheet 9 (moor road). *Sutherland.*

Despite its position so close to the through-route between the N. coast and the head of Strathnaver, this broch is one of the very few of which part of the wall stands more than 20 ft. in height. A small portion of the outer skin reaches an elevation of 22 ft. but as the corresponding section of the inner face has fallen, this is only sustained by a modern buttress. On either side of this portion the wall is reduced to about the level of the floor of the first gallery, up to about

12 ft. above ground level. The interior measures 27 ft. in diameter, the wall 14 ft. in thickness. A detail of interest is the large triangular lintel covering the outer opening of the entrance passage, which lies in the NE. below the highest surviving part of the wall. Such lintels have been observed elsewhere, and it has been noted that they occur in what have been thought to be later rather than earlier brochs.

Stoer, Broch (NC 036278), 5 miles NW. of Lochinver, Sheet 15 (A.837, B.869).
Sutherland.

This broch stands on a low eminence bordered to the W. by the sea and to the E. by a broad expanse of turf on sand beyond which the sharp peaks of Quinag loom over 10 miles of low, broken bare hills and innumerable intricate lochs. The ruin is handsome, composed of large rectangular blocks and standing exteriorly in places to a height of over 6 ft. above the tumbled ruins and probably twice as much above true ground level. The diameter of the interior is 32 ft., the thickness of the wall about 14 ft. The outer end of the entrance passage, which is in the E., is covered with a triangular lintel 4 ft. 6 in. long, 3 ft. 10 in. high and 1 ft. thick. Several details of the usual chambers and staircases are discernible.

The broch is defended by an outwork built of very large blocks and boulders; but another ruined wall lying some 100 yds. away is most probably a land boundary of later date.

Dun Mor Vaul, Broch (NM 046493), 3 miles N. of Scarinish, Sheet 44 (B.8069 and farm roads). *Tiree.*

At least six of the monuments on Tiree are either brochs or else circular galleried duns of closely similar appearance. This example, at the W. of Vaul Bay, measures 35 ft. in diameter within a wall about 13 ft. thick in which galleries and mural cells are apparent. It was excavated by Dr MacKie in 1962-64 with remarkable results including the discovery of a primary timber phase (about 6th century B.C.) and several successive reconstructions in stonework.

Stairhaven, Broch (NX 208534), 2¼ miles S. by E. of Glenluce, Sheet 82 (by-road and shore). *Wigtownshire.*

This structure, which is very well defended from casual approach by natural hazards, has been considered as a broch although there is still an element of doubt about the identification. A recent exposure of the wall faces at the entrance showed that when complete the wall measured 12 ft. 6 in. in thickness, but more than this will be required before a reliable judgement can be reached.

Teroy, Broch (NX 099641), 3 miles NE. of Stranraer, Sheet 82 (A.77, by-road and hill). *Wigtownshire.*

This structure, which is almost certainly a broch, stands on a promontory at the W. margin of Balker Moor, 150 yds. from the deep glen of the Kirklachie Burn. The wall measures 13 ft. in thickness, the interior 29 ft. in diameter. The entrance passage shows no sign of door-checks, but has a guard chamber. No galleries or other cells have been detected in the wall. The broch is defended to the ENE. by a deep broad ditch with a mound on the outer lip.

Ardwell, Broch (NX 066466), 3¼ miles SE. by S. of Sandhead, Sheet 82 (by-roads). *Wigtownshire.*

The broch on Ardwell Point lies on a narrow rocky spit cut off from the land by a wall and traversed by a ditch spanned by a built causeway. The broch, comparatively well preserved, has a normal entrance to seaward and another to landward, the latter possibly a secondary feature and certainly a very rare one. The broch wall measures about 13 ft. in thickness and the interior about 30 ft. in diameter.

Crammag Head, Broch (NX 088340), 3¼ miles WSW. of Drummore, Sheet 82 (B.7041 and by-roads). *Wigtownshire.*

This structure, situated on a little promontory defended on the landward side by a rampart and ditch, is most probably a broch, as the E. sector of the wall measured 15 ft. in thickness before it was demolished during the construction of a lighthouse. Existing descriptions speak of an original diameter overall of 60 ft. A sector of the W. arc of the wall still survives W. of the lighthouse.

DUNS

The word used to define this large and diverse category of monuments is the Gaelic *dùn* (pronounced *doon*), a fort or fortified dwelling place. Dr Euan MacKie has complemented his work on brochs by a valuable contribution which throws new light on duns and which is included in the work cited in the bibliography.

The class called galleried duns consists of circular or oval homesteads of a substantial kind, the main characteristic of which is a dry-stone wall perhaps 16 ft. thick pierced by an opening which is checked for a door, and containing passages or galleries the function of which is largely structural. The top of the wall could be reached by steps built either in the wall or on its inner face. This massive wall, enclosing an area measuring perhaps 50 ft. in diameter or 70 ft. by 40 ft. diametrically, contained timber-framed houses, tents or other unsubstantial shelters, and the main evidence for occupation is found in hearths. If they were to stand at all, walls so strong would have lasted a long time, and it is often the case that after their initial occupation at about the turn of the eras, they were reoccupied on and off for centuries.

The galleried promontory dun comprises an arc of walling similar in type to that already described, drawn across the neck of a coastal or inland promontory, the steep flanks of which were defended by a lesser wall.

Plain duns without galleries—circular, oval or oblong—also occur. Their walls range from 10 ft. to 20 ft. in thickness and have entrances checked for a door. Evidence from several of these shows occupation in the 1st and 2nd centuries A.D. and allows room for the assumption that they were built rather earlier than this.

The small duns built on a steep-sided rocky stack, numbers of which are found along the western seaboard, are at present virtually unexplored.

All the varieties of dun so far described belong in the homestead class. A larger type, lying on the border-line with the hill-forts, consists merely of a thick stone wall enclosing an area smaller than that usually considered appropriate to a hill-fort. In several examples of such duns vitrifaction occurs among the debris, indicating that the wall was of timber-laced construction (see section on Hill-forts). No works of this kind have been excavated, and their distribution is not as yet fully

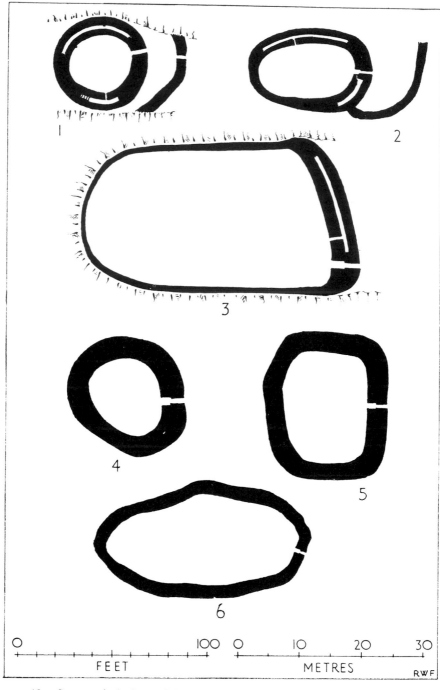

42　Some typical plans of Duns. 1, 2, 3: Round, Oval and Promontory
Galleried Duns. 4, 5, 6: examples of Simple Duns

known, but most are probably located in the west, in the Great Glen and in Cromarty.

Small insular duns, found in profusion in the Hebrides, are virtually unexplored, but there may be reason to suppose that some at least are of mediaeval date.

Turin Hill, Duns (NO 514534), 3½ miles NE. of Forfar, Sheet 54 (B.9133 and farm road). *Angus.*

See **Turin Hill** Fort.

Torbhlaran, Dun (NR 866943), 4 miles N. by E. of Lochgilphead, Sheet 55 (A.816, by-road and farm land). *Argyll, Mid.*

This site is interesting chiefly for the remarkable diorite needles which protrude from the E. flank of the hill and seem to form a natural quarry for such large standing stones as those at Ballymeanoch and other places in the vicinity. The dun is circular on plan, measuring about 50 ft. by 45 ft. within a ruined wall and defended on all sides by natural slopes except to the NE., where a ruined outer wall traverses the neck of the ridge.

Ardifuar, Dun (NR 789969), 7 miles NW. of Lochgilphead, Sheet 55 (A.816, by-road and footpath). *Argyll, Mid.*

This interesting structure embodies the entrance, mural cells, staircase and gallery and the scarcement which are appropriate to a broch and a galleried dun, but is probably unique in its plan. It is circular, measuring 65 ft. in diameter within a wall 10 ft. thick and now up to 10 ft. high. The scarcement runs round the inner face at a height of 5 ft. above ground level. A low platform, bordered by set stones, runs eccentrically round two-thirds of the interior. Relics found during excavations in 1934 include both Early Iron Age objects of stone and a piece of *terra sigillata* as well as several objects such as a crucible and stone moulds which are of later date.

Dun Mhuilig, Dun (NM 776019), 4 miles WNW of Kilmartin, Sheet 55 (A.816, B.8002). *Argyll, Mid.*

This promontory galleried dun occupies a rocky bluff on the NW. side of Loch Craignish. It consists of a galleried wall of a maximum thickness of 12 ft., some of the lintels of the gallery still remaining *in situ*. Two outer walls defend this structure from approach from the landward side.

Druim an Duin, Dun (NR 781913), 5½ miles WNW. of Lochgilphead, Sheet 55 (A.816, B.841, B.8025 and forest). *Argyll, Knapdale.*

This small, almost subrectangular galleried dun occupies part of a very narrow rocky ridge above the head of Loch Scotnish, in Knapdale Forest. It measures 50 ft. by 30 ft. within a wall up to 16 ft. thick at the base which still rises in places to a height of 9 ft. Entrances at the N. and S. ends are checked for doors, the latter having in addition a bar-hole and communicating mural cell or guard chamber.

Dun Mhuirich, Dun (NR 722845), 2¼ miles SW. of Tayvallich, Sheet 55 (B.8025). *Argyll, Knapdale.*

This interesting structure crowns a rocky knoll between the road and the shore of Linne Mhuirich. To the E. the flanks of this fall sheer to the water and the S. face is also steep, but in other directions access is fairly easy. The summit enclosure is an oval dun measuring about 55 ft. by 40 ft. within a comparatively well-preserved wall up to 7 ft. thick. This stands within an outer wall which can be followed all round the knoll except on the E. where the natural defences render it unnecessary. The foundations of several rectangular buildings of a later date than the dun lie inside and partly over the wall of the dun.

Dun a' Choin Dhuibh, Dun (NR 804641), 4¾ miles SW. of Tarbert, Sheet 62 (A.83, B.8024 and forest tracks). *Argyll, Knapdale.*

This dun, now embosomed in Achaglachgach Forest, is circular on plan, measuring about 40 ft. in diameter within a wall about 10 ft. thick. A normal entrance pierces the NE. arc of the wall and a curious Z-shaped passage the W. arc. The dun is defended to N. and S. by outworks.

Dun Skeig, Dun (NR 757571), 10 miles SW. of Tarbert, Sheet 62 (A.83, farm road and hill). *Argyll, Kintyre.*

See **Dun Skeig** Fort.

Kildonan Bay, Galleried Dun (NR

780277), 6½ miles NE. of Campbeltown, Sheet 68 (B.842). *Argyll, Kintyre.*

This comparatively well-preserved galleried dun, standing close to the road and overlooking Kilbrannan Sound from the W., is the most southerly outlier of the Early Iron Age structures of this class which occur farther N. along the coast and among the islands. Excavated in the 'thirties of this century, the remains of several features are still visible. The interior measures about 70 ft. by 40 ft. within an irregularly oval wall which varies in width from as little as 5 ft. to as much as 13 ft. The entrance is checked for a door, the wall pierced by a cell and by the entrance to a double stair. Small finds indicated that the original occupation was followed after a gap by a prolonged second phase in Early Mediaeval times.

Ugadale Point, Dun (NR 784285), 7 miles NE. of Campbeltown, Sheet 68 (B.842). *Argyll, Kintyre.*

This little structure is a fair example of what has been called a stack fort. It clings to a miniature rocky promontory at the N. end of Kildonan Bay and measures internally only about 55 ft. by 35 ft. within the ruin of a stone wall some 8 ft. thick. Much of the interior is occupied by rectilinear walls belonging to secondary structures. A trial excavation begun here during the inauspicious summer of 1939 produced evidence of desultory occupation embracing a period extending from the Early Iron Age to the 16th century A.D.

Suidhe Chennaidh, Dun (NN 029243), 1 mile NNW. of Kilchrenan, Sheet 50 (B.845 and moorland). *Argyll, Lorn.*

This dun measures about 40 ft. in dia-

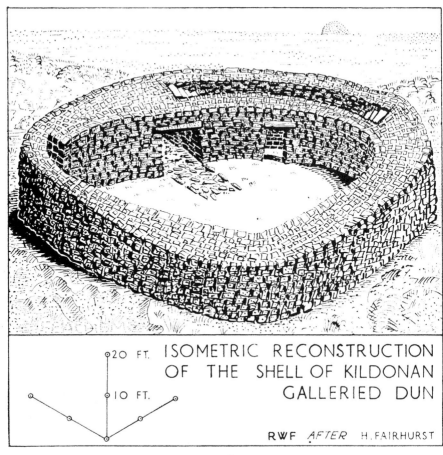

20 FT.
10 FT.

ISOMETRIC RECONSTRUCTION OF THE SHELL OF KILDONAN GALLERIED DUN

RWF *AFTER* H. FAIRHURST

meter within a wall about 14 ft. thick which is said to have stood to a height of 20 ft. early in the 19th century, before being pillaged for dyke-building. The entrance is checked for a door but has no bar-hole, and no mural galleries or cells exist in the wall. Several structures of this general type are on record both in Lorn and Mid Argyll and over the hills in NW. Perthshire.

Benderloch, Dun (NM 903382), 5¾ miles NE. of Oban, Sheet 49 (A.85, A.828 and private grounds). *Argyll, Lorn.*

See **Benderloch** Forts.

Rahoy, Dun (NM 633564), 8 miles NNW. of Lochaline, Sheet 49 (A.884, by-road and moorland). *Argyll, North.*

When this structure, standing above the NE. shore of Loch Teacuis, was excavated by Childe in 1936 and 1937, dynamite was used to assist in obtaining a section of the massive vitrified wall. The interior, measuring about 40 ft. in diameter, was found to be partially paved, and the centre occupied by a hearth. Relics included part of a bronze brooch of La Tène I type and a looped socketed axe of iron which together suggest a date early in the Iron Age, and also some saddle querns and a flint scraper.

Duniewick, Dun (NX 116851), 2½ miles NE. of Ballantrae, Sheet 76 (B.7044). *Ayrshire.*

The summit of Duniewick, a craggy knoll which rises from the N. foot of Knockdolian, measures 100 ft. by 85 ft., and is surrounded by a heavy spread of tumbled stones breached by an entrance in the SW. This structure may belong among the duns rather than the forts, for even though the thickness of the wall cannot be ascertained from surface indications, the situation and lack of outworks are more appropriate to the former than the latter.

Dunree, Dun (NS 347125), 3¼ miles NE. of Maybole, Sheet 70 (A.77, B.742). *Ayrshire.*

This dun stands on a conspicuous eminence 250 ft. above the River Doon, distant 700 yds. to the N. The summit of the knoll is surrounded by a grass-grown stony bank standing up to 6 ft. in height and spread to a thickness of as much as 20 ft. It encloses an area measuring 120 ft. by 100 ft. with an entrance in the WSW. The slight remains of two outer defences cover the approach from the N. It is probable that the main wall was originally 10 ft. or 12 ft. thick, but no precise measurements are available.

Monkwood, Dun (NS 337139), ½ mile SE. of Minishant, Sheet 70 (A.77). *Ayrshire.*

The remains of this dun crown a knoll on the left bank of the Water of Doon known as Mote Knowe. They consist of the grass-grown ruin of a wall originally about 15 ft. thick, which encloses a circular area about 50 ft. in diameter. Apart from a possible entrance in the SE. no details survive on the surface.

Kemp Law, Dun (NS 335336), 1 mile SW. of Dundonald, Sheet 70 (B.730 and by-road). *Ayrshire.*

The remains of this structure are both overgrown and much robbed and ruined, but they are of interest in that they include those of a timber-laced rampart partly vitrified. The main enclosure is an almost circular dun, measuring about 36 ft. in diameter within the ruin of a wall 14 ft. thick. At one point this was found to be vitrified for half its thickness, inwards from the inner face. A second wall can be traced round the dun at a distance of about 10 ft. outside it, but until the site is cleared the details of these and other possible features will remain masked.

Portencross, Dun (NS 171491), 2 miles WNW. of West Kilbride, Sheet 63 (B.7048). *Ayrshire.*

See **Portencross** Fort.

Dun Buidhe, Dun (NF 794546), 4 miles N. of Creagorry, Sheet 22 (A.865 and by-road). *Benbecula.*

This is one among several insular duns on Benbecula the majority of which conform in shape to the outline of the islet upon which they stand. The dun was originally reached by a massive stone causeway leading out from the shore by way of another islet, but when the water level was lowered this stood out partly on dry land. The fortified islet, measuring about 150 ft. in diameter, is surrounded by the debris of a wall now spread to 25 ft. in thickness. Within this is a dun, formed by a ruined wall about 13 ft. thick and measuring 30 ft. in diameter.

Berneray, Dun (NL 547802), 1 mile W. of Berneray pier, Sheet 31 (boat from Castlebay). *Berneray.*

This galleried promontory dun occupies a narrow headland on the W. side of Berneray 1 mile NW. of Barra Head, by the name of which both the dun and the lighthouse which stands close to it are known. The tip of the promontory is bounded to NW. and SE. by cliffs 600 ft. high, while on the landward side approach is cut off by a galleried wall 13 ft. thick comparable to many another at necessarily less imposing sites up and down the west coast. The entrance, towards the NW. end of the wall, is checked for a door and still exhibits part of a bar-hole. It has been reduced in width at a later date than that of its original construction. Stretches of the internal gallery can be recognised in the SE. sector of the wall.

Dun Burgidale, Dun (NS 063660), 1¼ miles NW. of Rothesay, Sheet 63 (farm road and moorland). *Bute.*

This dun, standing near the head of the St Colmac Burn, measures 67 ft. in diameter within a wall varying in thickness from 10 ft. to 14 ft. A gallery about 2 ft. 3 in. wide has been recorded as existing in the W. arc. The entrance, in the SE., was carefully opened in the 19th century by a Marquis of Bute.

Dun Scalpsie, Dun (NS 044580), 5 miles SW. of Rothesay, Sheet 63 (A.845 and pasture land). *Bute.*

This now ruinous dun occupies a rocky knoll 50 ft. above the Sound of Bute. It measures about 90 ft. by 80 ft. within a dry-stone wall varying in thickness between 9 ft. and 15 ft. The entrance is in the NW. Traces of what may have been outer walls are visible SE. of the dun.

Eilean Buidhe, Kyles of Bute, Dun (NS 018754), ½ mile ENE. of Buttock Point, Sheet 63 (boat, nearest at Colintraive). *Bute.*

This dun occupies the S. end of the northernmost of the Burnt Islands off the NE. tip of Bute. It measures about 55 ft. in diameter within a vitrified wall originally about 12 ft. thick.

Sgarbach, Dun (ND 373637), ½ mile E. of Auckingill, Sheet 12 (pasture land). *Caithness.*

This structure, apparently a kind of promontory dun, comprises the surface of a cliff-girt headland cut off from approach from the W. by a wall 62 ft. long, 12 ft. 6 in. thick and standing at best to a height of 4 ft. Near the centre it is pierced by an entrance passage 3 ft. 2 in. wide outside a pair of door-checks and 4 ft. 9 in. inside them. A bar-hole 8 in. square is formed in the wall. A mural cell measuring about 10 ft. by 7 ft. internally is entered by a narrow passage leading out of one side of the entrance passage.

These remains call to mind some of the promontory duns of the Western Isles rather than anything else local.

Dun Channa, Dun (NG 205047), 4¼ miles W. of Canna pier, Sheet 39 (farm tracks and moorland). *Canna.*

This dun occupies a stack of columnar basalt which stands on the W. shore of Canna 250 yds. S. of Garrisdale Point. The landward margin of the summit is defended by a dry-stone wall 6 ft. 6 in. thick, the entrance in which can now only be reached by means of a ladder or the use of rock-climbing techniques. The comparative thinness of the wall and the simplicity of the entrance suggest that this may possibly not be a prehistoric structure. Several mediaeval foundations lie within the dun.

Loch nan Cinneachan, Dun (NM 188568), 2¼ miles W. by S. of Arinagour, Sheet 46 (B.8070 and moorland). *Coll.*

This example of the insular duns of Coll, which compare with those of the Outer Isles and which are of uncertain date, is situated about 25 yds. from the E. shore of the loch to which it is connected by a causeway. The island, surrounded by the remains of a dilapidated and pillaged wall, contains the ruins of several rectangular buildings which may or may not belong to the dun.

Dun an Achaidh, Dun (NM 183546), 3¾ miles WSW. of Arinagour, Sheet 46 (B.8070). *Coll.*

Many of the dozen habitation sites recorded on the island of Coll are duns or small forts, built on stacks or isolated tables of rock situated either in land or on the sea shore, and presumably representing the defended residences of the families of Early Iron Age farmers and fishermen. The type, which is found from Kintyre to Skye, and even farther N., is also widely represented on Tiree. This example, situated on a steep-sided rocky eminence close to the S. side of the road, comprises two walls defending the summit plateau which measures 90 ft. by 24 ft. in extent. The entrance is in the N.

Dunan na Nighean, Dun (NR 415976), 2½ miles NNE. of Scalascaig, Sheet 61 (A.871, A.870 and moorland). *Colonsay.*

This small dun occupying an inland stack is entered from the NE. through a doorway midway in a straight stretch of walling 30 ft. long. Three lintel stones of the entrance passage are still *in situ*. The interior has been choked with tumbled wall stones and the ruin of a circular stone house.

Dunbuie Hill, Dun (NS 421752), 1 mile E. of Dumbarton, Sheet 64 (A.82 and by-road). *Dunbartonshire.*

The remains of this dun crown a hill which overlooks the estuary of the River Clyde from the E. and commands a splendid distant prospect of Dumbarton Rock. The dun was excavated in 1895, when it was found to measure 30 ft. in diameter within a wall 13 ft. thick, a fair amount of which can still be seen. The entrance, in the E., is 3 ft. wide. A tantalisingly brief part of the report suggests that there was a mural chamber on either side of the entrance. Finds included positively no pot-sherds; two implements of bone; stone pounders and whetstones and perforated stones; and parts of two rotary querns—a typical Early Iron Age assemblage, probably of pre-Roman date. The report also gives accounts and illustrations of several faked weapons of slate. It is interesting to note that only four years later, when a crannog was excavated on the foreshore of the Clyde estuary at a point about 1 mile S. of this dun, a larger collection of similar fantasies from the same source were "found".

Borvemore, Dun (NG 033940), 7 miles N. of Rodel, Sheet 18 (A.859 and moorland). *Harris.*

The remains of this structure stand on a rocky knoll ¾ mile S. of Borve Lodge. The wall is about 13 ft. thick, and the courtyard 20 ft. in diameter. The entrance, in the E., leads to an outer court 35 ft. long.

Craig Phitiulais, Dun (NH 930140), 2¼ miles NE. of Aviemore, Sheet 36 (A.970 and moorland). *Inverness-shire.*

This dun is situated far from the next example to have been recorded in any direction, at a point ½ mile ESE. of Pityoulish farmhouse, on a minor heather-clad eminence with a wide prospect northwards down Strathspey. It

measures 30 ft. by 20 ft. within the ruin of a substantial wall which must originally have measured about 11 ft. in thickness. The entrance is in the SW.

Onich, Dun (NN 029619), 1¾ miles WNW. of North Ballachulish, Sheet 41 (A.82 and moorland). *Inverness-shire.*

This little dun occupies a rocky knoll which is approached easily only from the NE., while to the W. it is bounded by a precipice 400 ft. high. It is oblong, measuring 45 ft. by 30 ft. within the ruins of a heavy stone wall in which small amounts of vitrified material can be discerned.

Auchteraw, Dun (NH 349070), 2½ miles SW. of Fort Augustus, Sheet 34 (forest roads). *Inverness-shire.*

This vitrified dun occupies a bold rocky promontory on the W. side of the valley of the River Oich overlooking the passage between Loch Ness and Loch Oich from a precipitous 200 ft. It measures 50 ft. by 25 ft. within a ruined wall containing masses of vitrified material. An outer wall bars approach from all directions other than the SE., and the entrance is in the SW.

This has the distinction of being one of the earlier vitrified structures on record in Scotland, having been visited and described by Thomas Pennant (*A Tour in Scotland*, 1796, i (1790), 222).

Am Baghan Galldair, Dun (NG 822207), 1 mile NE. of Glenelg, Sheet 33 (footpath). *Inverness-shire.*

This dun lies at a height of 475 ft. O.D. on the hill overlooking Glenelg Bay from the NE. It is formed by a wall 8 ft. thick which encloses an almost circular area measuring about 70 ft. in diameter. Two circular foundations in the N. sector are probably of later date than the dun.

Dun Grugaig, Galleried Dun (NG 852159), 3¼ miles SE. of Glenelg, Sheet 33 (by-road up Glen Beag). *Inverness-shire.*

This structure stands on a knoll on the brink of one side of a narrow, steep-sided gorge about 1½ miles above the upper of the two famous brochs. The wall, which still stands to a maximum height of 8 ft., is 14 ft. thick. It forms the arc of a D-shaped enclosure measuring 47 ft. along the chord formed by the precipitous side of the gorge by 38 ft. transversely. Mural chambers and a scarcement are discernible among the debris, as well as a blocked entrance passage with door-checks and bar-hole.

Dun Cul Bhuirg, Dun (NM 265246), 1½ miles W. of St Mary's Abbey, Sheet 48 (A.849 and ferry). *Iona.*

This small dun, occupying a steep-sided, towering rock near the western shore of Iona, measures about 75 ft. by 50 ft. within the now ruinous remains of a wall or rampart. Two platforms in the interior mark the sites of timber-framed houses, and there is room for two or three more. Excavations carried out in the dun in 1957 and 1958 revealed the remains of a very simple house, probably a mere rock shelter, on one of the platforms, and traces of a circular timber-framed house with a central hearth. A considerable amount of pottery, and certain other small finds, were recovered, suggesting an occupation in the Iron Age.

Castle Haven, Dun (NX 594483), 2¼ miles W. of Borgue, Sheet 83 (by-road and footpath to shore).
Stewartry of Kirkcudbright.

This structure was cleared of rubble and partly reconstructed in 1905. It is a D-shaped galleried dun of a type which is not otherwise recorded S. of Argyll and which stands partly on the chord of and partly within a larger enclosure of similar shape with which it may or may not be contemporary. The galleried dun measures internally 60 ft. by 35 ft., the outer court about twice as much. Relics found during the clearance include both Early Iron Age and early mediaeval objects.

Lochangower, Dun (NX 692661), 1 mile NE. of Laurieston, Sheet 83 (A.762, by-road and moorland).
Stewartry of Kirkcudbright.

This structure occupies a rocky knoll on a broken and rugged stretch of moorland. It is virtually subrectangular on plan, measuring about 100 ft. along either axis within the still substantial remains of a wall originally at least 12 ft. thick.

Auchencairn, Dun (NX 804508), ¼ mile SE. of Auchencairn, Sheet 84 (footpath and farm land).
Stewartry of Kirkcudbright.

The remains of this structure consist of a wall 12 ft. thick which encloses an area 110 ft. long by 80 ft. wide. It is comparable to the duns in the Mochrum district of Wigtownshire.

Lower Bayable, Dun (NB 516305), 6 miles E. by S. of Stornaway, Sheet 8 (A.866 and by-road). *Lewis.*

Whereas there is no evidence to show that the great majority of the crannogs in Scotland outside the SW. region were built in prehistoric times, there is likewise little guidance as yet available on the dating of the numerous insular non-galleried duns which pervade the Outer Hebrides. It will suffice to mention only a few of these, such as this example in Loch an Duin.

A small islet, connected with the shore by a man-made causeway 9 ft. wide and 90 ft. long, is ringed by a now ruinous wall. Several stretches of the outer face, built on the water's edge, indicate that the dun measures about 50 ft. in diameter over the wall.

Dun Cromore, Dun (NB 400206), 7½ miles S. by W. of Stornaway, Sheet 8 (A.859, B.8060 and by-road). *Lewis.*

This oval galleried dun is situated 50 yds. from the W. side of Loch Cromore. The interior measures 52 ft. by 44 ft. within a wall containing cells and a gallery, the latter reported to have had a stair within it which led up to a third gallery, passing by a second. All these upper works have now, however, been destroyed. An arc of walling forms a courtyard outside the entrance, to the NW.

Dun Baravat, Dun (NB 156356), 16½ miles W. of Stornaway, Sheet 13 (A.858, B.8011, B.8059, by-road and moorland).
Lewis.

This insular galleried dun occupies an islet connected to the shore of Loch Baravat by a causeway 100 ft. long. It measures internally 40 ft. by 30 ft. within the ruin of a galleried wall, the N. sector of which still stands to a height of 11 ft., measures 8 ft. in thickness and exhibits the remains of part of a scarcement and an upper gallery. A secondary building lies partly within and partly over the ruin of the wall.

An Sean Dun, Dun (NM 431563), 4½ miles W. by N. of Tobermory, Sheet 47 (A.848, estate road and moorland). *Mull.*

This structure measures 32 ft. in diameter within a wall about 10 ft. thick. The entrance, in the SSE., is not checked for a door. Mural galleries can be seen in the debris of the W. and E. arcs of the wall. The impression of a scarcement is probably due to the removal of the blocks from the highest remaining course of the inner face of the wall. The dun is covered on the S. by an outer wall about 6 ft. thick.

Loch Hunder, Dun (NF 905653), 2 miles SSW. of Lochmaddy, Sheet 18 (moorland and loch). *North Uist.*

This dun is representative of many examples of similar duns occuring in the Outer Isles the date of which is uncertain. It occupies an islet near the E. shore of the loch to which it is connected by a causeway. Another causeway connects it with a second islet and a third runs from this to the far shore. The dun is a flattened oval on plan, measuring about 40 ft. by 34 ft. over a wall which varies in thickness from 5 ft. to 10 ft. and includes at least one chamber and probably more. The second island bears traces of lesser fortifications.

Dun Torcuill, Dun (NF 888737), 3¼ miles NW. of Lochmaddy, Sheet 18 (A.865, moorland and loch). *North Uist.*

This structure and its neighbour, Dun Sticer, differ from classic brochs in the great variations in the thicknesses of the walls as well as by the fact that the walls are somewhat narrower in comparison with the diameter of the courtyards than is the case with brochs. These circumstances, combined with their situations on islets, point to the conclusion that they should rather be regarded as galleried duns than as brochs. The distinction is slight, since the two classes of monuments were doubtless virtually contemporary, but may imply that they were built by different people.

Dun Torcuill measures 38 ft. in diameter within a wall varying in thickness between 7 ft. 6 in. and 12 ft. 6 in. which contains a cell and galleries, and stands to a height of 10 ft. in the S. sector.

Clettraval, Dun (NF 749714), 10½ miles W. by N. of Lochmaddy, Sheet 18 (A.867, A.865 and moorland). *North Uist.*

See **Clettraval** Chambered Cairn.

Tom Orain, Dun (NN 867368), 2 miles W. of Amulree, Sheet 52 (by-road). *Perthshire.*

The remains of this dun stand on a low bluff round the base of which the road up Glen Quaich makes a slight bend. It now appears as an annular mound spread to a thickness of 25 ft. from which enough earthfast boulders

protrude to show that the dun originally measured about 63 ft. by 52 ft. within a wall about 12 ft. thick. This is the southernmost of the NW. Perthshire duns yet recorded.

Queen's View, Dun (NN 863602), 5 miles WNW. of Pitlochry, Sheet 43 (A.9, B.8019, forest track and footpath). *Perthshire.*

This is one of the better preserved examples of the duns of NW. Perthshire. It is situated in a clearing on the route of an overhead power line (and is therefore free from the conifers which surround it) only ¼ mile from the renowned viewpoint at the foot of Loch Tummel to which great numbers of people resort each year to enjoy the prospect of the E. end of the Road to the Isles so much valued by Queen Victoria.

The dun measures internally about 56 ft. in diameter. The wall, about 10 ft. thick, still retains several considerable stretches of the lower courses of the faces.

Balnacraig, Dun (NN 748476), ½ mile NE. of Fortingall, Sheet 51 (moorland and pasture land). *Perthshire.*

This well-preserved dun is situated on a fertile elongated shelf overlooking the lower reaches of the River Lyon from the N. The wall is in better condition than that of any other in the locality; all the stones of both faces are visible for at least one and as many as four courses. The interior measures 65 ft. by 58 ft., and the wall varies in thickness from 8 ft. to 13 ft. Several secondary structures lie within the dun and outside on the NE.

Roromore, Dun (NN 626468), 7 miles W. of Fortingall, Sheet 51 (by-road and farm road). *Perthshire.*

Those of the duns of NW. Perthshire which lie in Glen Lyon have long been famous, and none are better preserved than this one which is situated beside the farm road a few yards from the right bank of the Allt a' Chobhair. The wall appears as a considerable grass-grown mound from which numerous boulders of both faces protrude, but it has been robbed to build, amongst other things, a now ruinous rectangular building which occupies part of the interior of the dun. This measures about 50 ft. in diameter, the wall between 11 ft. and 14 ft. in thickness. The entrance is in the N.

Ceann na Coille, Dun (NN 807586),

$2\frac{3}{4}$ miles E. of Tummel Bridge, Sheet 52 (B.846 and by-road).   *Perthshire.*

Another well-preserved dun is situated only the length of a single field from the road which borders the S. shore of Reservoir Tummel. The lower courses of the wall have survived in a sound state, most of the inner face and about half the outer being visible among the debris and light brushwood. The interior measures 55 ft. in diameter and the entrance is in the E.

Braes of Foss, Dun (NN 753560), 6 miles E. by S. of Kinloch Rannoch, Sheet 51 (by-road).   *Perthshire.*

This, perhaps the highest of the many duns in NW. Perthshire, is situated at a height of 1050 ft. O.D. 400 yds. E. of the house at Braes of Foss, and an equal distance N. of the road from Kinloch Rannoch to Coshieville. The remains are a very good example of how slight such things can be and yet still be recognisable for what they are. They consist of a green mound from which a few boulders protrude, part of which has been erased by the plough. The dun originally measured about 85 ft. by 75 ft. internally within a thick stone wall.

Strathgarry, Dun (NN 890632), $1\frac{3}{4}$ miles WNW. of Killiecrankie, Sheet 43 (by-road, farmland and plantation).
                                                      Perthshire.

This oval dun, typical of the group in NW. Perthshire, measures about 60 ft. by 50 ft. within a wall varying in thickness about an average of 10 ft. Several large facing stones remain *in situ*, and the rubble core is spilled out in places. The interior may have been excavated to some slight extent to achieve a level surface. The hill upon which the dun is situated has been planted with conifers in recent times; and although the planters have respected the monument, the rank grass with which it is clothed may tend to obscure more detail as it luxuriates ungrazed.

Dun Borodale, Dun (NG 555364), $\frac{1}{2}$ mile W. of Raasay pier, Sheet 24 (by-road and woodland).   *Raasay.*

This oval dun, situated in Borodale Wood, measures axially 40 ft. by 30 ft. within the ruin of a wall 14 ft. thick. Traces of galleries or chambers can be seen in the debris, among them a cell a short distance S. of the entrance in the E.

Culbokie, Dun (NH 603587), 5 miles

NE. of Cononbridge, Sheet 27 (B.9163 and by-road).   *Ross & Cromarty.*

This is one of several duns in the neighbourhood which appear as triple rings in various stages of robbing and ruin. Carn Mor, as this one was called, is as good an example as any. The inner ring, a wall some 8 ft. thick, encloses an area 55 ft. in diameter. It is surrounded by a pair of ramparts with a median ditch which comprise together a formidable obstacle. The entrances of all the defensive elements are in the WSW. There is no reason to suppose that here, as in the other examples, all the defences should not be contemporary, and no proof that they are.

Kintail, Dun (NG 939207), 5 miles SE. of Dornie, Sheet 33 (A.87).
                                                      Ross & Cromarty.

Unnamed on the O.S. map, the village of Kintail stands on the N. shore of the head of Loch Duich at the mouth of the River Croe. The remains of this dun, standing immediately W. of an old manse on a little promontory, consist of an oval wall spread in ruin to a thickness of about 15 ft. The interior measures about 55 ft. by 25 ft., and the entrance may have been in the S.

Strathkanaird, Dun (NC 166019), 1 mile E. of Strathkanaird, Sheet 15 (moorland).   *Ross & Cromarty.*

This dun occupies a rocky knoll in the angle formed at the confluence of two small burns. It is D-shaped, measuring about 34 ft. by 32 ft. within a wall as much as 14 ft. thick in which it is most probable that there were chambers. The entrance is in the S.

Sandray, Dun (NL 637914), $\frac{3}{4}$ mile SW. of Bagh Ban, Sheet 31 (boat from Castle bay).   *Sandray.*

This dun, standing on an isolated rocky boss, is oval on plan, measuring about 50 ft. by 40 ft. within a galleried wall varying in thickness from 6 ft. to 12 ft. An outwork in the form of a stone wall bars approach from the W.

Dun Totaig, Dun (NG 235484), $1\frac{1}{4}$ miles W. by N. of Dunvegan, Sheet 23 (B.884 and moorland).   *Skye.*

Dun Totaig is almost oblong on plan, measuring axially about 24 ft. by 48 ft. within a wall varying from 10 ft. to 25 ft. in thickness. The entrance, in the short NW. end, is nearly 5 ft. wide and 19 ft. long. This is an example of a dun of unconventional type the date of which is uncertain.

Rudh an Dunain, Dun (NG 396160), 3¼ miles SSW. of Glenbrittle House, Sheet 32 (footpath). *Skye.*

This galleried promontory dun consists of a wall cutting off a headland which measures 80 ft. by 36 ft. in extent. The wall, built of large squared blocks, is 12 ft. thick at the base and stands to a maximum height of about 9 ft. The entrance, near the N. end, is checked for a door, and galleries can be distinguished within the wall.

Struanmore, Dun (NG 340390), 1 mile NNW. of Bracadale, Sheet 32 (A.863 and moorland). *Skye.*

This dun occupies an eminence 500 yds. N. of the broch of the same name. It is subrectangular on plan, measuring 175 ft. by 140 ft. within a wall varying in thickness from 8 ft. to 14 ft. and standing to a height of 5 ft. The entrance, over 6 ft. wide, is in the N. The remains of an outer work cover the dun to the NE. An almost circular stone foundation 6 ft. thick and about 33 ft. in diameter lies within the E. sector of the dun, and traces of two smaller circular structures can be seen between the dun and the outer wall.

Dun Skudiburgh, Dun (NG 374647), 1¼ miles NW. of Uig, Sheet 23 (A.855, farm road and moorland). *Skye.*

See **Dun Skudiburgh,** Fort.

Dun Liath, Dun (NG 360700), 4¾ miles NNW. of Uig, Sheet 23 (A.855 and moorland). *Skye.*

This galleried dun, situated on the cliffs NE. of the mouth of Loch Snizort, is drop-shaped on plan, measuring 150 ft. in length by 80 ft. in width within a galleried wall up to 12 ft. thick. The entrance is in the E. The wall stands in places up to 6 ft. in height, and must be one of the longest, if not the longest, such structures known. A row of earthfast stones like a diminutive *chevaux de frise* lies outside the dun to the S.

Dun Grugaig, Dun (NG 535124), 9¼ miles SW. of Broadford, Sheet 32 (A.881 and hill road). *Skye.*

This dun, on a headland on the E. side of Strathaird peninsula, is an example of the almost rectangular small but immensely strong galleried dun. It measures 50 ft. in length by 25 ft. in width within a wall, the landward sector

of which is 15 ft. thick. The entrance, in this sector, is checked for a door and fitted with bar-holes, and the wall is sufficiently well preserved for the remains of a gallery to have survived above it. At a point a few feet E. of the entrance an opening in the inner face of the wall leads to the beginning of a mural stair which gives access to the upper gallery.

Dun Vulan, Dun (NF 714297), 8¼ miles NW. of Lochboisdale, Sheet 22 (A.865, moorland and machar). *South Uist.*

This dun is characteristic of the many insular duns on South Uist. It stands on a spit between Loch Ardvule and the shore, an almost if not quite circular ruin about 56 ft. in outer diameter. The wall varies in thickness from 11 ft. to 15 ft., and traces of an internal gallery can be seen in the NE. sector. A later structure lies within it.

Castlehill Wood, Dun (NS 750909), 3 miles SW. of Stirling, Sheet 57 (by-road from Stirling). *Stirlingshire.*

This dun stands on a low, rocky eminence on the NE. face of the Touch Hills, just within a tract of land which at the time of writing is used as a testing ground for repaired Army vehicles, including tanks, so that caution is required both in walking to the dun and in leaving a car in the by-road which alone gives access to the site. The dun is oval on plan, measuring 75 ft. by 50 ft. along the axes within the ruin of a stone wall 16 ft. thick. The entrance is in the E. When the dun was excavated in 1955 the entrance passage was cleared and the door-checks revealed. Almost the whole of the interior was examined, but no post-holes or other sub-structures were discovered. Features noted included an external stair rising up the inner face of the wall at a point 10 ft. N. of the entrance passage, and two narrow mural chambers which appeared to have been used, though not necessarily originally constructed for, corn-drying kilns. Small finds, including Roman glass, pointed to occupation during the 1st century A.D., possibly extending into the 2nd and probably originating at a somewhat earlier period (saddle quern).

Craigton, Dun (NS 628872), ¾ mile NE. of Fintry, Sheet 57 (moorland). *Stirlingshire.*

This dun stands on a rocky knoll protruding from the SW. flank of the Fintry Hills below Double Craigs. The summit of the knoll is enclosed by the ruin of a wall about 10 ft. thick which defines an area measuring 48 ft. by 42 ft. Arcs of outer walling protect the easier approaches to this from the NW. and SE.

Loch Ardvair, Dun (NC 168332), 8½ miles NW. of Inchnadamph, Sheet 15 (A.837, A.894, B.869 and footpath). *Sutherland.*

The remains of this circular dun lie on a tidal rock at the S. end of the loch. They consist of a wall about 11 ft. thick which encloses an area 24 ft. in diameter. The interior has been partly cleared in the past, and considerable stretches of the face of the wall can be distinguished, together with the entrance, in the S.

Clashnessie, Dun (NC 055315), 6½ miles NW. of Lochinver, Sheet 15 (A.837, B.869 and farm road). *Sutherland.*

This small promontory dun occupies an almost completely isolated pillar of rock on the shore at the W. side of Clashnessie Bay. It is formed by a narrow ruinous wall which borders the rock to enclose an area measuring about 35 ft. by 25 ft. The entrance is in the SW. This structure is typical of a class found farther S. down the W. coast, but as far as is known is the northernmost example on the mainland.

Chang, Dun (NX 299481), 3¾ miles NW. of Port William, Sheet 82 (A.747 and farm road). *Wigtownshire.*

This is one of a group of walled enclosures which survive in various states of decay in the Mochrum district of Wigtownshire. Like the others, it consists of an oval enclosure, in this case measuring 110 ft. in length by 70 ft. in width within a ruinous stone wall about 12 ft. thick. Such structures occur in particular in Argyll, western Perthshire, Stirlingshire and Ayrshire, and where relics have been recovered from them they have been of Early Iron Age and Roman Iron Age date, and have suggested that the duns were defended homesteads.

Chippermore, Dun (NX 297483), 4 miles NW. of Port William, Sheet 82 (A.747 and farm road). *Wigtownshire.*

This is another of the dozen or so duns in the Mochrum group, comparable to that at Chang and others on the near-by farms of Corwall, Garheugh, Airyolland, Eldrig and Ringheel. This one measures about 90 ft. by 80 ft. within a wall about 9 ft. thick. It has been re-used as a sheepfold and a dump for cleared stones.

Craigoch, Dun (NX 012668), 5 miles NW. of Stranraer, Sheet 76 (A.718, B.798 and farm road). *Wigtownshire.*

This dun, perched on a rocky knoll close to the left bank of the Craigoch Burn, and cut off from the NE. and E. by a natural gully, measures about 27 ft. in diameter within an overgrown ruinous wall some 7 ft. in thickness.

Jamieson's Point, Dun (NX 033710), 6½ miles N. by W. of Stranraer, Sheet 76 (A.718 and by-road). *Wigtownshire.*

This structure has been called a broch at one time and an enclosure within a wall 4 ft. 6 in. in thickness at another, but the truth probably lies somewhere between these extremes. It is probably a simple circular dun, comparable to its neighbour at Craigton, an enclosure some 55 ft. in diameter within a wall some 10 ft. thick.

CRANNOGS

A crannog appeared when in occupation as a circular timber-framed thatched house apparently floating upon the surface of the lake or estuary or marsh in which it was situated. This watery protection was achieved either by building the house on a convenient small island or, as was almost always the case, by first making such an island where nature had not provided one. In the latter case, the first step was to select a position at a suitable distance from dry land, and mark it. There followed the task of rafting out boulders to the vicinity of the marker and there sinking them, until at long last a low, flat-topped island just breaking the surface of the water had been formed. As the uppermost level of this was likely to have been about 50 ft. in diameter, the amount of ballast required in anything but the shallowest water was enormous.

When this stage was completed, great numbers of stakes and piles of various weights and sizes were cut and assembled—a task comparable in degree to the collecting of material for building a broch or one of the smaller duns. The main sleepers upon which the framework of the house was to stand were incorporated into the uppermost layer of the stones of the island. A planked pathway, its inner side adjoining the outer wall of the house and its outer edge supported by piles, protruded a little way beyond the margin of the surface of the island. Access could be obtained from this to two other structural features—a dock in which canoes were kept, and a sinuous causeway leading to and from the shore. The surface of the causeway was arranged so that at normal water level it was just submerged, thereby forming a hazardous means of entry to an unwelcome stranger.

The crannog, yet another version of the circular house, has a debatable ancestry which extends far back in Ireland if not, indeed, in Scotland too. Once built, a crannog island lasts for ever even though the house rots away above water level. Many such an island was occupied in comparatively late mediaeval times, long after the original builders had abandoned it. Crannogs containing relics assignable to the end of the 1st millennium B.C. and the beginning of the 1st A.D. are comparatively few in number, and they are all in south-western Scotland. Little or no work has been done on crannogs in other parts of the country, however, and at present it is impossible to do more than speculate about the probability that the technique of crannog-building, like other very specialised methods such as broch-building, may never have been revived after the period of its natural demise.

Only two crannogs, revealed by the temporary lowering of the levels of lochs, have been excavated with technical competence in recent times. Most crannog islands are covered with scrub, but in a few cases it may be possible to distinguish the remains of timbers in them.

Loch Bruicheach, Crannog (NH 455368), 7 miles SW. of Beauly, Sheet 26 (A.9, A.833, by-road and forest tracks). *Inverness-shire.*
This crannog lies close to the N. shore of Loch Bruicheach. No evidence of the date of its construction, occupation or occupations has been published, but it is of considerable interest in that vitrified material is spread widely over it. This suggests more than the mere destruction by fire of a stone-and-timber building; and arouses speculation on whether the substructure may itself have contained timber which was ignited by such a fire.

Barean Loch, Crannog (NX 8655), 3½ miles SSE. of Dalbeattie, Sheet 84 (A.710 and farm roads). *Stewartry of Kirkcudbright.*
The crannog found when the level of the water in Barean Loch was lowered in 1865 was basically a timber structure. One of the relics found on it was a cooking pot, now preserved in the national collection, comparable to others found at the Roman Fort at Newstead; this indicated that the crannog was occupied at least as early as the 2nd century A.D., and probably built at an earlier date.

Loch Arthur, Crannog (NX 902690), ½ mile E. of Beeswing, Sheet 84 (footpath). *Stewartry of Kirkcudbright.*
This crannog near the NW. shore of Loch Arthur was noted in 1874 when oak piles and horizontal beams were found. At the same time a dug-out canoe 45 ft. long and 5 ft. wide at the stem was found in the loch. This is now in the national collection.

Lochrutton, Crannog (NX 898730), 5 miles W. by S. of Dumfries, immediately S. of Lochfoot, Sheet 84. *Stewartry of Kirkcudbright.*
This crannog is situated on the centre of Lochrutton Loch, 200 yds. SE. of a natural island called Dutton's Cairn. It was excavated in 1901 and 1902, when it was found to consist of a circular cairn of earth 80 ft. in diameter which rested on a foundation of logs. The wooden floor of the crannog lay beneath the earthen cap, the latter representing natural and artificial accumulations, the accretions of centuries. A few signs of the post structure of the crannog house were revealed, together with parts of the verandah. The relics recovered and recorded were all of mediaeval date, but the report of the exploration states that they all came from levels above the log floor, and there is little reason to doubt that the crannog is most probably of Early Iron Age date.

Milton Loch, Crannog (NX 839718), 9 miles W. of Dumfries, Sheet 84 (A.75 and by-road). *Stewartry of Kirkcudbright.*
When the level of the water in Milton Loch was reduced in 1953 two crannogs appeared to view, one in the SE. part of the loch and the other in the NW. They are ½ mile apart. The latter was excavated as far as the ever-rising level of the water would permit. The objects recovered ranged from a pre-Roman plough stilt and head, and part of the upper stone of a rotary quern of a type attributable to the 1st century A.D., to an enamelled bronze loop datable to the 2nd century A.D.

The crannog appears as a low circular, stone-covered island some 35 ft. in diameter, joined to the shore by a ragged double line of posts protruding from the soft mud. The house itself was floored with a great number of timbers; its roof was supported on several rings of posts, and the outer wall was made by resting split timbers between pairs of uprights. The interior was divided radially into compartments, and subdivided, and the hearth of clay and stones was placed not far from the centre. The timbers forming the floor of the house were extended outside all the way round to form a platform about 6 ft. wide, supported from beneath

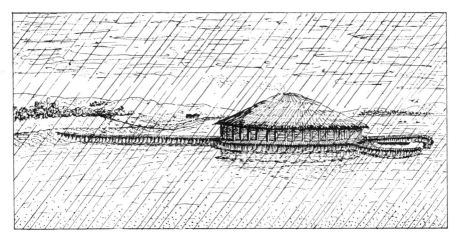

44 *Reconstruction of Milton Loch Crannog at a time of low water during a summer in the 1st century* A.D.

by piles. The causeway led directly from the door of the house to the shore, 100 ft. away to the W.

On the opposite side of the house from the causeway, wooden piles and mounds of stones were visible under the surface of the water when the excavation was in progress. These constituted a dock measuring about 35 ft. in greatest width by a little less in length, with its entrance in the SE., away from the house and facing the open waters of the loch.

No trace of a solid basis of boulders could be detected by probing immediately under the floor of the house, and the excavator concluded that if any such had ever existed it must have been separated from the floor of the house by a great layer of timbers.

Carlingwark Loch, Crannogs (NX 765615), immediately S. of Castle Douglas, Sheet 84.

Stewartry of Kirkcudbright.

Draining operations were carried out in Carlingwark Loch 200 years ago. During the time when the level of the water was lowered, at least four crannogs, two dams and a causeway were revealed, together with numerous relics of the pre-Roman and Roman Iron Age, including dug-out canoes, a bronze sword, a cauldron and numerous tools, implements and weapons, and a tankard handle of Corcoran's Class II, dated early in the 2nd century A.D.

Strathcashell Point, Crannog (NS 395930), 2¼ miles NW. of Balmaha, Sheet 56 (by-road and farm road).

Stirlingshire.

Although this crannog may date from early historic rather than from prehistoric times, it could as well be numbered among the Iron Age examples, all of which have been found in SW. Scotland, as no relics have yet been found in it. The artificial island, placed 450 yds. E. of the Early Christian cashel on the point, and 30 yds. from the nearest stretch of the shore, just breaks the surface when the level of Loch Lomond is normal, and supports a resolute tree and some seasonal herbs. It is possible to walk round its outer margin with the feet about 3 ft. below water level, and to see the great timbers which are embedded in it. The flat top, about 70 ft. in diameter, quickly gives way to sloping sides; the depth to which these fall has not been recorded.

Dowalton Loch, Crannogs (NX 4074), 2 miles W. of Sorbie, Sheet 77 (B.7052 and farm land). *Wigtownshire.*

The numerous crannogs reported from time to time when lochs in the Whithorn peninsula were drained are best represented by the Dowalton Loch crannogs excavated in 1863 and 1864. These produced evidence of timber buildings and foundations, and relics among which was a Roman *patera* which, with other objects, indicated an Early Iron Age date for these structures.

Black Loch, Crannog (NX 114612), 3 miles E. of Stranraer, Sheet 82 (within the Lochinch estate). *Wigtownshire.*

This crannog on an island in the Black Loch was investigated in 1870, when the wooden floor was found to be about 50 ft. in diameter. Traces of several successive occupations were revealed, and the relics included material datable to the 1st or 2nd century A.D. as well as to later periods, proving that the original structure was of Early Iron Age date.

PICTISH SYMBOL STONES

The remarkable assemblage of incised and carved boulders and slabs which have become known as Pictish Symbol Stones are almost all situated in the northern and eastern parts of the country, though a few occur in the north-west—regions in which the native Picts achieved the last flowering of their culture. It is now 60 years since these stones, together with many others of later date, were systematically studied for the first time by Joseph Anderson and Romilly Allen, and since then several attempts have been made to bring the subject up to date in the light of more recent work on comparative material elsewhere.

The original division of the incised and sculptured stones into three classes still forms a useful background against which the stones and their problems can be considered. The Class I examples comprise designs which are incised, not carved in relief, either on natural boulders or on stones only roughly dressed; and which include no Christian cross or other recognised attribute. They have been variously ascribed to the 7th and 8th centuries, to the 6th, 7th and 8th, to a period extending from the 4th to the 8th, and to the 7th, 8th and 9th centuries. Unless and until more support is forthcoming for the earliest dates, it may be as well to accept the last set listed above.

The symbols themselves comprise, on the one hand, what have been described as apparently abstract designs of a symbolic significance to those then in the know, and on the other delineations of objects recognisable to any beholder. The former group includes what are known as the Crescent and V-rod, the Double-disc and Z-rod, the Notched Rectangle and Z-rod, the Arch or Horseshoe, the Disc and Rectangle or Mirror-case, the Triple-disc and Cross-bar, the Pair of Discs (connected or not), the Flower, the Rectangular Figure or Comb-case and several other minor, rare, symbols allied to some of these. Among the latter is the Triple Disc without Cross-bar, in which the smaller outer discs are fashioned as if they formed link handles to a cauldron or bowl, the mouth of which is represented by the large central disc. The rest of the symbols are in animal form. The Serpent may appear by itself or with a Z-rod; the others are the Bull, the Boar, the Wolf or Hunting Dog, the Horse and the Stag, Fishes and various Birds. It may be remarked that the Ram is not known; but a fascinating, widely spread animal symbol is that of a fabulous, or unrecognisably stylised, beast with long snout, curled feet and tail, and a lappet, which is misleadingly known as the "elephant" symbol.

The origin of certain features of these designs has been traced to Early Christian manuscript and other decorative work, from such places as the Northumbrian centres. It is argued from this that they date from a time subsequent to the conversion of the Picts. It has been noted that the artistic influences are Northumbrian rather than Irish, as might perhaps have appeared at first sight; and that the distinct Mediterranean flavour of some of them must have been transmitted by way of the Anglo-Saxon monasteries.

Even after the subjection of the Picts by the Scoto-Irish in the middle of the 9th century, the stones—now of the Class II type on which the symbols are in relief and are usually accompanied by the representation of the Christian cross—continue to show Anglo-Saxon rather than Irish influence. The great Northumbrian monasteries were, after all, not far from eastern Pictland, while from the second half of the 7th century onwards the Anglo-Saxons held sway as far north as the River Forth, the southern boundary of Pictland.

The classic form of Class II stones is a heavy upstanding slab, with the carving in relief on one face. The Christian symbols—the cross and various allegorical forms—together with elaborate decorative interlace and other carvings, were in time allowed to cover the whole of the carved surfaces, and the old symbols, having become fewer and of less significance or importance in the whole design, finally died out altogether, perhaps by the end of the 10th century. The numerous elaborate slabs

45   *Objects and motifs among the principal Pictish symbols*

46 *Fish, Birds, and Animals selected from Pictish Symbol Stones. The framed Boar, taken from a low relief from Euffigneix, Haute Marne, and datable to the 1st century B.C. (after Powell), is inserted for comparison*

and free-standing crosses which followed form a separate study, as yet by no means concluded.

Most of the stones of Classes I and II described in this Guide stand near or close to where they were at the time they were made. Many others, including some of the finest, are to be seen in the National Museum of Antiquities in Edinburgh, while considerable quantities can be found in provincial museums such as Dunrobin, Inverness, Meigle, Perth, St Vigean's and Thurso, and in churches and private houses.

Some Pictish Symbol Stones have, in addition to the symbols, inscriptions in the Ogam alphabet. This is a kind of cipher, consisting of linear markings arranged on a base-line. It is thought to have been invented in Ireland in the 4th century, and to have been brought to Scotland by the colonists from Ulster. Ogams on Pictish Symbol Stones are for the most part of a variety known as "Scholastic Ogams", and are at present considered to date from the 8th or 9th century.

Dyce, Pictish Symbol Stones (NJ 887130), in Dyce, 5 miles NW. of Aberdeen, Sheet 38 (A.96, A.947).
Aberdeenshire.

A Class I stone in St Fergus' church, Dyce, is decorated with an "elephant" symbol above a double disc and Z-rod symbol, both clearly and very regularly incised.

A Class II stone set up beside the

47   *The Maiden Stone*

former is carved in relief with a floriated cross and shaft and the crescent and V-rod, mirror case, triple disc and double disc and Z-rod symbols.

Broomend of Crichie, Pictish Symbol Stone (NJ 779196), 1 mile S. of Inverurie, Sheet 38 (A.96).   *Aberdeenshire.*

See **Broomend of Crichie** Henge.

Brandsbutt, Pictish Symbol Stone (NJ 760225), ¼ mile NW. of Inverurie, Sheet 38 (Side road off A.96).   *Aberdeenshire.*

The Brandsbutt Class I stone is decorated with a crescent and V-rod and a serpent and Z-rod symbol, both incised, as well as being marked by a line of Ogams which are certainly contemporary with the symbols. It is a matter for regret that this stone was broken and partly lost in the past; and for congratulation that the remains have now been assembled and are under guardianship.

Logie Elphinstone, Pictish Symbol Stone (NJ 705259), 5 miles NW. of Inverurie, Sheet 38 (A.96 and private grounds).   *Aberdeenshire.*

A Class I stone, one of three found near by on the Moor of Carden, was taken to Logie Elphinstone. It bears two series of symbols on one face, one apparently erased in favour of the other. The erased symbol seems to have been a double disc and Z-rod, but parts of it still show, as the erasing was not completely effective. This is overlain in part by a crescent and V-rod and in part by another double disc and Z-rod symbol. Above all the symbols is a wheel Ogam, an incised circle to the circumference of which six or seven Ogam cipher characters are appended.

Maiden Stone, Pictish Symbol Stone (NJ 703247), 5 miles WNW. of Inverurie, Sheet 38 (A.96, by-road).
Aberdeenshire.

This beautiful pillar of red granite stands beside the by-road 1 mile NW. of Chapel of Garioch village. It is a Class II stone, carved in relief, showing at the front a man between fish monsters, an enriched cross and shaft, a panel with an enriched disc and other ornamental details. The back has beasts and a centaur-like figure, a rectangle and Z-rod, an "elephant" and a mirror and comb symbol. The sides have interlaced panels. This stone is one of the most beautiful to have survived *in situ.*

Picardy Stone, Pictish Symbol Stone (NJ 609302), 2 miles NW. of Insch, Sheet 37 (by-road). *Aberdeenshire.*

This Class I stone stands in a little enclosure close to a by-road between Netherton and Myreton farmhouses. It is incised with a double disc and Z-rod, a serpent and Z-rod and a mirror symbol.

Balluderon, Pictish Symbol Stone (NO 375375), 4¾ miles NNW. of Dundee, Sheet 54 (by-road through Downfield). *Angus.*

This stone of Class II, known as St Martin's Stone, is an upright slab of which the top is broken off. Sculpture in relief on one face comprises a horseman who is situated in the truncated lower arm of a cross; below to the left, a so-called "elephant" symbol and a serpent and Z-rod symbol; and below to the right another horseman.

St Vigean's, Pictish Symbol Stones (NO 638428), 1½ miles N. of Arbroath, Sheet 54 (by-road). *Angus.*

The collection of sculptured stones maintained by the Ministry of Works at St Vigean's includes six of Class II. The collection includes the "Drosten Stone" which bears an inscription in Hiberno–Saxon and examples of the double disc and Z-rod, crescent and mirror and comb symbols as well as beasts and men.

Dunnichen, Pictish Symbol Stone (NO 508488), 3¼ miles ESE. of Forfar, Sheet 54 (A.958 and by-road). *Angus.*

This splendid Class I slab, found in a field and re-erected in the garden of Dunnichen House, is inscribed on one face with, at the top, a flower symbol; in the middle, a double disc and Z-rod symbol; and below, mirror and comb symbols.

Aberlemno, Pictish Symbol Stone (NO 525555), 5 miles NE. of Forfar, Sheet 54 (B.9134). *Angus.*

(1) In a field ¾ mile N. of the church, a leaning sandstone pillar of Class I, inscribed on one face at the top with a serpent; below this a double-disc and Z-rod symbol; and at the bottom mirror and comb symbols. Two other inscribed slabs stand near by.

(2) In the churchyard, a trimmed slab beautifully decorated with Class II sculpture. On the front, a cross covered with decoration disposed in panels, the background carved with beasts. On the

48 *The elaborate "front" of the Pictish Symbol Stone which stands in the garden of the Manse at Glamis*

back, below a pair of beasts' heads interlocked, a bifurcated rectangle and Z-rod symbol and a triple disc symbol, below which are three rows of figures.

Glamis, Pictish Symbol Stone (NO 385466), 5 miles SE. of Forfar, Sheet 54 (A.94). *Angus.*

This slab standing in the grounds of the Manse is nearly 9 ft. high. One side is incised with a serpent symbol, a fish symbol and a mirror symbol. The other is beautifully decorated with an elaborate cross, the side panels beyond which contain a centaur, a dog-like beast, a pair of men fighting with axes, a head of a doe, a cauldron (from which a pair of legs protrude) supported on a bar by two ring-handles, and a triple disc symbol. The small outer circles of the latter are represented as being joined one to either side of the large central disc by bands in low relief, as if they were ring-handles. Several other examples of the triple disc symbol occur (e.g., another stone near Glamis (E.C.M. III, p.221) and others at Aberlemno (p.210),

Monymusk (p.193), Kintore (p.172), Inveravon, Banff (p.153) and Lindores (p.344)). The symbols on the stones at Kintore, Inveravon and Lindores all have a line or bar running across the discs; in the Kintore example, this is made to thread its way through the small outer circles and over the large inner one as if it passed through ring-handles.

Eassie, Pictish Symbol Stone (NO 352474), 2 miles W. of Glamis, Sheet 53 (A.94). *Angus.*

The Eassie Class II stone, standing in the ruins of the church, is richly ornamented on the front with a cross and figures in relief. On the back the carving includes a so-called "elephant" symbol, a double disc and Z-rod symbol and figures of men and beasts.

Cossans, Pictish Symbol Stone (NO 400499), 2¼ miles NNE. of Glamis, Sheet 53, 54 (A.928 and farm road). *Angus.*

St Orland's Stone, a handsome Class II slab, nearly 8 ft. high, is decorated on the front with a raised cross which, like the panels behind it, is elaborately ornamented in spiral and other relief.

49　*The simple designs on the "back" of the Glamis Stone*

The back carries, near the top, a crescent and V-rod symbol and a double disc and Z-rod symbol; below this, several horsemen and hounds, a boat containing six voyagers, and a cow being attacked by a monstrous beast.

Largo, Pictish Symbol Stone (NO 423035), in the gateway of the Parish Kirk, Sheet 59. *Fife.*

This stone has reached its present resting place after being discovered in 1839 in two pieces on the Largo estate and travelling thence in due course into Midlothian. One side has a late Celtic cross in relief and a pair of interlaced creatures with animal heads and fish tails. The other side has a Pictish scene in which three horsemen, two hounds and two deer move across the field, and also two symbols—the double disc and Z-rod and the so-called "elephant" symbol. All are much weathered and defaced.

Lindores, Pictish Symbol Stone (NO 262169), in Lindores. Sheet 59 (A.913). *Fife.*

This symbol stone originally stood on a near-by hill, but when this came under cultivation it was brought down and built into the garden wall of a cottage on the N. outskirts of Lindores, beside the road. Although incredibly defaced by a Government arrow, placed there by some surveyor in need of a handy place to inscribe a bench-mark, it presents very clearly two of the most common symbols —at the top a triple disc with cross bar, and below a crescent and V-rod symbol. The bench-mark is carved very precisely in the middle of the latter, while the large central disc of the upper symbol has been slit by the hole which once took the gnomon of a sun-dial. The divisions of this, and neatly carved Roman numerals, can also be detected. A curious additional feature which has not been studied or explained is a shallow pecked line following the outline of a rectangle which can be detected running across the lower half of the upper symbol, down through the extremities of the crescent and across the bottom of the face well below the latter. This outline appears to have been cut by the symbols; but an intensive examination would be necessary before its exact status could be accurately known, and whether perhaps the symbols have not been to some extent re-cut.

50 *Knocknagael, also known as the Boar Stone*

Knocknagael, Pictish Symbol Stone (NH 656412), 2¼ miles S. of Inverness, Sheet 26 (A.86 and by-road).
Inverness-shire.

This Class I slab, nearly 7 ft. high and standing near the roadside, is carved with the representation of a boar as well as with a mirror-case symbol.

Trusty's Hill, Pictish Symbols (NX 588561), ¼ mile W. of Gatehouse of Fleet, Sheet 83 (A.75 and footpath).
Stewartry of Kirkcudbright.

See **Trusty's Hill** Fort.

Burghead, Pictish Symbol Stones (NJ 109691), 8 miles NE. of Forres, Sheet 28 (B.9089).
Moray.

The renowned slabs from Burghead which include representations of bulls are no longer at their find-spot. As their interest and importance is great, it may be appropriate to mention that some of them are in the National Museum of Antiquities of Scotland in Edinburgh, and others in the British and Elgin Museums.

Pabbay, Pictish Symbol Stone (NL 605875), 150 yds. W. of highwater mark in Bagh Ban, Sheet 31 (boat from Castlebay).
Pabbay.

This interesting stone, found near the foundations of a church, bears the crescent and V-rod symbol above a lily symbol, but is most interesting for having also a cross potent. This rises from the crescent in such a way as to give no hint whether the latter was there first, as seems virtually certain, or whether the two were contemporary. Skye and the Outer Hebrides were still Pictish in St Columba's time.

Dunfallandy, Pictish Symbol Stone (NN 950560), 1¼ miles SSE. of Pitlochry, Sheet 53 (A.9 and by-road). *Perthshire.*

This Class II stone, originally from a disused chapel at Killiecrankie, is now near the mausoleum at Dunfallandy, some 5 miles down the valley. One side is ornamented with a decorated cross and nine side panels containing a figure of Jonah, beasts and Angels. The motifs on the other side include two Crescent and V-rod symbols, two "elephant" symbols, two saintly seated figures said to represent SS. Paul and Anthony, a warrior on horseback, an anvil, a hammer and a pair of tongs, all contained within a border composed of two elongated fish-tailed beasts.

Meigle, Pictish Symbol Stones (NO 287446), 4¾ miles NE. of Coupar Angus, Sheet 53 (A.94). *Perthshire.*

The Ministry of Works maintains a museum in Meigle in which are 25 sculptured stones of various kinds, about one third being stones of Class II.

Fowlis Wester, Pictish Symbol Stone (NN 928242), 4½ miles ENE. of Crieff, Sheet 58 (A.85 and by-road). *Perthshire.*

This Class II stone, 10 ft. high, stands within a railing in the village. Now much eroded by weather, it has been a magnificent example of Pictish sculpture, the front bearing a great ornamented cross and the back a number of carved features. The uppermost of these is a double disc and Z-rod symbol; below this comes a horseman, a hound, two horsemen one of whom has a hawk on his arm, a belled cow led by a man and followed by six other men, a crescent and V-rod symbol, a bird and a much worn representation of a beast consuming a man.

Abernethy, Pictish Symbol Stone (NO 190163), 6 miles SE. of Perth, Sheet 58 (A.90 and A.913). *Perthshire.*

This little Class I stone, situated not far from the round tower of Abernethy, is decorated with a so-called "tuning-fork" symbol, a hammer and an anvil, and a mutilated crescent and V-rod symbol.

Auchterarder, Pictish Symbol Stone (NN 924097), 2¼ miles SW. of Auchterarder, Sheet 58 (A.9). *Perthshire.*

This Class I stone standing in a field close to the S. side of the road is incised with a bird with its head turned back, which has been recognised as a goose, together with a rectangular grid representing a double-sided comb.

Raasay House, Pictish Symbol Stone (NG 546366), 200 yds. NNW. of Raasay House, Sheet 24. *Raasay.*

This stone bears a cross at the top and, beneath this, a "tuning fork" symbol and a crescent and V-rod symbol. The slab was removed from the vicinity of the pier, ¼ mile to the S.

Rosemarkie, Pictish Symbol Stone (NH 737576), 1 mile NE. of Fortrose, Sheet 27 (A.832). *Ross & Cromarty.*

This repaired Class II stone, standing against the wall of the church, measures 8 ft. 6 in. in height, and bears on the front a most elaborate and finely worked set of ornamented panels. On the back are, at the top, three crescent and V-rod symbols with a double disc and Z-rod symbol, two mirrors and a comb. Below these, an equal-armed cross within an elaborated border stands above a panel of key pattern.

Dingwall, Pictish Symbol Stone (NH 548589), ¼ mile NW. of the Railway Station in Dingwall, Sheet 26. *Ross & Cromarty.*

This Class I stone was found in use as a lintel over a doorway in Dingwall church, and set up on a base outside during restorations. One face is incised with a double disc and Z-rod symbol above one possibly unfinished or erased and one reasonably complete crescent and V-rod symbol. The other face has an arrangement of three circles and a crescent and V-rod symbol.

Edderton, Pictish Symbol Stone (NH 708850), on NW. border of Edderton village, Sheet 21 *Ross & Cromarty.*

This unhewn pillar of red sandstone standing 10 ft. high is incised on one face with a double disc and Z-rod symbol which is very crowded by a fish symbol.

Dunvegan Castle, Pictish Symbol Stone (NG 247490), 1 mile NNW. of Dunvegan, Sheet 23 (A.850). *Skye.*

This slab, found near a well beside the broch Dun Osdale, 1¼ miles S. by E. of the castle, is much weathered. It is still possible to identify on one side of it a crescent and V-rod symbol and two concentric circles, the outer of which measures almost 1 ft. in diameter.

Clach Ard, Pictish Symbol Stone (NG 421491), 5 miles NW. of Portree, Sheet 23 (A.850, B.8036 and by-road). *Skye.*

This stone, 4 ft. 5 in. high, has on its S. broad face a crescent and V-rod, a double disc and Z-rod and a mirror and comb symbol.

CONCLUSION

The monuments described in these pages, and the relics contemporary with them, provide virtually all the testimony there is of the social history of the successive and cumulative peoples who settled and exploited the Scottish countryside throughout a period extending over some three millennia before records were begun. Houses and henges, crannogs, brochs and hill-forts, standing stones, tombs and cairns, though tumbling and decayed, have left a pattern from which, practically exclusively, a picture can be built up to illustrate the developments introduced and superseded as time went by. To an ever-decreasing extent, the ensuing historic centuries too must be interpreted to some degree by the monuments and relics which they in turn have left behind them. Many of these later works are as conspicuous on the face of the land as are the earlier ones.

The rectilinear military works of the Roman armies assert themselves at various strategic points from Pennymuir or Birrens near the Border to as far north as Aberdeenshire; and it is only the erosive action of the plough that has obliterated more of them even farther north. The circular stone houses sprawling over the abandoned walls and ramparts of hill-forts and settlements in the southern part of the country bear witness to the years of enforced peace which preceded the final withdrawal of all Roman influence. The sinuous stone-lined tunnels of the souterrains represent a curious and still be no means fully understood episode, placed somewhere in the first half of the 1st millennium A.D.

Many of the mottes and baileys of the Normans, which occur in considerable quantities from the Solway to the Moray Firth, present a striking and imposing appearance. Earthworks which formed the bases of the defences of the somewhat later homestead moats, or moated granges, still survive in more limited numbers, chiefly in the southern and central counties. The grass-grown remains of farmsteads of later mediaeval date, eventually abandoned in favour of more convenient sites, occur in remote places almost everywhere that good land exists. Crofting communities, the inhabitants of which departed during the 18th or 19th centuries either voluntarily or by direction, to seek fortune and fame in the Colonies, appear in great numbers throughout the north and west.

The slopes of many of the hills in the southern parts of the country are corrugated with the often striking remains of cultivation terraces, or lynchets.

All these monuments have, of course, no place in prehistory, even though, together with the more substantial and familiar structures of stone or brick, they form a vital ingredient of history. It is as well to bear them in mind, however, since in the past the identification of some of them has been mistaken, through lack of knowledge of their origins and functions, and some of the older records and maps occasionally attribute them erroneously to prehistoric contexts. Now, however, the revised editions of the Ordnance Survey maps are giving their correct titles to those monuments which space allows to be included, and any confusion which may have existed is being eradicated.

A final cautionary word about trespass may save the visitor to a field monument embarrassment and delay. Although there is a well-known difference between the wording of the laws governing trespass in Scotland and those in force in certain other countries, the practical effect of the difference is virtually non-existent. It is therefore always advisable to ask permission to have access to any monument which is unprotected by such an organisation as the Department of the Environment or the National Trust.

BIBLIOGRAPHY

GENERAL

Including abbreviations used in the following pages

Ant., *Antiquity, A Quarterly Review of Archaeology*.

Arch J., *Archaeological Journal*, London.

Arch. Scot., *Archaeologia Scotica*, Edinburgh.

Atkinson, R. J. C., *The Henge Monuments of Great Britain*, chapter viii in Atkinson, R. J. C., Piggott, C. M., and Sandars, N. K., *Excavations at Dorchester, Oxon.*, Oxford, 1951.

C & T, Erskine Beveridge, *Coll and Tiree*, Edinburgh, 1903.

Chambers, W., *A History of Peeblesshire*, Edinburgh, 1864.

Childe, V. G., *The Prehistory of Scotland*, London, 1935; *Prehistoric Communities of the British Isles*, Edinburgh, 1940; *Scotland before the Scots*, London, 1946.

Cromar, Sir A. Ogston, *The Prehistoric Antiquities of the Howe of Cromar*, Aberdeen, 1931.

D & E, *Discovery and Excavation, Scotland*. Since its inauguration in 1947, the Scottish Regional Group of the Council for British Archaeology has published annually brief accounts of discoveries and excavations in Scotland. At first these were issued as parts of the Annual Reports of the Group, but in 1949 they were separated from the other items and issued as a printed booklet. The time was still not yet ripe for this to pay its way, and thereafter until 1955 the information was produced in duplicated typescript form as before, but separated from the rest of the Report. In 1955 a second attempt to sell a printed version succeeded, and printed booklets have appeared annually since that date.

E.C.M., III. J. Romilly Allen and J. Anderson, *The Early Christian Monuments of Scotland*, Edinburgh, 1903. Part III.

E.F.S., D. Christison, *Early Fortifications in Scotland*, Edinburgh, 1898.

Feachem, R., *Ancient Agriculture in the Highland of Britain*, P.P.S., XXIX (1973), 332-53

Henshall, A. S., *Prehistoric Chambered Tombs of Scotland*, Edinburgh. Vol. I, 1963, Vol. II 1972.

H.B.N.C., *History of the Berwickshire Naturalists' Club*, Edinburgh.

I.F.B., W. A. Gillies, *In Famed Breadalbane*, Perth, 1938.

Inv. The Royal Commission on the Ancient and Historical Monuments of Scotland periodically produces *Inventories* which supersede bibliographical references given here for the counties concerned. The reader should check with H.M.S.O. or the Commission.

Jarlshof, J. R. C. Hamilton, *Excavations at Jarlshof, Shetland*, H.M.S.O., 1956.

L & H, K. Jackson, *Language and History in Early Britain*, Edinburgh, 1953.

MacKie, E. W., *Dun Mor Vaul: An Iron Age broch on Tiree*, Glasgow, 1974.

MacKie, E. W., *Scotland: An Archaeological Guide*, London, 1975.

Mar, W. D. Simpson, *The Province of Mar*, Aberdeen, 1943.

N.M.A., The National Museum of Antiquities of Scotland, *Catalogue of Antiquities*, enlarged edition, Edinburgh, 1892.

P.M.A., J. Smith, *Prehistoric Man in Ayrshire*, 1895.

P.P.S., *Proceedings of the Prehistoric Society*, new series, Cambridge.
P.S.A.S., *Proceedings of the Society of Antiquaries of Scotland*, Edinburgh.
Pennant, J., *A Tour in Scotland and Voyage to the Hebrides*, London, 1776.
Picts, F. T. Wainwright, Ed., *The Problem of the Picts*, Edinburgh, 1955.
Piggott, S., *British Prehistory*, Oxford, 1949; *Neolithic Cultures of the British Isles*, Cambridge, 1954; *Scotland before History*, Edinburgh, 1958.
Powell, T. G. E., *The Celts*, London, 1958.
R & N, I. A. Richmond, Ed., *Roman and Native in North Britain*, Edinburgh, 1958.
Ross, A., *Everyday Life of the Pagan Celts*, London, 1970, 1972.
The Northern Isles, F. T. Wainwright, Ed., Edinburgh, 1962.
T.D.G.A.S., *Transactions and Journal of Proceedings of the Dumfriesshire and Galloway Natural History and Antiquarian Society*, Dumfries.
T.I.S.S., *Transactions of the Inverness Scientific Society*, Inverness.
Watson, W. J., *The History of the Celtic Place-Names of Scotland*, Edinburgh, 1926.
Williams, J., *An Account of some remarkable Ruins lately discovered in the Highlands and Northern Parts of Scotland*, London, 1777.
Wilson, D., *The Archaeology and Prehistoric Annals of Scotland*, Edinburgh, 1857 (2nd edn., *Prehistoric Annals of Scotland*, 2 vols., London & Cambridge, 1863).

The references shown below are to the page numbers of the volumes indicated, full details of which are in the General Bibliography

ABERDEENSHIRE

Balnagowan, *Cromar*, 84
Barmekin of Echt, *Mar*, 16
Barmkyn of North Keig, *Mar*, 61
Barra Hill, *Mar*, 61
Brandsbutt, *Mar*, 152
Broomend of Crichie, *P.S.A.S.*, LIV (1919–20), 154
Cairnmore, *Strathbogie*, 120
Cloghill, *P.S.A.S.*, LIX (1924–5), 21
Cullerlie, *P.S.A.S.*, LXIX (1934–5), 215
Dunnideer, *Mar*, 62
Dyce, *Mar*, 151
East Finnercy, *D & E*, 1952, 4
Knapperty Hill, *P.S.A.S.*, LXIII (1928-9), 34
Knockargetty Hill, *Cromar*, 102
Loanhead of Daviot, *P.S.A.S.*, LXIX (1934–5), 168
Logie Elphinstone, *Mar*, 153
Maiden Stone, *Mar*, 153
Memsie, *P.S.A.S.*, LXVIII (1933–4), 157, 176
Mither Tap of Bennachie, *Mar*, 60
Mortlich, *Cromar*, 89
Picardy Stone, *Mar*, 153
Pittodrie, *Mar*, 61
Tap o' Noth, *Strathbogie*, 35
Tomnaverie, *P.S.A.S.*, XXXIX (1904–5) 208

ANGUS

Aberlemno, *E.C.M. III*, 209
Balluderon, *E.C.M. III*, 215
Brown Caterthun, *P.S.A.S.*, XXXIX (1899–1900), 105
Cossans, *E.C.M. III*, 216
Craighill, *D & E*, 1957, 39
Denoon Law, *P.S.A.S.*, XXXIV (1899 1900), 91
Dunnichen, *E.C.M. III*, 206
Eassie, *E.C.M. III*, 217
Finavon, *P.S.A.S.*, LXX (1935–6), 347
Glamis, *E.C.M. III*, 221
Hurley Hawkin, *D & E*, 1958, 2: 1959, 1: 1960, 3: 1961, 5
Laws Hill, Drumsturdy, *Picts*, 70
St Vigean's, *E.C.M. III*, 234
Turin Hill, *Picts*, 74
White Caterthun, *P.S.A.S.*, XXXIV (1899–1900), 103

ARGYLL

Achnabreck, *P.S.A.S.*, VI (1864–6), App., 81: Pl. xxi, xxiii
Ardifuar, *P.S.A.S.*, XXXIX (1904–5), 259
Ardmarnock, *P.S.A.S.*, LXXVII (1942–3), 32

ARRAN

AYRSHIRE

BANFF

Little Conval, *E.F.S.*, 123, 254
Longman Hill, *P.S.A.S.*, LIX (1924–5), 24

BARRA

Dun Bharpa, *Inv. O.H.*, 457
Dun Cuier, *P.S.A.S.*, LXXXIX (1955–6), 290

BENBECULA

Airidh na h'aon Oidhche, *Inv. O.H.*, 350
Dun Buidhe, *Inv. O.H.*, 349
Stiaraval, *Inv. O.H.*, 351

BERNERAY

Dun Berneray, *Inv. O.H.*, 450

BERNERAY (HARRIS)

Cladh Maolrithe, *Inv. O.H.*, 126.

BERWICKSHIRE

Addinston, *Inv. Ber.*, 213
Blackchester, *Inv. Ber.*, 216
Coldingham Loch, *Inv. Ber.*, 81, 84, 85, 86, 87
Dean Castles, *Inv. Ber.*, 60
Earn's Heugh, *P.S.A.S.*, LXVI (1931–2), 152
Edinshall, *Inv. Ber.*, 121
Habchester, *Inv. Ber.*, 270
Haerfaulds, *Inv. Ber.*, 218
Longcroft, *Inv. Ber.*, 214
Marygold Hill Plantation, *Inv. Ber.*, 18
Overhowden, *P.S.A.S.*, LXXXIV (1949–50), 59
The Mutiny Stones, *P.S.A.S.*, LV (1924–5), 198

BUTE

Barone Hill, *P.S.A.S.*, XXVII (1892–3), 286
Bicker's Houses, *P.S.A.S.*, XXXVIII (1903–4), 18
Cairn Ban, *P.S.A.S.*, XXXVIII (1903–4), 27
Dunagoil, *P.S.A.S.*, XXVII (1892–3), 286
Dun Burgidale, *P.S.A.S.*, XXVII (1892–3), 287
Dun Scalpsie, *P.S.A.S.*, XXVII (1892–3), 282

Eilean Buidhe, *Arch. J.*, CXI (1954), 72
Glecknabae, *P.S.A.S.*, XXXVIII (1903–4), 37
Michael's Grave, *P.S.A.S.*, XXXVIII (1903–4), 33

CAITHNESS

Achanarras, *Inv. Caith.*, 141
Achavanich, *Inv. Caith.*, 293
Ben Dorrery, *Inv. Caith.*, 157
Ben Freiceadain, *Inv. Caith.*, 354
Broubster, *Inv. Caith.*, 163
Bruan, *Inv. Caith.*, 193
Camster, *Inv. Caith.*, 563
Camster, *Inv. Caith.*, 564
Dirlot, *Inv. Caith.*, 165
Dorrery, *Inv. Caith.*, 133
Earl's Cairn, *Inv. Caith.*, 72
Forse, *P.S.A.S.*, LXXXII (1947–8), 275
Garrywhin, *Inv. Caith.*, 559
Garrywhin, *Inv. Caith.*, 558
Garrywhin, *Inv. Caith.*, 528
Ham, *Inv. Caith.*, 65
Hill of Rangag, *Inv. Caith.*, 284
Holborn Head, *Inv. Caith.*, 438
Keiss, *Inv. Caith.*, 515
Langwell, *Inv. Caith.*, 250
Loch of Yarrows, *Inv. Caith.*, 567
Mid Clyth, *Inv. Caith.*, 292
Ormiegill, *Inv. Caith.*, 556
Ousdale, *Inv. Caith.*, 204
St John's Point, *Inv. Caith.*, 40
Sgarbach, *Inv. Caith.*, 45
Shebster, *Inv. Caith.*, 367
Shebster, *Inv. Caith.*, 369, 370
Shurrery, *Inv. Caith.*, 362
Shurrery, *Inv. Caith.*, 355
Skirza, *Inv. Caith.*, 35
Upper Dounreay, *Inv. Caith.*, 397
Warth Hill, *Inv. Caith.*, 41
Westerdale, *Inv. Caith.*, 105
Yarrows, *Inv. Caith.*, 543

CANNA

Dun Channa, *Inv. O.H.*, 681

CLACKMANNANSHIRE

Castle Craig, *Picts*, 73
Clackmannan, *Inv. Clack.*, 612

COLL

Dun an Achaidh, *C & T*, 7
Loch nan Cinneachan, *C & T*, 25.

Glassmount, *Inv. Fife*, 346
Greencraig, *P.S.A.S.*, LXXXII (1947–8), 264
Greencraig, *Inv. Fife*, 144
Greenhill, *P.S.A.S.*, XXXVI (1901–2), 635
Hare Law, *P.S.A.S.*, XXVI (1891–2), 114
Largo, *Inv. Fife*, 380
Lindores, *Inv. Fife*, 6
Lundin Links, *Inv. Fife*, 379
Newton of Collessie, *Inv. Fife*, 117
Norman's Law, *Inv. Fife*, 193
Norrie's Law, *Inv. Fife*, 378
Scotstarvit, *P.S.A.S.*, LXXXII (1947–8), 241
West Lomond, *Inv. Fife*, 501

Glen Nevis, *P.S.A.S.*, XXIII (1888–9), 371
Inverfarigaig, *P.S.A.S.*, XL (1905–6), 150
Knocknagael, *E.C.M. III*, 103
Laggan, *T.I.S.S.*, VIII (1912–18), 17
Loch Bruicheach, *T.I.S.S.*, VIII (1912–18), 113
Onich, *P.S.A.S.*, XXIII (1888–9), 374
Strone Point, *P.S.A.S.*, XL (1905–6), 149
Tighnaleac, *T.I.S.S.*, VIII (1912–18), 121

IONA

Dun Cul Bhuirg, *D & E*, 1957, 10: 1958, 10

HARRIS

Borvemore, *Inv. O.H.*, 125
Nisabost, *Inv. O.H.*, 135

ISLAY

Cragabus, *P.S.A.S.*, XXXVI (1901–2) 110

INVERNESS-SHIRE

Am Baghan Burblach, *P.S.A.S.*, XXIX (1894–5), 184
Am Baghan Galldair, *P.S.A.S.*, XXIX (1894–5), 185
Arisaig, *E.F.S.*, 171
Ashie Moor, *T.I.S.S.*, VIII (1912–18), 125
Auchteraw, *T.I.S.S.*, VIII (1912–18), 106
Avielochan, *T.I.S.S.*, I (1875–80), 59
Balnuaran of Clava, *P.S.A.S.*, LXXXVIII (1954–5), 188
Cabrich, *T.I.S.S.*, VIII (1912–18), 95
Castle Spynie, *Arch. Scot.*, IV (Pt. 1, 1831), 190
Corrimony, *P.S.A.S.*, LXXXVIII (1954–5), 173
Craig Phadrig, *T.I.S.S.*, VIII (1912–18), 90
Craig Phitiulais, *P.S.A.S.*, XLIV (1909–10), 193
Culdoich, *P.S.A.S.*, LXXXVIII (1954–5), 190
Dun Chliabhain, *T.I.S.S.*, VIII (1912–18), 117
Dun Grugaig, *P.S.A.S.*, LXXXIII (1948–9), 19
Dun Scriben, *T.I.S.S.*, II (1880–3), 145
Dun Telve, *P.S.A.S.*, L (1915–6), 241
Dun Troddan, *P.S.A.S.*, LV (1920–1), 83
Eilean nan Gobhar, *E.F.S.*, 173

KINCARDINESHIRE

Cairnton, *E.F.S.*, 195
Gourdon, *P.S.A.S.*, LVIII (1923–4), 33
Raedykes, *P.S.A.S.*, LVIII (1923–4), 20

KINROSS

Benarty, *Inv. Kin.*, 583
Dumglow, *Inv. Kin.*, 550
Dumglow, *Inv. Kin.*, 549
Dummiefarline, *Inv. Kin.*, 548
Orwell, *Inv. Kin.*, 577

KIRKCUDBRIGHT

Auchencairn, *Inv. Kir.*, 404
Barcloy, *Inv. Kir.*, 118
Barean Loch, *Inv. Kir.*, 122
Bargatton, *Inv. Kir.*, 46
Bargatton, *Inv. Kir.*, 47
Barnheugh, *Inv. Kir.*, 63
Blair Hill, *Inv. Kir.*, 367
Barstobric Hill, *Inv. Kir.*, 441
Boreland, *Inv. Kir.*, 362
Borness Batteries, *Inv. Kir.*, 60
Cairn Avel, *Inv. Kir.*, 94
Cairnderry, *Inv. Kir.*, 346
Cairnholy I and II, *P.S.A.S.*, LXXXIII (1948–9), 103.
Cairntosh, *Inv. Kir.*, 175
Cardoness House, *Inv. Kir.*, 20
Carlins Cairn, *Inv. Kir.*, 96

LANARKSHIRE

LEWIS

MIDLOTHIAN

Tormain Hill, *P.S.A.S.*, XVI (1881–2), 82–4

MORAY

Burghead, *E.F.S.*, 254
Burghead, *E.C.M. III*, 118
Doune of Relugas, *E.F.S.*, 195
Knock of Alves, *T.I.S.S.*, VIII (1912–18), 104

MUCK

Caisteal an Duin Bhain, *Inv. O.H.*, 691

MULL

An Sean Dun, *P.S.A.S.*, LXXVII (1942–3), 40
Dun nan Gall, *P.S.A.S.*, LXXVII (1942–3), 40
Port Donain, *D & E*, 1957, 5

NAIRN

Castle Finlay, *T.I.S.S.*, VIII (1912–18), 102
Dunearn, *T.I.S.S.*, VIII (1912–18), 105
Dun Evan, *T.I.S.S.*, VIII (1912–18), 108

NORTH UIST

Barpa Langass, *Inv. O.H.*, 224
Barpa nam Feannag, *Inv. O.H.*, 238
Caisteal Odair, *Inv. O.H.*, 190
Clach Mor a Che, *Inv. O.H.*, 252
Clettraval, *P.S.A.S.*, LXIX (1934–5), 480
Craonaval, *Inv. O.H.*, 219
Dun Torcuill, *Inv. O.H.*, 172
Loch Hunder, *Inv. O.H.*, 173
Uneval, *P.S.A.S.*, LXXXIII (1947–8), 1

ORKNEY

Blackhammer, *Inv. Ork.*, 573
Bookan, *Inv. Ork.*, 709
Burn of Mussetter, *Inv. Ork.*, 213
Burrian, *Inv. Ork.*, 193
Calf of Eday, *Inv. Ork.*, 245
Cutter's Tooer, *Inv. Ork.*, 952
Cuween, *Inv. Ork.*, 340
Dwarfie Stone, *Inv. Ork.*, 385
Gurness, *Inv. Ork.*, 263
Head of Work, *Inv. Ork.*, 414
Holland House, *Inv. Ork.*, 196
Holm of Papa, *Inv. Ork.*, 544, 545
Huntersquoy, *Inv. Ork.*, 217

Isbister, *P.S.A.S.*, XCII (1958–9), 25
Knowe of Lairo, *Inv. Ork.*, 577
Knowe of Smirrus, *Inv. Ork.*, 60
Knowe of Yarso, *Inv. Ork.*, 575
Knowes of Trotty, *Inv. Ork.*, 73
Maes Howe, *P.S.A.S.*, LXXXVIII (1954–5), 155
Mid Howe, *Inv. Ork.*, 583
Mid Howe, *Inv. Ork.*, 553
Netlater, *Inv., Ork.*, 13
Onstan, *Inv. Ork.*, 893
Oxtro, *Inv. Ork.*, 11
Quoyness, *D & E*, 1951, 12: 1952, 10
Ring of Bookan, *Inv. Ork.*, 732
Ring of Brodgar, *Inv. Ork.*, 875
Rinyo, *P.S.A.S.*, LXXIII (1938–9), 6
St Mary's, *Inv. Ork.*, 360
Sandyhill Smithy, *Inv. Ork.*, 224
Skara Brae, *Inv. Ork.*, 683
Staney Hill, *Inv. Ork.*, 39
Stenness, *Inv. Ork.*, 876
Stone of Setter, *Inv. Ork.*, 212
Taversoe Tuack, *Inv. Ork.*, 570
Too of Nugle, *Inv. Ork.*, 561
Via, *Inv. Ork.*, 714
Vinquoy Hill, *Inv. Ork.*, 216
Vola, *Inv. Ork.*, 889
Wheebin, *Inv. Ork.*, 34
Wideford Hill, *Inv. Ork.*, 410

PABBAY

Pabbay, *P.S.A.S.*, LXXIV (1939–40), 67

PEEBLESSHIRE

Cademuir Hill, *P.S.A.S.*, XXI (1886–7), 18
Cademuir Hill, *P.S.A.S.*, XXI (1886–7), 21
Caerlee Hill, *P.S.A.S.*, XXI (1886–7), 51
Chester Rig, *P.S.A.S.*, XXI (1886–7), 60
Dreva Craig, *P.S.A.S.*, XXI (1886–7), 21
Drumelzier, *P.S.A.S.*, LXV (1930–1), 363
Ford, *P.S.A.S.*, LXV (1930–1), 371
Glenachan Rig, *P.S.A.S.*, XCI (1958–9), 13
Green Knowe, *P.S.A.S.*, XCIV (1960–1), Forthcoming
Harehope, *P.S.A.S.*, XCIII (1959–60), 174
Harehope Rings, *P.S.A.S.*, XXI (1886–7), 30
Harestanes, *P.S.A.S.*, XXXVII (1902–3), 199

Helm End, *P.S.A.S.*, XXI (1886–7), 36
Henderland Hill, *P.S.A.S.*, XXI (1886–7), 34
Henry's Brae, *P.S.A.S.*, XXI (1886–7), 18
Kerr's Knowe, *P.S.A.S.*, XXI (1886–7), 62
Ladyurd Rings, *P.S.A.S.*, XXI (1886–7), 53
Langlaw Hill, *P.S.A.S.*, XXI (1886–7), 59
Mitchelhill Rings, *P.S.A.S.*, XXI (1886–7), 59
Muirburn Castle, *P.S.A.S.*, XXI (1886–7), 55
Northshield Rings, *P.S.A.S.*, XXI (1886–7), 38
Parkgatestone Hill, *P.S.A.S.*, XXI (1886–7), 49
Tinnis Hill, *P.S.A.S.*, XXI (1886–7), 70
White Hill, *P.S.A.S.*, XXI (1886–7), 42
White Meldon, *P.S.A.S.*, XXI (1886–7), 62
Whiteside Hill, *P.S.A.S.*, XXI (1886–7), 39
Woodend, *P.S.A.S.*, LXXIV (1939–40), 145

PERTHSHIRE

Abernethy, *P.S.A.S.*, XXXIV (1899–1900), 76
Abernethy, *E.C.M. III*, 282
Airlich, *P.S.A.S.*, XLIV (1909–10), 159
Auchterarder, *P.S.A.S.*, LXXXI (1946–7), 1
Balnacraig, *P.S.A.S.*, XLVII (1912–13), 41
Bareyra, *I.F.B.*, 33
Barry Hill, *P.S.A.S.*, XXXIV (1899–1900), 93
Bochastle, *P.S.A.S.*, XXXIV (1899–1900), 62
Braes of Fosse, *P.S.A.S.*, XLIX (1914–15), 26
Braes of Taymouth, *P.S.A.S.*, XCII (1958–9), 76
Castle Dow, *P.S.A.S.*, XXXIV (1899–1900), 71
Ceann na Coille, *P.S.A.S.*, XLIX (1914–15), 26
Clach na Tiompan, *P.S.A.S.*, LXXXVIII (1954–5), 112
Coldoch, *P.S.A.S.*, LXXXIII (1948–9), 12
Craigneich, *P.S.A.S.*, XLV (1910–11), 62
Croft Moraig, *P.P.S.*, XXXVII (1971), 1-15
Dalrulzion, *P.S.A.S.*, LXXX (1945–6), 130
Dowally, *P.S.A.S.*, XLII (1907–8), 144
Duncan's Camp, *P.S.A.S.*, XXXIV (1899–1900), 107
Dundurn, *Picts*, 82
Dunfallandy, *P.S.A.S.*, LXXVII (1942–3), 36
Dunfallandy, *E.C.M. III*, 286
Dun mac Tual, *P.S.A.S.*, XXXIV (1899–1900), 69
Dun Mor, *P.S.A.S.*, XXXIV (1899–1900), 67
Dunsinane, *P.S.A.S.*, XXXIV (1899–1900), 85
Evelick, *P.S.A.S.*, XXXIV (1899–1900), 56
Forgandenny, *P.S.A.S.*, XXXIV (1899–1900), 74
Fowlis Wester, *E.C.M. III*, 289
Glenlochay, *P.S.A.S.*, LXXXIV (1949–50), 172
Inchtuthill, *P.S.A.S.*, XXXVI (1901–2), 230
Kindrochat, *P.S.A.S.*, LXV (1930–1), 281: XCII (1958–9), 74
Kinnell, *P.S.A.S.*, XLIV (1909–10), 130
Machany, *P.S.A.S.*, LXXVII (1942–3), 38
Machulm, *P.S.A.S.*, XLIV (1909–10), 126
Meigle, *E.C.M. III*, 296
Moncrieffe Hill, *Picts*, 79
Monzie, *P.S.A.S.*, LXXIII (1938–9), 62
Newbigging, *P.S.A.S.*, XLIII (1908–9), 124
Queen's View, *P.S.A.S.*, XLIX (1914–15), 21
Roromore, *P.S.A.S.*, XLVII (1912–13), 39
Rossie Law, *P.S.A.S.*, XXXIV (1899–1900), 72
Rottenreoch, *P.S.A.S.*, LXXVII (1942–3), 31
Strathgarry, *P.S.A.S.*, LXXVII (1942–3), 48
Strathgroy, *P.S.A.S.*, LXXVII (1942–3), 36
Tom Orain, *P.S.A.S.*, XLVII (1912–13), 55

RAASAY

Dun Borodale, *Inv. O.H.*, 575
Raasay House, *Inv. O.H.*, 582

Muckle Heog, *Inv. Shet.*, 1559(2)
Nesbister Hill, *Inv. Shet.*, 1509
Ness of Burgi, *Inv. Shet.*, 1154
Ness of Gruting, *P.S.A.S.*, LXXXIX (1955–6), 346
Punds Water, *Inv. Shet.*, 1367
Ronas Hill, *Inv. Shet.*, 1365
Sae Breck, *P.S.A.S.*, LXXXVI (1951–2), 178
Scord of Brouster, *P.S.A.S.*, LXXXIX (1955–6), 370
Seli Voe, *Inv. Shet.*, 1428
Setter, *Inv. Shet.*, 1692
South Haven, *Inv. Shet.*, 1194
Stanydale, *P.S.A.S.*, LXXXIV (1949–50), 185
Stanydale, *P.S.A.S.*, LXXXIX (1955–6), 340
The Rounds of Tivla, *Inv. Shet.*, 1561
Uyea Breck, *Inv. Shet.*, 1552
Vementry, *Inv. Shet.*, 1493

SKYE

Boreraig, *Inv. O.H.*, 505
Carn Liath, *Inv. O.H.*, 632
Clach Ard, *Inv. O.H.*, 640
Dun Ard an t'Sabhail, *Inv. O.H.*, 478
Dun Cruinn, *Inv. O.H.*, 621
Dun Fiadhairt, *Inv. O.H.*, 508
Dun Gerashader, *Inv. O.H.*, 577
Dun Grugaig, *Inv. O.H.*, 651
Dun Hallin, *Inv. O.H.*, 509
Dun Liath, *Inv. O.H.*, 541
Dun Skudiburgh, *Inv. O.H.*, 542
Dun Suledale, *Inv. O.H.*, 618
Dun Totaig, *Inv. O.H.*, 519
Dunvegan Castle, *Inv. O.H.*, 528
Rudh an Dunain, *P.S.A.S.*, LXVI (1931–2), 183
Rudh an Dunain, *Inv. O.H.*, 483
Struanmore, *Inv. O.H.*, 479
Struanmore, *Inv. O.H.*, 489
Ullinish Lodge, *Inv. O.H.*, 493
Vatten, *Inv. O.H.*, 524

SOUTH UIST

Beinn a' Charra, *Inv. O.H.*, 407
Dun Vulan, *Inv. O.H.*, 375
Kilpheder, *P.P.S.*, XVIII (1952), 176
Loch a Barp, *Inv. O.H.*, 387
Reineval, *Inv. O.H.*, 389

STIRLINGSHIRE

Abbey Craig, *Inv. Stir.*, 69
Airthrey Castle, *Inv. Stir.*, 47, 48

Blochairn, *Inv. Stir.*, 11
Braes, *Inv. Stir.*, 74
Cairnhall, *Inv. Stir.*, 14
Castlehill Wood, *P.S.A.S.*, XC (1956–7), 24
Craigton, *Inv. Stir.*, 89
Dumgoyach, *Inv. Stir.*, 58
Dumyat, *Picts*, 77
Hill of Airthrey, *Inv. Stir.*, 6
Keir Hill of Gargunnock, *P.S.A.S.*, XCI (1957–8), 78
King's Park, *Inv. Stir.*, 42
Langlands, *Inv. Stir.*, 73
Meikle Reive, *Inv. Stir.*, 78
Myot Hill, *Inv. Stir.*, 75
Sauchie Craig, *Inv. Stir.*, 71
Stockie Muir, *Inv. Stir.*, 12
Strathcashel Point, *Inv. Stir.*, 107
Todholes, *Inv. Stir.*, 15
Torwood, *Inv. Stir.*, 100
Waterhead, *Inv. Stir.*, 61
West Plean, *P.S.A.S.*, LXXXIX (1955–6), 227

STROMA

Stroma Cairn, *Inv. Caith.*, 42

SUTHERLAND

Achany, *Inv. Suth.*, 447
Achu, *Inv. Suth.*, 82, 83
Altnacealgach, *Inv. Suth.*, 14
Badnabay, *Inv. Suth.*, 172
Ben Griam Beg, *Inv. Suth.*, 316
Castle Cole, *Inv. Suth.*, 25
Cinn Trolla, *Inv. Suth.*, 467
Clashnessie, *Inv. Suth.*, 5
Cnocan Daimh, *Inv. Suth.*, 169
Culkein, *Inv. Suth.*, 6
Duchary Rock, *Inv. Suth.*, 29
Dun Creich, *Inv. Suth.*, 54
Dundornadilla, *Inv. Suth.*, 155
Dun na Naigh, *Inv. Suth.*, 527
Dunrobin, *Inv. Suth.*, 270
Dun Viden, *Inv. Suth.*, 181
Glen Loth, *Inv. Suth.*, 474
Killin, *Inv. Suth.*, 44
Kilphedir, *Inv. Suth.*, 307
Kinbrace, *Inv. Suth.*, 372
Learable Hill, *Inv. Suth.*, 281
Loch Ardvair, *Inv. Suth.*, 4
Loch Loyal, *Inv. Suth.*, 538
Ospisdale, *Inv. Suth.*, 97
Portskerra, *Inv. Suth.*, 193
Skail, *Inv. Suth.*, 233
Skelpick, *Inv. Suth.*, 241
Stoer, *Inv. Suth.*, 7

Torboll, *Inv. Suth.*, 134

TIREE
Dun Mor Vaul, *MacKie*, 1974

WEST LOTHIAN
Bowden Hill, *Inv. W.Lot.*, 384
Cairnpapple, *P.S.A.S.*, LXXXII (1947–8), 68
Cockleroy, *Inv. W.Lot.*, 358
Craigie Hill, *Inv. W.Lot.*, 327
Earl Cairnie, *Inv. W.Lot.*, 328

WIGTOWNSHIRE
Ardwell, *P.S.A.S.*, LXXXI (1946–7), 54
Barsalloch Point, *Inv. Wig.*, 199
Bennan of Garvilland, *Inv. Wig.*, 245
Black Loch, *Inv. Wig.*, 32
Burrow Head, *Inv. Wig.*, 497
Cairnerzean, *Inv. Wig.*, 43, 44
Cairn Pat, *Inv. Wig.*, 413
Cairnscarrow, *Inv. Wig.*, 46
Caspin, *Inv. Wig.*, 76
Caves of Kilhern, *Inv. Wig.*, 269
Chang, *Inv. Wig.*, 190

Chippermore, *Inv. Wig.*, 191
Craigoch, *Inv. Wig.*, 72
Crammag Head, *Inv. Wig.*, 143
Crows, *Inv. Wig.*, 125
Cruise Back Fell, *Inv. Wig.*, 244
Doon of May, *Inv. Wig.*, 187
Dowalton Loch, *Inv. Wig.*, 423
Drumtroddan, *Inv. Wig.*, 225
Dunman, *Inv. Wig.*, 144
Fell of Barhullion, *Inv. Wig.*, 7
High Gillespie, *Inv. Wig.*, 346
Jamieson's Point, *Inv. Wig.*, 71
Kemp's Walk, *Inv. Wig.*, 174
Kirklauchlane, *Inv. Wig.*, 431
Knock Fell, *Inv. Wig.*, 305
Laigh Sinniness, *Inv. Wig.*, 306
Lingdowie, *Inv. Wig.*, 40, 41
Long Tom, *Inv. Wig.*, 49
Mid Gleniron, *Inv. Wig.*, 261, 263
Mid Gleniron, *Inv. Wig.*, 260
Milton of Larg, *Inv. Wig.*, 37
North Balfern, *Inv. Wig.*, 122
North Balfern, *Inv. Wig.*, 118
Portankill, *Inv. Wig.*, 140
Shennanton, *Inv. Wig.*, 101
Stairhaven, *Inv. Wig.*, 310
Teroy, *Inv. Wig.*, 28
Torhousekie, *Inv. Wig.*, 531

INDEX TO MONUMENTS